WordPerfect for Windows
Made Easy

Mella Mincberg

Osborne **McGraw-Hill**

Berkeley   New York   St. Louis   San Francisco
Auckland   Bogotá   Hamburg   London   Madrid
Mexico City   Milan   Montreal   New Delhi   Panama City
Paris   São Paulo   Singapore   Sydney
Tokyo   Toronto

Osborne **McGraw-Hill**
2600 Tenth Street
Berkeley, California 94710
U.S.A.

For information on translations or book distributors outside of the U.S.A.,
please write to Osborne **McGraw-Hill** at the above address.

WordPerfect for Windows Made Easy

1234567890 DOC 998765432

ISBN 0-07-881742-0

Publisher

Kenna S. Wood

Acquisitions Editor

Frances Stack

Associate Editor

Jill Pisoni

Project Editor

Judith Brown

Technical Editor

Dan Robinson

Copy Editor

Ann Krueger Spivack

Proofreading Coordinator

Kelly Barr

Proofreaders

K.D. Sullivan
Wendy Goss

Indexers

Phil Roberts
Peggy Bieber-Roberts

Word Processor

Lynda Higham

Director of Electronic Publishing

Deborah Wilson

Production Supervisor

Barry Michael Bergin

Quality Control

Bob Myren

Computer Designer

Helena Charm

Typesetters

Jani Beckwith
J. E. Christgau
Marcela Hancik
Peter Hancik
Susie C. Kim
Fred Lass
Stefany Otis
Lance Ravella
Michelle Salinaro
Marla Shelasky

Production Assistant

George Anderson

Cover Design

Mason Fong

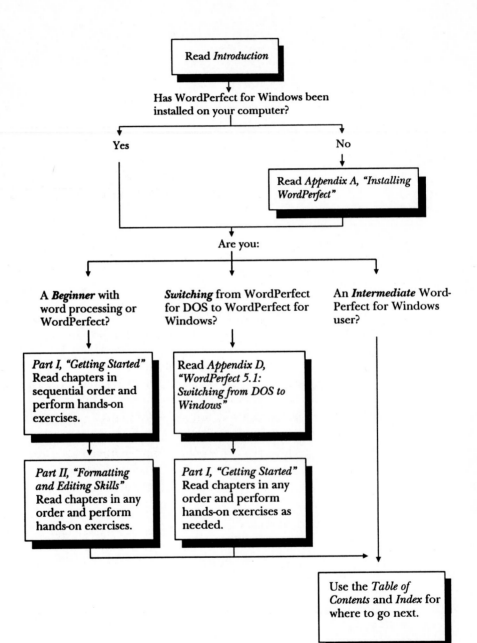

Read *Introduction*

Has WordPerfect for Windows been installed on your computer?

Yes

No

Read *Appendix A, "Installing WordPerfect"*

Are you:

A *Beginner* with word processing or WordPerfect?

Switching from WordPerfect for DOS to WordPerfect for Windows?

An *Intermediate* Word-Perfect for Windows user?

Part I, "Getting Started" Read chapters in sequential order and perform hands-on exercises.

Read *Appendix D, "WordPerfect 5.1: Switching from DOS to Windows"*

Part II, "Formatting and Editing Skills" Read chapters in any order and perform hands-on exercises.

Part I, "Getting Started" Read chapters in any order and perform hands-on exercises as needed.

Use the *Table of Contents* and *Index* for where to go next.

Contents at a Glance

Table of Contents

Acknowledgments

Thank you to all the people at Osborne/McGraw-Hill who worked so hard to make this book happen. Thanks also to copy editor Ann Spivack, who showed her talent for making my words say what I meant them to say, and technical editor and friend Dan Robinson, who made me feel more confident that what I said was true.

And, thanks to Ilene for listening, to Nea Vergain for remembering, and to Scott for giving me some needed pep talks throughout the writing process. "You're almost there," he'd say. "But, Scott," I'd reply, "I'm only on page 46."

Introduction

I wrote *WordPerfect for Windows Made Easy* to help make WordPerfect 5.1 for Windows quick and easy to learn. This book is for those of you who are:

- Beginners with word processing or WordPerfect
- Switching from a version of WordPerfect that does not run under Windows
- Intermediate users who want to increase your skills

This book covers everything you need to know to produce great-looking documents. You'll learn about the wide range of WordPerfect features, and you'll learn shortcuts to save you time.

How This Book Is Organized

WordPerfect for Windows Made Easy is divided into three main sections:

- Part I, "Getting Started", explains the fundamentals: how to start and exit WordPerfect for Windows, and how to type, edit, save, and print WordPerfect for Windows documents.
- Part II, "Formatting and Editing Skills", describes essential tasks such as: underlining and centering text, changing fonts, altering

margins and tabs, inserting headers and footers, moving sections of text, and checking your document for spelling errors.

- Part III, "Becoming a Sophisticated User", covers the special features of WordPerfect for Windows. Some features help you produce specific types of documents, such as newsletters and annual reports. Other features help you use WordPerfect for Windows more efficiently.

In all three parts, each chapter contains step-by-step explanations and a "Quick Reference" at the end, which serves as a chapter summary. Chapters 1 through 9 also contain hands-on exercises. Use these exercises as a tutorial to help get you started and make you a skillful user.

The Reference section contains appendixes that you will not want to ignore. Refer to Appendix A if you haven't yet installed WordPerfect for Windows. Appendix B describes the commands on the WordPerfect menus and lists WordPerfect's codes. Appendix C provides sources for additional support. Appendix D is devoted to how WordPerfect for Windows is different from WordPerfect for DOS.

At the back of this book, you will find a command card that you can tear out and put beside your computer. It is a condensed guide to WordPerfect's keyboard shortcuts.

How to Use This Book

What's the wisest method for tackling this book? That depends on your level of experience with WordPerfect for Windows.

If you're a beginner, you will want to read all of Part I to become comfortable with both the Windows environment and WordPerfect basics. I suggest you do the hands-on exercises as well, because the best way to learn is by doing. After you master the basics, proceed to Part II, where you'll sharpen your editing and formatting skills.

If you're switching from WordPerfect for DOS to WordPerfect for Windows, read Appendix D. It summarizes the main differences between the two, to help you make the adjustment. Then, review Part I to learn about the Windows environment; you must understand this environment before you'll feel comfortable with WordPerfect for Windows.

If you're an intermediate user, or once you become one, be sure to explore WordPerfect for Windows' more specialized capabilities, such as the Graphics and Tables features. What other special capabilities you investigate depends on the types of documents you produce. Look to the Table of Contents and Index for where to go next.

What the Notation Means

A specific notation is used throughout this book to indicate how to perform tasks.

Keys are enclosed in rounded boxes, such as (HOME) or (F10). Two or more keys that should be pressed simultaneously are joined by a plus (+) sign. For instance, (CTRL) + (DEL) means that you press the (CTRL) key, and while holding it down, press (DEL). Then release both keys.

Menus and menu items that should be chosen sequentially are joined by a comma (,). For instance, "File, Preferences" means that you select the File menu, and then select the Preferences menu item. You can use the underscored letters—the "F" in File and the "e" in Preferences—to do so.

Icons appear in the left margin of this book to set off special sections of text.

 A "note" icon (such as the icon to the left) marks text that is noteworthy; a "caution" icon marks text that warns about a potential problem; a "shortcut" icon marks text that offers a quick and easy alternative; and a "reminder" icon marks text with information that is important enough to repeat a second time.

 This hand icon points to the start of a hands-on exercise. You can choose to perform the exercise, or skip over it.

What to Expect if You're Switching from WordPerfect for DOS

Usually when a product is released for the first time, it is assigned the version number 1.0. WordPerfect Corporation has instead designated the new WordPerfect for Windows as version 5.1. This is to emphasize that WordPerfect 5.1 for Windows combines the advantages of Windows with the powerful capabilities of the best-selling WordPerfect 5.1 for DOS.

If you're accustomed to WordPerfect for DOS, you won't feel lost in unknown territory when you switch to WordPerfect for Windows. The basic approach to performing tasks is the same. Your main challenge is to adapt to the new interface—a different look to the main screen, a different look to the menus, a new level of prominence for the mouse, new commands, and new function key uses. If, however, you've become addicted to the WordPerfect 5.1 for DOS function key uses, there's a keyboard layout that mimics most of those keys.

In many ways, WordPerfect for Windows is an improvement. You'll appreciate the changes if you value seeing different fonts and graphics images right on screen—so that the result is a much more accurate image of the printed page. You'll like the changes if you enjoy (or at least don't mind) using a mouse, which can now be used to execute every command and to tap exciting new features like the Button Bar and Ruler. You'll be pleased if you need to work with up to nine WordPerfect documents at the same time. You'll be thrilled if you need to run two or more applications at one time—such as WordPerfect, a spreadsheet like Lotus 1-2-3, and a drawing program like CorelDRAW—and switch back and forth as you copy text and graphics between them.

Another plus is that features are now more accessible. You can hunt in menus if you can't remember how to execute a certain command, or if you want to uncover new options that are available to you.

WordPerfect for Windows is not an improvement, however, if you value speed above all else and don't have a high-powered computer. Tasks like spell-checking, executing a macro, or scrolling through a document take longer—maybe only seconds longer, but the seconds add up. I wrote this book using WordPerfect for Windows on a 386 SX machine with 4MB of memory and running at a speed of 20 MHz. At first, I desperately missed the snappy response of WordPerfect for DOS. The speed degradation is especially noticeable on a 286 machine.

WordPerfect for Windows is also a setback if you're resistant to change, because you *do* have to learn some new ways of doing things. There's no way around it.

Fortunately, documents created in WordPerfect 5.1 for DOS are completely compatible with WordPerfect 5.1 for Windows. So, you can go back and forth between the two. For instance, if you don't have a high-powered computer and you need to produce a lengthy document, use the DOS version to quickly type the raw, unadorned text, and then use the Windows version to tackle the layout of your pages.

Regardless of whether you're switching, are new to WordPerfect, or are an intermediate user, you can expect to have fun using WordPerfect for Windows. You'll be viewing colorful images and pop-up menus. You'll be dragging pictures and markers all over the screen. You'll be hopping from document to document, window to window. It's sure a long way from using a manual typewriter. I hope you enjoy WordPerfect for Windows, and I hope you enjoy using this book.

Mella Mincberg
Sonoma County, California

I

Getting Started

1

Exploring the WordPerfect for Windows Environment

If you're like me, the biggest hurdle when learning something new is getting over the initial awkwardness and uneasiness. The goal of this chapter is to provide an overview of the WordPerfect for Windows environment and get you comfortable with it.

I urge beginners to read the chapter from start to finish. You'll learn how to start up WordPerfect, how it appears on screen, and how it works with the mouse and keyboard. When you are ready to end your computer session, you will learn one more procedure—how to exit WordPerfect. The hands-on exercises in this chapter (and throughout the book) will help you learn by doing. Like every chapter in the book, this one concludes with a "Quick Reference" to recap what you've learned.

More experienced users may know some—and perhaps all—of the information provided in this chapter. For instance, those of you familiar with WordPerfect 5.1 for DOS know about the status line and the keyboard operations. Readers who have used Windows (or the Apple Macintosh) know about icons, and the mouse pointer. Rather than read this chapter from start to finish, more experienced users may want to skim its contents and read closely only those sections that deal with new information.

note *WordPerfect For Windows is ready to run only after it has been installed on the hard disk of your computer. Installation can be performed by you, by someone else who shares your computer equipment, or by your computer dealer. It is a one-time procedure. Once WordPerfect is installed, it is ready every time you turn on the computer. If WordPerfect has not been installed on your computer, see Appendix A before reading further.*

Starting WordPerfect for Windows

Getting WordPerfect for Windows to run on your computer is referred to as *starting, loading,* or *launching* WordPerfect. But WordPerfect is a *Windows application,* meaning that it operates only in the Windows environment. (An application that isn't designed to run under Windows, such as WordPerfect 5.1 for DOS, is called a *non-Windows application.*) So, before you can start using WordPerfect, you must start Windows.

Starting Windows

To start Windows, start up your computer as you usually do, either by turning on your computer or by inserting a startup disk in drive A and then turning it on. After a few moments, Windows appears on screen automatically. Your screen will resemble Figure 1-1, although the appearance and contents of your screen may be different (depending on which applications you installed and how you organized them). If Windows does not appear automatically, look for a prompt, such as C> or C:\>, on screen. At the prompt, type **win** and press (ENTER). Your computer screen will soon resemble Figure 1-1.

Windows is a *graphical user interface (GUI),* which means you can communicate with the computer using icons instead of typing hard-to-remember commands. An icon has two parts: a small picture and a caption. Figure 1-1,

Figure 1-1. *Six group icons in the Windows environment*

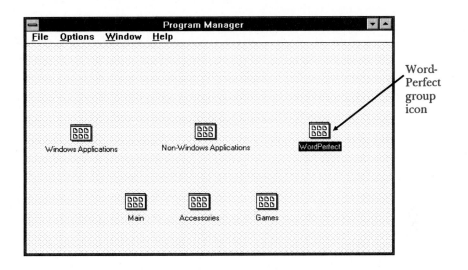

Word-
Perfect
group
icon

for instance, displays six icons with captions such as "Main", "Accessories", or "WordPerfect". Each of these icons represents a group of related applications, so these are called *group icon*s.

Starting WordPerfect

The procedure to start WordPerfect involves two icons. The first is the *WordPerfect group icon.* The second is the *WordPerfect program item icon,* one of the four related applications housed inside the WordPerfect group icon.

WordPerfect
group icon

WordPerfect
program item icon

If the WordPerfect group icon is on screen, begin with step 1, in the following
instructions, to start WordPerfect. If the WordPerfect program item icon is
on screen, begin with step 3.

1. Point to the WordPerfect group icon. *Point* means to slide the mouse
   until the tip of the arrow shown on screen, which acts as the mouse
   pointer, rests on the icon, like this:

WordPerfect

2. Double-click the left mouse button to choose that icon. *Double-click*
   means to press the left mouse button twice in rapid succession. Make
   sure to hold the mouse firmly before you double-click so that the
   mouse pointer does not move off the icon. In moments, the Word-
   Perfect group window opens, and a new set of icons appears on
   screen.

3. Point to the WordPerfect program item icon.

4. Double-click the left mouse button to choose the icon. An hourglass
   appears on screen, signifying that you must wait for the computer
   to load WordPerfect. Whenever an hourglass appears on screen, you
   do not want to use the keyboard or the mouse again until the
   computer has completed the task at hand and the hourglass disappears.

You will know that you have successfully started WordPerfect when, after
a few moments, you see the screen shown in Figure 1-2.

You can use your keyboard instead of your mouse to select the Word-
Perfect group and program item icons.

To choose the WordPerfect group icon, keep pressing (CTRL) + (TAB) or
(CTRL) + (F6) until the caption "WordPerfect" is highlighted, then press (ENTER).
To choose the WordPerfect program item icon, press the arrow keys (←), (→),
(↑), and (↓) until the caption "WordPerfect" is highlighted, then press (ENTER).

Figure 1-2. *WordPerfect application window*

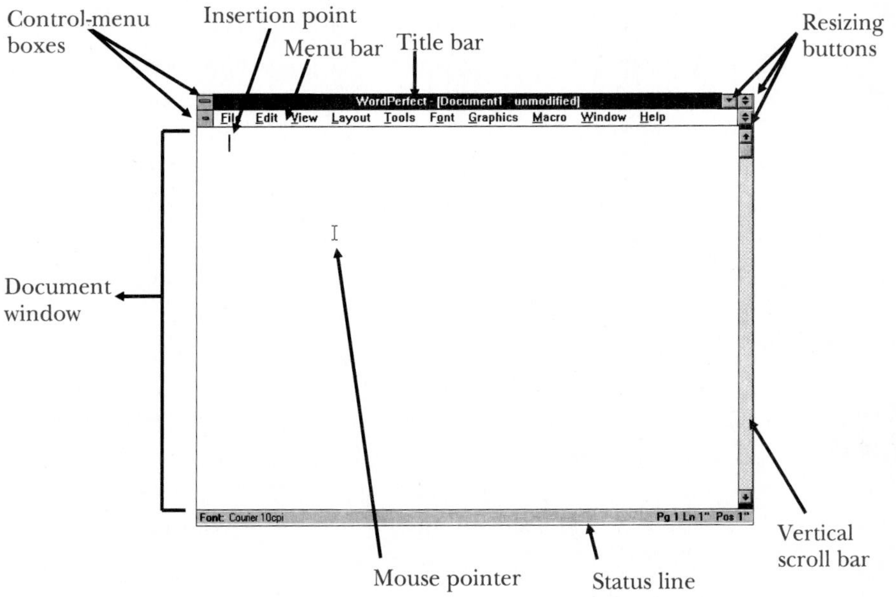
Control-menu boxes
Insertion point
Menu bar
Title bar
Resizing buttons
WordPerfect - [Document1 - unmodified]
File Edit View Layout Tools Font Graphics Macro Window Help
Document window
Font: Courier 10cpi
Pg 1 Ln 1" Pos 1"
Vertical scroll bar
Mouse pointer
Status line

Startup Messages

Sometimes you may encounter a problem or receive an error message on screen before WordPerfect will start. If your screen does not look like the screen shown in Figure 1-2, here's what may be happening:

- WordPerfect is asking for your license (or registration) number because this is your first time starting WordPerfect. Look at your WordPerfect package to find your license number, type it in, and press (ENTER). This number will then be easily accessible when you use the Help facility, as described in Appendix C.

- WordPerfect is requesting your user initials. If you're starting WordPerfect from a network, WordPerfect uses these initials–up to three characters–to keep special files needed to run WordPerfect on your computer separate from those of other individuals working simultaneously in WordPerfect on other computers. Type in one to three characters and press ENTER. (It is a good idea to use the same characters each time you start WordPerfect on the network.)

- WordPerfect is responding with a message asking you to rename, open, or delete backup files. Backup files help prevent you from losing documents because of a power failure or because someone shut off a computer before exiting WordPerfect properly. See Chapter 17 for more on the Backup feature and how to respond to this message.

- WordPerfect won't start, or it begins to load but then the computer freezes. This may indicate that WordPerfect has been installed improperly or that startup options are being used incorrectly; refer to Appendix A. Another possibility is that your computer does not have enough memory to run WordPerfect. WordPerfect requires at least 2 megabytes (2MB) of available Windows memory in order to load, so you can try starting WordPerfect without having other Windows applications already loaded or consider purchasing more memory for your computer.

Elements of the WordPerfect Window

Figure 1-2 displays the WordPerfect *application window,* a rectangular portion on the screen that is under the control of WordPerfect. Inside the application window is a smaller window, a *document window,* that displays any report, letter, or memo that you create. A window is bordered by a *frame,* an outside edge that defines its boundary.

The various elements of Figure 1-2 are described next; some are covered in great detail here, others mentioned only briefly will be discussed in more detail later in the book.

Title Bar

The title bar is located at the very top in Figure 1-2. The word "Word-Perfect" in the title bar indicates that the application controlling the window

1

is WordPerfect. The highlighting of the title bar tells you that the window is *active,* meaning that it is the one in which you are currently working.

A title bar can also display other information. If a document has been named, the name is displayed on the title bar; if the document has yet to be named, the title bar displays a generic name, such as "Document1". A title bar displays "unmodified" if the document on screen has not been changed since it was last saved on disk or if no document appears on screen.

WordPerfect - [Document1 - unmodified]

Resizing Buttons

When you first start up WordPerfect, both the WordPerfect application window and the document window are at their maximum sizes on screen. Three buttons located to the right of the title bar let you change the size of a window with your mouse:

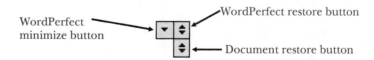

WordPerfect
minimize button

WordPerfect restore button

Document restore button

WordPerfect minimize button	Shrinks the WordPerfect application window
WordPerfect restore button	Returns the WordPerfect application window to a medium-sized window
Document restore button	Returns the document window to a medium-sized window

Whenever a restore button is selected, it is replaced by a maximize button, so that you can again expand a window to its maximum size. Chapter 10 discusses how to resize windows in detail.

Control-Menu Boxes

Two boxes located to the left of the title bar are used to close a window, or to display a list of options for moving, resizing, or switching between windows:

WordPerfect control-menu box

Document control-menu box

WordPerfect control-menu box	Governs the WordPerfect application window
Document control-menu box	Governs the document window

Menu Bar

The menu bar, located directly below the title bar, provides access to WordPerfect's powerful features. Features are organized by function into menus. A menu is simply a list of choices. You activate the menu bar with the mouse or with the (ALT) key, as described in Chapter 2.

 Directly below the menu bar on your computer screen, you may see a row of ten rectangular buttons. This is a WordPerfect Button Bar, which is hidden from view unless you or someone who shares your computer chooses to display it. Chapter 10 discusses the Button Bar feature.

Document Workspace

Located in the center of the document window, the *document workspace* is where the text of your document appears as you type. The document workspace takes up the largest portion of the window. In Figure 1-2, the document workspace is clear of text.

Notice in Figure 1-2 that a vertical bar sits at the top left corner of the document workspace. This bar, which blinks on the computer screen, is your *insertion point.* (In non-Windows applications, such as WordPerfect 5.1 for

DOS, the insertion point is referred to as the *cursor.*) As soon as you tap a key, a character will appear wherever the insertion point is located. The insertion point will automatically move forward to accommodate characters as you add them.

The insertion point can move only within the boundaries of the document on screen. So, for example, if you type a document that is two lines long, the insertion point can move only within the boundaries of those two lines; it cannot move to another part of the document workspace. If you type a ten-page document, the insertion point can move anywhere within those ten pages.

caution *If ever the insertion point stops blinking, you will be unable to type into the document workspace. Typically, the insertion point stops blinking because you pressed the* (ALT) *key, which activates the menu bar. If you inadvertently pressed* (ALT), *press it a second time (or press* (ESC)*) to deactivate the menu bar. The insertion point will start blinking again, and you'll be able to continue typing into the document workspace.*

Status Line

Located below the document workspace is the status line. The left side of the status line displays different messages depending on the status of the screen. In Figure 1-2, for instance, the left side indicates the current *font*— Courier, 10 characters per inch—the typeface that WordPerfect assumes for characters in the document. The current font is displayed if no commands or special features are active on screen.

The right side of the status line always contains three indicators—the page (Pg), line (Ln), and position (Pos) indicators—that inform you of the insertion point's present location in your document. For instance, in Figure 1-2, where the document workspace is clear and the insertion point is in the upper left corner, the status line reads:

```
Pg 1 Ln 1" Pos 1"
```

Pg 1 informs you that the insertion point is on page 1. Page numbers refer to the actual page numbers of the document once it is printed.

Ln 1" signifies that the insertion point is located one inch down from what will be the top of the page when the document is printed. When you first begin a document, WordPerfect automatically gives you a one-inch top margin for that document. You will see later in the book how to set the top margin to be as wide or narrow as you wish. A top margin is not displayed on screen.

Pos 1" means that the insertion point is located one inch from what will be the left edge of the paper when the document is printed. WordPerfect automatically gives you a one-inch left margin for your document (but you will see later in the book how to set the left margin to be as wide or narrow as you wish).

When the document workspace is empty, the insertion point cannot move. It stays fixed at the location Pg 1, Ln 1", Pos 1". As you begin to type text, the insertion point will move, and the status line will change to always reflect the insertion point's location.

If your document workspace appears clear but your status line reads something other than Pg 1 Ln 1" Pos 1", there is nothing wrong with your copy of WordPerfect. You may have pressed a key such as (SPACEBAR), which inserts a space into the document workspace. Or someone who shares your computer may have altered settings, such as margins, for your copy of WordPerfect. (Chapter 17 explains how it is possible to change initial settings.)

Scroll Bars

You use the scroll bars when you're using a mouse to move the insertion point quickly through a document. The vertical scroll bar, located just to the right of the document workspace in Figure 1-2, lets you scroll up and down through a document. This is especially useful when working on a long document. Moreover, you can request that a horizontal scroll bar appear as well (see Chapter 3). It will appear just above the status line:

Horizontal scroll bar

The horizontal scroll bar scrolls left and right through a document and is useful when a document is very wide.

Mouse Pointer

The *mouse pointer* is a graphical image that can move anywhere on screen. The pointer is controlled by the mouse and is used for almost any task other than typing text. The graphical image used to represent the mouse pointer can change depending on either its location on screen or the current state of the screen. Notice in Figure 1-2 that the mouse pointer appears as an I-beam. Examples of the different images that you'll encounter are shown in Figure 1-3.

 The mouse pointer and the insertion point appear on screen at the same time. Be sure never to confuse the two. Even though they are both pointers, they have quite different features and functions. Refer to Table 1-1 for a comparison.

The Mouse

The mouse is actually an optional piece of equipment, though to best use WordPerfect for Windows you need one. The mouse sits near the keyboard, either on a special pad or simply on the desk.

You operate a mouse by moving it to control the whereabouts on screen of your mouse pointer, and then pressing or holding down one of the mouse

Figure 1-3. *Different images used to represent the mouse pointer*

| Arrow | Hourglass | I-beam | Crosshair |
| Double arrow | Four-headed arrow | Hand | Prevent |

Table 1-1.   *Don't Confuse the Mouse Pointer with the Insertion Point*

Type of Pointer	Appearance on Screen	Location on Screen	How Controlled	Function
Mouse pointer	Varies	Anywhere	Mouse only	Points to a position on screen for completing tasks except for typing text
Insertion point	Blinking vertical bar	Remains in document workspace	Keyboard or mouse	Points to the current location in the document workspace for typing and editing text

buttons. Depending on your mouse, it will have either two or three buttons. In WordPerfect, the left mouse button is the principal button. Throughout this book, assume the left mouse button is the one to press unless otherwise instructed. Left-handed readers can change this setting so that the right button is the primary mouse button. (Instructions for doing this are given in Chapter 17.)

You can perform almost every task in WordPerfect—except for typing text—with a mouse. The terminology for using a mouse is as follows:

Term	Mouse Action
Point	Move the mouse until the tip of the mouse pointer rests on an item
Click	Press and release the mouse button
Double-click	Press and release the mouse button twice in rapid succession
Click and hold	Press and hold down on the mouse button
Drag	While holding down on the mouse button, move the mouse

Rather than say "point to X and then click the left mouse button", most users say simply "click X". This shorthand will be used throughout this book. So, for example, when you read, "Double-click the WordPerfect control-menu box", interpret that to mean you first point to the WordPerfect control-menu box and then double-click the left mouse button.

Those of you unaccustomed to the mouse will find that it takes just a bit of practice to become proficient using it. Here are some basic guidelines:

- Firmly grasp the mouse with your thumb on one side and your third and fourth fingers on the other side. The index finger should be held just above the mouse buttons, available for pressing the buttons when necessary. (Or, you may prefer to hold both the index and third fingers above the mouse buttons.)

- Move the mouse to the left or right along your desk to move the mouse pointer to the left or right on screen. Move the mouse away from or toward you to move the mouse pointer up and down on screen.

- If the mouse pointer ever disappears from the screen, move the mouse in a large circle on your desk until you again locate the mouse pointer.

- If you run out of room for moving the mouse because your hand is at the edge of your desk, lift the mouse up and then place it back down in the center of the desk. When you lift up the mouse, the mouse pointer remains immobile.

- When you click, you must hold the mouse steady, press sharply, and release quickly—especially important when double-clicking. If your hand shakes between the two clicks or if you don't double-click fast enough, the computer will record two regular clicks, rather than one double-click.

Hands-on Exercise: Use the Mouse

    These exercises will help you get accustomed to pointing with the mouse in the WordPerfect application window.

1. Point to the center of the document workspace. Notice that the mouse pointer is an I-beam when it's within the document workspace.

2. Point to the word "Font" in the lower left corner on the status line. The mouse pointer becomes an arrow.

3. Point to the position indicator ("Pos"), which is in the lower right corner on the status line.

4. Point to the word "WordPerfect" on the title bar at the top of the screen.

5. Point to the menu name "Tools" on the menu bar.

6. Point again to the center of the document workspace. The mouse pointer changes back to an I-beam whenever it is in the document workspace.

If you're not yet proficient at maneuvering the mouse, practice pointing to additional items on screen.

The Keyboard

In WordPerfect for Windows, the keyboard is used primarily to type text. Computer keyboards have an auto-repeat feature, which means a character will keep repeating if you hold its key down. (The exceptions include the following keys: CTRL, ALT, SHIFT, CAPS LOCK, and NUM LOCK.) It is important, therefore, to remember to press down on keys sharply, crisply, and briefly to avoid inadvertently repeating a keystroke.

In addition to typing text, you can use the keyboard as an alternative to the mouse for accessing features and moving the insertion point. If you don't have a mouse, you obviously must always use the keyboard options. Even if you use a mouse, you'll find that some keyboard options are actually shortcuts. Keyboard options are offered throughout this book.

Figure 1-4 shows a common keyboard style. Though keys may be positioned differently, all keyboard styles have three basic sections: the typewriter keypad, the numeric keypad, and the function keypad.

1

Typewriter Keypad

The typewriter keypad contains the standard typing keys as found on a typewriter, including numbers on the top row, letters in the middle three rows, and the (SPACEBAR) at the bottom. Some keys on this keypad either operate differently on a computer keyboard than on a typewriter, or are unique to the computer keyboard, as described in the following sections.

Letter Keys "O" and "L"

The letter keys should never be used when typing numbers. Unlike a typewriter, a computer knows the difference between the letters "o" and "l" and the numbers "0" and "1", and most printers display the letters and numbers differently. When typing numbers, be sure to use real zeros and real ones—found either on the top row on the typewriter keypad or on the numeric keypad.

Figure 1-4.   *Common keyboard style: the IBM enhanced keyboard*

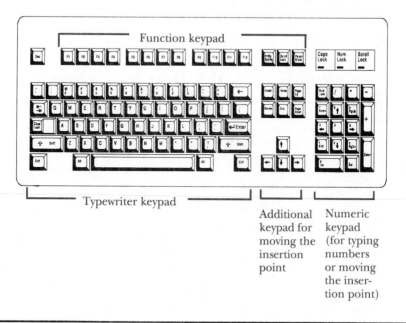

Spacebar

When you press the (SPACEBAR), a space is inserted into your document. This space occupies a place just like characters do. If you're used to a typewriter, you'll need to break the habit of relying on the (SPACEBAR) to move around in a document. Also, don't use the (SPACEBAR) to indent the first line of a paragraph, since the width and location of spaces can change in a computer-generated document; use the (TAB) key instead.

Enter Key

The (ENTER) key is usually on the right side of the keyboard. It is marked with the word "Enter", the word "Return", and/or a bent arrow symbol:

(Some keyboards have two (ENTER) keys where either one does the same task.) The (ENTER) key registers commands into the computer. In addition, the (ENTER) key is used when typing documents to end paragraphs and short lines of text, or to insert blank lines. On a computer keyboard you do *not* press the (ENTER) key to end each and every line in a paragraph, the way you do on a typewriter. (More on this in Chapter 3.)

Backspace Key

The (BACKSPACE) key is usually just above the (ENTER) key, marked with the word "Backspace" or with a symbol like this:

The (BACKSPACE) key is used to correct a mistake when you accidentally type the wrong character. It will erase the character just to the left of the insertion point.

Tab Key

The (TAB) key is marked either with the word "Tab" or with two arrows pointing in opposite horizontal directions:

Every time you press (TAB), the insertion point jumps to the next tab stop to the right, and the character you type will be fixed at that position. WordPerfect initially assumes that tab stop locations are every half inch. One important use for the (TAB) key is to indent the first line of a paragraph. Be sure to use the (TAB) key rather than the (SPACEBAR) in WordPerfect for indenting the first line in a paragraph or aligning text in tabular columns.

Shift Key

The (SHIFT) key is marked either with the word "Shift" or with an outline of an upward-pointing arrow:

The keyboard has two (SHIFT) keys located on either side of the (SPACEBAR). To use a (SHIFT) key to capitalize an individual letter, hold down the (SHIFT) key, and while holding it down, type the letter. You also use a (SHIFT) key just as you do on a typewriter to type symbols such as ! or $ or ?, which are located on the upper half of keys on the typewriter keypad.

Capitals Lock Key

(CAPS LOCK) acts like a toggle switch; press it once to turn capital letters on and off.

Status of Caps Lock	After Pressing a Letter Key
Active	Letter appears in uppercase
Inactive	Letter appears in lowercase

Keep in mind that (CAPS LOCK) affects *only letters;* you must still use the (SHIFT) key to type symbols such as ! and $ regardless of the status of (CAPS LOCK). You can tell when (CAPS LOCK) is active: the "Pos" indicator on the status line appears in uppercase—"POS". On some keyboards, there is also an indicator that lights up when (CAPS LOCK) is active.

Be aware that the (SHIFT) keys can reverse the status of the (CAPS LOCK) key. For instance, when (CAPS LOCK) is active, pressing (SHIFT) and a letter key will insert that letter in lowercase rather than in uppercase.

Alt and Control Keys

(ALT) and (CTRL) are used in combination with other keys—with function keys as well as typing keys such as **b**, **u**, and (TAB)—to change the behavior of those other keys. For instance, pressing (F1) by itself performs one task, (ALT) + (F1) performs another task, and (ALT) + (SHIFT) + (F1) a third task. Or, typing **u** will insert the character "u", but pressing (CTRL) + (U) will perform a different function. Or, pressing (TAB) will insert a tab, but pressing (ALT) + (TAB) has another purpose. There are numerous key combinations that use (ALT) or (CTRL) in WordPerfect, which you will learn about throughout this book. (ALT) is also used to activate or deactivate the menu bar, as described in Chapter 2.

 As mentioned in the Introduction, a plus sign between keys means that you press down on the first key, and while holding it down, press down on the next key. For instance, (ALT) + (F1) *means that you press down on* (ALT), *and while holding it down, press* (F1). *Then release both keys. Similarly,* (ALT) + (SHIFT) + (F3) *means that you press down on* (ALT) *and* (SHIFT), *and then while holding down both keys, press* (F3). *Then release all the keys.*

Numeric Keypad

The second section on the computer keyboard, the numeric keypad, serves two purposes. First, it can be used to enter numbers and is therefore an alternative to using the top row on the typewriter keypad. The numeric keypad is easier to use if you are accustomed to using number keys that are positioned in a ten-key layout—like on a calculator.

Or, the numeric keypad can be used to control the whereabouts of the insertion point. For instance, (←) moves the insertion point one space to the left, while (↑) moves the insertion point one line up.

The (NUM LOCK) key, which means "Numbers Lock", acts like a toggle switch; press it once to turn numbers on or off. It controls whether the numeric keypad is *active*—used for entering numbers—or whether it is *inactive*—used to move the insertion point.

Status of Num Lock	After Pressing a Key on Numeric Keypad
Active	Number appears on screen
Inactive	Insertion point moves

Be aware that the (SHIFT) key can reverse the status of the (NUM LOCK) key. For instance, when (NUM LOCK) is active, pressing (SHIFT) and a numeric keypad key will move the insertion point rather than insert a number.

Those of you with the keyboard style shown in Figure 1-4 have another set of keys for moving the insertion point. This second set is located between the typewriter keypad and the numeric keypad. If you have this second set, you may decide to use it for moving the insertion point. Then, you can keep (NUM LOCK) active and devote the numeric keypad solely to typing numbers.

Function Keypad

The third section on the keyboard is the function keypad, which sits on top of the keyboard with keys labeled (F1) through (F12). You can use function keys either by themselves or in combination with three other keys: (CTRL), (ALT), and (SHIFT). In WordPerfect, these combinations act as shortcuts for issuing commands. (You will learn more about commands in Chapter 2.)

A *keyboard template* provided with the WordPerfect package lists the shortcut assigned to each function key combination. This template should be placed next to your keyboard.

The template is actually two in one. One side of the template describes the *Common User Access (CUA) compatible keyboard,* with shortcut keys assigned in accordance with the standards set for all Windows applications. Word-Perfect Corporation shipped WordPerfect for Windows with the CUA keyboard as the *default*—meaning that the CUA keyboard is assumed to be the active keyboard. If you have remained with the default, look on the side of the template marked "CUA compatible" in the upper left corner.

The opposite side of the template describes the *WordPerfect (WP) 5.1 compatible keyboard,* with shortcut keys designed to mimic how function keys are used in WordPerfect 5.1 for DOS. Skillful users of WordPerfect 5.1 for DOS may have switched during installation to the WP 5.1 keyboard. In that case, use the side of the template marked "WP 5.1 Compatible".

Whichever side of the template you refer to, it is color-coded as follows:

Color Code on Template	Corresponding Key Combination
Black	Function key alone
Green	(SHIFT) + function key

Color Code on Template	Corresponding Key Combination
Blue	(ALT) + function key
Blue with green dot	(ALT) + (SHIFT) + function key
Red	(CTRL) + function key
Red with green dot	(CTRL) + (SHIFT) + function key

If you find the template confusing, you can instead bring up an onscreen list of function key shortcuts with the Help feature, as described in Appendix C. Or, look at the table provided in Chapter 2 for an alphabetical list of shortcuts using the function keys (and other keys as well). Those of you with a mouse could ignore the function keys entirely and issue commands exclusively with the mouse. I recommend, however, that you don't completely shy away from function keys. For those commands you issue often, you'll find that once you learn the key combinations, these really are shortcuts.

Whenever shortcuts are provided in this book, the keystrokes will refer to the Common User Access (CUA) compatible keyboard, the keyboard that is standard for most Windows applications. If you use (or wish to use) the WP 5.1 compatible keyboard, refer to Appendix D to learn more about that keyboard's assigned keystrokes.

Hands-on Exercise: Use the Keyboard

The following gives you some basic practice with the keyboard. First, watch how the keyboard's auto-repeat feature operates:

1. Press and hold down on the (R) key until a stream of letters appears halfway across the document workspace on screen. (If you attempt to type but the computer beeps instead, you may have accidentally activated the menu bar. Press (ALT) to deactivate it, and try typing again.)

   rrrrrrrrrrrrrrrrrrrrrrrrrrrrrrrrrrrrr|

   Your insertion point will be located at the end of the stream of letters, represented by the symbol | in this book.

2. Keep holding down the key, and watch as the characters are wrapped around to the beginning of the next line.

```
rrrrrrrrrrrrrrrrrrrrrrrrrrrrrrrrrrrrrrrrrrrrrrr
rrrrrrrrrrrrrr|
```

3. Hold down the (SPACEBAR) and watch as spaces are inserted instead of letters. The insertion point flies to the right.

```
rrrrrrrrrrrrrrrrrrrrrrrrrrrrrrrrrrrrrrrrrrrrrrr
rrrrrrrrrrrrrr                                 |
```

4. Press and hold down the (BACKSPACE) key until the screen is cleared of all those spaces and letters. Obviously, auto-repeat works not only with typing keys such as the (R) and the (SPACEBAR), but also with editing keys such as the (BACKSPACE) key.

Next, use the keyboard to type text into the document workspace. As you type, watch how, when the insertion point moves, the status line changes:

1. Type **Hello!!!** (Remember to tap the keys crisply so you don't accidentally trigger the auto-repeat feature. Also, remember to use the (SHIFT) key when typing the uppercase "H" and the three exclamation points.)

2. Press the (SPACEBAR) twice to insert two spaces.

3. Press (CAPS LOCK). When you do, notice that the position indicator on the status line reads "POS" rather than "Pos", signifying that uppercase has been activated.

4. Type **welcome**. All the letters appear in uppercase without your using the (SHIFT) key.

5. Type three more exclamation points. (Remember that, even though (CAPS LOCK) is active, you must still use the (SHIFT) key to insert the exclamation points.) Now the screen reads:

```
Hello!!!  WELCOME!!!|
```

6. Press (CAPS LOCK). Now the status line reads "Pos", since uppercase has been deactivated. The status line also indicates the current position of the insertion point. Suppose it reads as follows:

```
Pg 1 Ln 1" Pos 3"
```

This signifies that the insertion point is on page 1, 1 inch from the top of the page, and 3 inches from the left edge of the page when printed.

7. Press (ENTER). Now the insertion point moves down to the beginning of a new line. The status line reflects the fact that the insertion point is at the beginning of a brand-new line:

```
Pg 1 Ln 1.17" Pos 1"
```

This signifies that the second line of text will be 1.17 inches from the top of the page when printed. (You may find that the status line on your screen indicates another line location, such as Ln 1.16" or Ln 1.18". How WordPerfect spaces each line on a page depends partially on the printer defined to work with your copy of Word-Perfect and partially on the current font.)

Once text appears in the document workspace, you can move the insertion point within the text using the numeric keypad (or, if you have the enhanced keyboard, with the second set of movement keys):

1. Press the ⊕ key once. The insertion point moves to the top line on screen. (Remember that if you try to move the insertion point but a number appears instead, press (NUM LOCK) once to turn numbers off.)

2. Press the ⊖ key three times. The insertion point moves three characters to the right. Notice how the position indicator on the status line always indicates the change in location.

3. Press and hold down the ⊖ key. Auto-repeat will take effect, and the insertion point will fly to the end of the line.

4. Keep holding down the ⊖ key and the insertion point will wrap around to the beginning of the next line, which is the blank line that you created when you tapped the (ENTER) key.

5. Press ⊖. The insertion point refuses to move past the end of the document.

6. Press ⬇. Again, the insertion point will not move; it cannot move past the end of the document.

Exiting WordPerfect for Windows

At the end of a WordPerfect session, never simply turn off the computer. You will clutter your hard disk with unnecessary files by doing this. You should instead exit WordPerfect properly so that WordPerfect can handle all its internal housekeeping tasks.

You can exit WordPerfect easily and ensure that any documents you worked with during the session are closed in several different ways. All produce identical results. First, you can use the Exit command on the File menu, denoted as File, Exit. The procedure for selecting commands from the menu bar will be discussed in Chapter 2. The second method for exiting—and a shortcut for File, Exit—is to press (ALT) + (F4). The third method, for those of you with a mouse, is to double-click the WordPerfect control-menu box (the box in the uppermost left corner).

How WordPerfect responds will depend on the status of the text on screen. When the document workspace is clear or when text in the workspace has been saved on disk (more on saving in Chapter 4), the title bar reads "unmodified". In that case, when you issue the Exit command, it is executed immediately. In moments, you are returned to the Windows program.

When the document workspace contains text that has not been stored on disk, there is an additional step before WordPerfect is exited. After you issue the Exit command, WordPerfect displays a box called a dialog box, which you'll learn more about in Chapter 2. In the box, choose Yes or type y to save the text on screen before exiting. Choose No or type n to exit without saving. Or, choose Cancel or press (ESC) to repeal the Exit command.

Once you've returned to Windows, you can start up another software package or you can exit Windows and turn off the computer. You exit Windows the same way you exit WordPerfect: Choose File, Exit; press (ALT) + (F4); or double-click the Windows control-menu box.

Hands-on Exercise: Exit WordPerfect

   You'll become more familiar with how to execute commands in Chapter 2. For now, follow these instructions to exit WordPerfect:

1. Press (ALT) + (F4). Or, double-click the control-menu box. (Remember that this is the box in the upper left corner in the WordPerfect window. Also, remember when double-clicking to hold the mouse firmly and click twice quickly and crisply.)

    Since the document workspace contains text that has not been saved, WordPerfect displays a dialog box asking whether you wish to save changes to Document1.

2. Type **n** to choose <u>N</u>o, since what you typed was simply practice and not a document you would care to save.

    WordPerfect closes your practice document and returns you to the Windows environment.

Quick Reference

- To start WordPerfect with a mouse, double-click the Word-Perfect group icon and then the WordPerfect program item icon. When using the keyboard, highlight the WordPerfect group icon and press (ENTER) and then highlight the Word-Perfect program item and press (ENTER). In moments, the WordPerfect application window will display on screen.

- To mark the place where text will be inserted as you type, a flashing vertical bar appears in the document workspace. This is referred to as the insertion point.

- To keep track of the insertion point's current location, look to the status line, which is located in the lower right-hand corner of the document window. When you first start WordPerfect, the status line indicates the insertion point's location as

  ```
  Pg 1 Ln 1" Pos 1"
  ```

- To work with a mouse, you point the mouse pointer—a marker whose graphical image changes—to a location in the Word-Perfect application window. Then depending on the task to be performed, you click, double-click, or drag the mouse. The mouse can be used for any task except typing text.

- To learn about the function keys as shortcuts for performing tasks, WordPerfect provides a plastic keyboard template. The side of the template to which you should refer depends on whether you remained with the Common User Access (CUA) compatible keyboard or switched to the WordPerfect 5.1 for DOS (WP 5.1) compatible keyboard.

- To exit WordPerfect, select File, Exit. Or double-click on the WordPerfect control-menu box. Or, press (ALT) + (F4). You must always exit WordPerfect before you turn off your computer at the end of a working session.

2

Working with Menus, Commands, and Dialog Boxes

Like Chapter 1, this chapter offers fundamental information on how to work with WordPerfect. It describes how to gain access to all of WordPerfect's powerful features and commands. In fact, the information in this chapter is the foundation for working with the features and commands of all Windows applications. One of the most impressive aspects of Windows is that once you know the basics of one Windows application, you know the basics of all of them.

Read the chapter from start to finish and perform the hands-on exercises unless you are experienced with other Windows applications. Windows users who know about menu bars and dialog boxes can skim the chapter.

A word of warning to beginners: there are often several ways to accomplish the exact same task in WordPerfect (and, for that matter, in Windows). For instance, many commands can be executed using the mouse, using the keyboard, or with shortcut keys. Decide which of the available methods for accomplishing a given task is the easiest and most convenient for you. Focus on that method, ignoring the alternatives. Otherwise, WordPerfect can become more complicated than it should be.

About Menus and Commands

The menu bar provides access to WordPerfect's features. The ten menus listed on the menu bar enable you to do the following:

Menu	Action
Menu	**Action**
File	Open, save, and print documents
Edit	Change a document
View	Change what you see in the WordPerfect window
Layout	Change the text format in a document
Tools	Use tools to assist in creating and editing a document
Font	Change the appearance of printed text
Graphics	Add graphics boxes and lines to a document
Macro	Record or play a series of commands
Window	Change the document window display
Help	Get onscreen help

These menus are referred to as *drop-down* (or sometimes *pull-down*) menus because each "drops down" from the menu bar to display its *options* or *items*. Items on the menu bar are also referred to as *commands* because they "command" WordPerfect to execute the corresponding tasks. Figure 2-1 shows the File drop-down menu; you can see that this menu contains 13 commands, and that File, New is highlighted.

 As mentioned in the book's introduction, a comma placed between a menu and a command name is a shorthand form employed throughout this book. For example, File, New denotes the New command on the File menu.

Visual Clues

WordPerfect provides visual clues if it needs more input from you after you issue a command from a drop-down menu. The visual clues include these graphical marks: a check mark preceding a menu item, an arrowhead following a menu item, an ellipsis following a menu item, or a menu item that is faded in color.

Figure 2-1.   *The File menu drops down from the menu bar*

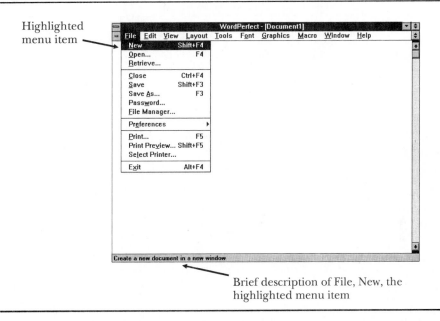

Highlighted menu item

Brief description of File, New, the highlighted menu item

A menu item *not* followed by one of these marks means that the command will be executed without additional input from you. Sometimes, the command affects the document workspace, as when you choose the New or Exit command. At other times, the command turns a feature on or off like a toggle switch. A feature will remain turned on until you turn it off. You can tell when a toggle is on by the check mark that appears next to the menu item. For instance, two of the features in the View menu shown here are on:

An item followed by an arrowhead (▶) brings up a second menu. This second menu is called a *cascading menu* because it tumbles down from the first

Figure 2-2.   *Choosing Preferences from the File menu results in a cascading menu*

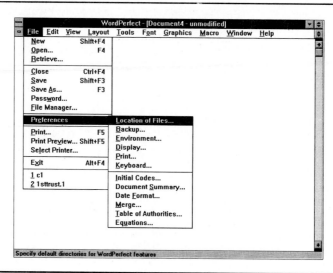

menu. A cascading menu will display additional items for you to choose from. For instance, the Preferences command in Figure 2-1 will bring up the cascading menu shown in Figure 2-2.

An item followed by an ellipsis, or three dots (...), opens a *dialog box*. A dialog box lets you carry on a conversation with WordPerfect. It can convey messages, options, or warnings. The Open, Retrieve, Save As, Password, File Manager, Print, Print Preview and Select Printer commands in Figure 2-1 will each open its own dialog box. (Dialog boxes are discussed in detail later in this chapter.)

Finally, when an item is faded or dimmed to a light shade (usually gray) it is unavailable in the mode or command you are currently using.

Issuing Commands from the Menu Bar

You can issue commands from the menu bar using either the mouse or the keyboard. Using your mouse, follow these steps:

2

1. Click a menu name. The corresponding drop-down menu appears, with the first item highlighted in reverse video. A brief description of that menu item displays on the status line at the bottom of the screen, as shown in Figure 2-1.

2. Click a menu item to choose it. (Or to cancel, click the menu name again or click in an empty area of the screen. The menu will close and disappear.)

As an example, to choose File, Preferences, you would click File. The File drop-down menu would appear. Then you would click Preferences.

You can also use your mouse to browse through the menus before choosing a menu item. Follow these steps:

1. Click and hold a menu name, and then drag the mouse left or right for a glimpse at other drop-down menus. As each menu name is highlighted, a brief description appears on the status line at the bottom of the screen.

2. Still holding down the mouse button, drag the mouse up or down through the menu items until the item that you wish to choose is highlighted. A brief description of the highlighted menu item appears on the status line.

3. When the menu item you wish to choose is highlighted, release the mouse button. (Or to cancel, point to an empty area of the screen and release the mouse button.)

reminder *To "click" something means to point to it and then press the left mouse button. To "click and hold" means to point to something and then press and hold down the left mouse button. To "drag" means to move the mouse while holding down the mouse button.*

When using your keyboard, a fast method relies on mnemonic keys. A *mnemonic key* is a letter key that can be employed to choose a menu or menu item. Mnemonic keys are indicated in WordPerfect's menu system and in this book as an underlined letter in a menu name or menu item. For instance, the mnemonic key for File is (F) and the mnemonic key for Preferences is (E). To issue a command with your keyboard, follow these steps:

1. Press (ALT) + a menu name's mnemonic key. The corresponding drop-down menu appears, with the first item highlighted in reverse video. A brief description of that menu item displays on the status line at the bottom of the screen, as shown in Figure 2-1.

2. Press a menu item's mnemonic key to choose that item. (Or to cancel, press (ALT); the menu will close and the menu bar will be deactivated. You can also press (ESC) to cancel the selection one level at a time. For instance, if the File menu appears on screen, press (ESC) once to close that drop-down menu and press (ESC) a second time to deactivate the menu bar.)

As an example, to choose File, Preferences, you would press (ALT) + (F). The File drop-down menu would appear. Then you would press (E).

A second keyboard method for choosing a menu item relies on the arrow keys and lets you browse before you choose a menu item. Follow these steps:

1. Press the (ALT) key or the (F10) key to activate the menu bar. The document control-menu box becomes highlighted.

2. Use the (←) and (→) keys to move left or right through the drop-down menus and use the (↑) and (↓) keys to move up or down within a drop-down menu's item. As each menu name or item is highlighted, a brief description appears on the status line at the bottom of the screen.

3. When the menu item you wish to choose is highlighted, press (ENTER). (Or to cancel, press (ALT).)

WordPerfect lets you display either full drop-down menus or short drop-down menus. Full menus display all the commands. Short menus show only those commands that you will probably use most often—to help you locate those items more quickly. During work sessions when you are typing straightforward documents, consider turning on the Short Menus feature. To do so, choose View, Short Menus. A check mark will be placed next to the Short Menus item and the menu will clear. To return to full menus at any time, choose View, Short Menus once again. The Short Menus feature is turned off.

2

Issuing Commands with Shortcut Keys

When you use shortcut keys, you can bypass the menu bar entirely when issuing certain commands. Only the most commonly used commands have shortcut keys. The shortcut keys are listed at the far right side on each drop-down menu. For instance, Figure 2-1 indicates that eight commands on the File menu have shortcut keys. For instance, you can press (SHIFT) + (F4) as a shortcut to using the menu bar to choose File, New. Or you can press (F4) as a shortcut for File, Open.

note | *The shortcuts listed on the drop-down menus reflect the keyboard that is currently selected on your computer. Thus, if you chose the WP 5.1 compatible keyboard, you'll see different shortcut keys listed on your computer screen than those shown in Figure 2-1.*

Keep in mind that not all shortcut keys are listed on the drop-down menus. Those that cannot fit within the narrow confines of the drop-down menu are excluded. For these, refer to the plastic template that came with your WordPerfect package (discussed in Chapter 1). Or, for a more complete list, see Table 2-1. Table 2-1 lists commands alphabetically in the left column, and provides the corresponding shortcut keys in the right-hand column. (There is also a list on the command card found at the back of this book.)

Table 2-1. *Shortcut Keys for Issuing Commands (CUA Compatible Keyboard)*

Command	Key Combination
Bold	(CTRL) + (B)
Cancel	(ESC)
Center	(SHIFT) + (F7)
Center Justify	(CTRL) + (J)
Clear	(CTRL) + (SHIFT) + (F4)
Close	(CTRL) + (F4)
Columns	(ALT) + (SHIFT) + (F9)
Copy	(CTRL) + (C) (or (CTRL) + (INS))
Cut	(CTRL) + (X) (or (SHIFT) + (DEL))
Date Code	(CTRL) + (SHIFT) + (F5)

Table 2-1.   *Shortcut Keys for Issuing Commands (CUA Compatible Keyboard)*
(continued)

Command	Key Combination
Date Text	`CTRL` + `F5`
Decimal Tab	`ALT` + `SHIFT` + `F7`
Define	`SHIFT` + `F12`
Document	`CTRL` + `SHIFT` + `F9`
Double Indent	`CTRL` + `SHIFT` + `F7`
Draft Mode	`CTRL` + `SHIFT` + `F3`
End Field	`ALT` + `ENTER`
End Record	`ALT` + `SHIFT` + `ENTER`
Exit	`ALT` + `F4`
Figure Edit	`SHIFT` + `F11`
Figure Retrieve	`F11`
Flush Right	`ALT` + `F7`
Font	`F9`
Full Justify	`CTRL` + `F`
Generate	`ALT` + `F12`
Goto	`CTRL` + `G`
Hanging Indent	`CTRL` + `F7`
Hard Page	`CTRL` + `ENTER`
Hard Space	`CTRL` + `SPACEBAR`
Help	`F1`
Help: What Is?	`SHIFT` + `F1`
Horizontal Line	`CTRL` + `F11`
Hyphen Dash Character	`CTRL` + `-`
Indent	`F7`
Italics	`CTRL` + `I`
Left Justify	`CTRL` + `L`
Line	`SHIFT` + `F9`
Line Draw	`CTRL` + `D`

Table 2-1. *Shortcut Keys for Issuing Commands (CUA Compatible Keyboard) (continued)*

Command	Key Combination
Macro Play	(ALT) + (F10)
Macro Record	(CTRL) + (F10)
Macro Stop	(CTRL) + (SHIFT) + (F10)
Margins	(CTRL) + (F8)
Mark Text	(F12)
Menu Bar	(ALT) (or (F10))
Merge	(CTRL) + (F12)
New	(SHIFT) + (F4)
Next Document	(CTRL) + (F6)
Next Pane	(F6)
Next Window	(ALT) + (F6)
Normal	(CTRL) + (N)
Open	(F4)
Page	(ALT) + (F9)
Page Down	(ALT) + (PGDN)
Page Up	(ALT) + (PGUP)
Paragraph Define	(ALT) + (SHIFT) + (F5)
Paragraph Number	(ALT) + (F5)
Paste	(CTRL) + (V) (or (SHIFT) + (INS))
Preferences	(CTRL) + (SHIFT) + (F1)
Previous Document	(CTRL) + (SHIFT) + (F6)
Previous Pane	(SHIFT) + (F6)
Previous Window	(ALT) + (SHIFT) + (F6)
Print	(F5)
Print Full Doc	(CTRL) + (P)
Print Preview	(SHIFT) + (F5)
Redisplay	(CTRL) + (F3)

Table 2-1.   *Shortcut Keys for Issuing Commands (CUA Compatible Keyboard)*
(continued)

Command	Key Combination
Replace	CTRL + F2
Reveal Codes	ALT + F3
Right Justify	CTRL + R
Ruler	ALT + SHIFT + F3
Save	SHIFT + F3
Save As	F3
Search	F2
Search Next	SHIFT + F2
Search Previous	ALT + F2
Select	F8
Select Cell	SHIFT + F8
Size	CTRL + S
Sort	CTRL + SHIFT + F12
Special Codes	ALT + SHIFT + F8
Speller	CTRL + F1
Styles	ALT + F8
Tables	CTRL + F9
Text Box Create	ALT + F11
Text Box Edit	ALT + SHIFT + F11
Thesaurus	ALT + F1
Undelete	ALT + SHIFT + BACKSPACE
Underline	CTRL + U
Undo	CTRL + Z (or ALT + BACKSPACE)
Vertical Line	CTRL + SHIFT + F11
WP Characters	CTRL + W

Hands-on Exercise: Choose Menus and Commands

   If WordPerfect isn't currently loaded on your computer you may wish to review Chapter 1 for instructions. Once WordPerfect is loaded, follow these instructions to practice working with drop-down menus and issuing commands:

1. Click and hold on File in the menu bar. The File drop-down menu temporarily overlaps the document workspace, and a short description appears on the status line.

2. Still holding down on the mouse button, drag the mouse pointer straight across (to the right) along the menu bar. Notice how you can browse through all the drop-down menus. Also notice that as each menu name is highlighted, a new description appears on the status line.

3. Once the Graphics drop-down menu is displayed, release the mouse button. The Graphics menu, which contains six items, remains on screen.

4. Clear the Graphics drop-down menu by clicking anywhere outside the drop-down menu (or by pressing (ALT)); the menu disappears. This cancels the Graphics command.

5. Choose View by clicking View or pressing (ALT) + (V). Notice on the View menu that no check mark appears after the Short Menus item, which means that this item is off.

6. Choose Short Menus by clicking Short Menus or pressing (M). Your command is executed immediately and the drop-down menu disappears.

7. Choose Graphics by clicking Graphics or pressing (ALT) + (G). Notice that on this drop-down menu only three items are listed, whereas before there were six. This is the Graphics short menu.

8. Press (ALT) to clear the Graphics drop-down menu.

9. Choose View and notice the check mark that appears beside the Short Menus item because you turned on the feature moments ago. Click Short Menus or press (M) to turn it off again.

10. Choose Ḟile, Pṟeferences. Since an arrowhead follows the Pṟeferences menu item, a cascading menu appears.

11. Click outside the menu or press (ALT) to clear the drop-down menu and the cascading menu at once.

12. Press (CTRL) + (SHIFT) + (F1). As indicated in Table 2-1 or on your template, this is the Preferences key—a shortcut for selecting Ḟile, Pṟeferences. The same cascading menu appears that you viewed moments ago.

13. Press (ALT) to clear the drop-down menu.

Elements of Dialog Boxes

A menu item followed by an ellipsis opens a dialog box. A dialog box provides a means for WordPerfect to request information from you and provide information to you. For instance, a dialog box appears when you select the Ḟile, Pṟint command letting you indicate which document and pages you wish to print, as shown in Figure 2-3. Another dialog box appears when you select the Ḟile, Ọpen command letting you indicate which document you wish to open (bring to the screen), as shown in Figure 2-4. A dialog box temporarily overlaps the document workspace.

Every dialog box is different, but all contain one or more of the following basic elements in common: title bar, control-menu box, group boxes, radio buttons, check boxes, text boxes, number/increment boxes, list boxes, pop-up list boxes, and command buttons.

You work with one element at a time—moving to it to make it active. To move within a dialog box using a mouse, click an element. Or, to move using your keyboard, press (TAB) or (SHIFT) + (TAB) to jump forward or backward between elements. To jump to a specific element, press (ALT) + the element's mnemonic key (if it has one).

To signify that an element is active, WordPerfect either displays a thin, dotted line around the element's name (such as around "Full Document" in Figure 2-3) or highlights an item inside the element in reverse video (such as the item next to "Filename" in Figure 2-4). Once you make a selection, you can move to another element or close the dialog box. The various elements

Figure 2-3. *Print dialog box*

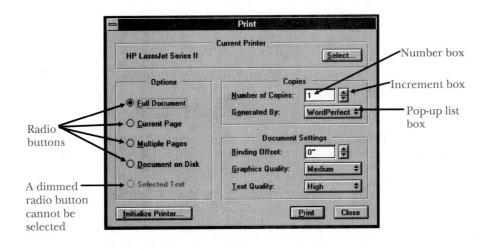

Figure 2-4. *Open File dialog box*

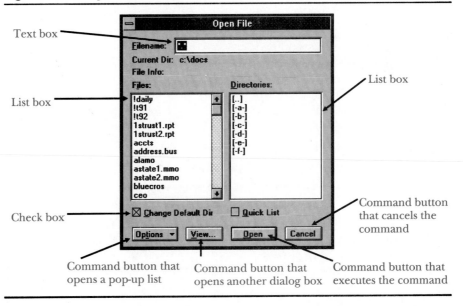

within dialog boxes and the procedure for making selections from them are described next.

note Inside a dialog box, only the Common User Access (CUA) compatible keyboard is preserved.

Title Bar

The title bar is located at the very top of a dialog box and indicates the command that opened the box, such as "Print" or "Open File". The highlighting of the title bar tells you that the dialog box is *active*, meaning that it is the one in which you are currently working.

A dialog box is like a small window, and the title bar enables mouse users to move the dialog box on screen. This ability is handy when a dialog box overlaps an area on screen that you wish to view before making a selection from the dialog box. To move a dialog box using a mouse, click and drag the title bar, moving the box in any direction. A box outline representing the dialog box will appear, mirroring the movements of your mouse. Release the mouse button once the outline is where you wish to relocate the dialog box. (Keyboard users can rely on the control-menu box to move a dialog box, as you'll see shortly.)

Control-Menu Box

Like an application window or a document window, a dialog box window has a control-menu box—a small rectangle located in the upper left corner. To close the dialog box, click the control-menu box, or press (ALT) + (SPACEBAR). A short drop-down menu appears:

Click Close or press © (the mnemonic key for Close).

2

shortcut *A quick way to close a dialog box with a mouse is simply to double-click the control-menu box. A quick way with the keyboard is to press (ALT) + (F4).*

The control-menu box also provides a keyboard option for moving a dialog box. With the dialog box on screen, press (ALT) + (SPACEBAR) and then press (M) (the mnemonic key for Move). The mouse pointer changes to a four-headed arrow. Now as you press the arrow keys, a box outline representing the dialog box appears. Move the box outline where you wish to relocate the dialog box. Press (ENTER).

Group Boxes

Group boxes, which are rectangular borders, organize dialog boxes into separate sections that are related by function. For instance, Figure 2-3 shows that the Print dialog box has four group boxes: Current Printer, Options, Copies, and Document Settings. On the other hand, the Open File screen shown in Figure 2-4 contains no group boxes.

Radio Buttons

Radio buttons, shaped like hollow circles, are options in which you can choose just *one* from among those that sit inside a group box. The circle of the currently selected radio button is filled in with a dot. For example, in Figure 2-3, Full Document is the current selection of the Options group box. In a group box, you cannot have more than one radio button in effect at once.

To choose a radio button with your mouse, click inside the radio button or click the name beside the radio button. The radio button is filled in, while all the other radio buttons in that group are unselected and preceded by hollow circles.

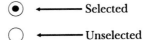

To choose a radio button with your keyboard, press (TAB) or (SHIFT) + (TAB) until you move to the group box containing that radio button. Then use the arrow keys to choose from among the radio buttons. Or, a faster method is to press (ALT) + the mnemonic key of the radio button you wish to choose.

Check Boxes

Check boxes, shaped like hollow squares, turn options in the dialog box on or off like a toggle switch. Using your mouse, click inside a check box or on the name beside the check box to turn it on; an X will appear inside the box. Click again to turn it off; the X disappears. Using your keyboard, first make the check box active (with (TAB) or (SHIFT) + (TAB)) and then press the (SPACEBAR) to turn it on or off. Or, a faster method is to press (ALT) + the mnemonic key of the check box you wish to turn on or off.

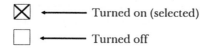

In Figure 2-4, for instance, there are two check boxes: the C̲hange Default Dir check box is on, while the Q̲uick List check box is off. Unlike radio buttons, with check boxes you can turn all of them on, all of them off, or have any combination in between.

Text Boxes

Text boxes provide space for you to input whatever information Word-Perfect is requesting. For instance, the F̲ilename text box in Figure 2-4 allows you to type in the name of a file that you wish to open. Using your mouse, type in a *new* entry in a text box by double-clicking inside the text box. The entry inside the text box is highlighted. When you start to type a new text entry, the previous entry is automatically erased.

To *edit* an entry that already exists in a text box, click (just once) inside the text box. The insertion point appears wherever you positioned the mouse

2

pointer before clicking. Then, use the (BACKSPACE), (DEL), arrow keys, and typing and editing keys to edit the text.

Using your keyboard, press (TAB) or (SHIFT) + (TAB) to make the text box active; the entry will be highlighted. To type a *new* entry, simply begin typing. To *edit* an existing entry, press the (←) or (→) key. The highlighting disappears and the insertion point appears inside the box. You can now edit the entry.

caution — *Don't press the* (ENTER) *key after you've finished typing into a text box. Pressing* (ENTER) *may execute the dialog box command prematurely, as described under the upcoming section entitled "Command Buttons".*

Number/Increment Boxes

Number boxes are similar to text boxes, except that they accept only number entries. Moreover, rather than typing in a number directly, you often have the option with number boxes of entering a new number using the nearby increment box, a box containing a pair of arrowheads separated by a line.

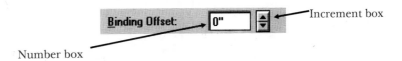

Number box

Increment box

In Figure 2-3, there are two such boxes: the Number of Copies number/increment boxes and the Binding Offset number/increment boxes. With your mouse, click the up arrowhead to increase the value in the corresponding number box by a predefined increment, or click the down arrowhead to decrease the value.

With your keyboard, make the corresponding number box active (with (TAB) or (SHIFT) + (TAB) or with (ALT) + the increment box's mnemonic key) and then press the (↑) or (↓) key to change the increment.

caution — *Don't press the* (ENTER) *key after you've finished typing into a number box. Pressing* (ENTER) *may execute the dialog box command prematurely, as described in the section, "Command Buttons".*

List Boxes

List boxes are like radio buttons in that you can choose one from among a group of options. But list boxes are used instead of radio buttons when: a group of items is too long to fit separately within the confines of the dialog box; or the items change periodically; or more than one item can be selected. For instance, the F<u>i</u>les list box in Figure 2-4 displays a list of filenames from which you can select the one you wish to open, a list that will change as you create new documents.

To select an item from a list box with your mouse, click the item; that item is highlighted. (In situations when you can select more than one item in a list, clicking works like a toggle switch. Click an item once to select it and click a second time to unselect it. When you click to select an item so that it is highlighted, any previously selected items in that list box will also remain highlighted.)

Sometimes, there are so many items in a list box that not all of them can be displayed at one time. In that case, a scroll bar will appear along the right side of the box, as shown in the F<u>i</u>les list box in Figure 2-4. A scroll bar in a dialog box operates just as a scroll bar in a document window. (Refer to Chapter 3 for information on how a scroll bar in a document window functions.)

To select from a list box using your keyboard, make that list box active (with (TAB) or (SHIFT) + (TAB) or with (ALT) + the list box's mnemonic key). Then use the arrow keys to select (highlight) the item you desire. Or, type the first few letters of the item to highlight it. In list boxes where you can select multiple items, use the (SPACEBAR) like a toggle switch.

Pop-up List Boxes

Pop-up list boxes contain items that are hidden until you're ready to select a new one. One item is currently in effect. The currently selected item, followed by two arrowheads pointing in opposite directions, is displayed on the face of the list box. Here's one example:

Pop-up list box

2

As shown in Figure 2-3, the Print dialog box contains three such pop-up list boxes. The current selection for Generated By is "WordPerfect"; for Graphics Quality is "Medium"; and for Text Quality is "High". To select with your mouse from a pop-up list box:

1. Click and hold on the pop-up list box. The entire list pops up on screen, and the currently selected item has a check mark next to it.

2. Still holding down the mouse button, drag the mouse up or down until you highlight the new selection.

3. Release the mouse button. The pop-up list box disappears, and the new selection is displayed.

To select with your keyboard from a pop-up list box:

1. Press TAB or SHIFT + TAB until you make that list box active. Or, press ALT + the pop-up list box's mnemonic key to make it active.

2. Press SPACEBAR; the entire list pops up on screen, and the currently selected item has a check mark next to it.

3. Use the ↑ and ↓ keys to highlight the new selection.

4. Press SPACEBAR. The pop-up list box disappears, and the new selection is displayed.

   You can also display each selection without viewing the entire list by following only steps 1 and 3.

Command Buttons

Command buttons are rectangles that appear three-dimensional to resemble push buttons. These buttons "command" WordPerfect to execute the

task listed on the face of the button. The two most common command buttons
are OK and Cancel:

The OK command button closes the dialog box and executes the command, while Cancel closes the dialog box and cancels the command. But
sometimes, command buttons other than OK or Cancel are provided. For
instance, in Figure 2-3, there is neither an OK nor a Cancel command button.
Instead, it is Print that executes the Print command and Close that closes the
dialog box and cancels the Print command. In Figure 2-4, it is Open that
executes the Open File command and Cancel that aborts the command.
Here's an example of a dialog box where command buttons are the only
elements that you can choose from.

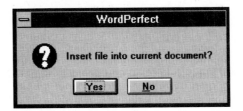

You can either choose the Yes or No command button to respond to
WordPerfect's question.

When you first open a dialog box, one command button has darker
borders, which means that it is preselected. You may have to look closely at
the screen to distinguish the command button with the darker borders. In
the dialog box above, for example, the Yes command button is preselected.
In Figure 2-4, look closely to see that Open is the preselected command
button.

Like menu items, command buttons provide visual clues as to what will
happen once you choose one:

2

- A command button that doesn't have a graphical mark beside the button name means that the command will be executed without further input from you. An example is the OK command button or the Cancel command button.

- A command button name followed by an ellipsis (three dots) opens a new dialog box that overlaps the first one. For instance, the View command button is followed by an ellipsis in Figure 2-4. Choosing View will open a new dialog box.

- A command button name followed by a downward-pointing arrowhead brings up a pop-up list that you can choose from. For instance, the Options command button in Figure 2-4 will display a pop-up list.

- A command button dimmed to a light shade (usually gray) is currently unavailable.

To choose a command button displaying a name without a graphical mark or one followed by an ellipsis, click it. Or, when using your keyboard, you have several alternatives: if the command button has been preselected, simply press (ENTER) to choose it; if the command button has not been preselected, either press (TAB) or (SHIFT) + (TAB) to make that command button active and press (ENTER); or press (ALT) + the command button's mnemonic key (if it has one). If command buttons are the only elements other than messages in a dialog box, simply press a command button's mnemonic key (without first pressing (ALT)). To choose the Cancel command button, the simplest method is to press (ESC).

shortcut *Double-clicking an item in a list box gives the same results as selecting the item and then choosing the OK command button.*

To choose a command button displaying a name followed by a downward-pointing arrowhead, the process is similar to working with a pop-up list box. When using your mouse, click and hold the command button. A pop-up list appears. Then, still holding down the mouse button, drag the mouse up or down until you highlight your selection. Release the mouse button. Or, when using your keyboard, either press (TAB) or (SHIFT) + (TAB) until you make the command button active, or press (ALT) + the command button's mnemonic key to make it active. Press (SPACEBAR) to display its pop-up list. Then, use the (↑) and (↓) keys to highlight your selection and press (SPACEBAR).

 Make sure to select OK or another command button that executes a command or to press (ENTER) only after you have selected from all the other elements in the dialog box. For instance, don't choose the Print command button shown in Figure 2-3 until you've made sure that the elements in all four group boxes—Current Printer, Options, Copies, and Document Settings—are correct for your present needs. Moreover, don't press (ENTER) while selecting from the elements in Figure 2-3 or you'll prematurely choose Print, because that is the preselected command button.

Hands-on Exercise: Work with Dialog Boxes

Here's a chance to select items within a dialog box:

1. From the menu bar, choose File, Print. The Print dialog box displays, as shown in Figure 2-3. It temporarily overlaps the document workspace.

   Notice the four group boxes in the dialog box, titled Current Printer, Options, Copies, and Document Settings. Also notice in Figure 2-3 that the group box named Options contains five radio buttons—Full Document is the selected item and Selected Text is dimmed, meaning that the item is not currently available for selection.

2. Click Document on Disk or press (ALT) + (D). When Document on Disk becomes the selected item, its radio button is filled in, and the radio button next to Full Document is hollow.

   Notice that the Text Quality pop-up list box has "High" or "Set In Driver" currently selected. (The available options depend on your printer.)

3. Click and hold the Text Quality pop-up list box or press (ALT) + (T) and then the (SPACEBAR). The list is opened, and a check mark appears next to the currently selected item.

2

4. Still holding down on the mouse button, drag the mouse down until "Draft" is highlighted, and then release the mouse button to select that item. Or press ⊙ to select "Draft", and then press the (SPACEBAR). The pop-up list box disappears, and "Draft" is displayed as the currently selected item. (You may find when you change the Text Quality selection, the Graphics Quality selection also changes. This depends on your printer.)

   Notice the Number of Copies increment box—the narrow box with arrowheads pointing in opposite directions, separated by a line. It sits beside a number box that shows that the current selection is "1" copy.

5. Click twice on the upward-pointing arrowhead. Or press (ALT) + (N), and then press (↑) twice. The number box changes to show a new selection, "3" copies. (If you click the downward-pointing arrowhead instead, WordPerfect will beep because the minimum number of copies is one.)

   Notice that the Print command button contains an ellipsis. When the Document on Disk radio button is selected, the Print command button brings up a second dialog box.

6. Click Print. Or, press (ALT) + (P). A second dialog box overlaps the first. An insertion point is located in a text box where you can type the name of a document.

7. Click Cancel or press (ESC) to close the Document on Disk dialog box. The Print dialog box remains.

8. Practice on your own to return the Print dialog box to its initial selections: Full Document, "1" copy, either "High" or "Set In Driver" Text Quality.

9. When the initial selections have been made, click Close or press (ESC) to close the Print dialog box.

Finally, here you'll move a smaller dialog box, the Password dialog box, on screen. To do so, use the mouse to drag the dialog box by its title bar.

1. Choose File, Password. The Password dialog box displays.

2. Click and hold the Password title bar.

3. Drag the mouse up, down, left, or right. Notice that a box outline appears that mimics the movements of your mouse.

4. Release the mouse button. The dialog box moves to the location where the box outline appeared a moment before.

5. Click Cancel or press (ESC) to close the Password dialog box.

If you've completed your WordPerfect session for today, remember from the discussion in Chapter 1 that you must exit WordPerfect properly before you turn to another Windows application or before you turn off your computer. To exit WordPerfect, choose <u>F</u>ile, E<u>x</u>it, press the shortcut keys (ALT) + (F4), or double-click the WordPerfect control-menu box.

Know About Help

WordPerfect offers a Help facility, whereby you can get onscreen assistance with all of WordPerfect's features and commands. For instance, if you can't remember how to use the Print command, you can find a brief explanation. Refer to Appendix C for a description on how to use Help. You may wish to get comfortable with the WordPerfect basics, dialog boxes, and WordPerfect terminology before you turn to the Help facility.

Quick Reference

- To issue a command via the menu bar, click a menu name and then a menu item. Or press (ALT) + a menu name's mnemonic key, and then press a menu item's mnemonic key. A mnemonic key is the underlined letter in a menu name or menu item.

- To issue a command via shortcut keys, press the key or key combination that, according to your template or Table 2-1, corresponds to that command. Not all commands have shortcut keys.

- To know what will happen when you choose a menu item, look for visual clues. No graphical mark means that a command will be executed without further input from you. An arrowhead following an item leads to a cascading menu. An ellipsis following an item brings up a dialog box. A command name faded to a light shade is currently unavailable.

- To move from element to element in a dialog box and make selections, click the element. Or press (TAB) or (SHIFT) + (TAB) to move forward and backward between elements. Or press (ALT) + the element's mnemonic key (if it has one). Make sure that all the proper selections are made before pressing (ENTER), choosing OK, or choosing another command button that executes the command.

2

3

Creating and Revising
Documents

Chapters 1 and 2 covered the mechanics of WordPerfect. This chapter shows a more practical aspect of learning WordPerfect—the actual creation of a document. You will learn how to type text, move the insertion point, fix typographical mistakes, and insert and delete text. And you'll use the Select feature, which allows you to mark off sections of text for easy editing.

This chapter also describes what goes on behind the scenes when you enter text. WordPerfect hides certain symbols, called codes, from you. These codes control how your words appear. You will uncover the codes from their hiding places and see how inserting or deleting a simple code can reshuffle paragraphs.

Typing Documents with Word Wrap and Automatic Page Breaks

Viewing a clear document workspace is like rolling a fresh sheet of paper into the typewriter; you're ready to type. You'll find that WordPerfect offers a feature known as WYSIWYG—what you see is what you get. When printed onto the paper, the document will be as close as possible to what you were viewing on screen.

Word Wrap

A feature called *word wrap* is one of the reasons computers are so much faster than typewriters. With classic typewriters, you slowed down near the end of each line to listen for the bell before pressing the carriage return. WordPerfect automatically senses the end of each line and "wraps" the next word down to the beginning of a new line. If you later insert or delete text, word wrap readjusts line breaks and reforms your paragraphs for you automatically. A line break created by word wrap is called a *soft return*—"soft" because its location may change later when you edit your text.

How does WordPerfect know when to wrap a word? WordPerfect assumes initially that you want left and right margins that are 1 inch wide. WordPerfect also assumes that you will print on standard-size paper, which is 8.5 inches wide. As a result, WordPerfect allows text only between the 1-inch position and the 7.5-inch position. Words that extend to the 7.6-inch position and beyond automatically wrap to a new line.

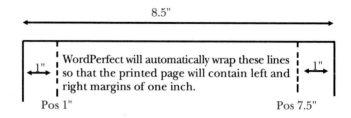

note ═══*The margin and paper size settings just described are the default or initial settings, the settings already in place when you first install WordPerfect. You can change default settings for a particular document, such as margins (see Chapter 6) or paper size (see Chapter 7), or you can change default settings more permanently, as described in Chapter 17.*

Because of word wrap, you never use the (ENTER) key like a carriage return. You don't press (ENTER) to end a line in the middle of a paragraph because WordPerfect will be unable to reformat paragraphs properly after you edit. Press (ENTER) only when you wish to:

- End a paragraph
- End a short line of text
- Insert a blank line in the text

A line break that you create with the (ENTER) key is called a *hard return*— "hard" because its location stays fixed.

Page Breaks

WordPerfect also saves you time by breaking your text into pages. There's no need to keep track of whether you're typing more lines than can fit on one page. WordPerfect automatically senses the end of a page and breaks the next line onto a new page. If you later insert or delete text, WordPerfect will automatically reformat your pages properly. The page break created by WordPerfect is shown on screen as a single line across the page:

Page break

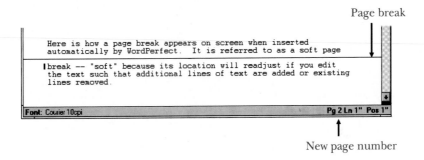

New page number

Figure 3-1.   *WordPerfect automatically breaks to a new page*

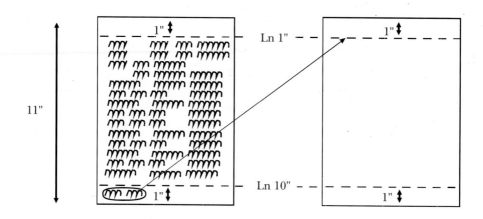

The status line indicates that the insertion point is at the start of a new page. The page break is called a *soft page break*—"soft" because, as with a soft return, its location may change later when you edit your text.

How does WordPerfect know when to break to a new page? WordPerfect assumes initially that you want top and bottom margins of 1 inch. Word-Perfect also assumes that you will print on standard-size paper, which is 11 inches long. To accommodate this, WordPerfect puts the first line of text at the 1-inch position from the top edge of the page and does not allow text below the 10-inch position. Text that extends beyond the bottom margin is placed on a new page (see Figure 3-1).

Hands-on Exercise: Type a Short Document

   This exercise lets you see how word wrap creates line breaks. You'll also learn when it is appropriate to use the (ENTER) key. The final document that you'll have on screen after this exercise is shown in Figure 3-2.

Figure 3-2. *Sample text to be typed*

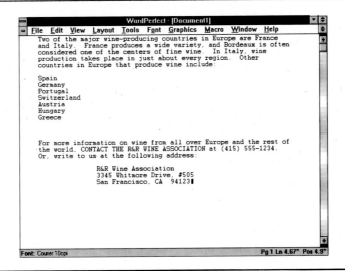

```
                        WordPerfect - [Document1]
  File  Edit  View  Layout  Tools  Font  Graphics  Macro  Window  Help
  Two of the major wine-producing countries in Europe are France
  and Italy.  France produces a wide variety, and Bordeaux is often
  considered one of the centers of fine wine.  In Italy, wine
  production takes place in just about every region.  Other
  countries in Europe that produce wine include:

  Spain
  Germany
  Portugal
  Switzerland
  Austria
  Hungary
  Greece


  For more information on wine from all over Europe and the rest of
  the world, CONTACT THE R&R WINE ASSOCIATION at (415) 555-1234.
  Or, write to us at the following address:

              R&R Wine Association
              3345 Whitmore Drive, #505
              San Francisco, CA  94123

  Font: Courier 10cpi                              Pg 1 Ln 4.67"  Pos 4.9"
```

reminder As you learned in Chapter 1, use the (BACKSPACE) key if you make a mistake and need to erase a character you just typed. Then type the correct character. (But, don't worry too much about typing mistakes; you will learn various ways to edit your text soon.)

1. If you haven't already done so, load WordPerfect as described in Chapter 1. The title bar on screen should read:

   WordPerfect - [Document1 - unmodified]

   You're in a clear document workspace and ready to type.

2. Type the following paragraph. Remember not to press the (ENTER) key at all while typing the paragraph; just keep typing and watch word wrap work. Also, when entering the word "wine-producing" in the first sentence, type the hyphen between "wine" and "producing" using the (-) key. (There are two (-) keys; one on the typewriter keypad and one on the numeric keypad. You can use either one.)

   Two of the major wine-producing countries in Europe are France and Italy. France produces a wide variety, and

Bordeaux is often considered one of the centers of fine
wine. In Italy, wine production takes place in just
about every region. Other countries in Europe that
produce wine include:

3. Press (ENTER) twice—once to end the paragraph (this moves the
   insertion point down to the next line) and the second time to insert
   a blank line.

4. Type the names of the following countries, making sure to press
   (ENTER) after each so that you type one country name on each line:

   Spain
   Germany
   Portugal
   Switzerland
   Austria
   Hungary
   Greece

   Your insertion point should now be on a blank line below
   "Greece".

5. Press (ENTER) three times to insert three blank lines.

6. Type the following paragraph. Again, do not press (ENTER) within the
   paragraph. While typing, remember from Chapter 1 that the
   (CAPS LOCK) key is available for typing a phrase in all uppercase
   letters. Also, remember to type real ones and zeros, rather than the
   letters "l" and "o" when typing numbers.

   For more information on wine from all over Europe and
   the rest of the world, CONTACT THE R&R WINE ASSOCIATION
   at (415)555-1234. Or write to us at the following
   address:

7. Press (ENTER) twice.

8. Press (TAB) three times.

As you learned in Chapter 1, tab stops are initially set 0.5 inch apart, and pressing the (TAB) key pushes the insertion point to the next tab stop. The (TAB) key is useful for indenting the first line in a paragraph or aligning text in tabular columns.

9. Type **R&R Wine Association** and press (ENTER).

10. Press (TAB) three times, type **3345 Whitmore Drive, #505** and press (ENTER).

11. Press (TAB) three times, type **San Francisco, CA 94123** and press (ENTER).

Congratulations to those of you who have just completed your first WordPerfect document! Your text may appear slightly different than the document shown in Figure 3-2. Where word wrap breaks text into lines depends on the font used when creating your document.

Moving the Insertion Point

The insertion point can move anywhere within a document. If your document is short, such as in the hands-on exercise you just did, you can see all the text on screen. If the document is long, however, you may see only about one-half of a full-length page at once. You must move through the document to view different sections of it. This is referred to as *scrolling* and is illustrated in Figure 3-3. It is as if your document is a roll of film that you are turning through a film projector to view it frame by frame.

You can use either the mouse or the keyboard to scroll through the document and move the insertion point. The mouse is convenient for skimming the text and for grand sweeps through a long document. You may find the keyboard is faster and easier when you want to make precise movements—such as to the beginning of the next paragraph or to the top of the page. A third option is the Go To feature.

Figure 3-3.   *Scrolling through your document on screen*

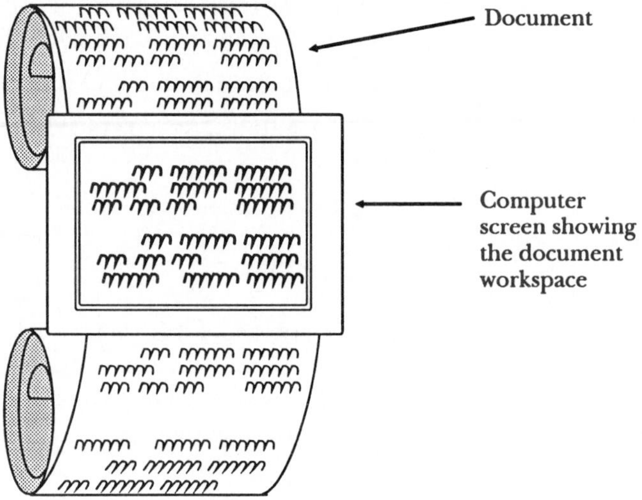

Document

Computer
screen showing
the document
workspace

Moving the Insertion Point with the Mouse and Scroll Bars

To relocate the insertion point anywhere on screen, follow these simple steps when using a mouse:

1. Point the mouse pointer (I-beam) at the spot in the document workspace where you want to move the insertion point.

2. Click the left mouse button.

Keep in mind that if you click directly on a character, the insertion point will appear just past that character (to the right of it).

reminder *As discussed in Chapter 1, the insertion point can only move through that portion of the document workspace in which you've previously typed characters or pressed* (ENTER) *to insert blank lines. The insertion point cannot move past the end of the document.*

For instance, if your document is five lines long and you click in a blank area at the bottom of the document workspace, the insertion point will move only as far as the end of the document, which is the fifth line.

When you wish to move the insertion point to a location in a document not currently displayed on screen, you must first scroll through the document to the spot where you want to place the insertion point. In other words, you have to be viewing the spot where you wish to place the insertion point before you can actually relocate it with your mouse. In a long document, scroll up and down with the mouse using the vertical scroll bar. In a wide document, scroll left to right using the horizontal scroll bar. (The horizontal scroll bar is hidden when you first start WordPerfect, but you can display it with the File, Preferences, Display command, as described in Chapter 17.)

A scroll bar is comprised of a *scroll box*, a *scroll area*, and two *scroll arrows*. These are labeled in Figure 3-4. The position of the scroll box tells you where

3

Figure 3-4. *Elements of the vertical and horizontal scroll bars*

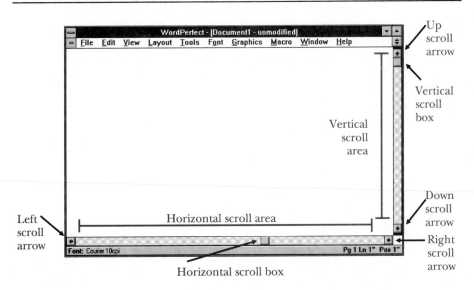

you are in relation to the document as a whole. For instance, if the vertical scroll box is at the top of the vertical scroll area (as shown in Figure 3-4), the top of the document is what you see on screen. If the scroll box is in the middle of the vertical scroll area, you see the middle of the document displayed on the screen.

To scroll short distances, use the scroll arrows. Click a scroll arrow once to scroll in the direction indicated by the arrow. For instance, click the up scroll arrow to scroll the document one line up. Click the down scroll arrow to scroll one line down. If you click and hold down on a scroll arrow, you can scroll in one direction continually.

To scroll longer distances in a lengthy document, use the scroll box. Click the scroll box and drag it to a new location in the scroll area. When you release the mouse button, the screen changes to display the text that corresponds to the scroll box's new position.

Once you scroll through a document using the scroll bar, point to a new location and click. The insertion point appears on screen right where the pointer was when you clicked.

caution *Keep in mind that the scroll bars allow you to move through a document without moving the insertion point. For instance, you may scroll through the middle of a document but still have the insertion point at the top. The insertion point does not move to the part of the document you're viewing until you point and click your mouse (or use the keyboard to move the insertion point). Don't attempt to edit text until you position the insertion point within the portion of the document that you're viewing.*

Scroll bars are found not only in the document window, but also in dialog boxes when there are too many items in a list box to display all at once. Use a scroll bar in a dialog box the same way you do here—display additional items in a list box one at a time by clicking a scroll arrow, or move quickly from one section of the list to another by clicking and dragging the scroll box.

Moving the Insertion Point with the Keyboard

Use the numeric keypad (or the second set of arrow keys) to move the insertion point when you're not using a mouse. Move horizontally one character at a time with the (←) or (→) key. Or press and hold down an arrow key to move in one direction continually.

As you move the insertion point with the arrow keys, word wrap brings it to the next line when appropriate—that is, if the insertion point is at the end of a line and you press ⊙, it wraps around to the beginning of the next line. If the insertion point is at the beginning of a line and you press ⊙, it moves back to the end of the last line:

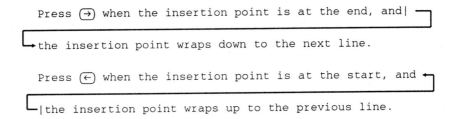

```
Press ⊙ when the insertion point is at the end, and|

the insertion point wraps down to the next line.

Press ⊙ when the insertion point is at the start, and

|the insertion point wraps up to the previous line.
```

Move vertically one line at a time with the ⊙ and ⊙ keys. As you move up and down, WordPerfect will attempt to maintain your current position on the line. For instance, suppose your insertion point is in the middle of the screen. When you press the ⊙ key, the insertion point will move down to the next line, preserving its position in the middle of the screen. But suppose that the next line of text is short, just three words long. When you press the ⊙ key, WordPerfect will move the insertion point down and place it just past the third word, which is as close to the middle of the screen as it can get in a short line.

To scroll longer distances, WordPerfect offers shortcut key combinations. These are summarized in Table 3-1.

- Use (CTRL) with the arrow keys to amplify the distance that the insertion point will move between words and lines. For example, (CTRL) + (←) or (→) moves the insertion point one word left or right; the insertion point lands before the first character of the word. Use (CTRL) + (↑) or (↓) to move the insertion point one paragraph up or down; the insertion point lands before the first character of the paragraph.

- Use (PGUP) or (PGDN)—either alone or in combination with (ALT) or (CTRL)—to move between screens or pages. (Remember that a screen is equivalent to approximately one-half of a full-length page.) (PGUP) or (PGDN) moves the insertion point to the top or bottom of the current screen. If the insertion point is at the top or bottom, (PGUP) or (PGDN) scrolls up or down one full screen. (ALT) + (PGUP) moves the insertion point to the top of the previous page, while (ALT) + (PGDN) moves the insertion point to the top of the next page. (CTRL) + (PGUP) or (PGDN) scrolls the screen to the left or right.

- Use (HOME) or (END)—either alone or in combination with (ALT) or (CTRL)—to move around the current page or to the edges of a line or document. (HOME) moves the insertion point to the beginning (left edge) of the line, and (END) moves the insertion point to the end (right edge) of the line. (ALT) + (HOME) or (END) moves the insertion point to the top or bottom of the current page. (CTRL) + (HOME) moves the insertion point to the top of the document, while (CTRL) + (END) moves the insertion point to the bottom of the document.

Table 3-1.   *Shortcut Keys for Moving the Insertion Point (CUA Keyboard)*

Movement	Key Combination
Word left	(CTRL) + (←)
Word right	(CTRL) + (→)
Paragraph up	(CTRL) + (↑)
Paragraph down	(CTRL) + (↓)
Screen left	(CTRL) + (PGUP)
Screen right	(CTRL) + (PGDN)
Screen up	(PGUP)
Screen down	(PGDN)
Top of page	(ALT) + (HOME)
Bottom of page	(ALT) + (END)
Previous page	(ALT) + (PGUP)
Next page	(ALT) + (PGDN)
Beginning of line	(HOME)
End of line	(END)
Beginning of document	(CTRL) + (HOME)
End of document	(CTRL) + (END)

Shortcut keys for moving the insertion point also work in dialog boxes. For instance, when a dialog box contains a text box, use the (HOME) key within the text box to move to the beginning of the line, or use the (END) key to move to the end.

Moving the Insertion Point with the Go To Feature

A final option for scrolling through a document and moving the insertion point is the Go To feature, which lets you specify that you wish to move to:

- The top of a specific page
- The top of the page where the insertion point is currently located
- The bottom of the page where the insertion point is currently located
- The insertion point's previous position (which is incredibly useful if you press the wrong key combination by mistake, and wish to return the insertion point to its location just before you made the error)

Use the Go To feature with these steps:

1. Choose Edit, Go To. The Go To dialog box appears on screen:

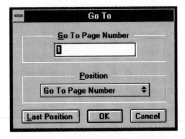

2. Type in a specific page number in the Go To Page Number text box and choose the OK command button (WordPerfect suggests the page number where the insertion point is currently located).

   Or, select Top of Current Page or Bottom of Current Page, from the Position pop-up list box, and then choose OK. (See Chapter 2 for a review of how to select an item from a pop-up list box.)

Or, choose the <u>L</u>ast Position command button.

The dialog box disappears and the insertion point relocates.

shortcut (CTRL) + (G) *is the shortcut for* <u>E</u>dit, <u>G</u>o To.

Hands-on Exercise: Move the Insertion Point

Let's practice moving the insertion point in the document you just typed, using both the mouse and the keyboard. As you become accustomed to WordPerfect, you will undoubtedly discover which method you prefer, depending on where the insertion point is and where it will be moved.

1. Click the "a" in "Spain" in the middle of the document. The insertion point moves just past the letter.

2. Click the empty spot just to the left of the "T" in "Two of the..." at the top of the document. The insertion point moves to the beginning of the document, just to the left of the letter "T".

3. Click an empty portion of the document workspace near the bottom of the screen. The insertion point moves only as far as the end of the document.

4. Press and hold down the (↑) key and watch the insertion point zoom up until it stops at the top of the document.

5. Press and hold down the (→) key for a few moments and watch the insertion point speed to the right. When it reaches the end of the line, the insertion point wraps down to the beginning of the next line and continues speeding along.

6. Press (CTRL) + (→) three times. The insertion point jumps forward three words.

7. Press (CTRL) + (←) three times to see the insertion point jump backward from word to word.

8. Press (←) until the insertion point is located at the left margin.

9. Press (↓) until the insertion point moves to the left margin of the line "3345 Whitmore Drive".

10. Press ⟶ three times. Since you used the TAB key before typing the address, the insertion point jumps from tab stop to tab stop.

11. Press CTRL + END. The insertion point moves down to the end of the document.

12. Press CTRL + HOME. The insertion point moves up to the beginning of the document.

Inserting Text

WordPerfect starts out in *Insert mode*. This means that any characters you type are placed at the insertion point and any text following the new characters is pushed to the right. Word wrap adjusts the text so that your paragraph fits properly within the margins. Thus, you can add as much text as you like in the midst of a document; WordPerfect will reformat the text for you. For instance, suppose you position the insertion point before the third word in this sentence:

```
For more |information on the seminar, please contact
Keith Michaels as soon as possible.
```

If you type **detailed** and then press the SPACEBAR once (to add a space between words), the word will be inserted as shown here:

```
For more detailed |information on the seminar, please
contact Keith Michaels as soon as possible.
```

An alternative way to insert characters is to switch to *Typeover mode*, where any new character you type will replace the character currently located at the insertion point. Use Typeover mode whenever you want to type over existing text—such as when you mistakenly transpose characters (like "teh" instead of "the", or "415" instead of "514"), or when the word you wish to replace has the same number of characters as the existing word. To switch into Typeover mode, press the INS key once. The message "Typeover" displays on the left side of the status line at the bottom of the screen. To switch back to Insert mode, press INS again.

For instance, suppose you position the insertion point before the third word in this sentence:

```
For more |detailed information on the seminar, please
contact Keith Michaels as soon as possible.
```

If you press (INS) once to switch into Typeover mode and then type **specific**, the word "specific" will replace "detailed" (both words have the same number of characters):

```
For more specific| information on the seminar, please
contact Keith Michaels as soon as possible.
```

Then you can press (INS) again to switch back to Insert mode.

The only key excluded in Typeover mode is the (TAB) key; pressing the (TAB) key moves the insertion point to the next tab stop, but never replaces a character even in Typeover mode.

A third method for inserting text involves the Select feature, described later in this chapter.

Deleting Text

You've already learned that the (BACKSPACE) key will erase the character you've just typed. (BACKSPACE) deletes the character to the *left* of the insertion point. For instance, suppose you position the insertion point after the third word in this sentence:

```
For more specific| information on the seminar, please
contact Keith Michaels as soon as possible.
```

If you press (BACKSPACE) nine times, you will erase "specific" and the extra space.

Another option is the (DEL) key (Delete), which deletes the character to the *right* of the insertion point. For instance, suppose you position the insertion point before the seventh word in this sentence:

```
For more information on the seminar, |please contact
Keith Michaels as soon as possible.
```

If you press (DEL) seven times, you will erase "please" and the extra space.

```
For more information on the seminar, |contact Keith
Michaels as soon as possible.
```

Whether you use (BACKSPACE) or (DEL) depends on where the insertion point is located when you notice the error in the text. Both the (BACKSPACE) key and the (DEL) key feature auto-repeat, so if you press and hold down either key you can erase as many characters in a row as you like without having to keep tapping the key.

You also have several shortcuts available to erase a whole word, a line, or page of words at once:

- To erase a word, position the insertion point anywhere within the word and press (CTRL) + (BACKSPACE).

- To erase everything to the end of the line, position the insertion point just before the first character that you wish to erase and press (CTRL) + (DEL). Everything to the right of the insertion point, all the way to the end of the line, will be erased.

- To erase everything to the end of the page, position the insertion point just before the first character that you wish to erase and press (CTRL) + (SHIFT) + (DEL). Everything to the right and below the insertion point, all the way to the end of the page, will be erased.

Besides deleting text with the keyboard, you can also delete using the Select feature. The Select feature is described later in the chapter.

Hands-on Exercise: Insert and Delete Text

 As you insert or delete text in the document you typed on screen, watch how WordPerfect reformats the document automatically.

Inserting Text

1. Position the insertion point at the beginning of the document if it isn't already located there. (Remember that an easy way to do this is to press (CTRL) + (HOME).)

2. Type the following sentence and watch how it is inserted as the rest of the text readjusts:

   ```
   Fine wines are produced all over the world.
   ```

3. Press the (SPACEBAR) twice to insert two spaces after the sentence.

4. Position the insertion point near the end of the first paragraph, just before the letter "O" that begins the sentence, "Other countries in Europe that ...."

5. Type the following, and again watch how the text readjusts to accommodate:

   ```
   In fact, Italy has been known to yield more wine per
   year than any other country in the world. Though white
   wines are manufactured here, it is Italy's red wines
   that have achieved a special reputation.
   ```

6. Press the (SPACEBAR) twice to insert two spaces after the last sentence you inserted.

7. Position the insertion point in the last paragraph just before the "1" in "1234".

8. Press the (INS) key once. The message "Typeover" appears on the status line.

9. Type **5678**. Notice how, since you've switched from Insert mode to Typeover mode, the new characters type right over the old ones.

10. Press the (INS) key once more to return to Insert mode.

Deleting Text

Now try deleting text:

1. Position the insertion point on the last line of the document, just to the right of the "A" in "CA", as follows:

```
San Francisco, CA| 94123
```

2. Press (DEL) until you erase the spaces and the zip code.

3. Position the insertion point anywhere within the word "and" in the last paragraph:

```
For more information on wine from all over Europe a|nd
the rest of the world, CONTACT THE R&R WINE
ASSOCIATION at...
```

4. Press (CTRL) + (BACKSPACE) six times to delete these six words: "and the rest of the world".

5. Press the (←) key to reposition the insertion point and then type a comma after "Europe". Now the sentence reads:

```
For more information on wine from all over Europe,
CONTACT THE R&R WINE ASSOCIATION...
```

Adding Extra Lines and Splitting Text into Paragraphs

After typing text, you can decide to insert or delete blank lines or to rearrange paragraphs. To insert a blank line, position the insertion point at the end of the line above where you want the blank line to appear and press (ENTER). To delete a line, position the insertion point either at the beginning of that line, and press (BACKSPACE), or at the end of the previous line, and press (DEL). For instance, position the insertion point after the first line in this text:

```
Jack Smith|
Miami, Florida
```

If you press (ENTER), you will insert a blank line, as shown here:

```
Jack Smith
|
Miami, Florida
```

Or make sure the insertion point is on the blank line and press (BACKSPACE) to delete the blank line just inserted:

```
Jack Smith|
Miami, Florida
```

To split a paragraph, position the insertion point where you want the new paragraph to begin and press (ENTER). You can press (ENTER) more than once to insert extra blank lines between paragraphs. To join two paragraphs, position the insertion point at the start of the second paragraph and press (BACKSPACE) as many times as necessary to bring it up to meet the first paragraph, or position the insertion point at the end of the first paragraph and press (DEL) as many times as necessary.

For instance, position the insertion point before the third sentence in this paragraph:

```
The seminar will be held on September 15th at the
Alhambra Gold Hotel, in downtown Oakland, CA. The topic
will be, "Wine Growing to the year 2000". |For more
information on the seminar, contact Keith Michaels as
soon as possible.
```

If you press (ENTER) twice, you will end one paragraph and then insert an extra blank line between the paragraphs:

```
The seminar will be held on September 15th at the
Alhambra Gold Hotel, in downtown Oakland, CA. The topic
will be,"Wine Growing to the year 2000".

|For more information on the seminar, contact Keith
Michaels as soon as possible.
```

To return this text to its original format, position the insertion point before the last paragraph and press (BACKSPACE) twice:

```
The seminar will be held on September 15th at the
Alhambra Gold Hotel, in downtown Oakland, CA. The topic
will be,"Wine Growing to the year 2000". |For more
information on the seminar, contact Keith Michaels as
soon as possible.
```

What you actually do when you reshuffle paragraphs is insert and delete codes that are hidden from you but that keep lines separated. Codes are described later in this chapter.

The Undelete and Undo Features

At some point you will make an editing change—such as erasing two sentences from a paragraph—and then realize you made a mistake. How nice it would be to recover all the text you've accidentally erased! Two features allow you to do just that—the Undelete and Undo features.

Undelete

The Undelete feature keeps track of your three most recent deletions, (a deletion is simply a character or group of characters that you erased before typing or moving the insertion point). For instance, suppose you press (CTRL) + (DEL) to erase a line; that's one deletion. Then you resume typing and press (DEL) twice in a row; that's another deletion. Now suppose you move the insertion point to the top of the document and press (CTRL) + (BACKSPACE) four times to erase four words; that's a third deletion. Any of your three most recent deletions can be restored anywhere in a document with Undelete. You restore a deletion with these steps:

1. Position the insertion point in the location where you want to recover the deleted text.

2. Choose Edit, Undelete. The last deletion appears on screen high-lighted in reverse video, and the Undelete dialog box appears. An example is shown in Figure 3-5 where the most recent deletion is the phrase, "from all over Europe,".

Figure 3-5.   *Recovering erased text with the Undelete feature*

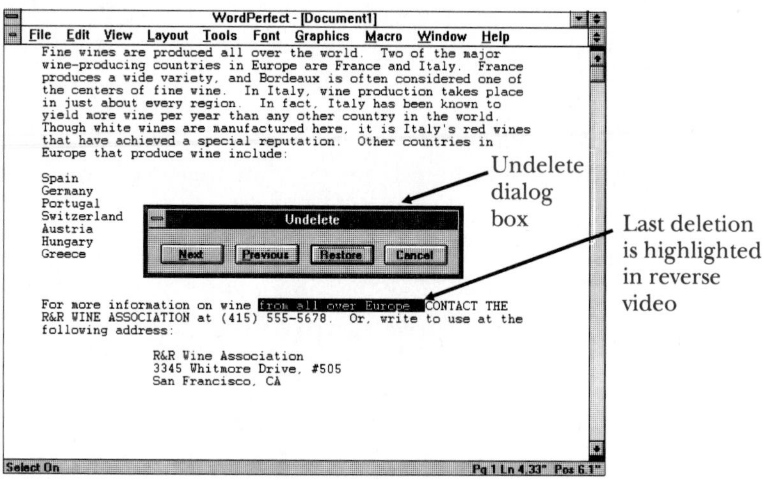

3. Choose <u>R</u>estore or simply press (ENTER) (since the <u>R</u>estore command
   button is preselected by WordPerfect) to restore the last deletion.
       Or, choose <u>N</u>ext or <u>P</u>revious to view the next-to-last or third-to-last
   deletion in reverse video on screen, and then choose <u>R</u>estore.
       Or, choose Cancel or press (ESC) to abort the Undelete procedure.

shortcut ═ (ALT) + (SHIFT) + (BACKSPACE) *is the shortcut for* <u>E</u>dit, U<u>n</u>delete.

Often the Undelete dialog box covers the display of the last deletion on
screen. If that's the case, you can move the Undelete dialog box out of the
way. See Chapter 2 for the procedure to move a dialog box.

Undo

The Undo feature reverses the very last change you made to the appearance of your document. If you just deleted a sentence, the sentence would be
restored to its original location. If you just typed a paragraph, the paragraph

would be deleted. If you just split a paragraph in two, the paragraph would be recombined. The procedure is simply to choose <u>E</u>dit, <u>U</u>ndo. You can revoke Undo by selecting <u>E</u>dit, <u>U</u>ndo a second time (before you do anything else to your document).

 Either (ALT) + (BACKSPACE) *or* (CTRL) + (Z) *is the shortcut for <u>E</u>dit, <u>U</u>ndo.*

Unlike the Undelete feature, Undo focuses not on the last *text deletion*, but on the very last *change*. For instance, if you delete a sentence, type three words, and then choose Undo, the three words just inserted will be removed. Also, Undo restores text to its *original* location—regardless of the insertion point's position.

Hands-on Exercise: Rearrange Paragraphs and Recover Deletions

Suppose you wish to break the first paragraph in your document on screen into separate paragraphs, and add some blank lines in the document. Follow these steps:

1. Position the insertion point just before the "I" that begins the sentence, "In Italy, wine production takes place...."

2. Press (ENTER) twice to create a second paragraph and then press the (TAB) key once to indent it. You should get these results:

   ```
   Fine wines are produced all over the world. Two of the
   major wine-producing countries in Europe are France and
   Italy. France produces a wide variety, and Bordeaux is
   often considered one of the centers of fine wine.

       In Italy, wine production takes place in just about
   every region....
   ```

3. Position the insertion point just before the "T" that begins the sentence, "Though white wines are manufactured here, ..."

4. Press (ENTER) twice and (TAB) once to create and indent the paragraph. Now the top of the document is split into three paragraphs.

5. Position the insertion point on the blank line below the third paragraph.

6. Press (ENTER) seven times to insert seven more blank lines before the list of countries. Notice now that the document is longer than can fit on one screen; the bottom of the document has scrolled off the screen.

7. Press (BACKSPACE) twice to reduce the number of blank lines by two.

Suppose you decide that you prefer your document without splitting that second paragraph:

1. Position the insertion point just before the "T" that begins the paragraph, "Though white wines are manufactured here, ..."

2. Press (BACKSPACE) three times to erase the tab and the two hard returns that separate the paragraphs.

Suppose you want to delete some words:

1. Position the insertion point at the top of the document. (A quick method is to press (CTRL) + (HOME).)

2. Press (CTRL) + (DEL) to erase the whole first line.

3. Press (↓) to move the insertion point down to the next line.

Oops! I didn't mean to have you delete the first line.

4. Press (↑) to move the insertion point back to the top of the document.

5. Choose Edit, Undelete. (Or, press (ALT) + (SHIFT) + (BACKSPACE).) The Undelete dialog box appears, and the line that you erased reappears.

6. Press (ENTER) to choose Restore, the preselected command button.

Revealing Codes

WordPerfect hides the codes that determine how your text appears on screen and prints on paper. Codes are hidden from you so they don't clutter the document workspace and make your typing more difficult. When you first type a document, you don't need to think about where these codes are hiding. However, when you wish to edit the text on screen, understanding the location of codes becomes important.

Codes in WordPerfect are represented by symbols, letters, or words enclosed in square brackets [ ]. (A complete list of codes can be found in Appendix B.) There are two general types of codes—single codes and paired codes.

- *Single codes* stand on their own. For instance, when you press the ⊝ key to hyphenate a word, WordPerfect inserts a [-] code. When you press (ENTER) to end a paragraph, WordPerfect inserts an [HRt] code, which stands for hard return. When word wrap creates a line break, WordPerfect inserts an [SRt] code, which stands for soft return. When you press the (TAB) key to jump to the next tab stop, Word-Perfect inserts a [Tab] code. (All these codes in brackets are invisible in your typed text.)

- *Paired codes* come in twos, marking off the borders of a chunk of text that they affect. Here's an example of a paired code:

```
[Bold On]Hello!![Bold Off]
```

The codes mark the word "Hello!!" to be bolded on screen and when printed. (More on bolding text and paired codes in Chapter 5.)

To reveal codes on screen choose View, Reveal Codes. A check mark is placed after the Reveal Codes menu item, and the document window is immediately split into two halves. The document workspace is on top and the reveal codes workspace is on the bottom—as shown in Figure 3-6. To close the reveal codes workspace, choose View, Reveal Codes again.

3

Figure 3-6. *Document workspace on top and reveal codes workspace on the bottom*

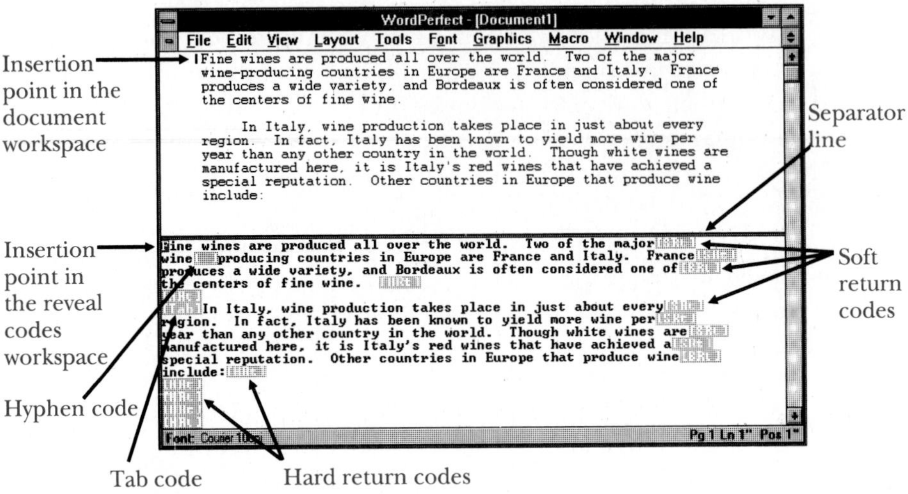

Insertion point in the document workspace

Insertion point in the reveal codes workspace

Hyphen code

Tab code

Hard return codes

Separator line

Soft return codes

shortcut **(ALT)** + **(F3)** *is the shortcut for* <u>V</u>*iew,* <u>R</u>*eveal* <u>C</u>*odes.*

When the screen is split, you see the insertion point twice, on top as the familiar blinking bar (|), and on the bottom as a rectangle highlighted in reverse video (usually orange in color, though the color can be changed). So, as you move the insertion point, you see it from two perspectives. In the document workspace, it moves between characters. But in the reveal codes workspace, it cannot move between characters. Instead, it is always highlighting a character or a code—as if "on" that character or code. You can delete a character or code when viewing the reveal codes workspace by positioning the insertion point on it and pressing **(DEL)**, or by positioning the insertion point on the next character and pressing **(BACKSPACE)**.

caution *WordPerfect keeps the insertion point on the middle line in the reveal codes workspace at all times. It scrolls the document to do this; so the portion of text you see in the reveal codes workspace at any given time may be different from what you see in the document workspace. This may be confusing at first.*

In the reveal codes workspace, you can complete your document normally. You can still insert and delete text. You can still use the menu bar and issue commands. You can still respond to dialog boxes. In fact, you can type a whole document with codes exposed. However, it can make typing confusing when all the codes appear.

It *is* an advantage to reveal codes when editing because you can see what's going on behind the scenes—how WordPerfect is marking the words you're deleting, inserting, and making changes to. For instance, as you're first learning WordPerfect, you could reveal codes before you combine two paragraphs so you don't have to "blindly" erase [HRt] codes that separate the paragraphs. It will also help to make sure you have erased them all. The reveal codes workspace is also a help if your document is not aligned the way you intended; you may discover a code that you accidentally inserted.

Mouse users should be aware that there is another method for revealing codes with an added benefit; it allows you to *size* (make larger or smaller) the reveal codes workspace:

1. Point to the narrow black space on either side of the vertical scroll bar. (That is, click the black space just above the scroll up arrow or below the scroll down arrow.)

   When you position the mouse pointer properly, it will change into a double-headed arrow.

2. Click and drag the mouse pointer (the double-headed arrow) to where you want the top of the reveal codes workspace to be.

3. Release the mouse button.

In this way, you can create a reveal codes workspace that is two lines or twenty lines in size.

Once the reveal codes workspace is displayed (regardless of whether you used the menu bar, a shortcut key, or the mouse to display it), you can resize it. Point to the line that separates the document workspace from the reveal codes workspace. The mouse pointer becomes a double-headed arrow. Then click and drag the mouse pointer up or down, and release the mouse button. If you drag it off the screen and release the mouse button, the reveal codes workspace disappears.

Creating Hard Spaces

You've just learned about codes in your text. A *hard space* is a special code that you insert when you wish to control word wrap. Hard spaces are useful because, while word wrap is a timesaver, there are times when it creates a line break at an awkward or inappropriate spot. For instance, word wrap may split a date between two lines like this:

```
According to my calendar, she will return on December
14th, 1993. If you wish to contact....
```

You don't want to correct this type of problem by pressing the (ENTER) key before "December" because this will break the paragraph in two. WordPerfect won't be able to reformat your paragraph properly when you edit later.

Instead, you can keep two words from being separated by inserting a hard space code between them. In the document workspace, the code is hidden and only a space appears. When you switch to the reveal codes workspace, the code [HdSpc] displays between the words. When you insert a hard space between "December" and "14th", here's the result:

```
According to my calendar, she will return on
December 14th, 1993. If you wish to contact....
```

When you switch to the reveal codes workspace, you'll see the hard space code that caused the change, as shown here:

```
According to my calendar, she will return on
December [HdSpc]14th, 1993. If you wish to contact....
```

WordPerfect now treats the two words "December" and "14th" as one unit, so if the second word crosses the right margin, both are wrapped to the next line. If you edit the text later, WordPerfect can still reformat the paragraph properly. To insert a hard space where there is an awkward line break, follow these steps:

1. Position the insertion point at the end of the line containing the awkward break.

2. Press (DEL) to delete the space between the words.

3. Choose <u>L</u>ayout, <u>L</u>ine, Special C<u>o</u>des. A dialog box appears listing a variety of special codes.

4. Select the Hard S<u>p</u>ace radio button, and then choose the <u>I</u>nsert command button. A hard space is inserted.

shortcut *The shortcut for steps 3 and 4 in the previous list is simply to press* (CTRL) + (SPACEBAR). *This is obviously a significant shortcut, so be sure to remember it if you want to insert hard spaces frequently.*

You may want to insert hard spaces as you type to prevent awkward line breaks before they happen. You simply type the first word, press (CTRL) + (SPACEBAR), and then type the second word. Here are a few examples where, by inserting hard space codes between the words, you can avoid clumsy line breaks in your documents:

```
December [HdSpc] 14th, [HdSpc] 1993
(415) [HdSpc] 555-5678
Mr. [HdSpc] Jones
P.T. [HdSpc] Barnum
```

The hard space code is shown in the preceding examples. In your document, however, the code will be shown only when you open the reveal codes workspace. (For information on preventing a hyphenated word from being split by a line break, such as the phone number 555-5678, see the section on hyphenation in Chapter 6.)

Hands-on Exercise: Reveal and Work with Codes

 View the reveal codes workspace and then delete and insert codes with these steps:

1. Position the insertion point at the top of the document. (Remember that (CTRL) + (HOME) is a fast way to do this.)

2. Choose <u>V</u>iew, Reveal <u>C</u>odes, or press (ALT) + (F3). Your screen should resemble Figure 3-6. Notice the two insertion points—one in each workspace—and the various codes.

Let's rearrange paragraphs as in the last hands-on exercise. This time, if you keep your eye on the reveal codes workspace as you proceed, you can watch as codes are deleted. Follow these steps:

1. Position the insertion point on the "I" that starts the paragraph, "In Italy, wine production takes place in...."

   In the reveal codes workspace (bottom), the insertion point is on the "I". In the document workspace (top), notice that the insertion point appears to be just to the left of the "I".

2. Press (BACKSPACE). The [Tab] code is deleted; the paragraph becomes flush against the left margin.

3. Press (BACKSPACE) twice. The two [HRt] codes are deleted, and the text is reformatted back into a single paragraph.

Let's add the hard space in the phone number listed in the last paragraph. This will safeguard against an awkward line break in the event that you later edit the text and the phone number falls at the end of a line.

1. Position the insertion point at the bottom of the document. (Remember that (CTRL) + (END) is a fast way to do this.)

2. Position the insertion point in the space between "(415)" and "555" in the last paragraph.

   In the reveal codes workspace (bottom), the insertion point is on the space. In the document workspace (top), notice that the insertion point appears to be just to the left of the space.

3. Press (DEL) to erase the space.

4. Press (CTRL) + (SPACEBAR). In the reveal codes workspace, you can see that you inserted a hard space code, as shown here:

   (415) [**HdSpc**] 555-5678

5. Choose <u>V</u>iew, Reveal <u>C</u>odes, or press (ALT) + (F3) to turn off the reveal codes workspace. The hard space code—and all codes—are again hidden from view.

Selecting Text

3

With the Select feature, WordPerfect lets you mark off one section of text on which you wish to perform an action. For instance, you can mark one paragraph and delete it. You can mark one sentence and bold it. Mark one word and underline it. You can mark six words and move them. Or mark eight lines and print them. You select text *before* you perform the action. To select text, you have four options. First, you can drag with a mouse. Follow these steps:

1. Position the mouse pointer at the beginning of the section of text you wish to select.

2. Click and drag the mouse to the opposite end of the section you wish to select. In this way you can select one word, three words, half a paragraph, one page—any amount of text you wish. The selected text is highlighted in reverse video and the status line displays the message "Select On".

3. Release the left mouse button.

Once a selection has been made, perform any action you like on the selected text. Or, click the mouse button to cancel the selection; the highlight disappears.

Second, there are shortcuts to dragging with a mouse when you want to select either a word, sentence, or paragraph. These shortcuts are summarized in Table 3-2.

• Use multiple clicks to quickly select a word, sentence, or paragraph. Double-click a word to select the word. Triple-click (three clicks in rapid succession) any word in a sentence to select the sentence—including the spaces following the sentence. Quadruple-click (four clicks in rapid succession) any word in a paragraph to select the paragraph—including hard return codes that follow the paragraph.

- Use the Edit menu to select a sentence or paragraph. Position the insertion point on a word and choose Edit, Select. Then choose Sentence to select the sentence and any spaces that follow the sentence. Or choose Paragraph to select the paragraph and any hard return codes that follow the paragraph. (As described in Chapter 8, you can also choose Tabular column to select a column that is aligned on tabs or indents, or Rectangle to select an area on screen shaped like a rectangle.)

- Use the (SHIFT) key to select from the insertion point to the mouse pointer. Position the insertion point at one end of the section of text you wish to select. Position the mouse pointer at the opposite end. Then, hold down the (SHIFT) key while you click the mouse button.

A third way to select text uses the keyboard rather than the mouse. The keyboard options all involve the (SHIFT) key. Position the insertion point at one end of the section of text you wish to select, and then press (SHIFT) + (→) or (SHIFT) + (←) to select to the right or left one character at a time. Press (SHIFT) + (↑) or (SHIFT) + (↓) to select up or down one line at a time. Or, press (SHIFT) + any key combination in Table 3-1 to select text up to the new location

Table 3-2.   *Shortcuts for Selecting Text with the Mouse*

Selection	Shortcut
Word	Double-click the word
Sentence	Triple-click the sentence or choose Edit, Select, Sentence
Paragraph	Quadruple-click the paragraph or choose Edit, Select, Paragraph
Insertion point to mouse pointer (I-beam)	(SHIFT) + click

indicated. For instance, press (SHIFT) + (CTRL) + (END) to select from the insertion point to the end of the document. Then perform an action on the selected text. If you attempt to move the insertion point without pressing down on the (SHIFT) key first, the selection is canceled and the highlighting disappears.

The fourth method for selecting text is similar to the WordPerfect 5.1 for DOS Block feature—you turn on the Select feature first and then mark off the section of text to be selected.

3

1. Position the insertion point at one end of the section of text you wish to select.

2. Press (F8) to turn on the Select mode. The words "Select Mode" appear on the status line.

3. Use the arrow keys or the shortcut keys shown in Table 3-1 to position the insertion point at the opposite end of the section of text. For instance, press (CTRL) + (END) to select all the text to the end of the document. The selection is highlighted in reverse video.

   Or, type the character that will be the last one included in the selected text (for instance, type a period if the selection will be one sentence that ends with a period). The selection is highlighted in reverse video.

4. Once a selection has been made, perform an action on the selected text. Or press (F8) to cancel the selection and the highlight disappears.

The Select feature is a critical feature in WordPerfect because it comes into play every time you want to do something to a portion of your document, rather than to the whole document.

For instance, you can insert or delete a portion of text by selecting the text first. The following are alternatives to the procedures you learned about earlier in this chapter:

- *Insert* After text is selected, type new text; this new text replaces the selected text. This procedure is similiar to how Typeover mode works, but is more versatile because the new text can have a different number of characters than the selected text. (This procedure works if you select the text with the mouse or the keyboard. However, it does not work if you use the (F8) key to select text.)

- *Delete*   After text is selected, press (DEL) or (BACKSPACE); the text is deleted.

You will see as this book continues that numerous features offered by WordPerfect can operate on selected text.

Keep in mind that when you mark off a section of text with the Select feature, any codes present will also be included in the selection. Therefore, when you select text, you may wish to choose <u>V</u>iew, Reveal <u>C</u>odes beforehand. That way, you can check for embedded codes while you're making a selection. You'll be able to include codes that you want as part of the selection, or exclude codes that you don't want in the selection.

Hands-on Exercise: Select Text

 Let's practice with the Select feature using both the mouse and the keyboard:

1. Position the mouse pointer (I-beam) at the bottom of the document just before the first "C" in the phrase, "CONTACT THE R&R WINE ASSOCIATION...."

2. Click and drag the mouse straight downward. WordPerfect highlights all the text from "CONTACT THE R&R..." to the end of the document, as shown here:

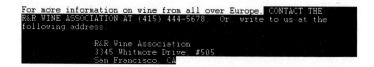

For more information on wine from all over Europe, CONTACT THE R&R WINE ASSOCIATION AT (415) 444-5678. Or, write to us at the following address:

        R&R Wine Association
        3345 Whitmore Drive, #505
        San Francisco, CA

3. Still holding down the mouse button, drag the mouse upward to the line just before the address. Some of the text is now excluded from the selection.

4. Release the mouse button to signify that you have completed the selection.

5. Click once. This cancels the selection.

6. Position the insertion point at the very top of the document. (Pressing (CTRL) + (HOME) is a shortcut.)

7. Press (SHIFT) + (→) five times. WordPerfect highlights the first five characters.

8. Press (SHIFT) + (CTRL) + (→) four times. WordPerfect highlights four more words.

9. Press (SHIFT) + (CTRL) + (↓). WordPerfect highlights the whole first paragraph plus the blank lines that follow that paragraph.

10. Press (SHIFT) + (↑) three times. Three lines are excluded from the selection.

11. Press (↑). The selection is canceled.

12. Position the insertion point just before the "R&R" in the address near the bottom of the document.

13. Select the entire address, either by clicking and dragging down with the mouse or by pressing (SHIFT) + (↓), (SHIFT) + (↓), (SHIFT) + (END). Here's how the selection will appear:

14. Press (DEL). The address disappears.

Suppose you wish you hadn't deleted the address. You can use the Undelete or Undo feature to get it back. Let's use the Undo feature. Choose Edit, Undo. The last change you made is canceled—so the address is reinserted.

To end this chapter's last exercise, exit WordPerfect; but save the document you have on screen first. Properly saving a document means you'll be able to recall and use it again.

1. Select File, Exit. Or double-click the WordPerfect control-menu box. Or press (ALT) + (F4). WordPerfect displays a dialog box asking whether or not you first wish to save the changes to Document1.

2. Click the Yes command button or type **y**. WordPerfect displays a Save As dialog box. (You will learn much more on this dialog box and on the Save feature in the next chapter.) Notice that the insertion point is inside the Save As text box, waiting for you to type in a name for that document. This is your first document, so let's make "first" its name.

3. Type **first** and press (ENTER).

In moments, the document is saved, and you've exited WordPerfect.

Quick Reference

- To use WordPerfect effectively, let word wrap create line breaks within paragraphs. Press (ENTER) only to end a paragraph, end a short line of text, or insert a blank line.

- To move the insertion point with a mouse, click at the new location. If the new location is not within view on your screen, use a scroll bar to bring it into view and then click.

- To move the insertion point with the keyboard, use the arrow keys. Or use any of the quick methods provided in Table 3-1.

- To switch between Insert and Typeover mode, press the (INS) key. (The (INS) key is a toggle, so when you press it once you'll be put into Typeover mode, and when you press it again you'll be back in Insert mode.) In Insert mode, characters are inserted at the insertion point. In Typeover mode, existing characters are replaced with new characters you type.

- To delete characters one at a time, press the (BACKSPACE) or (DEL) key. To delete a word, press (CTRL) + (BACKSPACE). To delete text to the end of the line, press (CTRL) + (DEL). To delete text to the end of the page, press (CTRL) + (SHIFT) + (DEL). To delete a section of text, use the Select feature to select the text and then press (DEL). Restore deletions by choosing Edit, Undelete.

- To reverse the last change made to a document, choose Edit, Undo.

- To select text using a mouse, either position the insertion point at one end of the text and click and drag the mouse to the opposite end, or use one of the shortcuts given in Table 3-2. Or to select text using the keyboard, position the insertion point at one end, and press (SHIFT) + arrow keys or any of the quick methods shown in Table 3-1. You can also press (F8) to turn on Select mode and then use the arrow keys or methods listed in Table 3-1.

- To make codes visible on screen, choose View, Reveal Codes. Codes are symbols enclosed in brackets that determine how your text will appear on screen and at the printer.

3

4

Saving, Recalling, and Printing Documents

Those glowing words on a computer screen that you may have spent hours getting just right are vulnerable. Follow the wrong procedure and they'll disappear, leaving you with the task of creating your document all over again.

The goal of this chapter is to make sure you don't accidentally lose an important document. You'll learn how to securely store a copy of a document on disk so that you can use it again in the future. You'll learn how to protect against power failures. And you'll learn how to get a listing of the stored documents, and bring up on screen any of those documents for review and editing. Finally, the chapter describes how to transform those glowing words into printed characters on paper. More advanced procedures for managing documents on disk and at the printer—which you'll want to know about once you're comfortable with the basics—are provided in Chapter 16.

Learning About Document Storage

Your computer stores information short-term in something called random-access memory or RAM. RAM contains and "remembers" your document while you work on it; RAM lets you edit it, format it, and do all the easy changes and enhancements that you cannot do with a typewriter. However, RAM is only temporary storage. When you turn off your computer, or if the electricity flowing to your computer stops due to a power failure, your screen goes blank and so does RAM; all the information stored in RAM disappears.

You must, therefore, store a copy of your document if you ever want to use it again. You store it on either your computer's hard disk or on a floppy disk. Once a document is stored it is referred to as a *file* that you have *saved* on disk. Once you save it, your document will be available for reviewing, editing, or printing every time you use WordPerfect in the future.

Understanding Drives and Directories

When you save a file, you must tell WordPerfect exactly where you will store it. If you plan to store the file on a floppy disk inserted into your computer's disk drive, the destination is usually referred to as drive A. If your computer has two disk drives, the one on the left or on top is usually referred to as drive A, and the other as drive B. If you plan to store the document on your hard disk, the destination is drive C. (If the hard disk is large enough you may have drives D, E, F, and so on, as well.) When you tell WordPerfect which drive to send your file to, you designate the drive with a letter followed by a colon, such as **a:** or **b:** or **c:**. (It makes no difference whether you use uppercase or lowercase letters.) Figure 4-1 shows a common floppy and hard disk placement on a PC unit.

When you store a document on your hard disk you must be more specific in your instructions to WordPerfect. Unlike a floppy disk, a hard disk holds an enormous amount of information and is typically divided electronically into sections, called *directories*. Each directory can hold files and can also be organized yet again into *subdirectories*. If a directory has a subdirectory, it is said to be the *parent* of that subdirectory.

If this discussion sounds abstract, think of a hard disk as the file cabinet shown in Figure 4-2. The directories of a hard disk work like the file drawers

Figure 4-1. *Floppy and hard disk drives on a PC*

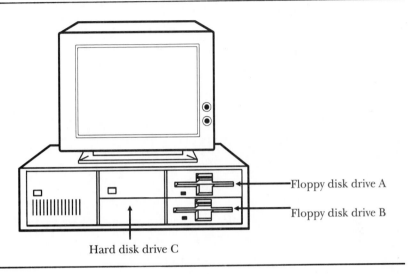

Floppy disk drive A

Floppy disk drive B

Hard disk drive C

Figure 4-2. *Think of your hard disk as a file cabinet*

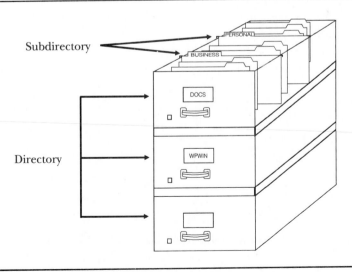

Subdirectory

Directory

Figure 4-3.   *Tree structure organization of the hard disk*

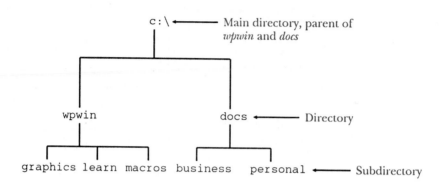

in a file cabinet. The directories are subdivided into subdirectories just like file drawers are subdivided with hanging file folders. So, if you imagine that the top drawer of the file cabinet is the directory *docs* (in which you store your documents), you can see that you can have subdirectories for your business documents, for your personal documents—you can organize the files that you create under any categories that you choose on your hard disk.

Another way to picture the organization of your hard disk is with the tree structure shown in Figure 4-3. This type of notation is very common in the world of computers.

So, if you store a file on the hard disk, you must specify not only a drive, but also a directory. To designate a directory, you add the backslash (\) symbol after the drive designation. For example, to indicate the main directory on drive C (before it is split into sections), the correct designation is *c:*. To indicate the directory named *docs*, the correct designation is *c:\docs*. To indicate the subdirectory named *business* within the *docs* directory, the correct designation is *c:\docs\business*.

Naming Files

Once you decide on a file location, you must also assign a name to your file, called a *filename*. There are some rules for naming files:

- Each filename must be unique in a directory. If you try to save a document with a filename already used in that directory, Word-Perfect will ask you if you want the new document to overwrite the existing file that already has that filename.

- A filename can contain from one to eight characters followed by an optional period and one to three extra characters. These extra characters after the period are referred to as a *file extension*. For instance, acceptable filenames are *myfirst*, (no file extension) or *myfirst.doc* (*doc* is a file extension).

- These characters are acceptable in a filename or its optional file extension: letters (uppercase or lowercase); numbers; and the following symbols:

  ! @ # $ % ^ ( ) - _ { } ' ' ~

- A filename cannot contain spaces.

- Certain file extensions are reserved and should be avoided. The extensions *.bat, .exe, .ini, .dll, .prs, .wwk,* and *.wcm* are used by WordPerfect or other programs for specific labeling purposes, so don't use these three-letter combinations in a file extension when naming your documents.

The following are examples of invalid filenames:

Invalid Filename	Reason Invalid
1st_document	Too many characters in filename
first.1234	Too many characters in extension
mmo+doc	Unacceptable character in filename
letter.*3	Unacceptable character in extension
10.15.93.rpt	Too many periods
bob brady.ltr	Contains a blank space

It is best to establish an organized system for naming files before you actually start naming them. How you devise an organized system depends on: the type of documents you produce; how structured you need (or like) to be; whether you save your files on a hard disk or floppy disk (or network); if you store on a hard disk, how that hard disk is organized; and whether other people share your computer. Figure 4-4 shows a few ideas. Each column represents a different filenaming scheme.

In the examples in Figure 4-4, document contents are abbreviated like this: "ltr" stands for letter, "rpt" stands for report, "mmo" stands for memo, and "bud" stands for budget. You can, of course, use any abbreviations that are easy for you to remember, and set up your naming system on whatever is most important in your work, whether it be the dates of your documents, the type of documents they are, the names of clients, or author names.

Indicating a Location for Your Documents

When you refer to a file, you specify the file's *path*, which includes its drive and directory location, a backslash (\), and its filename. For instance,

    c:\docs\smith01.ltr

indicates a file named *smith01.ltr* in *c:\docs*. Or,

    c:\docs\business\first

Figure 4-4.   *Three different filenaming schemes for documents*

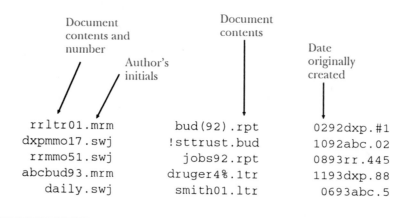

Document contents and number	Author's initials	Document contents	Date originally created
rrltr01.mrm		bud(92).rpt	0292dxp.#1
dxpmmo17.swj		!sttrust.bud	1092abc.02
rrmmo51.swj		jobs92.rpt	0893rr.445
abcbud93.mrm		druger4%.ltr	1193dxp.88
daily.swj		smith01.ltr	0693abc.5

indicates the file named *first* in *c:\docs\business.* Or,

    a:\ jobs92.rpt

is the path to a file named *jobs92.rpt* on a floppy disk in drive A.

In WordPerfect, one directory is the *default* or *current directory,* which is where WordPerfect assumes you wish to save and recall files. When referring to a file in the current directory, you can specify the filename only—not its full path. For instance, if the current directory is *docs* and you want to work with a file named *smith01.ltr* in that directory, specify the document simply as *smith01.ltr.* If the current directory is not *docs,* you must specify the document as *c:\docs\smith01.ltr.*

You should specify what directory is to be used as the permanent default each time WordPerfect is started. Otherwise, the default directory is assumed to be the same directory where the WordPerfect program files are stored, *c:\wpwin,* and this is not an effective way to organize files.

You specify a permanent default directory by choosing File, Preferences, Location of Files. Then, in the Documents text box, type the name of the directory where you want your document files to be kept, such as *c:\docs.* When you choose OK, the default directory is set for that day and for each time in the future when you start WordPerfect. (You may decide to store all your documents in multiple directories rather than one directory. For instance, you may decide to create several subdirectories, and then keep business documents in *c:\docs\business,* personal documents in *c:\docs\personal,* and so on. In that case, type into the Documents text box the name of the directory where a majority of your files will be kept.)

Hands-on Exercise: Change the Default Directory for All Working Sessions

 Depending on how WordPerfect was installed on your computer, you may or may not have had the opportunity to specify a default directory for each time you start WordPerfect. The following procedure lets you check the default directory and change it if necessary:

1. Choose File, Preferences, Location of Files. The Location of Files dialog box appears.

2. Notice whether or not a directory is specified in the Documents text box. In this example, the text box is blank:

3. If the Documents text box lists the correct directory for where you want your document files to be kept, choose Cancel or press (ESC) to close the Location of Files dialog box and cancel the command. You can skip the remainder of this hands-on exercise.

   On the other hand, if the Documents text box is blank or lists the directory where the WordPerfect program files are kept, you will want to specify a different directory by continuing with the following steps.

4. Choose Documents. The insertion point relocates into the Documents text box.

5. Type in a directory. For instance, type **c:\docs**. Or, type **c:\files** or **c:\wpwin\files**.

6. Choose OK or press (ENTER) to close the Location of Files dialog box.

7. If the directory you specified does not exist, WordPerfect asks if you wish to create it. Choose OK to create the directory.

Once you indicate a location for your document files, you can refer to your files by their filename only. You need to refer to a file by its full path only if the file is somewhere other than in the current directory. (See Chapter 17 if you want further details on the Location of Files dialog box.)

Saving a File

Once you understand the use of directories and filenames, you're ready to begin storing your reports, memos, or letters in files. The two features that you'll use frequently are Save As and Save. The first time you save a document, Save As and Save work the same way, with WordPerfect asking you for a filename to save the document with. For all future times when you save a document, however, the two features operate differently.

You use the Save As feature when you want to indicate a new filename or directory for your edited file. In this way you can save a new version of your document separately from the old version. For instance, suppose you create and save a document with the name *report*. Later, you edit it, but aren't sure whether you like the changes. In that case, use Save As to store the document a second time under a new name, such as *report#2* or *report.2*. You can also store it using the same name but in a different directory.

You use the Save feature when you want corrections to your document to overwrite the old file of the same name. A copy of what you see on screen, which is the new version of your document, automatically replaces the old version on disk. For instance, suppose you create and save a document with the name *letter*. Later, you edit it, and want to make the changes permanent. In that case, use Save. Without even asking for a new filename, WordPerfect inserts the new version of *letter* in place of the old version.

Let's see the step-by-step procedure for how Save As and Save work.

Using the Save As Feature

Follow these steps to use the Save As feature:

1. With the document displayed on screen, choose <u>F</u>ile, Save <u>A</u>s. The Save As dialog box appears as shown in Figure 4-5. The insertion point is inside the Save <u>A</u>s text box.

2. Notice the path that is listed next to "Current Dir:". This is the current directory. WordPerfect assumes you wish to save the next file to this directory.

4

Figure 4-5.   *Save As dialog box*

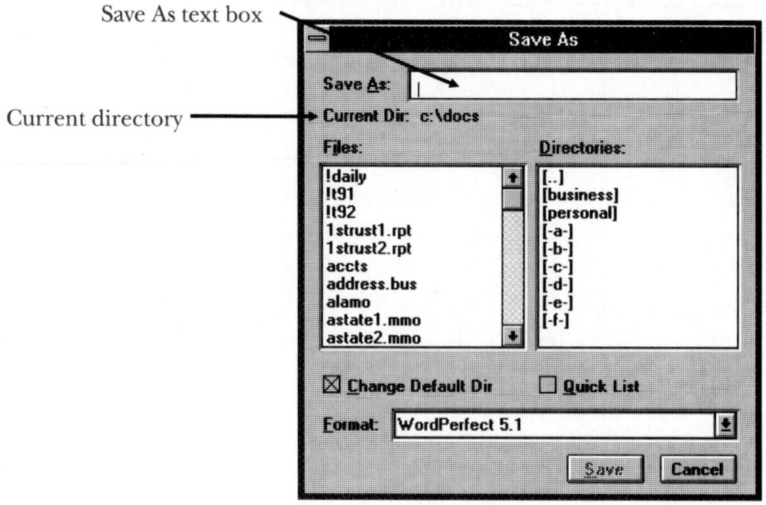

Save As text box

Current directory

3. If the current directory is where you wish to store the file, type the filename into the Save <u>A</u>s text box. For instance, type **boxer.ltr**.

   If the current directory is not the destination where you wish to store the file, type the complete path—the directory and filename separated by a backslash (\). For instance, if the current directory is not the *docs* directory, and you want *boxer.ltr* to be stored in the *docs* directory, type **c:\docs\boxer.ltr**. You can also type **a:\boxer.ltr** to store it on a floppy disk.

4. Choose the <u>S</u>ave command button, or press (ENTER) if <u>S</u>ave is pre-selected.

5. If the filename is unique, a mouse pointer switches to an hourglass, asking you to wait while WordPerfect processes. The document remains on screen, but in moments a copy is placed in the path you specified.

   If the filename already exists, a dialog box appears:

Choose Y̲es to replace the contents of the old file on disk with the document on screen. Choose N̲o if you don't want the old file overwritten, and the Save As dialog box reappears for you to type in another filename.

shortcut F3 *is the shortcut for* F̲ile, *Save* A̲s.

After you save a copy of a document on disk, the title bar indicates the document's path:

The title bar also displays the message "unmodified". As mentioned in Chapter 1, unmodified means that the document appearing on screen is identical to the copy stored on disk—it hasn't been modified since it was last saved.

caution *Whenever WordPerfect displays a dialog box asking whether you wish to replace an existing file, think carefully before you respond. If you choose Y̲es, the old file is erased when it is replaced. This can be disastrous if the old file is one that either you or someone else who shares your computer needed to keep. If you're not sure what the contents are of the file you're about to replace, it is safer to choose N̲o and save the new file under a different filename. Then, you can review the contents of the old file and decide whether or not you wish to erase it.*

Using the Save Feature

As soon as a document is edited, the message "unmodified" disappears from its title bar—even if only one word is changed. The file on disk is now different from what is displayed on screen. To save the document again, simply select File, Save.

If you have previously saved the document, WordPerfect already knows the file's path. You don't need to retype it when saving. WordPerfect immediately erases the old file contents, and replaces them with the updated version of the document. The document remains on screen so that you can continue working on it.

If you haven't yet saved the document when you select File, Save, it's as if you selected Save As; the Save As dialog box automatically appears.

shortcut (SHIFT) + (F3) *is the shortcut for* File, Save.

Saving frequently using the Save feature is a small price to pay for what could be huge dividends, especially if you're working on a lengthy document. Why save at regular intervals? Remember that every word you typed is stored in RAM, which is temporary storage and is dependent on electricity. Just imagine typing and extensively editing a 20-page document, only to experience a power failure. If you hadn't saved the document to disk at all, you'd have lost every word! If you had saved the document after typing but before editing, you'd still have the basic text, but you'd have lost all the editing changes. On the other hand, if you had saved your work ten minutes before the blackout, you'd have saved all but your last ten minutes of work. The Save command, therefore, is a quick and easy way to safeguard against a disaster.

There is a feature that automatically saves a document at regular intervals for you. The Backup feature is described in Chapter 17. Even with the Backup feature in use, it is good practice to save your work periodically yourself.

reminder *The Save feature replaces an old file with the new document. It does so without a warning message. If you wish to store a document in both its old and its new versions,* ***don't*** *use the Save feature. Instead, use Save As, and specify a different path and/or filename each time you save.*

Saving Selected Text

Rather than save an entire document, you may choose to save only a portion of it to a file. The file to which you save the document can be a new file or an existing file. If it is an existing file, you can either decide to overwrite (replace) the existing file with the selected text, or you can decide to append the selected text onto the end of the existing file. This concept is illustrated in Figure 4-6.

To save selected text and either overwrite or append to an existing file, follow these steps:

1. Select the text to be saved. (See Chapter 3 if you need a review on how to select text.)

2. Choose File, Save. A dialog box appears asking for the filename to which you wish to save this text. It is identical to Figure 4-5 except that the title bar reads "Save Selected Text".

3. Type a filename. (Or, type a full path to indicate a directory different from the current directory.)

4. Choose Save.

5. If the file does not already exist, WordPerfect creates it. If the file exists, WordPerfect displays a dialog box for you to select either Overwrite (replace) or Append.

6. Click the mouse button or press an arrow key to turn off the Select feature.

Figure 4-6. *Difference between append and overwrite*

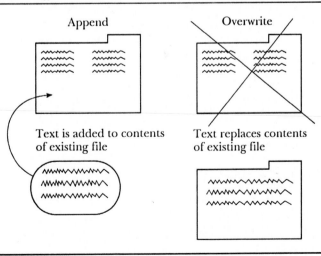

Closing a Document

When you've completed your work on a document, you must close the document window. When you do, WordPerfect gives you the option of saving changes you made to your document.

You close a document using the File menu. You can also use the document control-menu box. (Remember that, as described in Chapter 2, the document control-menu box is the smaller of the two boxes in the upper left corner of the window, just below the WordPerfect application control-menu box.)

How WordPerfect responds when you give the Close command will depend on the status of your document. If you have made no changes to your document since you last saved it, so that the title bar reads "unmodified", all you have to do is choose File, Close, or double-click the document control-menu box.

But, if you have made changes to your document, WordPerfect gives you the option of saving those changes:

1. Choose File, Close, or double-click the document control-menu box.

2. WordPerfect displays a dialog box asking whether or not you first wish to save the document.

3. To save the document before closing, choose Yes by clicking the Yes command button or typing **y**. If the document is being saved for the first time, WordPerfect will then display the Save As dialog box so that you can indicate a filename.

   To close without saving, choose No by clicking the No command button or typing **n**.

   To cancel the Close command, choose Cancel by clicking the Cancel command button or pressing (ESC). You can also press (ENTER) since the Cancel command button has been preselected.

shortcut (CTRL) + (F4) *is the shortcut for* File, Close.

Once you've closed the document, you will view a clear document workspace. You're now ready to work on a new document. (In WordPerfect you can work with more than one document at a time. Should more than one document be open when you use the Close feature, you will see one of the other documents that are still open rather than a clear workspace. More on this in Chapter 10.)

So Many Ways To Save

WordPerfect offers four features for saving changes you make to your documents. Three you've just learned about: Save, Save As, and Close. The fourth, Exit, was discussed in Chapter 1. Why are you given so many opportunities to save your document? WordPerfect is set up to help prevent you from losing anything that you want to keep for future use or reference. Here's how to manage the four features wisely.

- Use the Save As feature when you wish to save a document for the first time and continue working on it. Also use Save As when you wish to store the new version of a document as well as retain the old version.

- Use the Save feature to save a document at regular intervals while you continue to work on it, replacing the old with the new version automatically. Use Save only when you're confident that you won't accidentally overwrite a file you needed to keep.

- Use the Close feature when you wish to save a document and then exit that document workspace (but remain in WordPerfect). Or use Close to clear the document workspace without saving the document.

- Use the Exit feature to save a document, and then exit WordPerfect. Or use it to exit WordPerfect without saving the document.

note *Unfortunately, even if you are meticulous about saving your documents, there are instances when a hard disk "crashes", meaning that it stops functioning and loses all the information stored there. Floppy disks also can malfunction. If the loss of a specific file would be disastrous for you, make a backup copy of that file. For instance, if you store files on your hard disk, backup copies can be stored on floppy disks or on a tape backup system (if you have one), and you may even want to consider keeping these backups in a different location. For information on copying files, see Chapter 16.*

Hands-on Exercise: Create and Save a Document

          Figure 4-7 shows a document that, after the discussions in Chapter 3, you now know how to create. Type the document shown in Figure 4-7 to reinforce

Figure 4-7.   *Sample text to be typed and saved as* smith01.ltr

```
February 3, 1992


Mr. Barrett Smith
FST Accounting
1801 S. Harmon Street
Oakland, CA  94130

Dear Mr. Smith:

    As you requested, here is a list of full-time
employees who elected to accept the new vacation
option, along with their anniversary dates with us.
There are only three employees who chose the plan.
Please add their names to your records.

        Antonio Abbot        May 31st
        Lois Chang           April 27th
        Paul McClintock      August 7th

The new accrued vacation system should begin for these
employees immediately.


Sincerely,


Sandy Peterson
R&R Wine Association


P.S. I've enclosed a copy of our quarterly newsletter
for your enjoyment.
```

what you learned. (Remember to use the (TAB) key when aligning the table of names and dates.) When you're done typing this letter to Mr. Smith, store it on disk using these steps:

1. Choose <u>F</u>ile, Save <u>A</u>s (or press (F3)). The Save As dialog box appears on screen.

2. Notice your current directory, listed on the dialog box next to "Current Dir:". This is where your document is stored on your computer.

3. Type **smith01.ltr** and press (ENTER). A copy of the document is stored on disk in the current directory.

Once you've saved the document, practice the editing techniques you learned in Chapter 3 by editing the document as shown in Figure 4-8. Then, since the document has been modified, let's save it again. Choose <u>F</u>ile, <u>S</u>ave (or press (SHIFT) + (F3)). The edited version of the letter is stored on disk, replacing the original.

Make one more editing change to the document: delete the name "Sandy Peterson" and insert your own name as president. Now you've finished with this document, so let's close it. Because it has been modified since you last saved it, WordPerfect will remind you to save it again. Follow these steps:

1. Choose <u>F</u>ile, <u>C</u>lose (or press (CTRL) + (F4)). A dialog box appears asking if you wish to save the changes to *smith01.ltr* in the current directory.

2. Select <u>Y</u>es or type y. The newest version of the letter is saved, and the file is closed. On screen you now have a new blank document workspace.

Recalling a File

When you want to bring up on screen any of your saved documents, you have several methods for recalling them. Let's see how to open and retrieve files.

Figure 4-8.   *Sample text to be edited and saved again*

February 3, 199~~2~~
                      93

                  P.
Mr. Barrett∧Smith
FST Accounting
1801 S. Harmon Street
Oakland, CA 94~~130~~
                  413

              Barrett
Dear ~~Mr. Smith~~:

          we discussed   *complete*
    As ~~you requested~~, here is a∧list of full-time
employees who elected to accept the new vacation
option, along with their anniversary dates with us.
~~There are only three employees who chose the plan~~.
Please add their names to your records.

         Tim Fingerman
         Antonio Abbot   May ~~31st~~ *13th*
    └──→ Lois Chang   April 27th ── *May 20th*
         Paul McClintock   August 7th

The new accrued vacation system should begin for these
employees immediately. *Thank you* ⊗

Sincerely,

Sandy Peterson ← *President*
R&R Wine Association

            includ
P.S. I've ~~enclos~~ed a copy of our quarterly newsletter
for your enjoyment.

Opening a File

Use the Open feature to bring a copy of a document into a clear document workspace with these steps:

1. Choose File, Open. The Open File dialog box appears, as shown in Figure 4-9. Notice the information listed next to item "Current Dir:". WordPerfect assumes you wish to open a file from this directory.

2. If the current directory contains the file that you wish to recall, type its filename into the Filename text box. For instance, type **boxer.ltr**. (You can also use the Files list box, as described later in this section, to select the filename.)

    If the current directory is *not* the destination where you wish to recall the file from, type the file's full path. For instance, type **c:\docs\boxer.ltr** to indicate that the hard disk directory named *c:\docs* contains the filename *boxer.ltr*. (You can also use the Direc-

Figure 4-9.   *Open File dialog box*

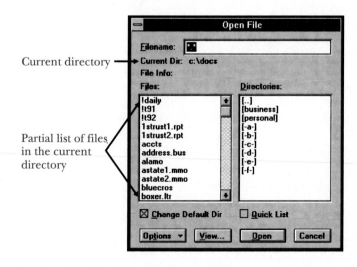

tories list box, as described later in this section, to search through different directories and then select the filename.)

3. Choose the Open command button. Or press (ENTER) if that command button is preselected.

4. If the file is found, the mouse pointer becomes an hourglass, requesting that you not use the mouse or keyboard until processing is done. In moments, the document appears on screen. (When you open a file, if the Document1 workspace contains any text whatsoever—even just one space—the file you're bringing up will be put into a new document workspace. More on having multiple documents open at once in Chapter 10.)

   If the file is not found, a new dialog box overlays the Open File dialog box:

   Choose OK. The Open File dialog box continues to display for you to try again. (You may have misspelled the filename or indicated the wrong path.)

shortcut (F4) *is the shortcut for* File, Open.

There is a quick method for opening frequently used files. WordPerfect keeps track of the four files that you opened most recently. When you open the File menu, these files are listed at the bottom of the menu, as shown in the example in Figure 4-10.

You can open one of the listed files by choosing File and then selecting a filename just as you would any other menu item. For instance, click "4 boxer.ltr" or type 4 to choose the last menu item in Figure 4-10. The file named *boxer.ltr* is opened.

Figure 4-10. *Last four files opened appear at the bottom of the File menu*

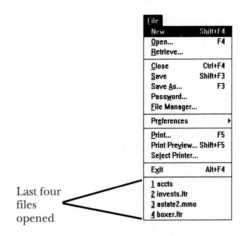

Last four files opened

Retrieving a File

You use the Retrieve feature when you already have one file open, and you want to bring in a copy of another file to the spot where the insertion point is located. So, for instance, if you wish to combine two already existing documents, use the Open feature to recall the first one, and then use the Retrieve feature to bring the second document into the first document on screen. Follow these steps:

1. Have your first document open, and position the insertion point in the location where you wish to insert the file that you'll retrieve.

2. Choose File, Retrieve. A dialog box appears, identical to the Open File dialog box shown in Figure 4-9 except that the title bar reads, "Retrieve File".

3. Type in (or select) a filename.

4. Choose the Retrieve command button, or press (ENTER) if that command button is preselected.

5. WordPerfect displays a dialog box to verify that you wish to retrieve the file into the current document. Select Y̲es to do so, or select N̲o to cancel the command.

Using the Retrieve feature to recall a file into a clear document workspace gives you the same result as using the Open feature.

Using Directories and Files List Boxes

The Open File and Retrieve File dialog boxes each contain two list boxes—the D̲irectories and the F̲iles list boxes. The D̲irectories and F̲iles list boxes are useful for: providing information on files and directories; providing a way to select a file by pointing with the mouse or the arrow keys instead of typing; and letting you change the current directory in order to search for a file whose name or location on disk escapes you. (Remember that Chapter 2 provides general information on list boxes, including how to select an item from a list box with either the mouse or the keyboard.)

The D̲irectories list box, shown on the right side in the Open File and Retrieve File dialog boxes, displays information on directories and drives.

The parent of the current directory is shown first (if the current directory has one) represented by two periods in brackets. Subdirectories are shown next (if the current directory has any) represented by the subdirectory name in brackets. Drives are shown last, represented by the drive letter between two dashes and in brackets. Here is a close-up of the D̲irectories list box from Figure 4-9, where the current directory is *c:\docs*, with a parent (*c:*)and two subdirectories (*c:\docs\business* and *c:\docs\personal*) on a computer with six drives:

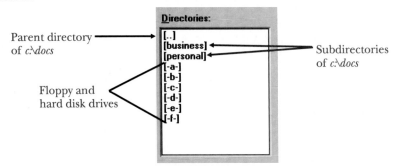

If you select a directory or drive from the Directories list box, the directory becomes highlighted. The date and time when that directory was created is displayed just above the Directories list box.

With a directory or drive highlighted, select the Open or Retrieve command button to make that drive or directory current. It is now displayed next to the "Current Dir:" item, and the Files and Directories list boxes update to show information on that new current directory. For instance, in the example just given, select [personal] and then select Open for information on the contents of *c:\docs\personal.* Or select [..] and then Open to display information on the contents of *c:\.* You can also select [-a-] and then Open to display information on the contents of the disk in drive A. (Note that you must have a disk in drive A before selecting it.) By making different directories current, you can search through your hard or floppy disks for a file whose location you do not know.

≡shortcut≡ If you double-click a directory or drive in the Directories list box, you get the same results as selecting the directory or drive and choosing Open or Retrieve.

You should know that, when you choose a new current directory, the long-term effect depends on the status of the Change Default Dir check box. This check box is located just below the Files list box in the Open File or Retrieve File dialog box. Notice in Figure 4-9, for example, that this box is checked, meaning that it is on. When this box is on and you select a new current directory, it becomes the default directory for the rest of the working session or until you change it again. When this box is off and you select a new current directory, the change is only fleeting; as soon as the Open File or Retrieve File dialog box is closed, the original default directory is reinstated. (This also applies to the Save As dialog box.)

WordPerfect also lets you assign descriptive names to directories with the Quick List feature. A Quick List box would then appear instead of a Directories list box. With a Quick List, you can avoid the confusion of having to maneuver through various levels of directories or the hassle of typing long paths. (See Chapter 16 for more on working with directories, changing the default directory, or using the Quick List feature.)

The Files list box, located on the left side in the Open and Retrieve dialog box, displays the list of files in the current directory. If you select a file from the Files list box, the filename becomes highlighted. Its name appears in the

<u>F</u>ilename text box. In addition, two types of information are provided for that file, as shown here:

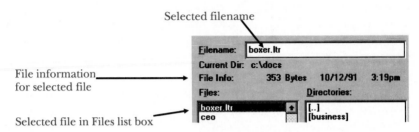

Selected filename

File information
for selected file

Selected file in Files list box

The first information is the size of the file, measured in bytes. A *byte* is a computer term of measurement equal to one character. Also provided are the date and time that the file was last saved to disk. By glancing at the file's date and time, you can tell when the most recent changes were made to that document.

Once a filename is selected in the list box, you can choose the <u>O</u>pen or <u>R</u>etrieve command button to recall that document to the screen.

 If you double-click a filename in the F<u>i</u>les list box, you get the same result as selecting the filename and choosing <u>O</u>pen or <u>R</u>etrieve.

Hands-on Exercise: Open a Document

You should be looking at a clear Document1 workspace. (You can be sure that it is clear if the message "unmodified" appears in the title bar.) Let's open a document:

1. Choose <u>F</u>ile, <u>O</u>pen (or press (F4)). The Open File dialog box appears on screen.

2. Notice the current directory. The files in that directory are displayed in the F<u>i</u>les list box. (If there are many files in that directory, not all of the files can be displayed at once.)

3. Type **smith01.ltr** and press (ENTER). A copy of the document is recalled from the current directory.

Now, we'll close this document and open a document using the F̲iles list box, rather than by typing the filename.

1. Choose F̲ile, C̲lose (or press (CTRL) + (F4)). Since the document has been unmodified, it closes immediately, and you are returned to a clear workspace.

2. Choose F̲ile, O̲pen (or press (F4)). The Open File dialog box appears on screen.

3. Visually locate the filename *smith01.ltr* in the F̲iles list box. If you can't see it, click the down scroll arrow until it comes into view. (Or press (TAB) to make the F̲iles list box active and then either press the (↓) until it comes into view or type the first few characters, **sm**, until the filename is highlighted.)

4. Double-click *smith01.ltr* to choose it. (Or highlight the filename and then select the O̲pen command button.) A copy of the document is recalled from disk.

Printing

Once you've typed and edited a document so that it says exactly what you want it to, you will want not only to save that document but also to print it on paper. Before you print, make sure that:

- The printer is connected to the computer and to the wall outlet.
- The printer is turned on.
- The "On Line" and/or "Ready" buttons on the face of the printer are lit (turned on).
- There is paper in the printer. (If your printer requires that you roll the paper into the printer, also make sure that the top of the first page is lined up properly at the printhead.)

You also must make sure that WordPerfect knows which printer you wish to use. You tell WordPerfect this information by selecting a printer—you usually do this when you first install WordPerfect. Once a printer is selected,

4

it is considered the document's *current printer*. To see what WordPerfect lists as your current printer, select File, Print. A Print dialog box appears, as shown in Figure 4-11. Your current printer is listed at the top of the dialog box under "Current Printer". This is the printer that WordPerfect will use to print out your documents. If the current printer name is correct, you are ready to print your document or you can choose Close to cancel the command.

If no printer is listed, if the name is incorrect, or if you wish to switch to another printer (because your computer is connected to more than one), then refer to Chapter 16. Chapter 16 describes how to select a different printer.

WordPerfect uses special files, called *printer drivers*, to obtain information on your current printer and how to print your documents. WordPerfect can work with printer drivers supplied with WordPerfect, which are installed just like the WordPerfect program is installed, usually at the same time. Word-Perfect can also work with printer drivers supplied by Windows. Chapter 16 describes the procedure to choose either WordPerfect or Windows printer drivers. If your current printer has a name followed by "(Windows)" it is a Windows printer driver. Otherwise, it is a WordPerfect driver.

Figure 4-11.   *Print dialog box*

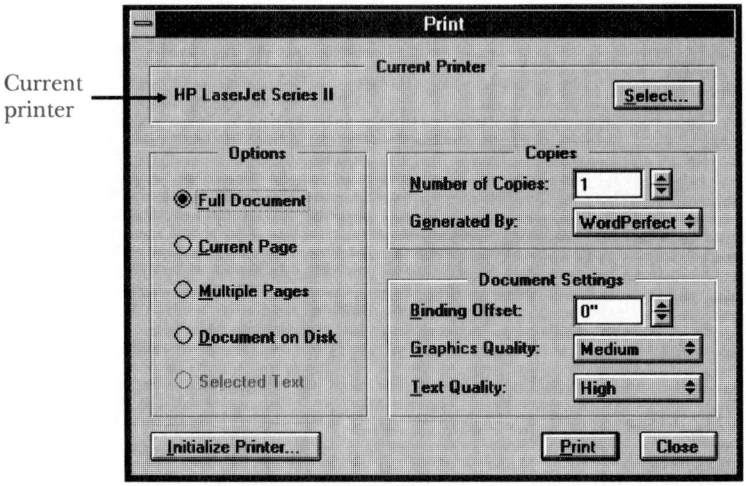

Printing Pages from the Document Workspace

When a document is displayed in the document workspace, printing one copy is quick and easy. Follow these steps to print a document that you've just typed or opened:

1. Choose File, Print. The Print dialog box appears, as shown in Figure 4-11.

2. Choose the Full Document or Current Page or Multiple Pages option.

3. Choose the Print command button.

shortcut (F5) *is the shortcut for File, Print.*
(CTRL) + (P) *is the shortcut for File, Print, Full Document, Print. In other words, you press* (CTRL) + (P) *when you wish to print the full document and bypass the Print dialog box altogether.*

When you select the Full Document or Current Page option, the command to print creates a *print job*, and a Current Print Job dialog box appears for a moment:

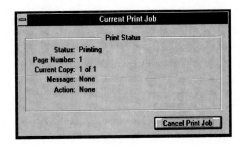

As soon as this dialog box disappears from the screen, the job begins printing; you can continue to work in WordPerfect while the job is printing. Or, if you like, before the Current Print Job dialog box disappears, select Cancel Print Job or press (ENTER) to abort the print command before the document is sent through to your printer.

When you select the <u>M</u>ultiple Pages option, the following dialog box appears:

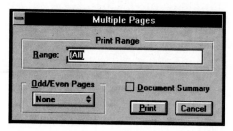

WordPerfect assumes you wish to print all the pages. To specify a different range of pages, type one of the variations of ranges shown next into the <u>R</u>ange text box:

To Print:	**Type:**
One page number	Page number, such as: 4
Consecutive pages	Page numbers joined by a dash, such as: 3-5
Nonconsecutive pages	Page numbers separated by commas or spaces, such as: 4, 6 or 4 6

When indicating consecutive pages, the first or last page is assumed. For instance, to print pages 1 through 5, type **-5**. Or, to print pages 8 through the end of the document, type **8-**.

Also, you can combine the specifications. For instance, to print pages 3 through 6 and page 10, type **3-6,10**. Make sure to type the page numbers in numerical order (for instance, type **3-6,10** rather than **10,3-6**) and be sure there is no space after the dash or comma.

You can also use the <u>O</u>dd/Even Pages pop-up list box to have Word-Perfect print only odd pages (pages 1, 3, 5, and so on) or only even pages (pages 2, 4, 6, and so on). You can also print odd or even logical pages. (See Chapter 7 for more on the Labels feature and logical pages.) And, you can turn on the <u>D</u>ocument Summary check box if you wish to print an existing document summary (see Chapter 16 for more on this feature).

After specifying page numbers, choose <u>P</u>rint. The Current Print Job dialog box appears for a moment, and then the printing begins.

Printing Selected Text

Rather than printing an entire page or document, you can print only a portion of it. For instance, you can choose to print two paragraphs only from your document, or select a page and a half that you want printed. The text you wish to print must be on screen. Follow these steps:

1. Select the text to be printed. (See Chapter 3 if you need a review on how to select text.)

2. Choose File, Print. The Selected Text option is preselected for you.

3. Choose the Print command button.

reminder (F5) *is the shortcut for File, Print.*

The selected text will print in the same position that it lies in the document. For instance, if you print a paragraph that starts at line 3" in the document workspace, it will print 3 inches down on the page.

Printing a Document from Disk

In addition to printing all or part of a document that appears on screen, you can print a document directly from disk—a convenience when you wish to print a long document, when you don't wish to recall it to the screen, or when you have many documents to print. Follow these steps:

1. Choose File, Print. The Print dialog box appears, as shown in Figure 4-11.

2. Choose Document on Disk.

3. Choose Print. A Document on Disk dialog box appears:

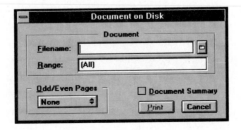

4. Type a filename into the Filename text box. (Or, type a full path to indicate a file stored in a directory other than the current directory.)

   You can also insert the document's path into the Filename text box by clicking the file button (the button containing a picture of a file folder that is next to the Filename text box), which displays the Select File dialog box. Then search through the Directories and Files list boxes that display, select a file, and choose Select.

5. Specify the range of pages (as previously described for the Multiple Pages option).

6. Choose Print. If the file is found, the Current Print Job dialog box appears and then the file is printed. If the file is not found, a dialog box appears indicating this; select OK and try again.

note *If the document you are printing from disk has been formatted for a printer other than the current printer, a dialog box will appear with this message: "Document has not been formatted for current printer. Continue?" Choose Yes to print the document with the current printer, or choose No to cancel the print command.*

Changing Print Settings

When viewing the Print dialog box, before choosing the Print command button you have the opportunity to change certain print settings:

- *Number of Copies*   This setting allows you to print multiple copies of a print job. For instance, rather than executing the print command three times for a document, change the Number of Copies item to 3, and execute the print command just once.

- *Generated By*   This setting determines whether WordPerfect or your printer is in charge of printing multiple copies. If your printer has its own command for printing multiple copies, printing may be faster by setting Generated By from "WordPerfect" to "Printer". The result will not be collated, however; your printer will print the multiple copies of page 1, page 2, and so on. On the other hand, when WordPerfect generates copies, the complete document is printed once, then printed a second time, and so on.

- *Binding Offset* This setting allows a provision for documents that you plan to bind in book format. For instance set a .25" offset and WordPerfect will shift the text of even-numbered pages a quarter-inch to the left and odd-numbered pages a quarter-inch to the right. This is important if the book will contain two-sided pages. (If you plan to bind one-sided pages, you can retain the binding offset at 0" and simply increase the left margin for the document.)

- *Graphics and Text Quality* The Graphics and Text Quality settings dictate the quality with which your graphics (including graphics lines, graphics images, some special characters, and equations) and text are printed.

When you are using a WordPerfect printer driver, you have four options to choose from for your graphics and text quality: Do Not Print, Draft quality, Medium quality, or High quality. The Do Not Print option allows you to print text and graphics separately. For instance, you can set Graphics Quality to "Do Not Print" and Text Quality to "High", so that only the text will be printed. Then, reverse the settings so that only the graphics will be printed. This is useful if your printer does not have the capacity to print both text and graphics at the same time. The Draft, Medium, and High options determine the resolution of the graphics or text on the printed page. The better the quality, the longer it takes to print. You can set the quality for graphics and text individually. For instance, you can set Graphics Quality to "High" and Text Quality to "Draft". (On certain printers, however, a change in quality from Draft to Medium or High has no effect on the printed page.)

When you are using a Windows printer driver, you have three options to choose from for your graphics and text quality: Do Not Print, Draft, or Set In Driver. The Do Not Print option allows you to print text and graphics separately. The Draft option directs the printer to print in draft mode, while the Set In Driver option directs the printer to print in whatever resolution is currently set for the driver. If you print both text and graphics, they must be printed in the same resolution. For instance, you cannot set Graphics Quality to "Draft" and Text Quality to "Set In Driver".

Once changed for a specific document, the Number of Copies and Generated By settings remain in effect until you change them again or until you close the document. So, for instance, if you change the Number of Copies setting to print 50 copies of a letter and then wish to print 1 more copy, remember to change Number of Copies back to 1. The Binding Offset, Graphics Quality, and Text Quality options remain in effect until you change them again, and are also saved with the document. So, if you change the Binding Offset setting, for instance, this setting remains in effect even when you close the document and then recall it to the screen another day.

Encountering Problems While Printing

When you attempt to print and nothing happens, it could be that your printer has not been set up properly for your equipment. Or the problem might be that the printer isn't turned on, or that there is no paper in the printer. A dialog box may appear indicating that there is a printer problem. You will either want to cancel the print job or resume the print job after correcting the problem. To resume, cancel, or pause a print job, you must use the Print Manager. The Print Manager is a Windows program that oversees print jobs, acting as the intermediary between WordPerfect and your printer.

If you experience a printer problem, see Chapter 16 for information on working with printers and printer drivers, and on how to access the Print Manager.

Hands-on Exercise: Print a Document

 Let's print a document stored on disk, the document you created in the last chapter, which you named "first". You don't have to bring the file to the screen, and it doesn't matter that another document is occupying the workspace. Follow these steps:

1. Turn your printer on. Make sure the Ready and/or On Line buttons on the printer are lit. Make sure the printer is connected to your computer. Make sure the paper is properly inserted.

2. Choose File, Print, or press (F5). The Print dialog box appears, as shown in Figure 4-11.

3. Choose <u>D</u>ocument on Disk.

4. Choose <u>P</u>rint. The Document on Disk dialog box appears.

5. Type **first** into the <u>F</u>ilename text box. (If you followed the hands-on exercise at the beginning of this chapter and changed the current directory, you will need to type the file's full path. Type **c:\wpwin\first**, for instance, if the default directory was *c:\wpwin* when you originally created and saved this file.)

6. Choose <u>P</u>rint. In moments, the Current Print Job dialog box appears. Soon after it disappears, the file is printed.

The file *smith01.ltr* should still be on screen from the previous hands-on exercise. Let's print out this document. Whenever you wish to print out the full document (which, for a one-page document, is the same as printing out the current page), there's a very short shortcut:

1. Press (CTRL) + (P). In moments, the Current Print Job dialog box appears. Soon after it disappears, the document is printed.

After the document has finished printing, remember to exit WordPerfect properly (as described in Chapter 1) if you've completed your computer session for the day.

4

Quick Reference

- To store a document on disk, decide which directory will store it and what its filename will be. A filename can contain eight characters or less with an optional period and three-character extension.

- To save a document for the first time or under a new filename, choose <u>F</u>ile, Save <u>A</u>s and indicate the directory and the filename that you wish to store it with.

- To save a document regularly, protecting against power failures, choose <u>F</u>ile, <u>S</u>ave.

- To close a document, choose <u>F</u>ile, <u>C</u>lose. Close a document whenever you're done working with it but want to remain in WordPerfect to work on another document.

- To open a file onto a clear document workspace, choose <u>F</u>ile, <u>O</u>pen and indicate the directory and the name of the file.

- To retrieve a file into the current document on screen wherever the insertion point is located, choose <u>F</u>ile, <u>R</u>etrieve and indicate the directory and the name of the file.

- To determine the default directory, where WordPerfect assumes you wish to recall files from and save files to, look at what's listed next to "Current Dir:" when you first display the Open File, Retrieve, or Save As dialog box.

- To print, choose <u>F</u>ile, <u>P</u>rint. Then, select the part of the document you want to print: full document, current page, or multiple pages. You can also print text that you previously selected or a document not currently in the document window.

II

Formatting and Editing Skills

5

Enhancing Characters

A *font* is a set of characters that defines how text will display in the document workspace and print on paper. In this chapter you'll see how to change font attributes, adding enhancements such as bold, underlining, or italics, or changing from very small to very large size. You'll also learn how to switch the typeface of your text to Helvetica or Times Roman or Century Schoolbook or any typeface you choose, and change the color of characters at the printer. Next, you'll learn about the Draft mode feature, where you specify that despite font changes, all characters on screen are uniform—as in WordPerfect 5.1 for DOS. You may find this makes the text more readable.

The chapter ends with a discussion on using special characters such as a bullet (•), the legal section symbol (§), or the one-half symbol (½). These are just three of the more than 1500 special characters available to you. Be aware that using colors, many fonts, and special characters depends on the capabilities of your printer.

Choosing Font Attributes

The font currently in effect for your text is called the *current font*. It is listed on the left side of the status line.

With WordPerfect, there are two categories of attributes that you can alter for the current font. First you can change the *appearance* of characters. You can make your readers notice words you want to stand out by adding emphasis or contrast. Appearance attributes include the following:

Bold	Characters are darkened
Underline	A single underscore appears below characters
Double Underline	A double underscore appears below characters
Italic	Characters are slanted to provide a cursive effect
Outline	Characters appear white and outlined in black
Shadow	The edges of characters are darkened or characters are printed twice—the second time just slightly to the right of the first printing—to produce a shadow effect
Small Cap	Letters appear as uppercase in miniature
Redline	Characters are marked either with a shaded background, a dotted line under the characters, a vertical bar in the left margin, or in a different color
Strikeout	A solid or dashed line is printed through the characters

The other way to alter a font attribute is to change its *size*. You're given the choice of how big or small to make characters. Size attributes include the following:

Fine	60	percent of normal size
Small	80	percent of normal size
Large	120	percent of normal size

Very Large	150 percent of normal size
Extra Large	200 percent of normal size
Superscript	60 percent of normal size, placed slightly above the standard line
Subscript	60 percent of normal size, placed slightly below the standard line

These size ratios may differ depending on your current font and printer, and also can be changed with the File, Preferences, Print command, as described in Chapter 17.

caution *When you change the size attribute in an existing document, it will reformat. For instance, line breaks, page breaks, and the alignment of text on tabs will be different. You may have to insert tabs or realign the text when you change the size of existing text.*

Underline, Bold, and Other Common Attributes

The most commonly used appearance and size attributes are illustrated in Figure 5-1.

All of these can be inserted in your document directly from the Font menu. The exact procedure depends on whether or not you've already typed

Figure 5-1. *Frequently used attributes*

Bold	<u>Underline</u>	~~Redline~~
Italic	<u>Double Underline</u>	~~Strikeout~~

Superscript shrinks and moves characters ^{up,} as in e^2.
Subscript shrinks and moves characters $_{down,}$ as in H_2O.

Fine, Small, Large, Very Large, Extra Large

the text you want to enhance. To choose an attribute before you type, follow these steps:

1. Position the insertion point where you wish to apply an attribute to the text.

2. Choose Font. The Font menu appears.

3. Choose from: Bold; Italic; Underline; Double Underline; Redline; Strikeout; Subscript; or Superscript.

    You can also choose Size to display a submenu, and then choose from: Fine; Small; Large; Very Large; or Extra Large.

    The attribute is turned on.

4. Type the text.

5. Repeat steps 2 and 3 to turn off the attribute. Or, choose Font, Normal to turn off any and all attributes in one command.

As an example, suppose you wish to underline one sentence. Choose Font, Underline, type the sentence, and then stop the Underline attribute at the end of that sentence by choosing Font, Underline again or by choosing Font, Normal.

You can apply more than one attribute to your text if you wish. Position the insertion point and then follow steps 2 and 3 as many times as there are attributes you wish to apply. For instance, choose Font, Bold and choose Font, Underline. Then type your text. When you're done typing the text, choose Font, Normal to turn off all the attributes at once. (Another method for applying multiple attributes is described in the next section, "Multiple and Less Common Attributes".)

To choose an attribute for existing text, you must employ the Select feature. (If you need a review of the Select feature, refer to Chapter 3.) Follow these steps:

1. Select the text. The text will become highlighted.

2. Choose Font.

3. Choose from: Bold; Italic; Underline; Double Underline; Redline; Strikeout; Subscript; or Superscript.

You can also choose Size to display a submenu, and then choose from: Fine; Small; Large; Very Large; or Extra Large.

The attribute is applied to the selected text only.

4. Click the mouse button or press an arrow key to turn off the Select feature.

As an example, suppose you wish to boldface a word that you've already typed. To do so, select the word so that it is highlighted. Next, choose Font, Bold, and click the mouse button to turn off the Select feature.

You can apply more than one attribute to your existing text if you wish. After you follow steps 1 through 3, the text remains selected, so you can apply additional attributes before turning off the Select feature with step 4. (A method for applying multiple attributes is described in the next section.)

≡shortcut≡ *Some of the attributes just discussed have shortcut keys:*

(CTRL) + (B) *is the shortcut for Font, Bold.*

(CTRL) + (I) *is the shortcut for Font, Italic.*

(CTRL) + (U) *is the shortcut for Font, Underline.*

(CTRL) + (N) *is the shortcut for Font, Normal.*

(CTRL) + (S) *is the shortcut for Font, Size.*

These are significant shortcuts, enabling you to completely bypass the Font menu. For instance, to choose bold before you type, simply press (CTRL) + (B) *type the text, and press* (CTRL) + (B) *again to turn off bold. As another example, to underline existing text, simply select the text, press* (CTRL) + (U)*, and click the mouse button or press an arrow key to turn off the Select feature.*

As you change a font attribute, notice how the Font menu indicates those attributes that are currently turned on in your text. When the insertion point is in a location where all attributes are currently off, choosing Font will display the Font menu with a check mark next to the Normal menu item, as shown here:

5

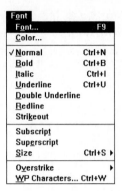

Once an attribute has been turned on, the check mark appears next to that attribute, rather than next to Normal. For instance, suppose you turn on Underline. When the insertion point is located where underlining is on and you choose Font, the Font menu displays like this:

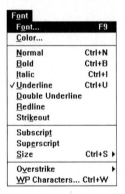

If two or more attributes are on, check marks will appear next to each of them.

When you select text before displaying the Font menu, either a check mark or a diamond-shaped bullet appears next to an attribute—depending on whether the attribute applies to *all* or only a *portion* of the selected text. For instance, suppose you select a sentence that has previously been underlined. When you display the Font menu, a check mark appears by the Underline menu item, as in the example just shown. However, if only two words in the sentence are underlined and the rest of it is normal, then when you choose Font, diamond-shaped bullets appear, as follows:

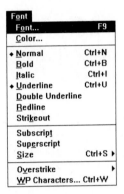

Multiple and Less Common Attributes

WordPerfect allows an alternative method for changing font attributes with a Font dialog box. The Font dialog box is convenient when you wish to apply several attributes to the same text—for example, to underline, bold, and italicize a heading. Moreover, three less commonly used attributes—Outline, Shadow, and Small Cap—can *only* be chosen from the Font dialog box. Follow these steps to apply attributes via the Font dialog box:

1. For text to be typed, position the insertion point where you want to apply the attribute(s). For existing text, select the text.

2. Choose Font, Font. The Font dialog box appears, as shown in Figure 5-2.

    The left side of the Font dialog box displays the current printer and the current font. The current font is the one that is highlighted in the Font list box.

    The right side displays check boxes for all the Appearance and Size attributes.

3. Choose those attributes that you wish to turn on or off. You can turn on more than one attribute at once; for example, text can be simultaneously italic and bold. You cannot, however, choose a size attribute when another is already selected, because text cannot be

Figure 5-2.   *Font dialog box*

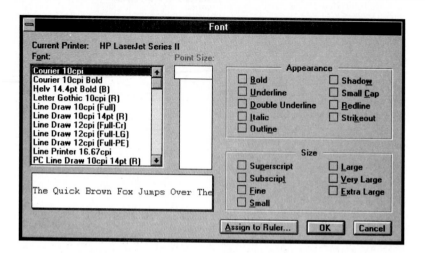

two different sizes at once. The change is shown in the preview box, which contains the words, "The Quick Brown Fox Jumps Over The Lazy White Dog".

4. Choose OK.

5. For text to be typed, type the text and then repeat steps 2 through 4 to turn off the attributes, or choose Font, Normal to turn off all the attributes at once.

   For existing text, click the mouse or press an arrow key to turn off the Select feature.

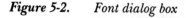 (F9) *is the shortcut for Font, Font.*

The Font dialog box indicates when an attribute is currently turned on in your text with an X in the attribute's check box. If you select text before displaying the Font dialog box, either an X or gray shading appears in the attribute's check box—depending on whether the attribute applies to *all* or only a *portion* of the selected text. For instance, suppose you select a sentence that has previously been underlined. When you choose Font, Font to display the Font dialog box, an X appears in the Underline check box. However, if only two words in the sentence are underlined, then when you display the Font dialog box, gray shading appears in the Underline check box.

How Attributes Display and Print

You don't necessarily need to view the Font menu or Font dialog box to see which attributes are currently on. When the insertion point is in an area controlled by an attribute, the left side of the status line reflects the change. For instance, with normal Courier, the status line reads as follows:

Font: Courier 10cpi	Pg 1 Ln 1" Pos 1"

When you choose underline and italics, the left side of the status line changes to show this:

Font: *Courier 10cpi*	Pg 1 Ln 1" Pos 1"

The document workspace displays the change as well. For instance, when you underline characters, an underscore appears on screen. If you italicize characters, they appear slanted on screen. That's the magic of WYSIWYG (what you see is what you get), which you learned about in Chapter 3. A few attributes, however, may display in a different foreground or background color, depending on the capabilities of your computer monitor and printer. Also, the Outline attribute always displays in another color.

At the printer, the results you get depend on: the capabilities of your printer, the fonts you have available for that printer, and the current font. Sometimes an attribute might not be available for the current font, or for *any* font available to your printer. In that case, the text will print without attributes, or the printer will substitute another attribute. Here's an example:

```
Italic was selected for this text. It appeared slanted
in the document workspace. But, since the printer
could not produce italic, words at the printer were
underlined instead.
```

Italic, Outline, Shadow, and Small Caps are four attributes that are often unavailable for a variety of printers. In other cases, various type sizes may be unavailable in the current font. If that occurs, WordPerfect will borrow sizes from another font that has the appropriate size available, as shown here:

This is Fine,
while this is Small size,
Notice how the typeface changes for Large,
AND AGAIN FOR VERY LARGE,
AND CAN'T GET BIGGER FOR EXTRA LARGE.

Other fonts may have all the different sizes available:

This is Fine,
while this is Small size,
Notice that this gets Large.
The same typeface gets Very Large,
and even prints in Extra Large.

Finally, sometimes you can print certain appearance attributes or change size attributes *only* by changing the current font, rather than by choosing an attribute. (The procedure to change the current font is described in the section, "Working with Fonts".) For instance, Italic may not be available for Courier on your printer, but may be available for Century Schoolbook.

To discover your own printer's attribute capabilities, consider creating a test document. Type text on screen using all the different attributes. Or open a test document provided by WordPerfect with the filename *printer.tst.* (If your WordPerfect program was installed in *c:\wpwin,* then *printer.tst* will also be found in that directory, so that the complete path for the file when you wish to open it on screen is *c:\wpwin\printer.tst.*) Print your own test document or print *printer.tst* to see how your printer handles attributes for the current font. Next, change the current font—as described later on in this chapter—and print again. Repeat this process to print the test file as many times as the number of fonts available to you. This way you can see which attributes your printer supports in each font.

There are special printing considerations for two attributes. For the Underline attribute, WordPerfect is initially set to underline spaces created with the (SPACEBAR), but not tabs created with the (TAB) key. For instance, if you turn on underlining and press the (SPACEBAR) repeatedly, you can create a blank line for signatures. However, if you turn on underlining and press the (TAB) key several times, no underline will appear until you start typing characters. You can change these settings to have WordPerfect not underline spaces but underline tabs—with the Typesetting feature, as described in Chapter 12.

For the Redline attribute, WordPerfect is set as printer dependent. Generally, this means characters are marked with a shaded background when printed. However, this might not be the case with your printer. Once you print a document containing Redline, you'll uncover what printer dependent means for your printer. You can change how Redlining appears in a specific document, so that rather than printer dependent, Redlining shows up as a character in the left margin or in alternating margins (in the left margin of odd pages and in the right margin of even pages). You can even specify what character shows up. To change the way in which Redlining appears, choose Layout, Document, Redline Method, and then select from the options provided.

Canceling an Attribute Change

When you make a font attribute change, behind the scenes WordPerfect places a pair of codes in the text on either side of the insertion point. For instance, if you turn on underline, the codes inserted are these:

```
[Und On]|[Und Off]
```

Any text typed between the code pair takes on that attribute. For instance, suppose you underline the word "Association". In the document workspace, the word appears as: <u>Association</u>. But, in the reveal codes workspace, the word appears as:

```
[Und On]Association[Und Off]
```

To cancel a font attribute, you have two alternatives. One involves selecting the text that you wish to remove the attribute from. Once the text is selected, you can do one of the following:

- Choose F<u>o</u>nt and then select the attribute with the check mark beside it that you wish to turn off
- Choose F<u>o</u>nt, <u>N</u>ormal to turn off all attributes
- Use the Font dialog box to unselect the attribute

With this method, you can cancel all or part of an attribute. For instance, if a sentence of six words is underlined, select all six words when canceling underlining for the entire sentence. Or select only three words to cancel underlining for half the sentence.

Another method to cancel a font attribute enables you to do so without selecting the text. Use the reveal codes workspace to locate either of the code pairs and then erase one of them. For instance, choose <u>V</u>iew, Reveal <u>C</u>odes to open the reveal codes workspace. Then, position the insertion point on the [Und On] code, and press (DEL). This removes underlining from the [Und On] code all the way to the [Und Off] code. Both codes of the code pair are erased.

Hands-on Exercise: Choose Font Attributes

 In a clear document workspace, open the file *smith01.ltr,* which you created in the last chapter. In this document, let's underline the word "complete" in the first paragraph, and both underline and boldface "accept the new vacation option":

1. Select the text "complete".
2. Choose F<u>o</u>nt, <u>U</u>nderline.
3. Turn off the Select feature by clicking the mouse or pressing an arrow key.
4. Select the text "accept the new vacation option".
5. Press (CTRL) + (U), the shortcut for choosing underline. Then, press (CTRL) + (B), the shortcut for bold.
6. Turn off the Select feature.

Next, let's insert text with a Large size attribute:

1. Position the insertion point just before the "Thank you" near the end of the letter.

2. Choose Font, Size, Large.

3. Type the following sentence: **Please keep this information confidential until February 6.** Then insert two spaces after the sentence.

4. Choose Font, Normal to turn off the Large size.

5. To see that Large size is no longer in effect, type the following sentence: **I'll call you then.**

Oops!! I only wanted the words "confidential until February 6" to be Large. Let's return the first half of that sentence back to normal:

1. Select "Please keep this information".

2. Choose (CTRL) + (N).

3. Turn off the Select feature by clicking the mouse or pressing an arrow key.

Working with Fonts

You can change not only the attributes for the current font, but you can change the font itself as well. A new font means a change in one or more of the following:

- *Typeface* This could be a change, for example, from Courier to Helvetica or Times Roman.

- *Type of horizontal spacing* You might have a *monospaced* font, where each character occupies the same amount of space, or a *proportionally spaced* font, where each character occupies a different amount of space in proportion to its width. A proportionally spaced font means a narrow letter like "i" is allotted less space than a wide letter like "m".

- *Size that is considered standard or "normal" for that font*   Size is measured in characters per inch (cpi) for monospaced fonts and in point size (pt) for proportionally spaced fonts.

- *Appearance attribute that is considered standard or "normal" for that font*   Usually, the Normal attribute signifies no bold or italics. Sometimes, however, the current font may be defined as a font with bold or italics or another attribute already turned on.

caution *When a change in the font results in a change in the font's size or horizontal spacing, an existing document will reformat. For instance, line breaks, page breaks, and the alignment of text on tabs will be different. You may, therefore, have to insert tabs or realign the text when you change the font in an existing document.*

Figure 5-3 shows six different fonts. Each font is an example of a different combination of typeface, horizontal spacing, normal size, and normal attribute. Notice how some of the fonts in Figure 5-3 have attributes already assigned to them. For instance, the last font is Cooper Black, which is bold. If you choose the last font in Figure 5-3 as the current font, your text will be bold without your having turned on the bold attribute. Bold will be considered a normal attribute for that font.

Which fonts are available for your printer? You will see a list of the fonts your printer can print when you attempt to change the font (described shortly).

Fonts come from three sources. First, all printers have at least one, and usually more, *internal fonts,* which are built in to your printer. Second, some printers have slots where you can change the *print wheel* or insert one or more *font cartridges.* Third, some printers can use *soft fonts,* which are stored in files on the computer's hard disk. Font cartridges and soft fonts contain a related group of fonts, and are purchased separately for your printer.

Once you purchase print wheels, font cartridges, or soft fonts, you may need to do one or more of the following before they become available for your documents: install the fonts for your printer driver, switch between Windows and WordPerfect printer drivers, or initialize your printer so that WordPerfect will recognize the fonts. (As described in Chapter 4, printer drivers are special files that provide information on how to print out your documents. These printer drivers can be supplied by WordPerfect or by Windows.) The procedures are described in Chapter 16.

Figure 5-3. *Examples of fonts with different typefaces, horizontal spacing, and attributes*

This is Courier typeface, 10 cpi, which is monospaced. Courier is the most common typeface.

THIS IS PRESENTATION TYPEFACE, 6.5 CPI, MONOSPACED & BOLDFACED. A DECREASE IN CHARACTERS PER INCH (CPI) MEANS FEWER CHARACTERS FIT ON A LINE.

This is Times Roman typeface, 10-point, which is proportionally spaced. Proportional spacing provides a more professional look to the text.

This is Century Schoolbook typeface, 14-point, which is proportionally spaced. An increase in point size results in a larger character.

This is Park Avenue typeface, 18-point, proportionally spaced and italicized.

Cooper Black! 24-point! Proportionally spaced! Boldfaced!

5

The sources for fonts—internal fonts, print wheels, font cartridges, and soft fonts—can be used in combination in a document. For instance, in Figure 5-3, Courier type is one of the printer's built-in fonts; Presentation and Times Roman come from cartridges that were purchased separately and inserted into the printer; and Century Schoolbook, Park Avenue, and Cooper Black are soft fonts (these shown here are from Bitstream, Inc.). The printer used was a Hewlett-Packard LaserJet Series II.

Your printer has one font associated with it that is set up as the default font for the printer: this is referred to as the *Printer Initial Font.* Whenever you begin a document, WordPerfect assumes the Printer Initial Font to be your current font. It lists this font in the left corner of the status line in a clear document workspace before you even start typing a new document. Typically, the Printer Initial Font is an internal font, such as Courier 10cpi.

The Printer Initial Font can be overridden for a particular document in one of three ways:

- Using the Document Initial Font dialog box, you can override the Printer Initial Font starting at the very top of the document. The entire document is affected.

- Using the Font dialog box, you can override the Printer or Document Initial Font at any location in the document.

- Using the Font button on the ruler, you can override the Printer or Document Initial Font at any location in the document.

These three methods are described more fully next.

Changing the Document Initial Font

You can change a font for an entire document starting at the top of the document. The Document Initial Font feature establishes the current font in the document workspace, not only for the main text, but also for elements such as headers, footers, footnotes, equations, and captions for graphics boxes. Follow these steps:

1. The insertion point can be located anywhere within the document.

2. Choose Layout, Document, Initial Font. A Document Initial Font dialog box appears, as shown in Figure 5-4. The currently selected font is highlighted in the Fonts list box. Other available fonts are also listed.

3. Select a new font from the Fonts list box. This becomes the current font. The preview box, located below the Fonts list box and containing the words, "The Quick Brown Fox Jumps Over The Lazy Dog", changes to reflect the selection. You can thus see how the current font will appear in your document. This is an example of *WYSBYGI,* or "what you see before you get it".

4. For a *scalable* font—or one in which you can change the size of the characters in a typeface—indicate a point size by typing or selecting from the Point Size list box. This becomes the normal size for the current font.

   You can tell if a font is scalable by the Point Size element. It is not scalable if the Point Size element is dimmed to a light shade of gray.

Figure 5-4. *Document Initial Font dialog box*

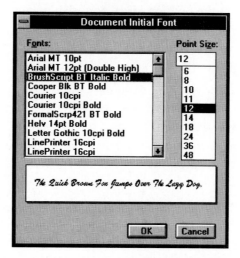

On the other hand, the highlighted font in Figure 5-4 is scalable, since the Point Size element displays possible point size options.

5. Choose OK.

The font is changed for the entire document. Any existing text in the document workspace will display in the new font. Moreover, the left side of the status line notes the name of the new font. If you later decide on a different Document Initial Font, repeat steps 1 through 5.

Changing the Font in the Font Dialog Box

The second way to change a font is in the Font dialog box (the same dialog box previously described for changing appearance and size attributes). Using this dialog box, you can change the current font starting at a specific location. For instance, you can change the font starting at the top of the document, or starting at the fifth paragraph, or starting on the sixth page. You can also change the font for just selected text, such as for paragraphs four and five only. Follow these steps:

1. Position the insertion point where you wish to change the font. Or select the text for which you wish to change the font.

2. Choose Font, Font. The Font dialog box appears, as shown in Figure 5-2. The Font list box, located on the left side in the Font dialog box, highlights the current font.

3. Select a new font from the Font list box. This becomes the current font. The preview box, located below the Font list box, changes to reflect the selection.

4. For a *scalable* font, indicate a point size by typing or selecting from the Point Size list box. (A font is not scalable if the Point Size element is dimmed to a light shade. For instance, the current font in Figure 5-2 is not scalable.)

5. If you desire, you can also turn on appearance or size attributes for the current font on the right side of the Font dialog box (as previously described).

6. Choose OK.

shortcut (F9) *is the shortcut for Font, Font.*

For a font change at the insertion point, WordPerfect inserts a single code. The font code indicates the type of font change, such as

```
[Font:Presentation 6.5cpi Bold]
```

This code causes a font change in the document workspace starting from where it was inserted and continuing to the end of the document (or up to the point where you insert another font code later in the text). It changes the font for headers or footers created beyond the text from the font code. You can also change the font for an element such as a header, footer, or footnote by inserting a font code within the text of the element.

For a font change restricted to selected text, WordPerfect inserts two codes. At the beginning of the selected text, a font code is inserted to change the current font. At the end of the selected text, a font code is inserted to return the font to its previous status. For instance, suppose the current font is Courier 10cpi. You select one sentence and change the font for that one sentence to Presentation 6.5cpi Bold. In the document workspace, only that one sentence is affected by the font change. In the reveal codes workspace, here's the result:

```
[Font:Presentation 6.5cpi Bold]Here's the one
sentence that was selected.[Font:Courier 10cpi]
```

To cancel a font change, repeat steps 1 through 6, but select the original font. Another alternative is to view the reveal codes workspace, and then find and delete the font code(s). This second alternative allows you to delete unnecessary codes, which lessens the possibility of problems later on with an errant code.

Changing the Font on the Ruler

An alternative to the Font dialog box for changing the current font—but with the exact same effect—is to use the Font button and Size button on the ruler. The ruler is a quick way to execute font and other layout changes. You must have a mouse to take advantage of the ruler.

5

Figure 5-5.   *Ruler Fonts Menu dialog box*

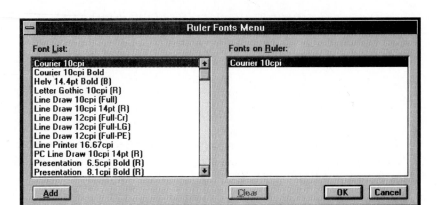

The ruler lets you choose from a list of commonly used fonts. Before you can rely on the ruler, you must assign the commonly used fonts to the ruler with these steps:

1. Choose Font, Font.

2. Choose Assign to Ruler, to display the Ruler Fonts Menu dialog box shown in Figure 5-5. The default font, Courier 10cpi in Figure 5-5, is always listed in the Fonts on Ruler list box because it is assigned to the ruler automatically.

3. Select a font from the Font List list box and choose Add; the font also appears in the Fonts on Ruler list box. Repeat until you've added all the fonts you use often. (You can also select a font from the Ruler list box and choose Clear to delete it.)

4. Choose OK.

The fonts you add to the Ruler list box are, in turn, assigned to the ruler. You only need to assign each font to the ruler once. After that, each font you assigned is easily accessed whenever the ruler is on screen.

Display the ruler by choosing <u>V</u>iew, <u>R</u>uler. Here's what will appear in the document workspace just below the menu bar:

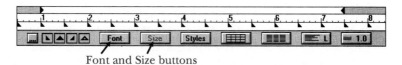

Font and Size buttons

The ruler slightly reduces the size of the document workspace. This is a small price to pay, however, for the convenience the ruler provides. If you're making numerous font or other layout changes in a document, it makes sense to keep the ruler on screen at all times. (See the next chapter for additional information on the ruler.)

shortcut (ALT) + (SHIFT) + (F3) *is the shortcut for <u>V</u>iew, <u>R</u>uler.*

Once the ruler is displayed on screen, every time you wish to change the current font, follow these steps:

1. Position the insertion point where you wish to change the font, or select the text for which you wish to change the font.

2. Click and hold the Font button. A list appears of the fonts previously assigned to the ruler.

3. While still pressing the mouse button, drag the mouse to select a new font, and then release the mouse button.

4. If the font is scalable, click and hold the Size button. Drag the mouse to select a point size, and release the mouse button. (A font is not scalable if the Size button is dimmed to a light gray.)

This has the same result as when you select a font in the Font dialog box: for a font change at the insertion point, a single font code is inserted; for a font change restricted to selected text, one font code is inserted at the beginning of the selected text and another font code that returns the font to its previous status is inserted at the end of the selected text.

shortcut *Double-click the Font button to display the Font dialog box from the ruler. This is convenient if you wish to select a font that you use less frequently and have therefore not assigned to the ruler.*

5

Hands-on Exercise: Change Fonts in a Document

The document *smith01.ltr* should still be in your document workspace. Notice the current font for your text, which is listed on the left side of the status line. Let's change the font for the entire document. In other words, let's change the Document Initial Font.

1. Choose Layout, Document, Initial Font. A dialog box will appear, like the one shown in Figure 5-4, except that only the fonts available for your printer will be listed.

2. Select a new font from the Fonts list box.

3. If the font is scalable, select or type a point size using the Point Size list or text box.

4. Click OK or press (ENTER).

In the document workspace, the status bar changes to reflect the new current font. Also, you may notice a change in the look or size of characters. If the font change resulted in a size or horizontal spacing change, the text will reformat automatically. In some cases after reformatting, parts of the document may look awkward. For instance, the list of names and dates may not be aligned properly, as shown here:

Antonio Abbot	May 31st
Lois Chang	April 27th
Tim Fingerman	May 20th
Paul McClintock	August 7th

This could be corrected by inserting or deleting tab codes, either in the document workspace or the reveal codes workspace. Don't bother here because you're about to make another font change. Let's change the font only for the list of names and dates:

1. Select the list of names and dates.

2. Choose Font, Font. Or, press (F9).

3. Select a new font from the Font list box.

4. If the font is scalable, select or type a point size using the Point Size list or text box.

5. Click OK or press (ENTER). Then turn off the Select feature.

Now as you move your insertion point, notice how the status line changes to indicate the current font for each section of the document; there is one font for the list of names and dates, and another font for the rest of the document.

You may wish to print out your document. One example is shown in Figure 5-6. Century Schoolbook is in effect for most of the document; Helvetica is in effect for the list of names and dates. Notice also that attributes were applied to "complete", "accept the new vacation option", and "confidential until February 6", as directed in the previous hands-on exercise.

Working in Draft Mode

Draft mode offers a display on screen with the same uniform characters found on the reveal codes workspace (and the same characters that Word-Perfect 5.1 for DOS users are familiar with). Draft mode is oriented toward text, rather than graphics. The characters are monospaced and all of the same size. Font attributes are shown on screen in a different color, rather than with actual character changes. Graphics are not displayed.

Draft mode is useful when you wish to focus on your document's contents rather than its layout. It is also useful if you've changed the font or font attributes and either the text is slow to respond when you edit or the text is hard to read. To turn on Draft mode, choose View, Draft Mode. To return to normal mode, choose View, Draft Mode again.

You may find using the document workspace when in Draft mode is easier on your eyes. (You can even change the colors on the display to whatever combination is most comfortable for you. The File, Preferences, Display feature accomplishes this, and is described in Chapter 17). When you're ready

Figure 5-6.   *Different fonts and attributes applied to* smith01.ltr

February 3, 1993

Mr. Barrett P. Smith
FST Accounting
1801 S. Harmon Street
Oakland, CA 94413

Dear Barrett:

As we discussed, here is a <u>complete</u> list of full-time employees who elected
to **accept the new vacation option**, along with their anniversary dates with us.
Please add their names to your records.

Antonio Abbot	**May 31st**
Lois Chang	**April 27th**
Tim Fingerman	**May 20th**
Paul McClintock	**August 7th**

The new accrued vacation system should begin for these employees immediately.
Please keep this information confidential until February 6.   I'll call you then.
Thank you.

Sincerely,

Your Name
President
R&R Wine Association

P.S. I've included a copy of our quarterly newsletter for your enjoyment.

---

to format your document or see graphics lines and boxes inserted into your
document, switch back to normal mode.

reminder *Switching to Draft mode only affects the display of text on screen, not text at the printer.*

Figure 5-7. *Select Text Color dialog box*

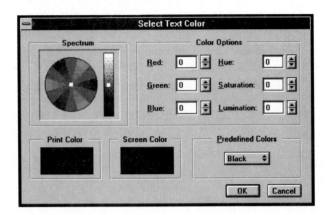

Printing Text in Color

You can take advantage of the Color feature, which specifies the color for text on the printed page, if you have a color printer. Follow these steps:

1. Position the insertion point where you want to change the color.

2. Choose Font, Color. The Select Text Color dialog box appears, as shown in Figure 5-7.

3. Choose a color from the Predefined Colors pop-up list box. The Print Color and Screen Color boxes show how your color choice will affect the text, both on paper and on screen. (The printed text colors and screen text colors are independent.)

   You can also create a custom color. Specify a number between 0 and 255 in the Red, Green, and Blue number boxes to select a color combination; specify a number between 0 and 360 in the Hue number box to adjust the gradation of color (the ratio in which Red,

Green, and Blue combine); and specify a percentage between 0 and 100 in the Lumination and Saturation number boxes to adjust the intensity of the color and the amount of white it contains.

Or create a custom color by using a mouse to drag the tiny rectangular shapes in the two Spectrum pallets. The Spectrum pallet shaped like a circle controls hue and saturation, while the Spectrum pallet shaped like a rectangle changes the lumination.

4. Choose OK.

Behind the scenes, WordPerfect inserts a single code that controls the color change, such as [Color:Red]. This single code takes effect starting from where it was inserted until the end of the document, or up to the point where you insert another color code farther forward in the text. For instance, two paragraphs after changing the color to red, you can insert a [Color:Black] code to return the text to black. To cancel a color change, switch to the reveal codes workspace and delete the color code.

When the insertion point is in a location affected by a color change, the font listed on the left side of the status bar will display in the new color. The characters in the document workspace affected by the color change will also change color, but *only* if the Text In Windows Systems Color check box—the first item on screen when you choose File, Preferences, Display—is turned off.

Using Special Characters

With WordPerfect, you are not limited to the characters on the computer keyboard. You can produce special characters—for example, bullets of various sizes (such as ● or • or ○), the one-half symbol (½), the section sign (§), the paragraph symbol (¶), and many others. You can also produce *digraphs* (two vowels or consonants combined to express a single sound) or *diacritics* (a vowel or consonant combined with a diacritical mark to express a single sound) such as Æ, á, or ö. In fact, depending on your printer, with WordPerfect you can include a variety of multinational, mathematical, scientific, Greek, and Hebrew symbols in documents—over 1500 special characters in all. You can either use WordPerfect's character sets to do so, or take advantage of the Overstrike feature.

WordPerfect Character Sets

In WordPerfect, characters are separated into 13 *character sets*. Each character set has a name and a corresponding number, as listed in Table 5-1.

To insert a character from any character set into a document on screen, follow these steps:

1. Position the insertion point where you want the character to appear.

2. Choose Font, WP Characters. The WordPerfect Characters dialog box appears, as shown in Figure 5-8.

3. Choose a character set from the Set pop-up list box. When you select a new character set, the display in the Characters list box changes to show the characters in that set.

Figure 5-8. *WordPerfect Characters dialog box*

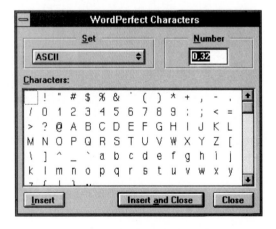

Table 5-1.   *WordPerfect Character Sets*

Name	Character Set Number	Contents
ASCII	0	ASCII set (space through tilde) found on the computer keyboard
Multinational 1	1	Common capitalizable multinational characters, diacritics, and noncapitalizable multinational characters
Multinational 2	2	Rarely used noncapitalizable multinational characters and diacritics
Box Drawing	3	Double/single box drawing characters
Typographic Symbols	4	Common typographic symbols not found in the ASCII set
Iconic Symbols	5	"Picture" (icon) symbols
Math/Scientific	6	Nonextensible, nonoversized math/scientific characters not found in the ASCII set
Math/Scientific Extension	7	Extensible and oversized math/scientific characters
Greek	8	Full Greek character set for ancient and modern applications
Hebrew	9	Full Hebrew character set for ancient and modern applications
Cyrillic	10	Full Cyrillic character set for ancient and modern applications
Japanese	11	Characters for Hiragana or Katakana (the type is determined by the typeface)
User-Defined	12	255 user-definable characters

4. Select a character from the Characters list box. (Not all the characters can fit in the list box, so be sure to use the scroll bars or down arrow to see more.)

   When you select a character, that character's WordPerfect character number displays in the Number text box. A *WordPerfect character number* is comprised of a character set number, a comma, and a character number from the set (such as 2,16 or 4,0).

5. Choose Insert and Close if you wish to insert the character at the insertion point and close the dialog box in one command.

   Or, choose Insert if you wish to insert the character and keep the dialog box open to insert additional characters. You can then switch back and forth between the WordPerfect Characters dialog box and the document workspace—typing keyboard characters and then special characters again—by clicking with the mouse in the document workspace or the dialog box, or by pressing (ALT) + (F6). When you're done inserting special characters, choose Close or press (ESC) to close the dialog box.

5

shortcut (CTRL) + (W) *is the shortcut for Font, WP Characters.*

WordPerfect offers a similar, but speedier procedure, when you need to insert one of the more common symbols, digraphs, or diacritics. Rather than hunt in the character sets for the special character you need, simply type a character combination directly into the Number text box, one character after the other, without commas or spaces. Table 5-2 provides a list of the available character combinations and their corresponding special character.

Every special character is inserted in the text as a code. But you can only see this code if you switch to the reveal codes workspace and position the insertion point on the special character. The code indicates the special character's WordPerfect character number. For instance, suppose you insert the section sign (§) in the text. In the document workspace, the section sign displays. When you switch to the reveal codes workspace and position the insertion point on the section sign, the following code is shown: [§:4,6]. This is because the section sign's WordPerfect character number is 4,6.

Whether or not special characters will print depends on your printer. If your printer cannot print graphics, you can print only those special characters available for the current font. If your printer can print graphics, then you can

Table 5-2. *Character Combinations and Their Corresponding Special Characters*

Character Combination	Resulting Special Character	Character Combination	Resulting Special Character
* .	•	- n	-
* *	•	- m	—
* o	°	= =	≡
* O	O	~ ~	≈
/ o	ø	Y =	¥
- f	ƒ	P t	₧
- L	£	P ¦	¶
/ c	¢	< <	«
+ -	±	> >	»
/ 2	½	< =	≤
/ 4	¼	> =	≥
? ?	¿	= /	≠
! !	¡	t m	™
c o	©	s m	SM
r x	℞	r o	®
= a	ª	o x	¤
= o	º	' i	í
A E	Æ	, c	ç
a e	æ	^ a	â
O E	Œ	` e	è
I J	IJ	' e	é
" u	ü	@ a	å
		~ n	ñ

print every special character, because those unavailable for the current font are printed graphically.

To discover your own printer's special character capabilities, you can create a test document by typing special characters in various fonts. You can also open a document provided by WordPerfect with the filename *charmap.tst*. (If your WordPerfect program was installed in *c:\wpwin*, and if you installed the Printer Program files there, then *charmap.tst* will also be found in that directory. If you did not install the Printer Program files, *charmap.tst* is unavailable. See Appendix A.) Print your test document or *charmap.tst* to see which special characters will print for the current font. Next, change the current font, and print again. Repeat this process to print the test file as many times as you have fonts available, to discover which special characters your printer supports in each font.

The Overstrike Feature

The Overstrike feature is an alternative for inserting digraphs or diacritical marks that your printer might not otherwise produce. The Overstrike feature gives you the ability to print two or more characters in the same position. To use Overstrike, follow these steps:

1. Position the insertion point in your document where you want the digraph or diacritical mark to appear.

2. Choose Font, Overstrike, Create. The Create/Edit Overstrike dialog box appears.

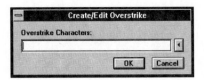

3. In the Overstrike Characters text box, type the characters to be printed as an overstrike. For instance, type /o, which will produce ø in the text. Or, type ` a, which will produce à in the text.

You can also use the arrowhead button, located beside the Overstrike Characters text box, to display a pop-up list for choosing attributes such as bold or underline for the overstrike.

4. Choose OK.

An overstrike code, such as [Ovrstk:a'], is inserted behind the scenes, so that both characters will be printed at the same position. You can also alter an existing overstrike by placing the insertion point forward from the code and choosing Font, Overstrike, Edit. The Overstrike dialog box reappears for that overstrike character.

Hands-on Exercise: Insert Special Characters

 In the *smith01.ltr* document, which should still be displayed on your computer screen, you'll add a name—Roberto Peña—where a diacritic must be inserted. Then, you'll insert another special character—the double exclamation point (where the two exclamation points are much closer together than if you typed two exclamation points from the keyboard)—into the document. Here's how the middle of the document will appear when you're done:

Antonio Abbot	**May 31st**
Lois Chang	**April 27th**
Roberto Peña	**June 16th**
Tim Fingerman	**May 20th**
Paul McClintock	**August 7th**

Special characters

The new accrued vacation system should begin for these employees immediately‼

1. Place the insertion point at the end of the second line in the tabular column of names and dates, just past April 27th.

2. Press (ENTER) and then tab once so that the insertion point is positioned to add a name.

3. Type **Roberto Pe**.

4. Choose F<u>o</u>nt, <u>W</u>P Characters (or press (CTRL) + (W)).

5. Type **n~** into the <u>N</u>umber text box.

6. Choose Insert <u>a</u>nd Close.

7. Type **a** to complete the name Peña.

8. Position the insertion point after the sentence, "The new accrued vacation system....immediately.", and press (BACKSPACE) to erase the period at the end of the sentence.

9. Choose F<u>o</u>nt, <u>W</u>P Characters (or press (CTRL) + (W)).

10. Select Iconic Symbols from the <u>S</u>et pop-up list box.

11. Select the double exclamation point (!!) from the <u>C</u>haracters list box.

12. Choose Insert <u>a</u>nd Close.

Notice that you have inserted two special characters into your text. You may wish to print out *smith01.ltr* to see the printed results. Then save and close the document.

5

Quick Reference

- To apply a font attribute before typing, choose F̲ont and then choose the attribute to turn it on. Then type the text. When you're finished typing, choose F̲ont and the attribute to turn off the attribute. Certain common attributes have shortcuts, such as bold ((CTRL) + (B)), underline ((CTRL) + (U)), and italic ((CTRL) + (I)).

- To apply a font attribute to existing text, select the text before choosing F̲ont and the attribute.

- To change the current font starting at the top of a document, choose L̲ayout, D̲ocument, Initial F̲ont.

- To change the current font beginning at a specific location and continuing to the end of the text (or until you alter it again further forward in the text), choose F̲ont, F̲ont. To change the font for a section of existing text, select the text before choosing F̲ont, F̲ont.

- To make frequent font changes, the ruler is a handy tool. If the ruler is hidden, choose V̲iew, R̲uler to display it. To select a new font, click and hold the Font button located on the ruler, and then drag the mouse to select a font. The fonts listed on the ruler are limited to those that you previously assigned to the ruler.

- To switch to Draft mode, so that all the characters are uniform and easy to read while typing and editing, choose V̲iew, D̲raft mode.

- To insert a special character, choose F̲ont, W̲P Characters. For commonly used special characters, type the corresponding character combination, as listed in Table 5-2. For other special characters, select a character set and then the special character that you want to insert.

6

Changing the Layout: Margins, Lines, and Paragraphs

When you make decisions about how text will appear on the printed page, you are setting the document's *format* or *layout*. This chapter focuses on the layout of lines and paragraphs. It explains how to alter the settings for margins, justification (the horizontal alignment of text between the margins), spacing, hyphenation, tab stops, and the alignment of text on tab stops. You'll learn about two methods for modifying these settings, the Layout menu and the ruler.

The Layout menu is the method described first. It is the basic method and highly flexible; with it you can make any type of layout modification you desire.

The ruler, discussed later on in the chapter, is a convenient alternative for only the most common changes, including altering margins, changing justification, setting line spacing, and changing tab stops. It simplifies your work because you make the format changes while viewing your document, and you see the effects instantaneously. To take advantage of the ruler, your computer must be equipped with a mouse. Mouse users should make sure to learn not only about the Layout menu, but about the superb ruler feature as well.

About Initial Settings and Layout Codes

The initial settings, also referred to as default settings, for lines and paragraphs in a document are as follows:

Setting	Default
Margins	1-inch border on each side
Text alignment	Left justification
Spacing	Single
Line height	Automatically set by WordPerfect
Hyphenation	Off
Tab settings	Every half-inch across the page width (for 14 inches across)

Figure 6-1 shows how these settings affect your printed document. You can change any or all of these initial settings for a particular document using the Layout menu.

When you make a layout change, a layout code (which is hidden like all codes in WordPerfect) is inserted in the text to override one of the initial settings. The code takes effect from its location *forward,* for all text either to the end of the document or to the next code of the same type that Word-Perfect encounters in the document. For instance, a margin code at the top of page 2 has an effect from page 2 all the way to the end of your document unless you change margins later in your document.

There are two additional initial settings related to how WordPerfect operates that are important to know about before you begin inserting layout

Figure 6-1. *Initial settings for lines and paragraphs on a page*

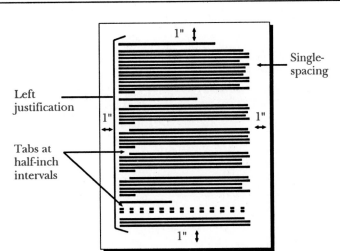

codes in your document. They are the Auto Code Placement and Units of Measure features.

Auto Code Placement Feature

WordPerfect is set up with the Auto Code Placement feature turned on. This gives you more flexibility in where you place the insertion point before changing margins, tabs, and so on. Specifically, when the Auto Code Placement feature is on, any top/bottom margin change will insert a code *at the top of the page* where the insertion point was located when you made the change. Any left/right margin, justification, tab, or spacing change will insert a code *at the beginning of the paragraph* where the insertion point was located when you made the change. When the Auto Code Placement feature is off, WordPerfect places the layout code exactly where the insertion point was located, even if in the middle of a paragraph. The File, Preferences, Environment command controls the Auto Code Placement feature. (See Chapter 17 for more information.)

Units of Measure Feature

WordPerfect assumes that layout changes involving distances are measured in inches. As a result, you can indicate an inch measurement simply by typing a number, such as **2**. You could also type a number followed by a double quote, **2"**, or a number followed by the letter "i", **2i**. Measurements can be indicated in other units, however, including centimeters, points, and 1200ths of an inch. The File, Preferences, Display command controls the Units of Measure feature. (See Chapter 17 for more information.)

Changing Margins

WordPerfect assumes margins of 1 inch on all sides of the page. To change margins, follow these steps:

1. For a top/bottom margin change, place the insertion point on the page where you want the margin change to begin.

   For a left/right margin change, place the insertion point just before or within the paragraph where you want the change to begin.

   For a left/right margin change that you want to affect only a section of existing text, select the text. (See Chapter 3 if you need to review the Select feature.)

2. Choose Layout, Margins. The Margins dialog box appears.

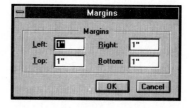

3. Type new margin settings in the Left, Right, Top, or Bottom number boxes.

4. Choose OK.

≡shortcut≡ (CTRL) + (F8) *is the shortcut for* <u>Layout</u>, <u>Margins</u>.

WordPerfect inserts margin codes in the text to enforce the new margin settings. As with all codes, margin codes are displayed only if you switch to the reveal codes workspace.

A top/bottom margin change inserts a code such as [T/B Mar:2",2"] at the top of the page. This new top/bottom margin setting will remain in effect until the end of the document, or until WordPerfect encounters another top/bottom margin code later in the document. The top and bottom margins are *not* displayed in the document workspace, but the status line does show the change. For instance, if the top margin is changed to 2 inches, then when you position the insertion point at the top of the page, the line indicator on the status line reads Ln 2".

A left/right margin change inserts a code such as [L/R Mar: 1.5",1"] at the start of the current paragraph. The margin change takes effect from that point forward, until the end of the document or until another left/right margin code is encountered farther on in the text. The text shifts on screen to abide by the new left/right margin settings, and the status line reflects the change. For instance, if the left margin is changed to 1.5 inches, then when the insertion point is at the left margin, the position indicator on the status line reads Pos 1.5".

≡reminder≡ *If the Auto Code Placement feature is off, you must position the insertion point at a more precise location before initiating a margin change, such as just before a certain paragraph (rather than anywhere in the paragraph) or at the very top of a specific page (rather than anywhere on that page).*

A left/right margin change for selected text inserts two codes, one at the beginning of the first paragraph in the selected text, and a second code at the end of the last paragraph in the selected text. The second code returns margins to their original setting. For instance, suppose left/right margins are originally set at 1 inch and you select a paragraph of text as follows:

```
Two of the major wine-producing countries in Europe are France and
Italy   France produces a wide variety, and Bordeaux is often
considered one of the centers of fine wine.

In Italy, wine production takes place in just about every region.
In fact, Italy has been known to yield more wine per year than any
other country in the world.
```

Once you change the left margin to 2 inches for the selected text, the left/right margin codes inserted are as shown here:

```
[L/R Mar:2",1"]
         ┗━━▶ Two of the major wine-producing countries in Europe are
              France and Italy.  France produces a wide variety, and
              Bordeaux is often considered one of the centers of fine
[L/R Mar:1",1"]   wine.
         ┗━▶ In Italy, wine production takes place in just about every region.
             In fact, Italy has been known to yield more wine per year than any
             other country in the world.
```

≡*note*≡ *Learn about the ruler later in this chapter for another simple way to change left/right margins.*

Justifying Text

Justification refers to the alignment of lines and paragraphs against the left and right margins. WordPerfect has two methods for justifying text—one for individual lines, and another for paragraphs of multiple lines.

Centering or Right-Justifying a Single Line

WordPerfect automatically *left-justifies* text, meaning that each line starts flush against the left margin. You can tell WordPerfect to center a line between the margins rather than left-justify it, as with this line:

```
                    Journey to the Center
```

You can also *right-justify* text, meaning that the last character of the line sits at the right margin, as shown in the following date:

```
                                          June 16, 1993
```

To center or right-justify one line of text, follow these steps:

1. Position the insertion point at the left margin.

2. Choose Layout, Line.

3. Choose Center or Flush Right, (whichever you prefer for your line).

4. If the text has yet to be typed on the line, type it, and then press (ENTER) to stop centering or right-aligning.

WordPerfect places a hidden [Center] or [Flsh Rgt] code directly before the text.

shortcut (SHIFT) + (F7) *is the shortcut for* Layout, Line, Center. (ALT) + (F7) *is the shortcut for* Layout, Line, Flush Right.

You can use Center and Flush Right on the same line, provided that the text entries are short. Here's an example:

```
Anita Robbins          President          ABC Company
```

To produce these results, place the insertion point at the left margin, and follow these steps (using the shortcut keys this time):

1. Type **Anita Robbins**.

2. Press (SHIFT) + (F7) and type **President**.

3. Press (ALT) + (F7) and type **ABC Company**.

You can also produce a dot leader when centering or aligning text flush right. To do so, choose Center or Flush Right twice in a row. Here is an example:

```
Anita Robbins............President..........ABC Company
```

Justifying Paragraphs and the Document

There are four alternatives for justifying multiple lines of text—whether one paragraph or an entire document. *Left justification*, which is the initial WordPerfect setting, aligns text at the left margin while text is *ragged*, or not aligned, at the right margin. *Right justification* does just the opposite, aligning text at the right margin while text is ragged at the left margin. *Center justification* centers text between the margins. *Full justification* aligns text at both the left and right margins; space between words is expanded or compressed to fully justify the text. Examples are shown in Figure 6-2. To change the justification, follow these steps:

1. Place the insertion point just before or within the paragraph where you want the justification change to begin.

   For a justification change confined to a section of existing text, select the text.

2. Choose Layout, Justification.

3. Choose Left, Right, Center, or Full. The text shifts on screen to correspond to the new justification.

shortcut (CTRL) + (L) *is the shortcut for Layout, Justification, Left.*
(CTRL) + (R) *is the shortcut for Layout, Justification, Right.*
(CTRL) + (J) *is the shortcut for Layout, Justification, Center.*
(CTRL) + (F) *is the shortcut for Layout, Justification, Full.*

Changing justification inserts a justification code such as [Just:Right] at the start of the paragraph where the insertion point is located, which affects text to the end of the document or up to the next justification code. For a section of text, two codes are inserted—one before the first paragraph in the selected text, and a second code below the last paragraph in the selected text. The second code returns justification to its original setting.

When you select full justification, you can decide on the justification limits. In other words, you can determine how much WordPerfect is able to expand or compress spacing between words in order to right-justify each line of text. The Layout, Typesetting command controls justification limits, as described in Chapter 12.

Changing Vertical Spacing

Two features determine the amount of white space that WordPerfect inserts between lines of text. The first is Line Spacing; the most common settings for line spacing are single-spacing and double-spacing. The other feature is Line Height, which is the distance between the baselines in single-

Figure 6-2. *Four justification options available*

Left justification

Two of the major wine-producing countries in Europe are
France and Italy. France produces a wide variety, and
Bordeaux is often considered one of the centers of fine
wine. In Italy, wine production takes place in just
about every region. In fact, Italy has been known to
yield more wine per year than any other country in the
world.

Right justification

Two of the major wine-producing countries in Europe are
France and Italy. France produces a wide variety, and
Bordeaux is often considered one of the centers of fine
wine. In Italy, wine production takes place in just
about every region. In fact, Italy has been known to
yield more wine per year than any other country in the
world.

Center justification

Two of the major wine-producing countries in Europe are
France and Italy. France produces a wide variety, and
Bordeaux is often considered one of the centers of fine
wine. In Italy, wine production takes place in just
about every region. In fact, Italy has been known to
yield more wine per year than any other country in the
world.

Full justification

Two of the major wine-producing countries in Europe are
France and Italy. France produces a wide variety, and
Bordeaux is often considered one of the centers of fine
wine. In Italy, wine production takes place in just about
every region. In fact, Italy has been known to yield more
wine per year than any other country in the world.

6

spaced text. (A *baseline* is where the letters sit on a line, not including the tail of "y" or "g" or "p", which drops below the baseline.) The amount of space between lines of text is determined by multiplying the line spacing by the line height.

It is most common to alter the white space between lines with the Line Spacing feature. WordPerfect assumes that you want your text single-spaced. To alter line spacing for all or part of your document, follow these steps:

1. Place the insertion point just before or within the paragraph where you want the change to begin.

    For a spacing change that you wish to affect only a section of existing text, select the text.

2. Choose Layout, Line, Spacing. The Line Spacing dialog box appears:

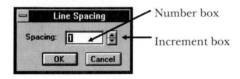

3. Type a number into the Spacing number box, either in whole numbers (such as **2**), in decimal numbers (such as **1.5**), or in fractional numbers (such as **1 1/2**).

    You can instead indicate a number in half-inch increments by clicking on the up or down arrow on the Increment box located just to the right of the Spacing number box.

4. Choose OK.

shortcut SHIFT + F9 *is the shortcut for Layout, Line.*

A code such as [Ln Spacing:2] is inserted at the start of the current paragraph. The spacing changes on screen to abide by the new line spacing code. For a spacing change confined to a section of text, two codes are inserted—one before the first paragraph in the selected text, and a second code at the end of the last paragraph. The second code returns spacing to its original setting.

note *Learn about the ruler later in this chapter for another simple way to choose among single, one-and-a-half, and double-spacing.*

The initial line height setting is set automatically by WordPerfect and depends on your printer and the current font's size. For Courier at 10 cpi, for instance, the line height is .167 inch, resulting in six lines per one vertical inch. But, because the line height is set automatically, it will be adjusted when you change to a font with a different size.

Here's a line of text with a line height of .167".

Line height

Here's a taller font, so the line height is adjusted to .227".

You can instead switch from automatic to a fixed line height setting, which remains constant even if you change the font size. This is useful if you must fit a limited number of lines in a certain amount of space (as in a fill-in-the-blanks form, for example). Follow these steps:

1. Place the insertion point just before or within the paragraph where you want the change to begin.

   For a height change that you want to affect only a section of existing text, select the text.

2. Choose Layout, Line, Height. The Line Height dialog box appears:

6

The current line height setting is displayed in the Fixed number box. This setting fades to pale gray when Auto is the option selected, indicating to you that the current line height can change.

3. Choose Auto. Or, choose Fixed, and then you can type a new line height measurement into the Fixed number box.

4. Choose OK.

reminder (SHIFT) + (F9) *is the shortcut for* Layout, Line.

A code, such as [Ln Height:2"] for a fixed line height of 2", is inserted at the start of the paragraph where the insertion point is located. Existing text changes on screen to abide by the new line height code. For a change confined to a section of text, two codes are inserted—one before the first paragraph in the selected text and the second code at the end of the last paragraph. The second code returns line height to its original setting.

Revising Layout Changes and Maneuvering Around Codes

You may decide after formatting a document—perhaps with new margins, a different justification, or other change—that you don't like the results. You have three alternatives:

- *You can override an existing layout change with a new setting by repeating the procedure.* A new layout code replaces the previous code. For instance, suppose you position the insertion point in the first paragraph in a document and change left/right margins to 2 inches. A [L/R Mar: 2",2"] code is inserted. If you later decide you'd prefer margins to be 1.5 inches, reposition the insertion point in the first paragraph and change the margins again. The old margin code is replaced by a new [L/R Mar: 1.5",1.5"] code. (This assumes that the Auto Code Placement feature is on.)

- *You can cancel the effect of a layout change by deleting the layout code.* To do this, select View, Reveal Codes to open the reveal codes workspace. Locate the code, and then either position the insertion point on the code and press (DEL), or position the insertion point to the right of the code and press (BACKSPACE).

- *You can undo a layout change that you just made with the Undo feature.* Select Edit, Undo. Keep in mind, however, that the Undo feature will only work if the layout change was the very last change you made to the document. (See Chapter 3 for more on this feature.) The layout code that you just inserted will be erased, and the document will look as it did before you made the layout change.

You always want to watch for errant codes, because these codes can lead to problems in formatting your text. It is easy to mistakenly press the wrong key and insert a layout code that you didn't intend in the text. For instance, instead of entering (SHIFT) + (R), you may accidentally press (CTRL) + (R) in the middle of a paragraph. This simple mistake will insert a [Just:Right] code at the beginning of the paragraph, and your text will suddenly shift to the right. Or you may inadvertently press (SHIFT) + (F7), which, as you've learned, inserts a [Center] code in the text. A [Center] code can lead to overlapping text if it is accidentally inserted to the right of the center point on a line. Whenever the layout of your document is awkward or not what you anticipated, switch to the reveal codes workspace to see if an errant code is causing the trouble. If so, delete that problem code.

Even when the proper layout codes are in your document, it's a good idea to be mindful of them as you continue to type and edit. There may be a string of codes; for instance, suppose you change left/right margins, line spacing, and turn on justification at the top of the document. If you reveal codes, you'll see something like this:

```
[L/R Mar:2",1"][Ln Spacing:2][Just:Full]
```

Be sure to position the insertion point properly before you select text that is near layout codes. For example, if you wish to delete a paragraph and there are codes at the beginning of it, you may or may not want the codes included in the selection—depending on whether you want to delete the codes along with the text. Place the insertion point to the left of codes to include them when you select text. Place the insertion point to the right of codes to exclude them when you select text.

6

WordPerfect offers several extra shortcut keys for maneuvering the insertion point around codes without having to switch to the reveal codes workspace. You learned in Chapter 3 (see Table 3-1) that pressing (HOME) moves the insertion point to the beginning of the line and pressing (CTRL) + (HOME) moves the insertion point to the top of the document. If there are codes in those locations, press these shortcut keys twice. In other words:

Movement	Key Combination
Beginning of line	(HOME)
Beginning of line before codes	(HOME), (HOME)
Beginning of document	(CTRL) + (HOME)
Beginning of document before codes	(CTRL) + (HOME), (CTRL) + (HOME)

note *WordPerfect offers the ability to place most layout codes that would otherwise clutter the top of the document on a special screen. With the Document Initial Codes feature, you can change features such as margins and justification starting at the top of the document, but without inserting the codes in the document. This safeguards against accidentally moving or erasing a code. See Chapter 7 for more on the Document Initial Codes feature.*

Hands-on Exercise: Change the Layout

 Start with a clear document workspace. You'll type a memorandum and change its layout in the process. But let's change the memo's top margin to 2 inches before typing the text.

1. With the insertion point at the top of the document, choose <u>L</u>ine, <u>M</u>argins (or press (CTRL) + (F8)).

2. Choose <u>T</u>op, type **2"**, and then click OK or press (ENTER). Notice that the status line reads:

```
Pg 1 Ln 2" Pos 1"
```

The top margin has been changed to 2 inches.

3. Choose <u>V</u>iew, Reveal <u>C</u>odes or press (ALT) + (F3).

   Notice that the code [T/B Mar:2",1"] has been inserted. This code will affect the entire document. If the memorandum was many pages long, every page would have a 2-inch top margin when printed.

4. Choose <u>V</u>iew, Reveal <u>C</u>odes (or press (ALT) + (F3)). The reveal codes workspace is hidden again.

Now let's type the memorandum shown in Figure 6-3:

1. Choose <u>L</u>ayout, <u>L</u>ine, <u>C</u>enter (or press (SHIFT) + (F7)). The insertion point jumps halfway between the left and right margins.

Figure 6-3. *Sample memorandum to be typed and formatted*

```
                          URGENT NOTICE

To: All Employees                   From: Sandy Peterson
Date: October 23, 1992              Re: Vacation Option


As you know, we announced on September 15th a new
vacation opportunity for employees who are full-time or
who consistently work more than twenty hours per week.
Here is the list of employees who have already signed up:

Antonio Abbott
Lois Chang
Tim Fingerman
Paul McClintock

If you wish to sign up, but your name is not on the list,
telephone the personnel office by October 30th at
(415) 333-9215. Thank you.
```

6

2. Type **URGENT NOTICE.** (Remember that an easy method for typing words in uppercase letters is to use the (CAPS LOCK) key.) The words are automatically centered as you type.

3. Press (ENTER) twice to end the line and insert a blank line.

4. Type **To: All Employees.**

5. Choose Layout, Line, Flush Right (or press (ALT) + (F7)). The insertion point jumps to the right margin.

6. Type **From: Sandy Peterson.**

7. Press (ENTER) once to move to the next line.

8. Type **Date:.** Then type today's date. (An alternative to typing today's date is to have WordPerfect insert it for you with the Date feature, described in Chapter 8.)

9. Press (ALT) + (F7) and type **Re: Vacation Option.**

10. Type the remainder of the memorandum as shown in Figure 6-3.

WordPerfect's initial setting is for left justification, left and right margins of 1 inch, and single-spacing for all your documents. Let's change these. Follow these steps:

1. Position the insertion point at the top of the document to change justification starting at the top.

2. Press (CTRL) + (F), the shortcut for fully justifying the document.
   Notice that the text readjusts on screen; the lines in the two paragraphs are fully justified. Spaces have been inserted to achieve this effect.

3. In the last paragraph, insert the word "immediately" before the word "telephone". Because WordPerfect attempts to maintain full justification, you may find that the line of text expands or compresses as you type.

4. Keep the insertion point in the last paragraph in order to change left/right margins starting in that last paragraph.

5. Choose Line, Margins (or press (CTRL) + (F8)).

6. Type **2"** in the Left number box and then click OK or press (ENTER).
   Notice that one paragraph adjusts on screen for a left margin of 2 inches and a right margin of 1 inch.

7. Position the insertion point at the left margin before "Antonio Abbot".

8. Select the text up to the last name on the list, "Paul McClintock" to change line spacing for that list of names.

9. Choose Layout, Line, Spacing.

10. Type **2** for double-spacing and press (ENTER).

11. Click the mouse or press an arrow key to turn off the Select feature.

Notice that the list of names is double-spaced. If you reveal codes, you'll find that a [Ln Spacing:2] code is located before the first name on the list, and a [Ln Spacing:1] code is located at the end of the list of names, which returns the last part of the memorandum to single-spacing.

After the change, you may notice that the left margin of the last paragraph looks awkward. Let's cancel that left margin change in the last paragraph, returning it to its initial setting. Follow these steps to delete the margin code:

1. Choose View, Reveal Codes and locate the [L/R Mar: 2", 1"] code positioned just before the last paragraph.

2. Position the insertion point on that code and press (DEL).

3. Choose View, Reveal Codes (or press (ALT) + (F3)).

Make sure that you save this document before you read on, so that you protect against a power failure or human error. Use the Save or Save As feature, and type **vacation.mmo** as the filename. Keep the document on screen.

Using Hyphenation

WordPerfect automatically wraps words that extend beyond the right margin to the next line. If you wish to have WordPerfect hyphenate long words at the right margin instead of wrapping them, you can turn on hyphenation. Figure 6-4 illustrates the line-by-line differences for identical text with and without hyphenation. When a document is left-justified, as in Figure 6-4, the right margin becomes less ragged when the automatic hyphenation feature is turned on. (When a document is set to full justification, less space is necessary between words with automatic hyphenation turned on.)

Hyphenation is a personal preference. Some people never use it; other people always do. Or, you may prefer it only in certain instances, such as when text is formatted into narrow columns. You can have WordPerfect hyphenate automatically for you, or you can hyphenate on your own.

Figure 6-4.   *Paragraphs typed with hyphenation on have a less ragged right margin*

Hyphenation off

```
Here is a standard paragraph to show the
noticeable effects of hyphenation in your
documents. Hyphenation is off initially but
can be turned on easily enough. Hyphenation
is preferred by some people but avoided by
others.
```

Hyphenation on

```
Here is a standard paragraph to show the no-
ticeable effects of hyphenation in your docu-
ments. Hyphenation is off initially but can
be turned on easily enough. Hyphenation is
preferred by some people but avoided by oth-
ers.
```

Automatic Hyphenation

When hyphenation is turned on, words are hyphenated by WordPerfect when they completely span the width of the *hyphenation zone.* This zone has a left boundary and a right boundary, each measured as a percentage of the line length. The default settings are for a left boundary of 10 percent and a right boundary of 4 percent. For instance, assume the standard line length is 6.5 inches. The left hyphenation zone equals .65 inch (6.5 inches x 10 percent), and the right hyphenation zone equals .26 inch (6.5 inches x 4 percent). Figure 6-5 illustrates a paragraph where the word "considered" would be hyphenated since it spans the entire width of the hyphenation zone.

(You may be surprised that the initial setting for the right hyphenation zone is greater than 0. This allows for a more reliable average right margin setting.)

You can turn on hyphenation anywhere in a document, either before or after you type the text. You can widen or narrow the hyphenation zone at the same time. You widen the hyphenation zone by inserting larger percentages, which results in *fewer* words being hyphenated. You can also narrow the hyphenation zone by inserting smaller percentages, which results in *more* words being hyphenated.

6

Figure 6-5. *The word "considered" is a candidate for hyphenation*

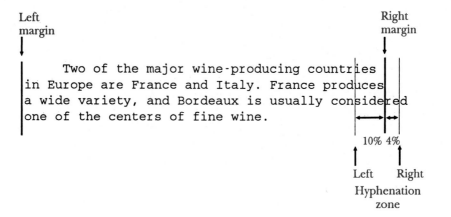

To turn automatic hyphenation on or off, follow these steps:

1. Position the insertion point where you want the change in hyphenation or the hyphenation zone to begin. (To turn hyphenation on or off, it is critical to position the insertion point exactly; the Auto Code Placement feature does not operate when turning hyphenation on or off.)

2. Choose Layout, Line, Hyphenation. The Line Hyphenation dialog box appears:

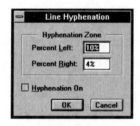

3. To turn hyphenation on, select the Hyphenation On check box so that an X appears in that box. To turn it off, select the Hyphenation On check box until no X appears.

    To change the hyphenation zone, type a new left hyphenation zone setting in the Percent Left number box and/or a new right hyphenation zone setting in the Percent Right number box. Type only the number; WordPerfect will insert the percent sign (%) for you.

4. Choose OK.

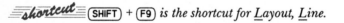 (SHIFT) + (F9) *is the shortcut for* Layout, Line.

When you change the hyphenation zone, WordPerfect inserts a code such as [HZone:6%,0%] at the start of the current paragraph. When you turn on hyphenation, WordPerfect inserts a [Hyph On] code at the insertion point location, turning on hyphenation for the remainder of the document (or up to a [Hyphen Off] code located farther forward in the document).

With hyphenation on, WordPerfect hyphenates words that completely span the hyphenation zone. It searches its own dictionaries to determine where to place each hyphen. The hyphen inserted is referred to as a *soft hyphen*; it's called "soft" because the hyphen will disappear from a word later if the text is edited such that the word no longer crosses the right margin.

Sometimes, when WordPerfect cannot determine where to place a hyphen, it will request your assistance. A dialog box will appear providing various options, as in this example for the word "SPACEBAR":

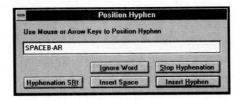

A hyphen appears incorrectly in this instance. Use the mouse or the ⬅ and ➡ keys to reposition the hyphen. Then, choose one of the following command buttons:

- *Insert Hyphen* Choose Insert Hyphen if you want a soft hyphen inserted (the kind that WordPerfect uses to hyphenate words). It is temporary; it will disappear if you later edit your document and the hyphenated word no longer crosses the right margin.

- *Hyphenation SRt* Choose Hyphenation SRt if you do not want a hyphen, but still want the word split. This is useful for compound words that are broken with something other than a hyphen, such as "black/white". The hidden code [HyphSRt] is inserted.

- *Insert Space* Choose Insert Space if you want a regular space inserted rather than a hyphen. This is useful if you mistakenly left out the space between two words.

6

You can also choose one of the following command buttons without first positioning the hyphen:

- *Ignore Word*   Choose Ignore Word to wrap the entire word down to the next line, and insert the hidden code [Hyph Ign Wrd] before the word, ensuring that it remains unhyphenated.

- *Stop Hyphenation*   Choose <u>S</u>top Hyphenation to halt hyphenation temporarily. The word is wrapped down to the next line. (If the word is too wide to fit on the line, such as a long word that extends beyond the width of a narrow column, the word is split by a line break. A [DSRt] code, which stands for deletable soft return, is inserted at the split.)

═══*note*═══ *Consider turning on hyphenation only after you've typed and done an initial edit on your document. If you turn on hyphenation before you edit, Position Hyphen dialog boxes may continually appear and slow you down.*

After WordPerfect hyphenates text, you may wish to override some hyphenation decisions. If you want to change the hyphen location or cancel hyphenation for a particular word, make the change manually (as described in the next section), and then delete the soft hyphen that WordPerfect inserted. If you wish to cancel hyphenation on some or all of the words that WordPerfect previously hyphenated, delete the [Hyph On] code that turned on hyphenation in the first place. Then delete the soft hyphens that you no longer want in the text.

You should be aware that the operation of the Hyphenation feature can be changed using the <u>F</u>ile, Pr<u>e</u>ferences, <u>E</u>nvironment command. See Chapter 17 for more details.

Manual Hyphenation

You can hyphenate the occasional word manually, without WordPerfect's assistance. You may also wish to hyphenate manually when hyphenation is on but you wish to override one of WordPerfect's hyphenation decisions.

There are three types of hyphens that you can insert in a document: regular hyphen, dash character, and soft hyphen. All look identical (like a dash or minus sign) in the document workspace, but are different in the reveal codes workspace. The hyphen you insert depends on the word you are hyphenating. In addition, there are two related codes that you need to know about when hyphenating on your own.

The *regular hyphen* remains fixed in a word, and splits the word if it crosses the right margin. Use the regular hyphen whenever you are typing compound words that should be permanently hyphenated, such as "wine-producing" or "mother-in-law". In these examples, the hyphen must be present whether or not hyphenation is on. You can identify a regular hyphen in the reveal codes workspace because the code [-] is inserted.

The *dash character*, also referred to as a hard hyphen because it is similar to a hard space (described in Chapter 3), remains fixed in a word but ensures that the word is never split. If the word crosses the right margin, it will be wrapped down to the next line in its entirety. Use the dash character for phone numbers such as 555-1234, or for phrases containing minus signs such as 5000 yards –532 yards, or in other situations where you believe that a line break at the hyphen would prove awkward. You can identify a dash character in the reveal codes workspace because no code is inserted; instead, the hyphen appears like any other character. The hyphenated word is treated as if it contained no hyphen at all.

The *soft hyphen*, as previously described, is temporary. It remains in a word only when the word crosses the right margin. Use the soft hyphen to hyphenate a word if the sole purpose of the hyphen is to split the word by a line break because it crosses the right margin. You can identify a soft hyphen in the reveal codes workspace because the code inserted is -.

The *hyphenation soft return* produces no hyphen or space, but does split a word by a line break. Use the hyphenation soft return to manually split a compound word that is broken with something other than a hyphen, such as "black/white". The hyphenation soft return disappears if you later change the document so that the word no longer crosses the right margin. You can identify a hyphenation soft return in the reveal codes workspace because the code [HyphSRt] is inserted.

The *hyphenation ignore word* code can be inserted when automatic hyphenation is on, or will be turned on later, but you wish to ensure that a certain word is never hyphenated. The word is wrapped down to the next line, and the hidden code [Hyph Ign Wrd] is inserted before the word.

Here's how to manually insert hyphens or related codes into your text:

6

1. Position the insertion point where you want the hyphen or related code to be inserted.

2. Choose Layout, Line, Special Codes. The Insert Special Codes dialog box appears, as shown in Figure 6-6.

3. Select an option from the Hyphenation Codes group box for the type of hyphen you desire and choose Insert.

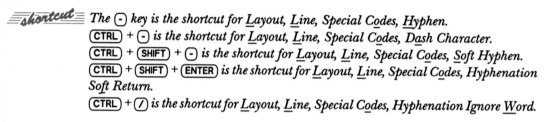 *The* (-) *key is the shortcut for* Layout, Line, Special Codes, Hyphen.

(CTRL) + (-) *is the shortcut for* Layout, Line, Special Codes, Dash Character.

(CTRL) + (SHIFT) + (-) *is the shortcut for* Layout, Line, Special Codes, Soft Hyphen.

(CTRL) + (SHIFT) + (ENTER) *is the shortcut for* Layout, Line, Special Codes, Hyphenation Soft Return.

(CTRL) + (/) *is the shortcut for* Layout, Line, Special Codes, Hyphenation Ignore Word.

Figure 6-6.   *Insert Special Codes dialog box*

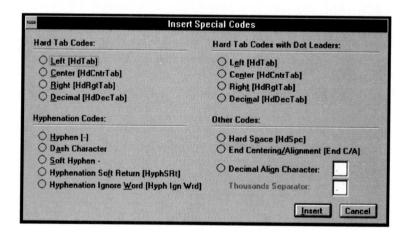

Hands-on Exercise: Hyphenate a Document

 In this exercise, you'll use automatic hyphenation to hyphenate the document on screen. You'll narrow the hyphenation zone so that more words will be hyphenated than would be if you used the default hyphenation zone settings.

1. Position the insertion point at the top of the document, so that hyphenation will begin for the first and all succeeding paragraphs.

2. Choose Layout, Line, Hyphenation.

3. In the Percent Left number box, type **5**. (Remember, DON'T press (ENTER) after typing into the number box.)

4. In the Percent Right number box, type **0**.

5. Select the Hyphenation On check box to turn on hyphenation.

6. Click OK or press (ENTER).

Notice that any words that would otherwise cross the narrow hyphenation zone are hyphenated. For instance, the word "opportunity" in the first paragraph may be hyphenated on your computer screen.

After you finish working with this practice document, close the document, saving it again under the filename *vacation.mmo* (or whatever you chose to name it).

Customizing Tab Settings

As previously mentioned, tabs in WordPerfect are preset in half-inch intervals across the full width of a page (up to 14 inches in width). Text entries are left-aligned at the tab stop. For many documents, the preset tabs are sufficient. But you may need to add or delete a tab stop. Or you may want to

6

change all your tab settings, such as for typing tabular columns, where it's most convenient to press (TAB) only once to move from column to column. In WordPerfect, you can set tabs at regular intervals, or the tabs can be spaced unevenly.

You can change not only the location of tab stops, but the style of tab stops as well. You can choose from four different styles:

Left Align	Text is aligned with its left edge at the tab stop (this is the initial setting for all tab stops)
Right Align	Text is aligned with its right edge at the tab stop
Decimal Align	Text is aligned with a specific character (usually the decimal point) at the tab stop
Center	Text is centered at the tab stop

In addition, each of these styles can be preceded by a *dot leader* (which looks like a row of periods). The results of using these different styles in tabular columns are shown in Figure 6-7.

You can also decide whether to set tab locations in relative or absolute terms. *Relative* (the default setting) means that you set tabs in relation to the left margin. The left margin is position 0", with negative numbers to the left (such as -0.5 inch) and positive numbers to the right (such as +0.5 inch). If you change the left margin, tabs shift so that they remain the same distance from the left margin. This option is useful when you want tab stops to remain the same distance from the left margin (such as every half-inch) even if you change the margins or format the text into newspaper columns with the Columns feature.

Absolute means that you set tabs that stay anchored to the left edge on the page. The left edge of the page is position 0", with positive numbers to the right. This option is useful when you want tabs fixed at a particular location regardless of any left margin or other format changes.

To change tab stop locations, follow these steps:

1. Place the insertion point just before or within the paragraph where you want the change to begin.

   For a tab set change confined to a section of existing text, select the text.

Figure 6-7. *Tabular columns aligned on tab stops in various ways*

Four tabular columns without dot leaders:

Left	Right	Decimal	Center
↓	↓	↓	↓
Dan	Gillespie	5,564.00	Portland
Jeannette	Redman	12,333.50	San Francisco
Ilene	Bean	880.55	Long Beach
Jim	Frances	14,999.70	Bellevue
Scott	Johnberg	33.50	Sebastopol
Gayle	Smith	25,999.00	Oakland
Sarika	Robinson	50.00	Beaverton

Two tabular columns, one with a dot leader:

Left   Decimal

↓   ↓

```
Dan Gillespie..........5,564.00
Jeannette Redman......12,333.50
Ilene Bean..............880.55
Jim Frances..........14,999.70
Scott Johnberg...........33.50
Gayle Smith..........25,999.00
Sarika Robinson..........50.00
```

6

2. Choose Layout, Line, Tab Set. The Tab Set dialog box appears:

The current tab settings are listed in the Position list box, located in the center of the dialog box. You can use the scroll bar or the arrow keys to move through the list of current settings.

3. To switch between relative and absolute tab settings, select Left Margin or Left Edge from the Position From group box.

4. To delete an individual tab type a tab location into the Position number box or select (highlight) an existing tab from the Position list box, and choose Clear Tab.

   To delete all tabs, choose Clear Tabs.

5. To set an individual tab or change an existing tab, select a tab style (such as Left Align or Center) and choose whether to turn on or off dot leaders by selecting Dot Leader Tabs. Then type a tab location into the Position number box or select an existing tab from the Position list box, and choose Set Tab. Repeat for each tab you wish to set.

   To set evenly spaced tabs, turn on the Evenly Spaced check box so that an X appears in that box. The Tab Set dialog box now presents new options. Type a location for the first tab stop in the Position number box, type the amount of space you want between each tab stop in the Repeat Every number box, select a tab style and whether or not you want dot leaders from the Tabs group box, and choose Set Tab.

   To return to the initial (default) settings—which means evenly spaced tab stops every half-inch, left-aligned, and relative to the left margin—choose Default.

6. Choose OK.

A [Tab Set:] code is inserted at the start of the paragraph where the insertion point is located. This code does not indicate the style of each tab stop, but does list each tab location and also whether the tabs were set as absolute or relative locations. For instance, the code [Tab Set:Rel: -1", every 0.5"] is inserted when you choose to return to the initial (default) settings. The code [Tab Set:Rel: +0.75",+1.5"] is inserted when you set just two tab stops relative to the left margin. If you set many individual tab stops, the code can be quite long. The Tab Set code affects all text forward from the code, to the end of the document or until another Tab Set code is encountered. Or, if you selected text before changing tab stops, two codes are inserted—one before the first paragraph in the selected text, and a second code at the end of the last paragraph in the selected text. The second code returns tabs to their original setting.

note *Learn about the ruler later in this chapter for another simple way to set tabs.*

With the decimal align tab style, you can change the character on which the text aligns from a decimal point to another character. For instance, you can align a tabular column on the dollar sign or the colon.

1. Position the insertion point where the change in the current decimal align character is to take effect.

2. Choose Layout, Line, Special Codes. The Insert Special Codes dialog box appears, (refer back to Figure 6-6).

3. Select the Decimal Align radio button, type a new character into the Decimal Align character text box, and choose Insert.

A code, such as [Decml/Algn Char:$,,] is inserted that will affect all text positioned on decimal-aligned tabs from that location forward, to the end of the document or until another code is encountered.

6

Working with Tab Stops

Whether you stay with the default tabs or create customized ones, you can use more than just the (TAB) key to align text on tab stops.

Aligning Lines on Tab Stops

When you wish to override a tab style for a single line, use a hard tab instead of (TAB). There are four styles of hard tabs to choose from (just like the four styles of tab stops), each with or without dot leaders: hard left align, hard right align, hard center, and hard decimal align. For instance, suppose you change tab settings and the first tab stop is a decimal-aligned tab. If you want to temporarily override that decimal-alignment by centering text on that tab stop, use a hard center tab to do so.

Hard tabs are especially useful when you want the first line of a tabular column to be a column header that you wish to align differently than the rest of the column. Insert a hard tab using these steps:

1. Position the insertion point where you want to insert the tab code.

2. Choose Layout, Line, Special Codes. The Insert Special Codes dialog box appears (refer back to Figure 6-6).

3. Choose an option from the Hard Tab Codes group box or the Hard Tab Codes with Dot Leaders group box.

4. Choose Insert.

The insertion point jumps to the next tab stop, and a code, such as [HdTab] for a hard left align, or [HdRgtTab] for a hard right align, is inserted.

shortcut (ALT) + (SHIFT) + (F8) *is the shortcut for* Layout, Line, Special Codes.
(ALT) + (SHIFT) + (F7) *is the shortcut for* Layout, Line, Special Codes, Decimal Hard Tab.

Aligning Paragraphs on Tab Stops

You already know that the (TAB) key is used to indent the first line of a paragraph one tab stop to the right. Four features are available for aligning whole paragraphs on tab stops. Examples are shown in Figure 6-8.

- *Indent* The Indent feature indents the entire paragraph one tab stop to the right, creating a left margin change restricted to that one paragraph. The code [Indent] precedes the paragraph.

- *Double Indent* The Double Indent feature indents the entire paragraph one tab stop to the right and also to the left, creating a left/right margin change for that one paragraph. This is convenient when typing a long, indented quote. The code [Dbl Indent] precedes the paragraph.

- *Hanging Indent* The Hanging Indent feature indents the entire paragraph except for the first line one tab stop to the right. The first line hangs out farther, helping to provide emphasis to individual

Figure 6-8. ***Paragraphs aligned on a tab stop in various ways***

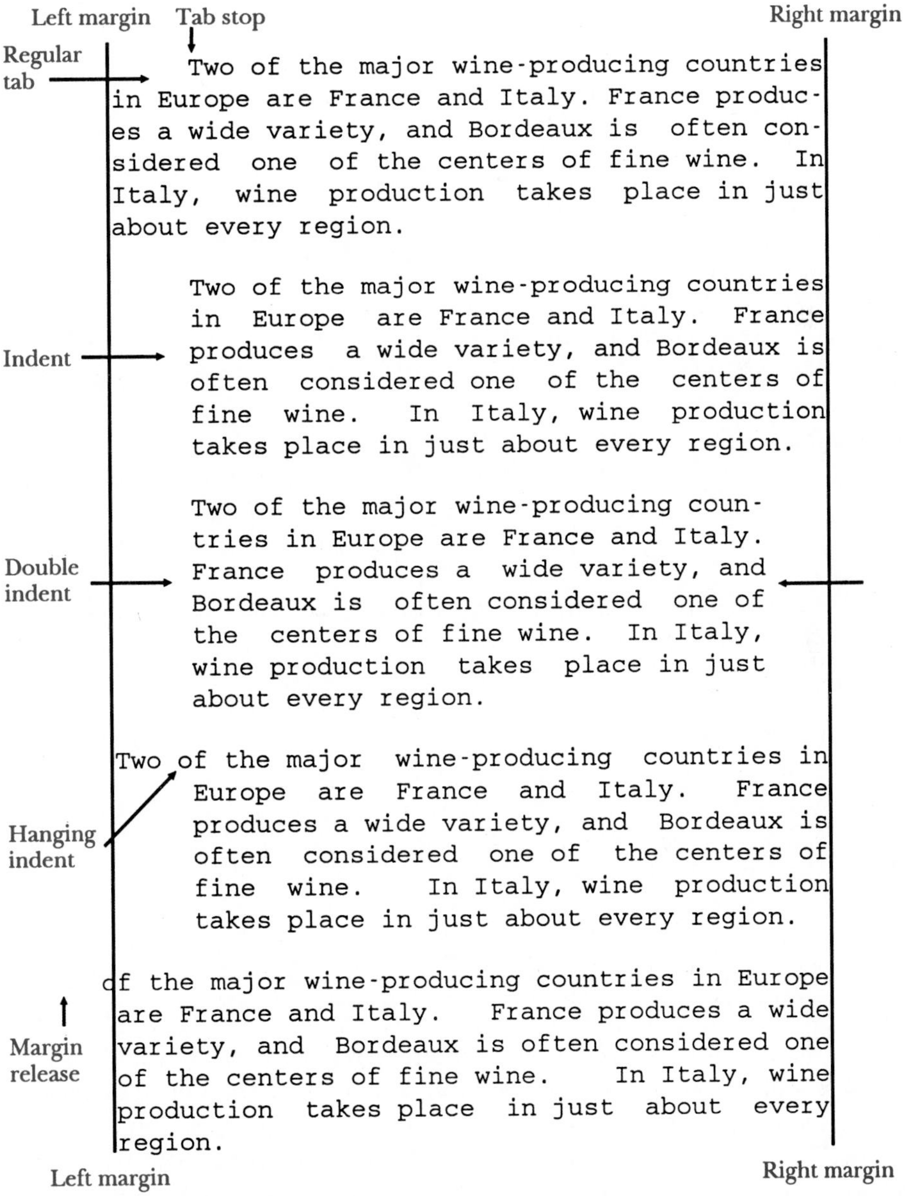

Left margin   Tab stop   Right margin

Regular
tab

    Two of the major wine-producing countries
in Europe are France and Italy. France produces a wide variety, and Bordeaux is often considered one of the centers of fine wine. In
Italy, wine production takes place in just
about every region.

Indent

        Two of the major wine-producing countries
        in Europe are France and Italy. France
        produces a wide variety, and Bordeaux is
        often considered one of the centers of
        fine wine. In Italy, wine production
        takes place in just about every region.

Double
indent

        Two of the major wine-producing coun-
        tries in Europe are France and Italy.
        France produces a wide variety, and
        Bordeaux is often considered one of
        the centers of fine wine. In Italy,
        wine production takes place in just
        about every region.

Hanging
indent

Two of the major wine-producing countries in
        Europe are France and Italy.   France
        produces a wide variety, and Bordeaux is
        often considered one of the centers of
        fine wine.   In Italy, wine production
        takes place in just about every region.

Margin
release

of the major wine-producing countries in Europe
are France and Italy.   France produces a wide
variety, and Bordeaux is often considered one
of the centers of fine wine.   In Italy, wine
production takes place in just about every
region.

Left margin   Right margin

6

paragraphs in the same way that bulleted paragraphs do. The codes [Indent][Mar Rel] precede the paragraph.

- *Margin Release*   The Margin Release feature indents the first line in a paragraph one tab stop to the left—even beyond the left margin. The code [Mar Rel] precedes the paragraph.

To align paragraphs either using one of the indent styles or Margin Release, follow these steps:

1. Position the insertion point precisely where the indentation will begin.

2. Choose Layout, Paragraph.

3. Choose Indent; Double Indent; Hanging Indent; or Margin Release.

 (F7) *is the shortcut for* Layout, Paragraph, Indent.

(CRTL) + (SHIFT) + (F7) *is the shortcut for* Layout, Paragraph, Double Indent.

(CTRL) + (F7) *is the shortcut for* Layout, Paragraph, Hanging Indent.

(SHIFT) + (TAB) *is the shortcut for* Layout, Paragraph, Margin Release.

The same steps apply whether you are about to type the paragraph or for an existing paragraph. The code or codes inserted affect the text up to the hard return [HRt] code that marks the end of the current paragraph.

To remove an indent or margin release, you must delete the corresponding code. One way is to position the insertion point on the first character of the paragraph and press (BACKSPACE). Unlike other layout codes, indent and margin release codes can be deleted without switching to the reveal codes workspace. In that respect they are more similar to tab codes.

Hands-on Exercise: Tabular Columns

Start with a clear document workspace. (If you haven't yet closed the document from the previous exercise, close that document, saving it with the filename *vacation.mmo*.) The goal is to create the document displayed in Figure 6-9. First, let's create the top half of this document:

1. Type the short paragraph at the very top of Figure 6-9, which starts with "I spoke to David Michaels...." Then press (ENTER) twice to move down two lines.

2. To represent a bullet, type the letter **o**.

    Or, to type a bullet as a special character, select F<u>o</u>nt, <u>W</u>P Characters (or press (CTRL) + (W)) and select from the various bullets in the Typographic Symbols set. (See Chapter 5 for a review of the Special Characters feature.)

3. Press (F7) (the shortcut key for the Indent feature) and type the first bulleted paragraph in Figure 6-9, which starts with "He is meeting

Figure 6-9. *Sample text to be aligned on tab stops*

I spoke to David Michaels on January 3rd about our financial situation. He reported the following highlights:

•   He is meeting with a venture capitalist next week who is interested in investing with us.

•   Our debt stands at $159,000 as of December 31st, 10 percent lower than we anticipated. Financial forecasts project that we'll be out of debt within two years. Here are the debt figures (in thousands):

Amount Owed	Name of Bank
$48.5	Floyd Interstate Bank
9.8	Center Bank
100.7	Bank of Stevenson
55.0	Savers Bank of Milwaukee
2,000.5	Regina Bank

with ...." Notice that the paragraph is indented one tab stop from the left margin. Then press (ENTER) twice to move down two lines.

4. Type the letter **o** or a bullet.

5. Press (F7) and type the second bulleted paragraph. Then press (ENTER) twice.

Now we're ready to change tabs. It's necessary to set two tab stops, one as a decimal align 1.5 inches from the left margin, and the other as a centered tab 4 inches from the left margin:

1. Choose Layout, Line, Tab Set.

2. Choose Clear Tabs.

3. Select Decimal Align.

4. In the Position number box, type **1.5"** and then choose Set Tab.

5. Select Center.

6. In the Position number box, type **4"** and then choose Set Tab.

7. Click OK or press (ENTER).

A tab set code is inserted in the text. Entries in the first tabular column will be aligned on the decimal tab, while those in the second will be center aligned. That is perfect for all except the header "Amount Owed". To center that one entry, use a center hard tab to override the decimal-align tab stop:

1. Select Layout, Line, Special Codes (or press (ALT) + (SHIFT) + (F8)).

2. Select Center [HdCntrTab] and then choose Insert.

3. Type **Amount Owed**. This header is centered on the tab stop.

4. Press (TAB), type **Name of Bank**, and press (ENTER) twice. This header is centered, too, because the tab stop is a center type.

5. Press (TAB) and type **$48.5**.

6. Press (TAB) and type **Floyd Interstate Bank**.

7. Continue to type the remainder of the tabular columns, and then press (ENTER) twice to move down to a blank line.

Though this document is complete, assume just for the moment that it continues for several pages. Return tabs to their initial (default) setting so that you can continue on with more bulleted paragraphs. Follow these steps:

1. Select Layout, Line, Tab Set.
2. Choose Default.
3. Click OK or press (ENTER).

Close this document, and save it under the filename *finance1.mmo.*

Layout Changes on the Ruler

If you use a mouse, the ruler is a wonderful alternative to using the Layout menu for many common setting changes. The ruler makes changing the text layout a simple process that's easy to follow on screen. You see your current settings displayed, and can watch as changes you make in settings affect your document. For instance, you can move a tab stop, examine how existing text adjusts, and then move the tab stop again.

Of the layout features already described in this chapter, only the most common ones can be changed using the ruler—left/right margins, justification, line spacing, and tab settings. You can also change the font (see Chapter 5), create text columns and tables (see Chapter 11), and turn on styles (see Chapter 15) using the ruler. You change the layout by clicking and dragging a ruler marker or button. You must have a mouse to use the ruler.

Display the ruler by choosing View, Ruler. Figure 6-10 shows the ruler in a clear document workspace. The Ruler reduces the size of the document workspace by about an inch. Most users find that the loss of this inch of space is a small price to pay for the convenience the ruler provides.

shortcut (ALT) + (SHIFT) + (F3) *is the shortcut for* View, Ruler.

The ruler shows the current settings with markers or buttons. For instance, in Figure 6-10 you see that the margin markers show margin settings at positions 1" and 7.5"; the tab markers show left-aligned tabs positioned

6

Figure 6-10.   *The ruler simplifies the process for certain layout changes*

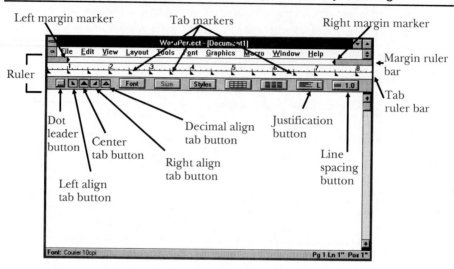

every half-inch; the justification button displays an "L", representing left justification; and the line spacing button displays "1.0", representing single-spacing. These are all the default settings.

As you move the insertion point through the text, the ruler markers and buttons will update to reflect any change in the current settings.

To change a setting with the ruler, be sure to first place the insertion point just before or within the paragraph where you want the change to begin. Or, if you want the change to affect only a specific section of existing text, select the text it will affect. Then proceed as follows depending on the layout change you want to make:

- To change a margin, click and drag the margin marker left or right on the margin ruler bar to a new location. Release the mouse button. To return the margin marker to its original position, drag it up to the top of the document window before releasing the mouse button.

- To delete a tab, click and drag a tab marker downward, off the tab ruler bar. Release the mouse button.

- To move a tab, click and drag the tab marker left or right on the tab ruler bar to a new location. Release the mouse button. To return the tab to its original position, drag the tab marker up to the top of the document workspace before releasing the mouse button.

- To copy a tab, hold down (CTRL) while you drag a tab marker to a new location.

- To work with a selected group of tabs, click between two tab markers, move the mouse pointer left or right to select any number of tab markers, and release the mouse button. The selected tabs are highlighted. Then, delete the selected tabs by dragging them downward, off the tab ruler bar. Or, move the selected tabs by dragging them to a new location. Or, move the selected tabs where they replace (rather than add to) existing tabs by holding (SHIFT) while dragging the tabs to a new position. Or, copy the selected tabs by holding down (CTRL) while dragging the tabs to a new position.

- To insert a new tab, click and drag the tab button corresponding to the tab style that you want to a location on the tab ruler bar. Release the mouse button. (The dot leader button is like a toggle switch that controls whether or not the tab styles are with or without dot leaders. To insert a tab with a dot leader, click the dot leader bar so that dots appear on each of the tab buttons before you click and drag one.)

- To change the justification, click and hold the justification button. Drag the mouse to select a new setting and release the mouse button.

- To change the line spacing, click and hold the line spacing button. Then drag the mouse to select a new setting and release the mouse button. (Your options are limited to single-spacing, one-and-a-half-spacing, and double-spacing on the ruler.)

WordPerfect inserts codes at the beginning of the current paragraph (assuming that the Auto Code Placement feature is on), just as if you had altered the layout using the Layout menu.

shortcut *Double-click on any of the ruler markers or buttons to display the dialog box for the corresponding layout feature (if that feature has one). This comes in handy for accessing features in the dialog boxes that aren't available on the ruler. For instance, double-click on a margin marker to display the Margins dialog box, where you can change not only left/right margins, but also top/bottom margins. Or double-click on the line spacing button to display the Line Spacing box, where you are not restricted to single-spacing, one-and-a-half-spacing, or double-spacing. Or double-click on a tab marker to display the Tab Set dialog box. In that dialog box, you can quickly clear all tabs; then choose OK and return to the ruler to set individual tabs.*

Note that the operation of the ruler can be changed using the File, Preferences, Environment command. See Chapter 17 for more details.

Quick Reference

- To change the layout, use the Layout menu. Choose Layout, Margins to change margins. Choose Layout, Justification to change justification. Choose Layout, Line, and the corresponding menu item to change line spacing, line height, or tab settings, or to turn hyphenation on or off.

- To change the layout beginning at a specific location, be sure to position the insertion point before choosing from the Layout menu. A layout code that you insert affects text from where it is inserted all the way to the end of the document, unless another code of the same kind is inserted later in the text.

- To change the layout for a section of existing text, select the text before choosing from the Layout menu.

- To align a paragraph on a tab stop, choose Layout, Paragraph and select from four different indentation options: Indent, Double Indent, Hanging Indent, and Margin Release. These options offer a quick method for a margin change that is restricted to an individual paragraph.

- To make the most common layout changes—left/right margins, justification, line spacing, tab settings—the ruler is a handy alternative to the Layout menu. Choose View, Ruler to show the ruler. Then click and drag items on the ruler to make the changes. You must have a mouse to use the ruler.

7

Adjusting the Page and Document Layout

When you type a lengthy document, WordPerfect formats the text into pages for you. The Automatic Page Break feature is a timesaver, but sometimes it can lead to awkward splits in your text. This chapter will show how to control the location of page breaks or create your own. You'll also learn how to include headers or footers and place page numbers on each page of your document automatically.

This chapter introduces two useful features that can help you get the results you want at the printer. With the Advance feature, you can specify where on a page certain text should appear—a convenience when filling in a preprinted form or for desktop publishing. And with the Paper Size feature, you can tell WordPerfect you are using something other than standard-size paper, when you want to type sideways on the page or address an envelope, for example.

Also, you'll learn about Document Initial Codes. With this feature, you can avoid placing layout codes in your text and reduce the clutter of codes in a document.

note *The procedures in this chapter, as in the previous chapter, are based on the initial setting of Auto Code Placement turned on. With it on, layout codes are automatically placed where they should fall in your text—either at the beginning of the current paragraph or the current page. If the Auto Code Placement feature is off, however, all layout codes are inserted at the insertion point, which means you must position the insertion point more precisely. Chapter 17 describes this feature in more detail.*

Controlling Automatic Page Breaks

WordPerfect breaks to a new page based on a document's paper size and top/bottom margin settings. For instance, if you don't change the initial settings—a paper size of 11 inches long, with top/bottom margins of 1 inch—WordPerfect allows 9 vertical inches of text on a page (11 inches minus 1-inch top margin minus 1-inch bottom margin). If you change both the top and bottom margins to 2 inches, WordPerfect allows 7 vertical inches of text on a page (11 inches minus 2 inches minus 2 inches), and thus creates a page break sooner on every page. This is illustrated in Figure 7-1. On the document workspace, a single line marks the page break. On the reveal codes workspace, an [SPg] code marks the page break. It is called a "soft" page break because its location may shift later when you edit your text.

Sometimes WordPerfect creates a page break at an awkward spot. Examples of such situations are shown in Figure 7-2. WordPerfect gives you several features that help avoid awkward soft page breaks: the Widow/Orphan, Conditional End of Page, and Block Protect features.

Protection Against Widows and Orphans

You can prevent one line of a paragraph being left stranded by itself on a page. When the first line of a paragraph appears at the bottom of the preceding page (as in the first example in Figure 7-2), it is called a *widow*. When the last line of a paragraph appears at the top of the following page, it is called an *orphan*. By activating the Widow/Orphan feature, you allow WordPerfect to break the page one line earlier or later than it might otherwise, to avoid an awkward widow or orphan.

Figure 7-1. *Top/bottom margins and paper length determine how much text WordPerfect allows on a page*

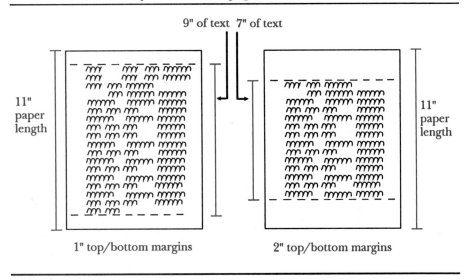

Figure 7-2. *WordPerfect sometimes creates awkward page breaks*

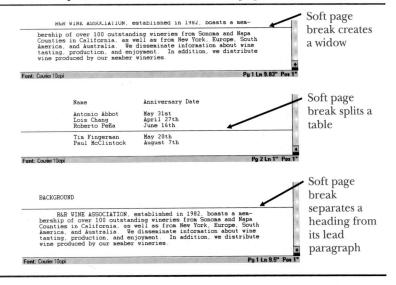

The Widow/Orphan feature is turned on and off like a toggle switch. Simply position the insertion point just before or anywhere within the paragraph where you want the change to begin. Choose Layout, Page, Widow/Orphan.

shortcut (ALT) + (F9) *is the shortcut for* Layout, Page.

If the feature was off, it will be turned on, and a [W/O On] code is inserted just before the paragraph. If the feature was on, it will be turned off with a [W/O Off] code. You may wish to turn on Widow/Orphan protection at the top of a document, so that the feature is active throughout the entire document.

Protecting a Block of Text

You can protect one section of text—perhaps a chart or tabular columns—from being split by a page break, using these steps:

1. Select the text.

2. Choose Layout, Page, Block Protect.

3. Click the mouse or press an arrow key to turn off the Select feature.

reminder (ALT) + (F9) *is the shortcut for* Layout, Page.

A [BlockPro:On] code is inserted before the selected text, and a [BlockPro:Off] code is inserted at the end, grouping together the lines that you don't want separated by a page break. You can add or delete text between the codes, and still the block will remain intact on one page (unless the block is more than one page in length).

Using Conditional End of Page

You can protect against a specific number of lines being split by a page break. For instance, suppose you type a heading followed by two hard returns and then a leading paragraph. You can request that WordPerfect keep the heading, the blank lines, and the first line or two of the paragraph on the same page. This prevents the unattractive situation of having a heading at the bottom of one page and the paragraph at the top of the next (this is shown in the last example in Figure 7-2).

1. Count the number of lines you wish to keep together. For example, a one-line title, two blank lines, and two lines of text equal five lines.

2. Move the insertion point to the line immediately *above* those that you want to keep together.

3. Choose Layout, Page, Conditional End of Page.

4. Type the number of lines you wish to keep together (in this case type 5) and choose OK.

WordPerfect inserts a code into the text, such as [Cndl EOP:5], which means that the next five lines will be treated as a unit, and moved to the next page if a soft page break would otherwise split them apart.

Creating Manual Page Breaks

You can specify that a page break appear at a particular location when you haven't yet filled the entire page with text. This is appropriate, for example, after typing a cover page, or when you complete one letter and wish to begin a new one, or upon completing a section of a report when you want the next section to start on a new page. To end one page manually and begin another, position the insertion point where you want the page break to occur, and select Layout, Page, Page Break.

shortcut (CTRL) + (ENTER) *is the shortcut for Layout, Page, Page Break.*

A hard page code [HPg] is inserted—"hard" because the page end will not change, no matter how you edit the text. A page boundary will always be located at that spot. Of course, the code is hidden in the document workspace. You will see a double line across the document workspace, rather than a single line, to distinguish the hard page break from the soft page break that WordPerfect inserts.

7

caution *Be sure not to end each page with a hard page break because WordPerfect will be unable to reformat pages properly after you edit. Instead, rely on WordPerfect's Automatic Page Break feature, and insert a hard page only where you definitely want a permanent page break, regardless of how the text will be formatted later on.*

Centering a Page from Top to Bottom

You can center a short page of text vertically between the top and bottom margins as shown in Figure 7-3. Maybe you've typed a short letter that you wish to center on the page. Or perhaps you've created a cover page for a report or a title page for a term paper. To center a page, position the insertion point anywhere on the page you want to center and choose Layout, Page, Center Page.

A [Center Pg] code is inserted at the top of the current page. Unlike most layout codes, which affect text to the end of the document, the center page code affects *only the current page*. You must repeat the procedure just described for each page you wish to center top to bottom.

Keep in mind that the centering occurs only at the printer; the document window does not display centering. (You can use the Print Preview feature, described in Chapter 16, to see where the text will appear on the printed page.)

Hands-on Exercise: Create and Center a Title Page

Suppose you wish to begin compiling into one file all the letters regarding new policies at R&R Wine Association. In Chapter 4, you typed one of these letters to Mr. Barrett Smith. Let's recall that file and create a cover page for the compilation of such letters, with these steps:

1. Open the file named *smith01.ltr*.

2. Make sure the insertion point is located at the top of the document by pressing (CTRL) + (HOME).

3. Choose Layout, Page, Page Break to create a hard page (or press (CTRL) + (ENTER)). Notice the double line that appears to mark the page break.

4. Press (↑) to move the insertion point back up to the top of the document, above the double line.

5. Press (SHIFT) + (F7) and type the head, **CHANGES IN POLICIES AND PROCEDURES** to center this title.

6. Press (ENTER) three times to create several blank lines.

7. Press (SHIFT) + (F7) and type **R&R WINE ASSOCIATION**.

8. Choose Layout, Page, Center Page to center the cover page.

What you've created doesn't resemble a cover page on screen, but if you print it out, you'll find the text centered between the top and bottom margins,

Figure 7-3. *A cover page centered top to bottom*

**Ten Secrets of
Fine Wines**

Presented
by

The R&R Wine Association

7

giving you a well-spaced cover page. If you want to check that the page will be centered top to bottom without actually printing, switch to the reveal codes workspace and look for the [Center Pg] code at the top of the cover page, or use your Print Preview feature, described in Chapter 16.

Using the Advance Feature

The Advance feature allows you to indicate exactly where text should appear on the current page when printed. This feature is useful for printing on a preprinted form, where you must "fill in the blanks" on screen. It is also useful for some desktop publishing situations, such as printing two items in the same location (a paragraph of text and a graphics image), or for creative spacing of characters in a title or heading. You can also use the Advance feature for simple formatting. For example, to accommodate letterhead, you could use Advance to position the first line of a letter at a precise position below the letterhead logo that will appear when printed.

Depending on the Advance option you choose, you can move vertically or horizontally with these selections:

- Up, Down, Left, or Right moves in relation to the current location of the *insertion point*. For instance, if the insertion point is at position 1" and you enter a Right measurement of 3.5", the insertion point moves horizontally to position 4.5".

- To Line or To Position moves in relation to the top or left *edge of the page*. For instance, if you enter a To Line measurement of 5", the insertion point moves vertically to line 5". If you enter a To Position measurement of 8", the insertion point moves horizontally to position 8".

You cannot advance both vertically and horizontally at the same time; you must use the feature twice if you wish to move in both directions. For instance, if you wish to print text starting at line 8" and position 3", first use the To Line option and specify a measurement of 8", and then use the To Position option and specify a measurement of 3". Follow these steps to use Advance:

1. Choose Layout, Advance. A dialog box appears.

```
┌─────────────────────────────────────┐
│ ─ │            Advance              │
├─────────────────────────────────────┤
│        ┌─ Advance ──────────────┐   │
│        │ ○ Up        ○ Left     │   │
│        │ ○ Down      ○ Right    │   │
│        │ ○ To Line   ○ To Position│ │
│        │                        │   │
│        │ Advance: [0.001"]      │   │
│        └────────────────────────┘   │
│           [  OK  ]  [ Cancel ]      │
└─────────────────────────────────────┘
```

2. Choose one of the six Advance options shown.

    If you select Up, Down, Left, or Right, WordPerfect suggests .001" in the Advance number box. If you select To Line, WordPerfect displays the current line measurement (the line where the insertion point is currently located). If you select To Position, WordPerfect displays the current position measurement.

3. Type a measurement into the Advance number box.

4. Choose OK.

A hidden Advance code is inserted into the document, such as [AdvDn:0.5"] or [AdvToLn:3"], and the insertion point moves to the new location on the page. If you selected Down, Left, Right, or To Line, the document window will display the move. If you selected Up or To Position, the document window will not display the move, so check the status line to verify the change.

Keep in mind when positioning text vertically from the top of the page that WordPerfect is initially oriented to measure to the top of the text line, rather than to the text's baseline. As a result, when you select To Line and enter a vertical measurement, WordPerfect will print the *top* of the text line at the measurement specified.

You may prefer that WordPerfect print the *baseline* (bottom) of the text line at the measurement specified. At the top of the document, choose Layout, Line, Height and set a fixed line height. Then choose Layout, Typesetting and turn on the First Baseline at Top Margin option (more on typesetting in Chapter 12). Now when you use Advance to enter a To Line measurement, WordPerfect will print the baseline of the text line, rather than the top, at the measurement specified. The difference is illustrated in Figure 7-4. Consider turning on this option before typing information on screen that will later be printed on a preprinted form. That way, you can measure from the top of the form to each blank line, which is a more straightforward process.

Hands-on Exercise: Use Advance

 Let's return to the cover page created in the last hands-on exercise. Suppose that on all cover pages you wish to insert a signature line for the Chief Executive Officer (CEO) as shown in Figure 7-5.

First, suppose you decide that you no longer want to center the page top to bottom. You want the first line of text to appear at the top of the standard page:

1. Choose <u>V</u>iew, Reveal <u>C</u>odes (or press (ALT) + (F3)). Now you can view the codes.

2. Locate and delete the [Center Pg] code.

3. Choose <u>V</u>iew, Reveal <u>C</u>odes.

Figure 7-4.   *Differences in the Advance feature with First Baseline At Top Margin option turned off and on*

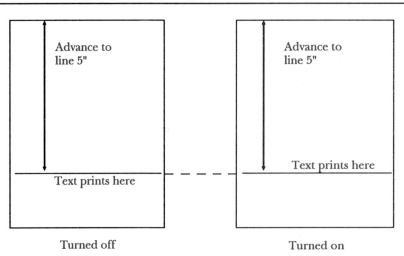

Advance to line 5"

Text prints here

Advance to line 5"

Text prints here

Turned off

Turned on

Now let's add a signature line for the CEO. Suppose that the signature line always appears at line 7" and position 4".

1. Position the insertion point just to the right of the head, "R&R WINE ASSOCIATION" on the cover page, and press (ENTER) to move down to a blank line.
2. Choose Layout, Advance.
3. Select the To Line option.
4. Select Advance and type **7"**.
5. Choose OK or press (ENTER). Notice that the insertion point zooms straight down to line 7".
6. Choose Layout, Advance.
7. Select the To Position option.
8. Select Advance and type **4"**.
9. Choose OK or press (ENTER). Notice that the insertion point moves over to position 4".
10. Type **CEO signature:.**
11. Press the (SPACEBAR) a couple of times, press (CTRL) + (U) to turn on underlining, press the (SPACEBAR) until you've created a line sufficiently long for a signature, and press (CTRL) + (U) to turn off underlining.

You can print out this page to get the results shown in Figure 7-5. Then save this modified document. But let's save it under a new name, so that the letter to Mr. Smith can be preserved as it was, and this new document can be stored in a new file.

1. Choose File, Save As (or press (F3)).
2. Save this file under the name *policies.ltr.*

Establishing Headers, Footers, and Page Numbers

A *header* prints the same line or lines of text at the top of every page, while a *footer* prints text at the bottom of every page. In multiple-page documents,

Figure 7-5.   *Sample cover page*

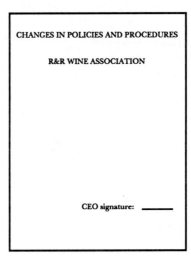

CHANGES IN POLICIES AND PROCEDURES

R&R WINE ASSOCIATION

CEO signature: _____

it is common to insert headers or footers. For instance, each chapter of a report might contain a header with the chapter title. A letter might contain a header with the recipient's name and page number. These can be inserted with the Headers or Footers features.

You have a second option for numbering your pages. Use the Page Numbering feature when you wish to specify a new page number or establish a special numbering type.

Headers and Footers

You can create up to two headers and two footers for each page of your document. You can also create up to two headers or footers that appear on alternating pages. Examples are shown in Figure 7-6. A header or footer can be one, two, or many lines long, and can contain just text or text and the page number.

1. Position the insertion point anywhere on the page where you want the header or footer to begin.

Figure 7-6. *Header and footer examples*

One header
and one footer
on every page

R&R Wine Association

Draft Page 1

Two different
headers for
alternating
pages

R&R Wine Association

Page 1

Wine Tasting

Page 2

One footer on
every page

2. Choose <u>L</u>ayout, <u>P</u>age, <u>H</u>eaders or <u>F</u>ooters. A dialog box appears, such as this one for Headers:

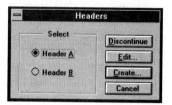

3. Select the <u>A</u> or <u>B</u> option. (There is no difference between how a Header/Footer A or B works; the A and B are conventions to distinguish between the two different headers or footers that you can create.)

4. Choose <u>C</u>reate to establish a new header/footer A or B, or choose <u>E</u>dit to alter an existing header/footer A or B.

   A Header or Footer window appears on screen, with the header or footer number (A or B) listed in the title bar at the top. An example for Header A is shown in Figure 7-7.

Figure 7-7.   *Header A window for Document 1*

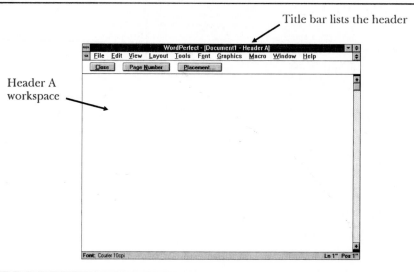

5. Type the text of the header or footer, and change the font or font attributes (such as adding underline or bold) if you want. The current font is listed in the status line at the bottom of the Header or Footer window.

6. If you wish to include the page number as part of the header/footer, position the insertion point where the page number should appear in the header/footer text and choose Page Number. A ^B code is inserted to represent the current page number. In the reveal codes workspace, this code will appear as [Insert Pg Number:^B].

7. Choose Placement to determine the pages on which the header or footer will appear. Your choices are: Every Page, Odd Pages, or Even Pages.

8. Choose Close to return to the document window.

WordPerfect inserts a code at the top of the current page, such as [Header A:Every page;R&R Wine Association]. This indicates the type, placement, and text of the header or footer (or a portion of the text if it is lengthy). The header or footer prints on the page where you inserted the code (as long as the code remains at the very top of the page) and on each subsequent page that you specified (every page, even pages, or odd pages).

The margins will be retained so headers and footers will not print in the top or bottom margins. Instead, a header will start just below the top margin, and will be followed by one blank line to separate it from the first line of the main text. A footer will appear just above the bottom margin, and will be preceded by a blank line. (To add more blank lines separating a header or footer from the main text, insert hard returns in the header or footer.) The number of text lines in the body of the text will be reduced on the page to accommodate the header or footer, as illustrated in Figure 7-8. As a specific example, if a header is two lines long, the number of text lines will be reduced by three—to accommodate two lines containing the header, and one blank line between the header and the body of the text.

Headers and footers are two of the few elements that are *not* displayed in the document workspace. To view the headers and footers, use the Print Preview feature, as described in Chapter 16. You can also print out the text to see the results.

Figure 7-8.   *Top/bottom margins preserved even when headers or footers are added*

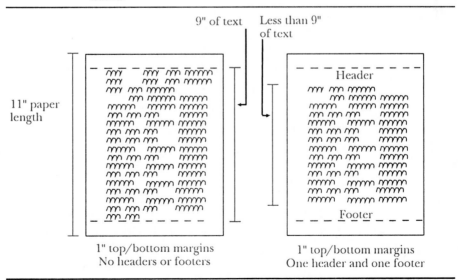

caution *A header/footer code must remain at the top of the page, before any text, to take effect for that page. If you position the insertion point before the header/footer code and type a sentence, the code is pushed forward, away from the top of the page, and won't take effect until the following page. Therefore, be careful to keep track of where a header/footer code is located whenever editing your document. You may wish to insert a hard page break just before a header/footer code that is on a page other than page 1 in your document.*

You have several alternatives for canceling or suppressing a previously created header or footer within your document. You can:

- Cancel the header/footer for the entire document. To do so, switch to the reveal codes workspace and delete the code.

- Suppress the header/footer on one particular page of the document. This will be described later in this chapter.

- Change the header/footer on a page farther forward in the document. To do so, create a new header/footer on that page to replace the old one. Only a Header A can replace a Header A, only a Footer A can replace a Footer A, and so on.

- Discontinue the header/footer on a page farther forward in the document. To discontinue a header/footer, follow these steps:

  1. Position the insertion point anywhere on the page where you want the header or footer to stop.

  2. Choose Layout, Page, Headers or Footers.

  3. Select the Header/Footer A or Header/Footer B option.

  4. Choose Discontinue. A code, such as [Header A: Discontinue] is placed at the top of the current page.

Page Numbering

To number your pages, you can insert a header or footer in the text with a ^B code in the header or footer, as previously described. But if page numbering is your main objective or if you wish to renumber pages or establish a special numbering type, it's easier to use the Page Numbering feature. Follow these steps:

1. Position the insertion point anywhere on the page where you want page numbering to begin.

2. Choose Layout, Page, Numbering. A dialog box appears, such as the one for Headers shown in Figure 7-9.

3. Select a page number position from the Position pop-up list box. The options include: Top Left, Top Center, Top Right, Alternating Top (top left on even pages and top right on odd pages), Bottom Left, Bottom Center, Bottom Right, and Alternating Bottom (bottom left on even pages and bottom right on odd pages). When you select an option, the outcome is displayed on the Sample Facing Pages in the dialog box shown in Figure 7-9.

4. If you wish to change from Arabic numbers (1, 2, 3, 4) to another type, select from the Numbering Type pop-up list box. You can

Figure 7-9. Page Numbering dialog box

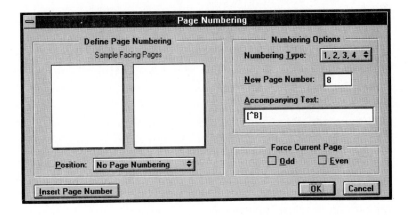

choose between lowercase Roman numerals (i, ii, iii, iv) and upper-case Roman numerals (I, II, III, IV).

5. If you wish to renumber pages in your document, select New Page Number and type into the number box. WordPerfect suggests the current page number in the number box.

     You may, for instance, wish to renumber pages so that the first two pages of a document are introductory pages 1 and 2 (with lowercase Roman numerals i and ii), while the rest of the pages are the main text, 1, 2, 3, 4, and so on (with Arabic numbers).

6. If you wish to insert page numbers with accompanying text, select Accompanying Text and add text into the text box. The [^B] code in the text box represents the page number. So, for instance, if you insert the insertion point before the [^B] and type **Page** and press the (SPACEBAR) to produce Page [^B], the document will be numbered Page 1, Page 2, and so on. The change is displayed in the Sample Facing Pages in the dialog box.

7. If you want to make sure that a certain page has either an even or odd page number, select the Odd or Even check box. You may, for instance, want to ensure that the first page of each chapter in your report is odd-numbered, which is customary if you're printing double-sided copies.

8. Choose OK.

When you initiate page numbering, WordPerfect inserts a code at the top of the current page, for example [Page Numbering: Bottom Center]. If you make other selections, other codes may be inserted as well, such as [Pg Num:5] if you renumbered the page to page 5 or [Force:Odd] if you forced the current page to be odd. Page numbers print on the page where you inserted the code (as long as the code remains at the very top of the page) and on each subsequent page.

Like headers and footers, page numbers will not print in the top or bottom margins. These margins will be retained. Instead, a page number will appear either below the top margin or above the bottom margin (depending on your page numbering selection), and will be separated from the main text by a blank line.

Also, as for headers and footers, page numbering does not display in the document workspace. To view page numbers, you can use the Print Preview feature, as described in Chapter 16. Or print out the text.

caution *A page numbering code must remain at the top of the page, before any text, to take effect for that page. Be careful to keep track of where a page numbering code is located whenever editing your document. You may wish to insert a hard page break just before a page numbering code that is on other than page 1 in your document.*

You have several options for canceling or suppressing page numbering:

- Cancel the page numbering for the entire document. Switch to the reveal codes workspace and delete the code.

- Suppress the page numbering on one particular page of the document. The Suppress feature is described in the next section.

- Discontinue page numbering on a page farther forward by positioning the insertion point on the page where you want the page numbering to cease, returning to the Page Numbering dialog box, and selecting the No Page Numbering option from the Position pop-up list box.

You should know that if you renumber pages, WordPerfect uses the new page numbers for printing the pages. For instance, suppose the first page of your document is renumbered as page 25. If you wish to print the first and second pages, you can choose the Multiple Pages option in the Print dialog box and specify that you wish to print 25-26. If you renumber pages several times in a document, the document is considered to be divided into sections. When you specify pages to be printed, you can indicate a section by typing the section number, a colon, and then the pages to be printed in that section. For instance, suppose the first section of a document is numbered as pages i-vii and the next page is renumbered to page 1. Specifying that you wish to print pages 1:1-4, for example, will print pages i-iv. Specifying that you wish to print pages 2:1-4 will print pages 1-4 in that second section.

One final option in the Page Numbering dialog box is that you can simply insert the current page number in the main text, without turning on page numbering. Position the insertion point where you want the page number to appear and choose Layout, Page, Numbering, and the Insert Page Number command button.

7

Suppress Headers, Footers, and Page Numbers

To suppress the printing of headers, footers, and/or page numbering on one specific page, follow these steps:

1. Position the insertion point on the page where you want to suppress headers, footers, and/or page numbering.

2. Choose Layout, Page, Suppress.

3. Select the check boxes for one or more items you wish to suppress; these could include: Header A, Header B, Footer A, Footer B, and Page Number.

4. If you want to move the page number to the bottom center of the current page only, select the check box for Print Page Number at Bottom Center. (This option is unavailable once you select Page Number.) This option is useful, for instance, when a full page is occupied by a table or figure.

5. Choose OK.

reminder (ALT) + (F9) *is the shortcut for Layout, Page.*

WordPerfect inserts a code at the top of the page to suppress items for that page. For instance, if you suppress Header A and Page Number, the code inserted is [Suppress:HA,PgNum]. Unlike most other layout codes, which affect text to the end of the document, the suppress code affects *only* the current page. Therefore, repeat the preceding steps 1 through 5 on each page where you wish to suppress headers, footers, and/or page numbers.

The suppress code must be located at the top of the page, before any text, to take effect. Therefore, you may wish to place a hard page break just before the code.

Suppress is especially useful when inserting a header/footer or page numbering on all but page 1. Insert the header/footer or page numbering code at the top of page 1, immediately followed by a suppress code. The header/footer or page numbering code will sit at the top of the document, with less chance of getting in the way than if on page 2, but the header/footer or page numbering will not appear until page 2.

Hands-on Exercise: Insert a Header

 Suppose your policies and procedures document is a draft. At the top of every page, you wish to include the page number on the left and the word "DRAFT" and today's date on the right, separating the header from the main body of the text by two blank lines. Let's say this is the header you want to appear at the top of page 1:

1	DRAFT–February 1, 1993

CHANGES IN POLICIES AND PROCEDURES

R&R WINE ASSOCIATION

And this is the header you want for page 2:

2	DRAFT–February 1, 1993

February 3, 1993

Mr. Barrett P. Smith
FST Accounting
1801 S. Harmon Street
Oakland, CA 94413

Dear Barrett:

1. Position the insertion point on the cover page, which is the first page of *policies.ltr*.
2. Choose Layout, Page, Headers.
3. The options Header A and Create are already preselected, so simply press (ENTER).
4. Choose Page Number to insert ^B, which will insert a page number in the header.

5. Choose Layout, Line, Flush Right (or press (ALT) + (F7)).

6. Type **DRAFT —**.

7. Type in today's date. (Or simply use the Date feature by choosing Tools, Date, Text, as described in Chapter 8.)

8. Press (ENTER) to create a blank line as part of the header. Since WordPerfect automatically inserts one line, pressing (ENTER) once means now that two blank lines will separate the header from the main text when the document is printed.

9. Choose Close.

If you choose, you can print out this document to view the header on both pages.

Changing the Paper Size and Type

In WordPerfect, you change the dimensions of a page by selecting a *paper definition* for the current printer. The initial setting is for a paper definition with the name, or *paper type*, of standard. The initial setting is also for a paper definition with a *paper size* that is 8.5 inches wide by 11 inches long, the norm for a business letter. (For versions of WordPerfect not sold in the United States, the default paper size will vary.) Also, this paper definition contains other settings to determine how the paper is fed into the printer—these will vary depending on the current printer.

How you change the paper definition depends on whether, for the current printer the associated printer driver—the special file that indicates to WordPerfect how your printer functions—is supplied by WordPerfect or Windows. (Chapter 16 describes how to select a different printer, which allows you to switch between a WordPerfect and a Windows printer driver.)

If you are using a Windows printer driver, you can select only one paper definition for each document, and you change that paper definition by changing the setup of the printer driver itself, as described in Chapter 16. The exception is labels. You can create a limited paper definition for labels when using a Windows driver.

If you are using a WordPerfect printer driver, you have far greater flexibility. You can change the paper definition starting on any page in your document. Depending on your printer, WordPerfect supports standard (8.5-by-11-inch) paper, legal (8.5-by-14-inch) paper, envelopes, labels, and other paper definitions. The procedure for working with paper definitions is described below.

Selecting a Paper Definition

To select a paper definition when using a WordPerfect printer driver, follow these steps:

1. Position the insertion point on the page where you want to specify a new paper size/type combination.

2. Choose Layout, Page, Paper Size. The Paper Size dialog box appears for the current printer; an example is shown in Figure 7-10. The current paper definition is highlighted, such as the Standard 8.5" x 11" paper definition in Figure 7-10.

3. Select a paper definition from the Paper Type list box for the paper size/type combination that you desire. Not all the paper definitions may be displayed at one time, so you may need to scroll through the list box to find the paper definition that you want.

4. Choose Select.

≡*note*≡ *Select the [ALL OTHERS] paper definition, which is the last one listed in the Paper Type list box, if you plan to print a document on different printers. Or select this definition if the paper size/type combination you wish to specify is rare, one that you won't be using again, and that therefore doesn't necessitate the creation of a new paper definition. When you select [ALL OTHERS], you can then specify the Paper Type and Paper Size settings that you want for that situation. WordPerfect uses the [ALL OTHERS] paper definition if the current printer doesn't have a paper definition that matches the paper size/type code in your document.*

WordPerfect inserts a code at the top of the current page, such as [Paper Sz/Typ:9.5" x 4",Envelope]. This code affects all pages from the current page

7

Figure 7-10.   *Paper Size dialog box lists paper definitions for the current printer*

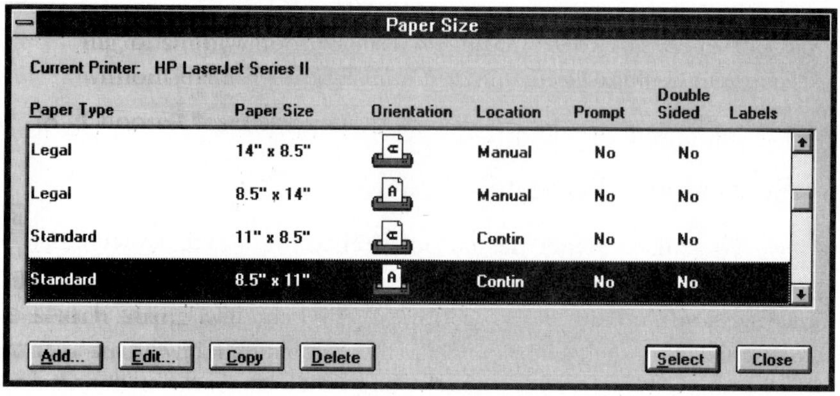

forward. Therefore, if you wish to change the paper size for an entire document, make sure that the insertion point is on page 1 before you insert a paper size/type code. If you wish to change the paper size for just one page in the middle of a long document, remember to change the paper definition twice—once on that page, and a second time on the next page.

Always take into account the current margin settings whenever you change the paper definition. The initial margin settings of 1 inch on all sides may become inappropriate if the paper size changes. For instance, if you choose a paper definition with a paper length of 4 inches, only 2 vertical inches of text will be printed on the page unless you change top and bottom margins (4-inch paper length minus 1 inch for the top margin, minus 1 inch for the bottom margin).

Also, keep in mind that you can't select a paper definition when the paper size would result in overlapping margins and no room for text. For instance, suppose your top and bottom margins are both 1 inch. In that case, you can't choose a paper definition with a paper size that is less than 2 inches in height unless you change margins *first* and then select the paper definition.

Text will be too wide to display across the screen if you change to a paper definition with a wide page width—such as to 11 by 8.5 inches standard landscape (which is the standard 8.5-by-11-inch page turned sideways). In that case, mouse users may wish to turn on the horizontal scroll bar, an aid for moving quickly across a line. You can turn on the horizontal scroll with File, Preferences, Display, as described in Chapter 17. Keyboard users can use the (HOME) and (END) keys to move quickly from one end of the line to the opposite end.

Creating or Editing a Paper Definition

If there is no existing paper definition for the size and type combination that you desire, you can create a new paper definition. View the Paper Size dialog box as shown in Figure 7-10 and choose Add. An Add Paper Size dialog box appears, as displayed in Figure 7-11. Change the options in this dialog box and then choose OK to confirm the changes. The new paper definition now appears in the Paper Type list box, and can be selected like any other paper definition.

You can alter an existing definition by selecting (highlighting) that paper definition and choosing the Edit command button at the bottom of the Paper Size dialog box. A dialog box appears like the one shown in Figure 7-11, except it will be titled "Edit Paper Size". To create a paper definition similar to an existing one, select the existing definition, choose Copy, and edit the results until it has the characteristics you wish it to have. Finally, the Delete command button allows you to erase an obsolete paper definition.

The options that you can change when adding or editing a paper definition are described next.

Paper Type

The Paper Type option on the Add or Edit Paper Size dialog box allows you to name the new paper definition. The name can be one of the predefined names from the Paper Type pop-up box, such as Standard, Bond, Letterhead, Labels, Envelope, Transparency, and Cardstock. You can also select Other and type a new name into the Other text box.

Paper Size

The Paper Size option allows you to select a predefined size from the Paper Size pop-up list box, such as Standard (8.5 by 11 inches), Standard

Figure 7-11.   *Use the Add Paper Size dialog box to specify a new paper definition*

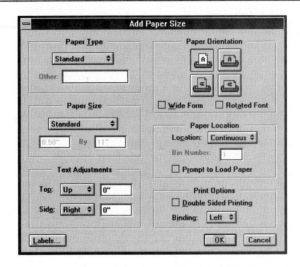

Landscape (11 by 8.5 inches), Legal (8.5 by 14 inches), Legal Landscape (14 by 8.5 inches), Envelope (9.5 by 4 inches), Half Sheet (5.5 by 8.5 inches), and several others. Or select <u>O</u>ther and type width and height dimensions into the number boxes.

Paper Orientation

The Paper Orientation options tell WordPerfect the direction that paper is fed into the printer and text is printed on the paper. There are two check boxes you can turn on or off. What you select depends on your printer.

You may use a printer where the carriage is wide enough so that paper can be fed into the printer either in the portrait (short) orientation or the landscape (wide) orientation:

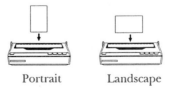

Portrait   Landscape

If you wish to print in portrait orientation, leave both boxes unchecked. If you wish to print in landscape orientation, turn on the W̲ide Form check box and turn the paper sideways when you feed it into the printer.

You may use a laser printer where the paper can be fed into the printer only in the portrait orientation. In that case, if you wish to print in portrait orientation, leave both boxes unchecked. If you wish to print in landscape orientation, you must direct the printer to print the text sideways by turning on the Rota̲ted Font check box. Only those fonts that can print sideways on the page will be available from the Font menu.

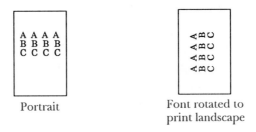

Portrait

Font rotated to
print landscape

Depending on the status of the two check boxes, WordPerfect highlights the visual picture of the orientation you selected:

Portrait, nonrotated, currently selected

Portrait, rotated

Landscape (wide), nonrotated

Landscape (wide), rotated

note *When you select a predefined paper size that is marked with the landscape orientation (such as Standard Landscape or Legal Landscape), the appropriate check box will be turned on for you automatically. In that case, you don't have to change the orientation manually.*

Paper Location

The Paper Location options let you specify from the Loca̲tion pop-up list box how paper is fed into the printer—whether the paper-feed will be

Continuous, Manual, or from a Bin (paper tray or sheet feeder). If you select Bin, you must then specify a particular bin number.

When using continuous-feed paper with perforations at the edges connected to a tractor feed, the correct option is Continuous. When using a printer that feeds paper from a *single* paper tray (typically a laser printer), the correct option for feeding paper from the paper tray is usually Continuous, while the correct option for feeding a single sheet yourself from a slot above the paper tray is Manual. When using a printer with numerous paper trays or sheet feeder bins—perhaps with plain paper in bin 1, letterhead in bin 2, and envelopes in bin 3—the correct option is Bin, and the bin number you choose depends on which paper type you plan to use.

When you select the Manual option, you may wish to turn on the Prompt to Load Paper check box. When this check box is turned on, WordPerfect will pause during printing and sound a beep to remind you to manually feed a piece of paper into the printer. You then resume printing by switching to the Print Manager and selecting the Resume option (see Chapter 16).

Text Adjustments

The Text Adjustment options are used only if the text is not located where it should be on the printed page. Select Top or Side, and specify a direction and a measurement. (Before you specify a Text Adjustment option, make sure that the problem isn't that the top of the paper is misaligned in the printer. For instance, make sure that when using continuous-feed paper that the perforations between pages are lined up with the *printhead,* which is the mechanism that puts ink to paper.)

Print Options

If your printer has the capability to print on both sides and you wish to do so, select Double sided. Then, select Binding and indicate whether the binding edge for the final document will be on top (as it would be for a calendar) or on the left (as it would be for a book).

Envelopes

Envelopes are one common reason to change from the standard paper definition. With most WordPerfect printer drivers, WordPerfect has a predefined paper definition for 9.5-by-4-inch envelopes, which is the standard size of a business envelope. You can view the Edit Paper Size dialog box for the envelope to determine exactly how the envelope paper definition has been defined for your printer. Choose Layout, Page, Paper Size, and select (highlight) the Envelope paper definition. Then, choose Edit. After reviewing the paper definition, either choose Cancel to back out of this dialog box or edit the definition if necessary.

You can create a new paper definition for envelopes if your printer has no predefined definition for them. You would usually want to make the following selections: Envelope from the Paper Type list box; Envelope from the Paper Size list box; landscape orientation for laser printers or portrait orientation for dot-matrix printers; Manual from the Location pop-up list box; and perhaps also Prompt to Load Paper so that the computer signals a beep when it is time to put the envelope in the printer.

Should you also need to print addresses on envelopes with a different paper size—other than 9.5 by 4 inches—you can create another paper definition. One easy way to do this is to select (highlight) the existing Envelope paper definition, choose the Copy option, and then edit the copy by changing the paper size setting.

When you wish to print an address on an envelope, use the envelope paper definition as shown in these steps:

1. Position the insertion point on the page where you want to place the envelope address.

2. Choose Layout, Page, Paper Size. The Paper Size dialog box appears for the current printer.

3. Select a paper definition for the envelope type from the Paper Type list box.

4. Choose Select to insert the page size/type code for envelopes at the top of the page and to return to the document workspace.

5. Change margins for the envelope. For example, for an envelope with the return address preprinted and assuming the standard 9.5-by-4-inch size, try the top and left margin settings shown in Figure 7-12.

   For a 9.5-by-4-inch envelope where the return address is not preprinted, change top and left margin settings, and also create a

Figure 7-12.   *Settings for a 9.5-by-4-inch envelope*

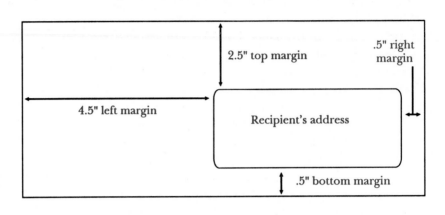

single tab stop to type the recipient's address. Try the settings shown
in Figure 7-13.

Once the page layout is established, you're ready to type the recipient's
address, like this:

```
Mr. Barrett P. Smith
FST Accounting
1801 S. Harmon Street
Oakland, CA  94413
```

If the return address is not preprinted, the page will look like this:

```
R&R Wine Association
3345 Whitmore Drive, #505
San Francisco, CA 94123
```

```
                              Mr. Barrett P. Smith
                              FST Accounting
                              1801 S. Harmon Street
                              Oakland, CA 94413
```

Figure 7-13.   *Settings for a 9.5-by-4-inch envelope with the return label not preprinted*

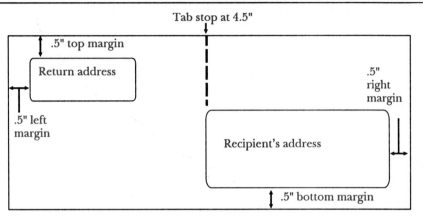

If you wish to prepare another envelope, press (CTRL) + (ENTER) to insert a hard page, and then type a new name and address.

How you print out the envelope will depend on the current printer. Typically, feed the 4-inch (narrow) edge of the envelope into a laser printer, and the 9.5-inch (wide) edge of the envelope into a printer with a long carriage, such as a dot-matrix printer, as shown in Figure 7-14.

The Edit Paper Size dialog box for your envelope paper definition will indicate the setup for your current printer.

note   *The Merge feature, discussed in Chapter 14, gives you a shortcut to produce multiple envelopes for mass mailings.*

Labels

Large envelopes with clasps can't be fed into a printer, so the alternative is to produce labels that you can adhere to the large envelopes. You'll also want to produce labels for bulk mailings. WordPerfect usually has no pre-defined paper definition for labels because their form and size vary so tremendously. If you have a laser printer, you probably use sheets of labels that are 8.5 inches wide by 11 inches long with labels in any of a variety of sizes on the sheets (such as 4 inches wide by 1 inch high or 4 inches wide by 2 inches high). If you have a dot- matrix printer, you may use continuous-feed labels with perforations at the edges, connected to a tractor feed.

You can create a paper definition for labels whether the current printer uses a WordPerfect or a Windows printer driver, but the procedure is slightly different. For WordPerfect printer drivers, you specify the paper size, orientation, type, and the label dimensions. For Windows printer drivers, you specify only the label dimensions, while the paper size, orientation, and type are defined when you edit the printer setup (as described in Chapter 16). To specify a paper definition for labels, follow these steps:

1. Choose Layout, Page, Paper Size. The Paper Size dialog box appears for the current printer.

2. Select Add to display the Add Paper Size dialog box. If using a Windows printer driver, choose OK and the Edit Labels dialog box

Figure 7-14.   *Feeding envelopes into dot-matrix and laser printers*

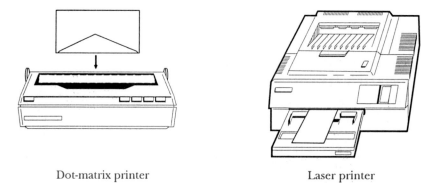

Dot-matrix printer   Laser printer

appears; skip to step 7. If using a WordPerfect printer driver, continue with step 3.

3. Select Labels from the Paper Type pop-up list box. (You can also select Other and type in a new name.)

4. If the labels are not on 8.5-by-11-inch sheets (standard size), select Paper Size. For sheets of labels on paper of other sizes, type in the correct dimensions. For continuous-feed labels on a long roll, as shown in Figure 7-15, specify the width as the total width of the labels across the roll, and the height as measured from the top of one label to the top of the next.

5. If the location for the labels is incorrect, select a different option (such as Manual) from the Paper Location pop-up list box. You may also wish to select Prompt to Load Paper.

6. Choose the Labels command button. An Edit Labels dialog box is displayed as shown in Figure 7-16. WordPerfect suggests some label dimensions. For instance, with standard size sheets WordPerfect assumes three labels across and ten labels down on a sheet.

Figure 7-15.   *A long roll of continuous-feed labels*

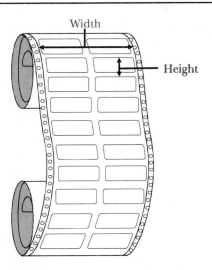

7

Figure 7-16.   *Edit Labels dialog box*

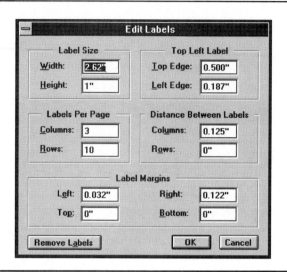

7. Change the label dimension settings to fit the type of labels you have including: label size, number of labels per page (sheet), label margins, the location of the top left label from the edge of the page (sheet), and the distance between labels. An example of how to determine these different measurements is shown for a sheet with three labels across and ten labels down in Figure 7-17. (For continuous-feed labels as in Figure 7-15, the Left Edge and Top Edge should be set to 0", the Rows of labels per page set to 1, and the other measurements set according to the label dimensions.)

8. Choose OK and return to the document workspace.

Once a paper definition for labels is created, you can select this new paper definition on any page in a document as follows:

1. Position the insertion point on the page where you want to type labels.

2. Choose Layout, Page, Paper Size. The Paper Size dialog box appears for the current printer.

Figure 7-17. *Measurements used when creating a paper definition for a sheet of labels*

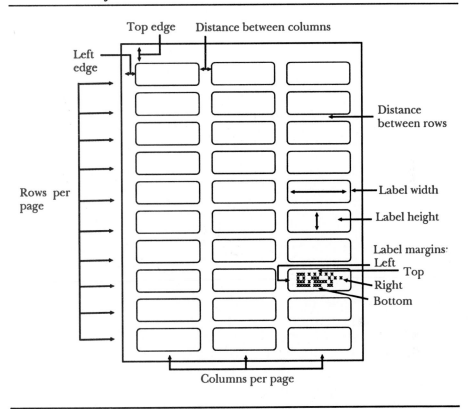

Top edge   Distance between columns

Left edge

Distance between rows

Rows per page

Label width

Label height

Label margins:
Left
Top
Right
Bottom

Columns per page

3. Select the paper definition for labels from the Paper Type list box.

4. Choose Select to insert the page size/type code for labels at the top of the page.

Once the paper size/type code is inserted at the top of the page, type one label, like this:

```
Mr. Barrett P. Smith
FST Accounting
1801 S. Harmon Street
Oakland, CA 94413
```

Then, to prepare a second label, press (CTRL) + (ENTER) to insert a hard page, and type a new name and address.

With a paper definition for labels, WordPerfect distinguishes between two types of "pages", and this affects how the labels are printed. The sheet to which the labels are attached (such as an 8.5-by-11-inch sheet) is the *physical page*. Each label on a sheet is a *logical page*. Thus, if a sheet holds thirty labels, WordPerfect knows that there are thirty logical pages on each physical page.

When you print the full document of labels, logical pages are printed across the physical page from left to right and from top to bottom.

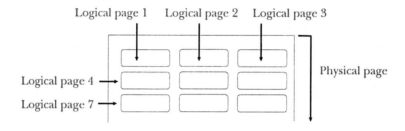

If you type less than thirty addresses, when you print the document, the remaining labels on the sheet will be left blank.

When you specify individual pages, it is the logical pages that are printed. For instance, if you print the current page rather than the full document, only one label will be printed. Similarly, if you print selected pages, only the corresponding labels will be printed.

How you actually print out the labels will depend on the current printer. You may manually feed a sheet of labels into a laser printer, or place labels on continuous-feed tractors for dot-matrix printers. The Edit Paper Size dialog box for your label paper definition will indicate the setup for your current printer.

note *The Merge feature, discussed in Chapter 14, gives you a shortcut to produce multiple labels for mass mailings.*

Hands-on Exercise: Suppress a Header and Print an Envelope

 Let's create a business envelope for the letter addressed to Mr. Smith. You should still have the document named *policies.ltr* on screen.

1. Position the insertion point at the bottom of the document. A quick way to do this is to press (CTRL) + (END).
2. Press (CTRL) + (ENTER) to create a new page for typing the envelope.

Before using this new page to type the envelope, suppress the header created in the previous hands-on exercise; otherwise, the header will print on the envelope, too.

1. With the insertion point on the new, blank page, choose Layout, Page, Suppress.
2. Select the Header A check box.
3. Choose OK.

Now, let's change the paper size and margins for this document. (The following exercise assumes that your current printer uses a WordPerfect printer driver, and that your printer already has a paper definition for a 9.5-by-4-inch envelope. If not, you must create a paper definition for envelopes, as previously described, before continuing.) Suppose the envelope is already preprinted with the return address:

1. With the insertion point on the new, blank page, choose Layout, Page, Paper Size. The Paper Size dialog box appears for the current printer.
2. Select a paper definition for the 9.5-by-4-inch envelope from the Paper Type list box.
3. Choose Select.

7

4. Choose <u>L</u>ayout, <u>M</u>argins (or select (CTRL) + (F8)), and change the left margin to 4.5", the right margin to .5", the top margin to 2.5", and the bottom margin to .5". Then press (ENTER). (Remember not to press (ENTER) until you've changed all four margin settings; otherwise, you'll have to choose <u>L</u>ayout, <u>M</u>argins to return to the dialog box again. Refer to Chapter 6 if you need a review on changing margins.)

   Notice that with the insertion point at the top of the page, the status line changes to reflect the new margin settings:

   ```
   Pg 1 Ln 2.5" Pos 4.5"
   ```

5. Type the recipient's address:

   ```
   Mr. Barrett P. Smith
   FST Accounting
   1801 S. Harmon Street
   Oakland, CA 94413
   ```

   (Actually, it would be quicker to copy the address from the letter to the envelope rather than type the address a second time; Chapter 8 discusses the Copy feature.)

If you have a blank envelope, you may wish to practice printing this envelope. The orientation of the envelope and the way it is fed into the printer will depend on your printer (your printer manual will tell you whether envelopes can be fed and if so how to do it) and on how the envelope paper definition has been set up.

You've finished working on this document. Close the document, saving it again under the name *policies.ltr* to preserve the changes you've made.

Inserting Initial Codes in a Document

It is easy when formatting a document to amass many layout codes together in a document, usually at the top. For instance, suppose you change the paper definition to legal paper, change top/bottom and left/right margins, set new tab stops, switch to full justification, and add page numbering.

The following is an example of what might be hidden at the top of the document:

```
[Paper Sz=Typ:8.5"x14",Legal[T/B Mar:2",2"]
[Pg Numbering:Bottom Center][L/R Mar:1.5",2"]
[Tab Set:Rel:+0.5",+2.5",+5",+6"][Just:Full]
```

WordPerfect offers the ability to hold many layout codes that would otherwise be placed at the top of the document on a special screen, the Document Initial Codes workspace. (Codes that cannot be inserted in this workspace include header/footer codes and paragraph indent codes.) By inserting layout codes in the Document Initial Codes workspace rather than in the document itself, you reduce the clutter at the top of the document and safeguard against accidentally moving or erasing a code, something that is all too easy to do when a code is in the document itself.

note   *Place a layout code in the Document Initial Codes workspace only if that code affects the document beginning at the top. Layout changes that take effect starting somewhere other than page 1 must be inserted directly into the document.*

You can insert or delete a code in the Document Initial Codes workspace at any time while working on a document. Follow these steps:

1. Choose <u>L</u>ayout, <u>D</u>ocument, Initial <u>C</u>odes. A special Initial Codes window appears (split into two sections like the reveal codes workspace) displaying codes. An example is shown in Figure 7-18, with a code for left justification displayed as the only initial code for the document.

2. Insert layout codes as you normally would. For instance, choose <u>L</u>ayout, <u>M</u>argins, and then type new margin settings. A margin code is inserted. You can also delete codes as you normally would.

3. Choose <u>C</u>lose.

The codes inserted in the Document Initial Codes workspace don't appear in the document itself, but affect text in the document—including the main text as well as headers, footers, footnotes, endnotes, equations, and the captions of graphics boxes.

7

Figure 7-18.   *The Document Initial Codes workspace is split to reveal codes*

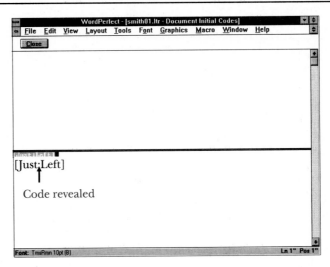

You can edit the initial codes for a document at any time by returning to the Document Initial Codes workspace; simply repeat steps 1 through 3. This Document Initial Codes workspace is saved along with the document. If you clear the document workspace and begin typing a new document, the new document starts out with the default settings.

Codes inserted in the document itself override codes on the Document Initial Codes workspace. That way, you can specify initial codes, and then change the layout farther down in the document. The hierarchy is given here:

DEFAULT SETTINGS establish the layout for all *new documents*
↓

DOCUMENT INITIAL CODES override the default settings
starting at the *top of the current document*
↓

CODES in the current document override
Document Initial Codes *wherever*
they are inserted

note *You can even change the default settings established by WordPerfect Corporation. In this way, you can customize WordPerfect to your needs for all new documents that you create. For more information about the File, Preferences, Initial Codes command see Chapter 17. Once you make changes to the default settings, codes reflecting these changes will appear in the Document Initial Codes workspace for each subsequently created document.*

If you have already inserted various layout codes at the top of a document, you can move them to the Document Initial Codes workspace. Use the Cut feature to remove the codes. Then, display the Document Initial Codes screen, and use the Paste feature to insert the codes there. For more on the procedure to move text and/or codes, see Chapter 8.

7

Quick Reference

- To control automatic page breaks, you can: choose Layout, Page, Widow/Orphan to protect against single lines of a paragraph stranded on a separate page; select text and choose Layout, Page, Block Protect to prevent text from being split by a page break; or choose Layout, Page, Conditional End of Page to keep a number of lines from being split by a page break.

- To create a manual page break, choose Layout, Page, Page Break, or press (CTRL) + (ENTER).

- To center a short page of text between the top and bottom margins, choose Layout, Page, Center Page.

- To advance text vertically or horizontally on the page, choose Layout, Advance.

- To insert a header or footer, choose Layout, Page, and then Headers or Footers. To establish page numbering, choose Layout, Page, Numbering. When you need to suppress a header, footer, and/or page numbering on the current page, choose Layout, Page, Suppress.

- To select a new paper definition, which specifies a new paper size and/or type, choose Layout, Page, Paper Size. Choose a new paper definition, for instance, print envelopes, labels, or on odd-sized paper. When you change the paper definition, be sure to consider whether a change in margins is also called for.

- To reduce the clutter at the top of the document, insert layout codes on the Document Initial Codes screen. Choose Layout, Document, Initial Codes.

8

Cutting, Copying, and Using Special Editing Tools

Reworking words, rearranging sentences, reordering paragraphs—you'll perform these tasks frequently when editing documents. WordPerfect makes the rewriting process less arduous with some special editing enhancements. One handy feature enables you to "cut-and-paste" text within a document or from one document to another without using scissors or tape. You can also copy text from one page or document to another.

Another editing timesaver is the Search feature. WordPerfect can look through a long document and position the insertion point on a specific word or phrase you can't seem to locate, or it can find a hidden code that is eluding you. A related feature is Replace, in which WordPerfect locates a certain word or phrase and swaps it for another phrase of your choice.

If you would like to edit your document and keep track of editing changes, you can use the Document Compare feature to display the differences between the old and edited versions. The Comments feature lets you place nonprinting notes in a document. Document Compare and Comments are especially useful if you are part of a team of people who participate in the writing, typing, and revising of a document.

Two final editing tools discussed in this chapter are the Case Conversion feature, which allows you to switch between upper- and lowercase on letters that are already typed, and the Date feature, a handy way to quickly date or time stamp your document.

Cutting, Copying, and Appending

The *Clipboard* is a place in the computer's memory (RAM) where information—text or graphics—can be stored. Once information is stored in the Clipboard, you can transfer that information to another location. Word-Perfect offers three features that take advantage of the Clipboard:

- *Cut*   Cut erases information from its current location and places it onto the Clipboard.

- *Copy*   Copy copies information without removing it from its current location, and places it onto the Clipboard.

- *Append*   Append copies information, removing it from its current location and adding it to what is already contained on the Clipboard.

The differences between these three procedures are shown in Figure 8-1. Cut or Copy are used when you wish to move or copy a single section of text. Append lets you keep adding to the contents of the Clipboard. It is convenient when you wish to copy many sections of text from different locations and transfer them together to another location.

Working with Standard Text

The Cut, Copy, and Append features can quickly reverse the order of two sentences or copy a paragraph from one part of a report to another. Being aware of the shortcuts available for selecting various units of text—such as a word, a sentence, a paragraph, or a page (as described in Chapter 3)—will

Figure 8-1. *Differences between cutting, copying, and appending to the Clipboard*

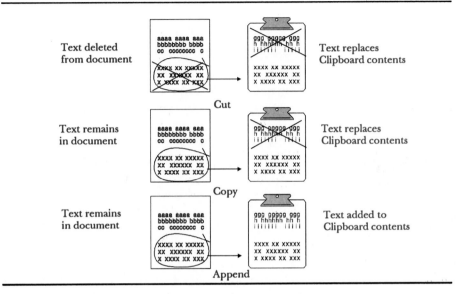

increase your speed and skill in cutting, copying, or appending. To cut, copy, or append a section of text in a document:

1. Select the text.

2. Choose <u>E</u>dit and then choose Cu<u>t</u>, or <u>C</u>opy, or Appen<u>d</u>.

3. If you choose Cu<u>t</u> or <u>C</u>opy, click once or press an arrow key to turn off the Selection feature.

shortcut *Either* (SHIFT) + (DEL) *or* (CTRL) + (X) *is the shortcut for <u>E</u>dit, Cu<u>t</u>.*
Either (CTRL) + (INS) *or* (CTRL) + (C) *is the shortcut for <u>E</u>dit, <u>C</u>opy.*

Once you place text in the Clipboard, you are ready to *paste* that text into another location. To paste, follow these steps:

1. Place the insertion point where you wish to insert (paste) the contents of the Clipboard.

8

2. Choose <u>E</u>dit, <u>P</u>aste. The text is inserted, and the insertion point moves to the end of the pasted information.

≡*shortcut*≡ *Either* (SHIFT) + (INS) *or* (CTRL) + (V) *is the shortcut for* <u>E</u>dit, <u>P</u>aste.

Even after you paste the contents of the Clipboard into a new location, the contents remain in the Clipboard. Therefore, you can paste the same information into many different locations; just repeat steps 1 and 2 of the previous instruction as many times as is necessary. The Clipboard contents change only when you cut or copy once again to replace it, or when you append to add to it. The contents remain even after you exit WordPerfect because the Clipboard is created by Windows, and not by WordPerfect. But once you exit Windows, the contents are cleared.

You can work with the Clipboard not only within one document, but between two or more documents. For instance, you can cut text from one document, switch to a second, and then paste the text into the second document. Chapter 10 describes how to switch between multiple documents in WordPerfect. Moreover, because the Clipboard is created by Windows, you can work with the Clipboard between applications. For instance, you can cut text from a WordPerfect document, switch to a different word processor or to a spreadsheet like Lotus 1-2-3, and then paste the text. Chapter 16 discusses how to work between multiple applications.

There is another method for moving text to different locations within a WordPerfect document. Instead of cutting and pasting, you can use the Undelete feature, which was described in Chapter 3. Since the Undelete feature lets you restore text anywhere in your document, use this feature to move text as follows: delete the text using any of the standard deletion methods (for instance, select the text and press (BACKSPACE)), reposition the insertion point where you want to insert the deleted text, and choose <u>E</u>dit, Un<u>d</u>elete.

Keep in mind that deleting text is a very different operation than cutting text. Deleted text is stored in a different place in your computer; not in the Clipboard. If you delete text, reposition the insertion point and use the Undelete feature to restore it. If you cut text, reposition the insertion point and use the Paste feature—not the Undelete feature—to restore it. (As described in Chapter 3, you can restore text to its *original* location—as long as the deletion or cut was the last thing you did to your document—with the Undo feature, by choosing E̲dit, U̲ndo.)

Working with Tabular Columns and Rectangles

You can cut, copy, or append not only standard sections of text, but also tabular columns and rectangles. A *tabular column* is a column of text aligned on a tab stop with tabs or indents. A *rectangle* is a rectangular section of text located on lines that end with hard returns. You can rearrange tabular columns or rectangles without disturbing other parts of text on a page. For a tabular column, proceed as follows:

1. Position the insertion point just before the first character in the first line of the tabular column, and select text up to any character in the last line in that column. Here's an example where the goal is to cut the column labeled "Month/Day":

Name	Month/Day	Year	Department
Antonio Abbot	May 31st	1974	Personnel
Lois Chang	April 27th	1980	Sales
Roberto Peña	June 16th	1990	Marketing
Tim Fingerman	May 20th	1990	Sales
Paul McClintock	August 7th	1991	Finance

   (For two or more tabular columns, you can select text up to any character in the last line of the right-most column you wish to select.)

2. Select E̲dit, S̲elect, T̲abular Column. WordPerfect highlights the column(s) and the tab or indent codes that precede it (so that the tabs or indents will be cut or copied along with the column).

Name	Month/Day	Year	Department
Antonio Abbot	May 31st	1974	Personnel
Lois Chang	April 27th	1980	Sales
Roberto Peña	June 16th	1990	Marketing
Tim Fingerman	May 20th	1990	Sales
Paul McClintock	August 7th	1991	Finance

3. Choose E̲dit and then choose Cu̲t, C̲opy, or Appen̲d. Or, you can press (BACKSPACE) or (DEL) if you want simply to delete the column(s).

4. If you choose to cut or copy the column(s), reposition the insertion point where you wish to insert the column(s) and choose Edit, Paste.

Keep in mind that the steps just described are for one or more columns aligned on tab stops, not for text formatted using the Column or Table features (described in Chapter 11).

Working with rectangles is useful when you wish to work with only a portion of a tabular column, with text separated by spaces rather than tabs, or with text combined with graphics created with the Line Draw feature. For a rectangle, proceed as follows:

1. Position the insertion point at one corner of the rectangle (such as the upper left corner) and select text to the opposite corner (the lower right corner). Here's an example where the goal is to cut the number "19" from each entry in the column labeled "Year":

Name	Month/Day	Year	Department
Antonio Abbot	May 31st	1974	Personnel
Lois Chang	April 27th	1980	Sales
Roberto Peña	June 16th	1990	Marketing
Tim Fingerman	May 20th	1990	Sales
Paul McClintock	August 7th	1991	Finance

2. Select Edit, Select, Rectangle. WordPerfect highlights only that rectangle:

Name	Month/Day	Year	Department
Antonio Abbot	May 31st	1974	Personnel
Lois Chang	April 27th	1980	Sales
Roberto Peña	June 16th	1990	Marketing
Tim Fingerman	May 20th	1990	Sales
Paul McClintock	August 7th	1991	Finance

3. Choose Edit and then choose Cut, Copy, or Append. Or, you can press (BACKSPACE) or (DEL) if you want simply to delete the rectangle.

4. If you choose to cut or copy the rectangle, reposition the insertion point where you wish to insert it and choose Edit, Paste.

caution *Be sure to save your document before attempting to edit a tabular column or rectangular section of text. How that text reappears will depend on tab stops and/or margin settings, and you may get unexpected results. If, after you move or copy text, the document is in disarray, you can clear the workspace, recall the document you have just saved to the screen, and try again. (The Undo feature does not work when selecting tabular columns or rectangles.)*

Hands-on Exercise: Cut and Paste Text

 You created a document in Chapter 6 named *finance1.mmo*. Open that file so that you can practice cutting and pasting. The editing that you will perform is illustrated in Figure 8-2. First, change the order of the leading sentence in the second bulleted paragraph.

1. Select the phrase "stands at $159,000" and the blank space that precedes it, as shown here:

```
●     Our debt stands at $159,000 as of December 31st, 10% lower
      than we anticipated.  Financial forecasts project that we'll
      be out of debt within two years.  Here are the debt figures
      (in thousands):
```

2. Select Edit, Cut.
3. Position the insertion point between the date, "December 31st", and the comma that follows the date.
4. Select Edit, Paste.

Now try moving the leading bulleted paragraph down to the bottom of the document. But this time, use shortcut keys.

1. Select the first bulleted paragraph along with the hard returns that follow it, as shown here:

```
●     He is meeting with a venture capitalist next week who is
      interested in investing with us.
```

8

Figure 8-2.   *Text to be rearranged in* finance1.mmo

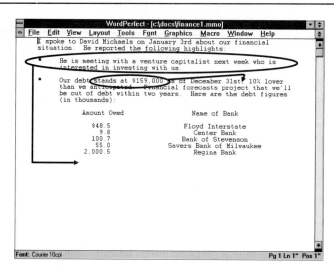

(One quick method is to quadruple-click the paragraph. Or, position the insertion point anywhere in the paragraph and choose Edit, Select, Paragraph.)

2. Press (SHIFT) + (DEL) (or press (CTRL) + (X)).

3. Position the insertion point at the bottom of the document (one quick method is to press (CTRL) + (END)), and press (ENTER) to position the insertion point on a blank line.

4. Press (SHIFT) + (INS) (or press (CTRL) + (V)).

Searching and Replacing

WordPerfect offers two sophisticated features for locating information in your document. The Search feature helps you find a character, phrase, or hidden code. The Replace feature goes one step further than Search, substituting new information for the character, phrase, or hidden code that it finds.

Searching for Text

Searching through the text for a specific character, word, or phrase can be a time-consuming process. Imagine, for instance, needing to reread an entire 50-page report just to find one reference to sales of champagne. Perhaps you want to reference the information provided about champagne. Or you may have new information about champagne sales to add. Rather than scroll through the document yourself, WordPerfect's Search feature can find the phrase "champagne" for you in moments. What you search for is referred to as the *search text* or *search string*, and it can be up to 80 characters in length.

1. Position the insertion point where you want the search to begin.

2. Choose Edit, Search. The Search dialog box appears as shown here:

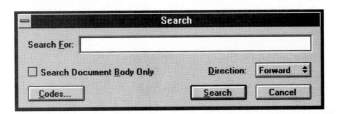

3. In the Search For text box, type the search string you wish to find.

4. If you wish to change the search direction, select Forward or Backward from the Direction pop-up list box.

5. If you wish to limit the search to the main text of the document, turn on the Search Document Body Only check box. If you wish to search not only the main text but also headers, footers, footnotes, endnotes, graphics box captions, or text boxes in the document, then make sure that this check box has no X in it.

6. Choose Search.

shortcut F2 *is the shortcut for Edit, Search.*

In moments, the insertion point will move just after the first occurrence of the search text and the Search dialog box will close, disappearing from the screen. Or, if the text is not found, WordPerfect will prompt with a message on the status line, such as:

8

```
String not found: champagne
```

The Search dialog box will then close.

Keep in mind that WordPerfect is sensitive to uppercase letters in the search string. An uppercase string will match *only* uppercase in the text, while a lowercase string will match either. For instance, suppose you type "CHAMPAGNE" into the Search For text box. WordPerfect will find "CHAMPAGNE", but will not find "Champagne" or "champagne". However, if you type "champagne" into the Search For text box, then WordPerfect will find any of the three variations. Be careful of typos, though. If the string you typed is "hcampagne", then the word "champagne" would not be found at all in the text.

The search string is retained until you change it again or exit WordPerfect, so you can continue the search easily. To move forward to the next occurrence of the search string, choose Edit, Search Next. To move backward to the previous occurrence of the search string, choose Edit, Search Previous. Until at least one search is attempted where you type a search string into the Search For text box, the Search Next and Search Previous options are unavailable, and are therefore dimmed to gray on the Edit menu.

shortcut   (SHIFT) + (F2) *is the shortcut for* Edit, Search Next
(ALT) + (F2) *is the shortcut for* Edit, Search Previous.

The Search feature can even be used as a timesaver when you are selecting text and know the last phrase, word, or character in the block you wish to select. For instance, suppose you wish to select text starting at the top of a page, up to and including the word "champagne". Position the insertion point at the top of the page and either select the first few characters or press (F8), so that the Select feature is turned on. Then, perform a search for the string "champagne". The text up to and including "champagne" will be highlighted.

Including Codes in a Search String

You can also include codes in a search string. You'll save time by using the Search feature instead of manually hunting for elusive codes in the reveal codes workspace. For instance, you can search for the code that turns on hyphenation: [Hyph On]. You can search for a combination of characters and codes, such as the bullet (•) followed by a tab code: •[Tab]. Or search for the phrase "San Francisco" only when it is flanked by a pair of boldface codes: [Bold On]San Francisco[Bold Off]. After choosing Edit, Search to initiate the search so that the Search dialog box appears on screen, follow these steps to include a code in the search string:

1. Choose Codes. Now, as shown in **Figure 8-3**, a second dialog box—the Codes dialog box—appears on screen.

2. Select (highlight) a code from the Codes dialog box. Codes are listed alphabetically in the Search Codes list box, so to select a code, use the arrow keys or the scroll bar located at the right side of the Search Codes list box. Or, type the first few letters of a code to move directly to the code you wish to select.

    You can also choose Merge Codes to turn on the Merge Codes check box, and then select a merge code. (Merge codes are discussed in Chapter 14.)

3. With a code selected, choose Insert. The code is inserted into the Search For text box.

4. Continue typing the search string, and then execute the search.

shortcut *Double-clicking on a code in the Search Codes list box gives you the same results as selecting a code and choosing Insert.*

Once the Codes dialog box is open, it remains on screen until you close it or execute the search. Therefore, you can insert multiple codes into a search string easily by switching back and forth between the Search dialog box and the Codes dialog box. Click in either dialog box to switch. Or, press (ALT) + (F6). For instance, suppose you wish to search for the phrase "San Francisco" when it is boldfaced. Follow the steps just described to choose "Bold On"; a [Bold On] code is inserted into the Search For text box. Next, type **San Francisco** into the Search For text box. Then, click in the Codes dialog box or press (ALT) + (F6) to make the Codes dialog box active again, so that you can choose "Bold Off". A [Bold Off] code is inserted into the Search For text box. The results in the Search For text box are: [Bold On]San Francisco[Bold Off].

8

Figure 8-3.   *Both the Search and Codes dialog boxes on screen*

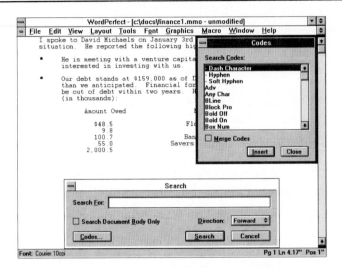

Keep in mind that, while layout codes can be searched for, there's no way to specify a particular parameter within a layout code. For example, you can search for an [L/R Mar] code, which is a generic Left/Right Margin code, but not specifically for a Left/Right Margin code with left/right measurements of 1.5".

note   Appendix B provides a complete list of codes. Refer to it to more easily decipher any unfamiliar codes as you edit your text and include codes in search strings.

One special code in the Search Codes list box is the [Any Char] code, which stands for "any character". This is a wildcard that can be included in the search string to represent either a single character, a space, or a tab. So, for example, the string "wa[Any Char]t" would match "wait", "want", "wart", "watt", "wa t" or "wa[Tab]t". [Any Char] can sit in for any character but the first character in the search string—a wildcard cannot begin a search string. To include a wildcard while typing the search string, follow the steps given earlier and select Any Char from the Search Codes list box.

Replacing Text and/or Codes

The Replace feature is a powerful editing tool. It finds text or codes in your document, and changes them. Depending on how you replace text, it can serve as a straight substitution, an insertion, or a deletion. For example, if you searched for "ABC Company" and replaced it with "XYZ Corporation", that would be a substitution wherever the corporation name appeared. If you searched for "Jack" and replaced it with "Jack F. Johnson", that would be an insertion wherever the name appeared. If you searched for a beginning underline code "[Und On]" and indicated no replacement text, all underlining would be deleted. With the Replace feature, these actions take just moments.

1. Position the insertion point where you want the search to begin.
   Or to search only a section of text in a document, select that text.

2. Choose Edit, Replace. The Search and Replace dialog box appears:

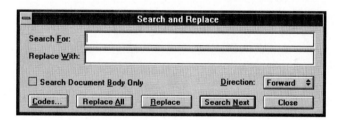

3. In the Search For text box, type the search string you wish to find.

4. In the Replace With text box, type the replacement text. (Leave this text box blank if you want to carry out a deletion.)

5. If you want to change the search direction, select Forward or Backward from the Direction pop-up list box.

6. If you want to limit the search to the main text of the document, turn on the Search Document Body Only check box. When this check box is off, the search extends to headers, footers, footnotes, endnotes, graphics box captions, or text boxes in the document.

7. If you want WordPerfect to replace every occurrence of the search string in a single action, choose Replace All.

8

Or if you want to make changes selectively, choose Search <u>N</u>ext to move to the first occurrence of the search string (in whichever direction selected in step 5). Next either choose <u>R</u>eplace and then Search <u>N</u>ext to replace that single occurrence and continue searching, or simply choose Search <u>N</u>ext to move on to the next occurrence without making a replacement. Continue for all occurrences.

8. Choose Close or press (ESC) to close the Search and Replace dialog box.

shortcut (CTRL) + (F2) *is the shortcut for <u>E</u>dit, <u>R</u>eplace.*

Like the Search feature, the Replace feature is case sensitive. An uppercase search string will match *only* uppercase letters in the text, while a lowercase string will match either. Also, if a word in the search string contains a capitalized letter (as in "Jack"), the replacement word will be capitalized the same way.

Again like the Search feature, the Replace feature lets you include codes in either the search string or in the replacement string, including the [Any Char] code as a wildcard. But, fewer codes can be included. For instance, you cannot include layout codes in the replacement string because there is no method for specifying a measurement, such as left/right margins of 1.5". When you attempt to insert such a code, a message box appears to inform you that it cannot be included.

caution *When you execute a search and replace by choosing Replace <u>A</u>ll, WordPerfect changes every occurrence of a string, even if it's part of another word; the results may surprise you. For instance, if you replace all occurrences of "pen" with "ballpoint", you'd also change "pencil" to "ballpointcil" and you'd swap "indispensable" for "indisballpointsable". You could search for "pen" both preceded and followed by a blank space. But then WordPerfect wouldn't find the word if, for instance, it were preceded by a tab code at the beginning of a paragraph or followed by a punctuation mark at the end of a sentence. The safest method for replacing a fairly common character string is to execute the search and replace selectively with Search <u>N</u>ext and <u>R</u>eplace.*

Hands-on Exercise: Replace Text

The document *finance1.mmo* should still appear on screen. Notice in that document that the word "financial" appears twice. Suppose you wish to change that word to "monetary".

1. Position the insertion point at the top of the document.
2. Choose <u>E</u>dit, <u>R</u>eplace (or press (CTRL) + (F2)). The Replace dialog box appears.
3. In the Search <u>F</u>or text box, type **financial**. (Type the word in lowercase letters to make sure that all occurrences are found.)
4. Choose Replace <u>W</u>ith, and type **monetary**.
5. The <u>D</u>irection pop-up list box should indicate a forward search. If not, choose <u>D</u>irection and select Forward.
6. Choose Replace <u>A</u>ll.
7. Choose Close (or press (ESC)).

When you move up to the top of the document, you'll notice that the word "monetary" appears twice. WordPerfect properly capitalized the word in the second occurrence, to start the sentence "Monetary forecasts...", because the word "Financial" had been capitalized previously.

Comparing Documents After Editing

WordPerfect offers a feature called Document Compare in which any editing changes made to a document on screen can be compared to the original version on disk. Perhaps you are part of a work group, where one person writes the draft version and several others make suggestions for revisions. The Document Compare feature lets you compare the revised

8

article, report, or contract with the draft version. The documents are compared phrase by phrase. A *phrase* here is defined as text between punctuation marks (such as a period, colon, question mark, exclamation point, or comma), hard return codes, hard page codes, footnote and endnote codes, and the end of the document.

Added phrases on screen are *redlined*: this means that the codes [Redln On] and [Redln Off] are inserted around the added text, so that on screen, the phrase appears in red. At the printer, the phrase may appear in shading, as a vertical bar in the left margin, or in a different color. How redline appears on the printed page depends on your printer. For more on redlining, see Chapter 5.

Deleted phrases are recalled onto the screen and marked with strikeout; the codes [Stkout On] and [Stkout Off] are inserted around the deleted phrases. A line is drawn through the phrases, both on the screen and at the printer.

Moved phrases are bordered by two messages. "THE FOLLOWING TEXT WAS MOVED" is inserted before the phrase, and "THE PRECEDING TEXT WAS MOVED" is inserted after the phrase.

To compare the current document with another document on disk, follow these steps:

1. Make sure that the edited document is on screen.

2. Choose Tools, Document Compare, Add Markings. The Add Markings dialog box appears:

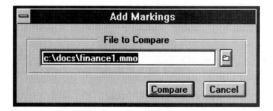

If the document on screen has previously been saved, its filename is automatically suggested in the File to Compare text box.

3. To accept the suggestion that the document on screen be compared with the original version on disk, choose Compare.

You can also type the filename of a different document and choose <u>C</u>ompare. If you don't remember the filename of the document on disk, click the file button, the button with the picture of the file folder located to the right of the File to Compare text box. A Select List dialog box displays so that you can scroll through a list of directories and files—just like in the Open File dialog box—to find the one you want. Select (highlight) the file, and choose OK.

WordPerfect compares the documents and, after a few moments, marks the onscreen document. An example of the result (after it is printed) is shown in Figure 8-4.

After WordPerfect has compared two documents, you have a variety of options. First, you can simply print out the result. That way you can see the

Figure 8-4. *Printed document showing redline and strikeout after comparison to previous draft*

I spoke to David Michaels on January 3rd about our monetary
situation. ~~I spoke to David Michaels on January 3rd about our~~
~~financial situation.~~ He reported the following highlights:

•   Our debt as of December 31st stands at $159,000, 10% lower
     than we anticipated. Monetary forecasts project that we'll
     be out of debt within two years. ~~Financial forecasts~~
     ~~project that we'll be out of debt within two years.~~ Here
     are the debt figures (in thousands):

              Amount Owed   Name of Bank

                 $48.5   Floyd Interstate
                   9.8   Center Bank
                 100.7   Bank of Stevenson
                  55.0   Savers Bank of Milwaukee
               2,000.5   Regina Bank

~~THE FOLLOWING TEXT WAS MOVED~~
•   He is meeting with a venture capitalist next week who is
     interested in investing with us.

     ~~•   Our debt stands at $159,000 as of December 31st,~~
~~THE PRECEDING TEXT WAS MOVED~~

8

changes clearly and can even solicit suggestions for the final version of your document by distributing the printed text.

Second, you can move the insertion point to each revised phrase in the text and decide which version of the phrase you prefer. (The Search feature is convenient for moving to each [Redln On] or [Stkout On] code.) When you delete the text you don't want, be sure to also delete the accompanying Redline or Strikeout codes.

Third, you can request that WordPerfect either restores the document on screen to the way it was before you initiated the Document Compare feature, or restores it while maintaining the redline markings. By leaving the redline markings in the document, you will have a version that marks only the added phrases (and does not display in strikeout the text that has been deleted). Follow these steps:

1. Choose Tools, Document Compare, Remove Markings. The Remove Markings dialog box appears:

2. To remove all markings (including Redline and Strikeout codes you may have inserted manually), choose OK.

   You can also remove all but the redline markings by turning on the Leave Redline Marks check box and then choosing OK.

Inserting Comments

Using the Comments feature, you can type notes that will appear in a shaded box on screen, but will not appear on the printed page. It's a convenient way to leave a reminder to yourself or someone else who will be viewing this document on screen. For instance, in a draft document, you can insert comments containing questions that you'd like to resolve later.

The Comments feature is also handy for indicating what information should be typed at a specific location in a document; such as in a form that you designed and that other people will be filling out on screen. To insert a document comment, follow these steps:

1. Position the insertion point where you want the comment to appear.

2. Choose Tools, Comment, Create. The Create Comment dialog box displays as shown here:

3. Type the text of your comment, using the Bold, Underline, and Italic command buttons to turn on or off these font attributes if you so desire.

4. Choose OK.

The comment appears as a shaded box with rounded edges on screen. An example is shown in Figure 8-5. Behind the scenes, a [Comment] code is inserted—which can be viewed if you switch to the reveal codes workspace.

A comment can be deceiving. While it may occupy numerous lines on screen, it is always considered a single code. Therefore, you can use the arrow keys to pass over the comment in one keystroke. If the [Comment] code is positioned in the middle of a line of text, the comment will divide that line on screen (as in Figure 8-5), but not affect the text at the printer since it occupies no space at all in the actual printed document.

You cannot edit the contents of a comment within the document workspace, but must redisplay the dialog box that contains the contents of the comment. To edit a comment, it is best to position the insertion point just below the comment; WordPerfect searches backward first to locate the

8

F*i*gure 8-5.   *A comment appears as a shaded box with rounded edges*

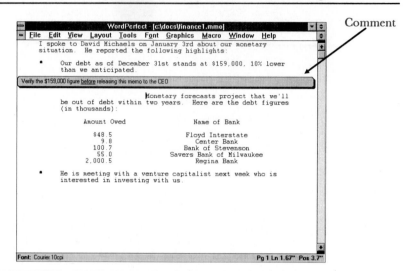

comment, and searches forward only after no comment is found in the backward direction. After positioning the insertion point, choose Tools, Comment, Edit. The comment is redisplayed in a dialog box, which is identical to the Create Comment dialog box except that the title bar reads "Edit Comment". Choose OK when you are finished editing the comment.

shortcut *Double-clicking a comment is the shortcut for Tools, Comment, Edit.*

You can also convert the contents of a comment box into regular text. This would be useful, for instance, if you created a comment that you now wish to include as part of the document, or that you now wish to print out. (Remember that comments don't print.) Position the insertion point below the comment and choose Tools, Comment, Convert to Text. The shaded comment box disappears, while its contents are incorporated into the document as regular text.

Conversely, you can convert a section of text into a comment. Perhaps you typed text into a document that you want to save as part of the document but don't wish to print. Select the text that you wish to convert into a comment and choose Tools, Comment, Create.

There are two methods for removing comments, along with their contents, from your text. If you wish to erase a comment permanently, choose View, Reveal Codes to switch to the reveal codes workspace and find the [Comment] code (or you can use the Search feature to do so), and then delete the code. If you wish to hide all comments temporarily (for example, if you wanted to edit a document without the distraction of comments or to see exactly how it will print without the comments), choose View, Comments. The comments are hidden from view. Choose View, Comments again when you're ready to redisplay the comments.

Hands-on Exercise: Add a Comment

To create a comment like the one shown in Figure 8-5, follow these steps:

1. Position the insertion point before the sentence that starts "Monetary forecasts project that we'll...."

2. Choose Tools, Comment, Create.

3. Type **Verify the $159,000 figure**, choose Underline, type **before**, choose Underline to turn off underlining, and type **releasing this memo to the CEO**.

4. Choose OK.

If the comment does not appear on screen, then comments may be hidden from view; choose View, Comments.

Converting Between Uppercase and Lowercase

Once you've typed text on screen, you can have WordPerfect switch the text's case for you, without any retyping. For instance, suppose that you

8

inadvertently press (CAPS LOCK) and type a full sentence before you realize that all the letters are in uppercase. The Convert Case feature can switch those letters to lowercase. The Convert Case feature works on selected text, as shown in these steps:

1. Select the text to be converted.

2. Choose Edit, Convert Case, and then choose Uppercase or Lowercase.

3. Click the mouse button or press an arrow key to turn off the Select feature.

WordPerfect is case sensitive, so if you select lowercase, it still keeps the following in uppercase: "I"; contractions with "I" such as "I'll" and "I've"; and the first word of a sentence. However, WordPerfect recognizes the first word of a sentence only if you include the ending punctuation mark (such as a period) from the preceding sentence in the selected text. Be sure to include the ending punctuation from the previous sentence when you are converting a sentence to lowercase so that the first word remains capitalized.

Inserting the Date

As long as the date is kept current on your computer, the Date feature can automatically insert the date for you. To insert today's date as regular text, simply follow these steps:

1. Position the insertion point where you want to type the date.

2. Choose Tools, Date, Text. The date is inserted as "Month Day, Year", as in January 13, 1993.

shortcut (CTRL) + (F5) *is the shortcut for* Tools, Date, Text.

The date is inserted as text just as if you typed it yourself—only faster. You can edit or delete the date just like text.

As an alternative, you can insert today's date as a code. If inserted as a code, the date will *change* each time you open the document or print it. For instance, if you insert a date code in your document today, it will display today's date. If you use that same document tomorrow, it will display tomorrow's date. If you print out the document in a year, it will print next year's date. The date code is useful when creating a form letter that you send out periodically and want updated with the current date. But it is not useful when you wish to stamp a document on a certain date and maintain that date as part of a permanent record. Follow these steps to insert the date as a code:

1. Position the insertion point where you want to insert the date code.

2. Choose <u>T</u>ools, <u>D</u>ate, <u>C</u>ode. In the document workspace, the date is inserted as "Month Day, Year", as in the example January 13, 1993. If you use the reveal codes workspace, however, you will see that the code inserted is [Date: Month DayofMon, Yr<4>].

shortcut (CTRL) + (SHIFT) + (F5) *is the shortcut for* <u>T</u>ools, <u>D</u>ate, <u>C</u>ode.

You also have the option of changing the way that the Date is displayed—from the "Month Day, Year" format to something else. Follow these steps:

1. Choose <u>T</u>ools, <u>D</u>ate, <u>F</u>ormat. The Document Date/Time Format dialog box appears as shown here:

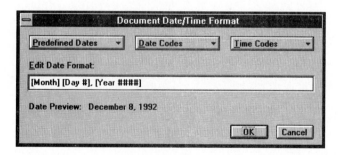

Notice that next to the heading "Date Preview" is an example of how the currently selected date format will appear in your document.

2. Choose an option from the <u>P</u>redefined Dates pop-up list box.
   You can also create a custom date format by combining codes from the <u>D</u>ate Codes pop-up list box and the <u>T</u>ime Codes pop-up

list box. You can separate the codes with words, letters, spaces, commas, colons, or dashes. Numbers and certain symbols (such as $ or %) are not allowed.

3. Select OK.

Once you change the date format, this new format will appear each time you use the Date feature from then on for the rest of the work session—whether you insert the date as text or as a code. A change in the date format will have no effect, however, on preexisting date text or codes.

The Predefined Dates pop-up list box contains the following date format options:

March 4, 1992   Wednesday, March 4, 1992
Mar 4, 1992   Wednesday, 4 March, 1992
4 March, 1992   3/4/92

Here's just one example of a custom format that you can create; it is functional for documents that need to be both time- and date-stamped:

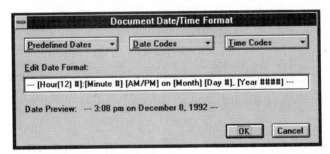

Keep in mind that WordPerfect does not set the date and time. It is your computer clock that keeps track of the date and time. If the date and/or time are incorrect, you can reset them using the Windows Control Panel. (Refer to Chapter 17 for details.) Also see Chapter 17 for information on the File, Preferences, Date Format command, which allows you to edit the date format for all future work sessions in WordPerfect; not just for the current work session.

Hands-on Exercise: Insert the Date

Suppose you wish to insert today's date at the top of the document on screen. You want *today's* date to remain (and not change tomorrow or the next day), so you'll insert the date as text. Watch how quickly the date can be inserted in your document with these steps:

1. Position the insertion point at the top of the document, press (ENTER) twice to insert blank lines, and then move back up to the top of the document.

2. Select Tools, Date, Text (or press (CTRL) + (F5)).

You get the same results as if you typed the date yourself, except that WordPerfect types it much faster.

Since this is the last hands-on exercise in this chapter, save and close *finance1.mmo*.

8

Quick Reference

- To cut a block of text, select the text. Then, choose Edit, Cut, or press (CTRL) + (X), or press (SHIFT) + (DEL). The text is removed and placed on the Clipboard—a temporary storage facility.

- To copy a block of text, select the text. Then, choose Edit, Copy, or press (CTRL) + (C), or press (CTRL) + (INS). A copy of the text is placed on the Clipboard.

- To append a block of text, select the text. Then, choose Edit, Append. A copy of the text is added to the contents of the Clipboard.

- To insert the contents of the Clipboard into a document, choose Edit, Paste, or press (CTRL) + (V), or press (SHIFT) + (INS).

- To search for a combination of characters and/or codes in your document, choose Edit, Search or press (F2). Then, type the search text, which is the word or phrase that you wish to search for.

- To replace a combination of characters and/or codes in your document, choose Edit, Replace or press (CTRL) + (F2). Type in the search text and the replacement text.

- To compare a revised document on screen with an original document on disk, choose Tools, Document Compare, Add Markings. Redline codes are inserted around text added to the revision, while Strikeout codes are inserted around text that was deleted.

- To insert a comment into the document that will display but not print, choose Tools, Comment, Create.

- To switch existing text from uppercase to lowercase or vice versa, select the text and choose Edit, Convert Case.

- To insert the date automatically, choose Tools, Date, Text or press (CTRL) + (F5). You can also insert the date as a code in a document that will update whenever you open or print that document; to do so, choose Tools, Date, Code or press (CTRL) + (SHIFT) + (F5).

III

Becoming a Sophisticated User

9

Using the Speller and Thesaurus

WordPerfect offers an on-line Speller and Thesaurus so that you can tap keys rather than lift heavy, hardbound reference books. The Speller can check that the words in your document are spelled correctly. The Thesaurus can help you find just the right word as you're writing a document, and is also useful when you're not sure of the exact meaning of a word. You can even use a Speller and Thesaurus for documents written in another language. A related bonus is the Word Count feature, which WordPerfect uses to count the words in your document for you. All of these features are covered in this chapter.

The Speller

The Speller is a stand-alone application, separate from WordPerfect, that checks for misspelled words in your WordPerfect documents. The Speller compares the spelling of each word in your document with the spellings of those contained in the Speller's *main dictionary*. The main dictionary is actually split into two separate parts: a common word list of 2500 words and a main word list of 115,000 words. The common word list is always checked first, to speed up each spelling check, and the main word list is checked next.

 The filename where the dictionary is stored is called *wp{wp}xx.lex*, where the *xx* is a two-letter *language code* that denotes the language of the dictionary. For instance, if you purchased WordPerfect in the United States, the filename for the main dictionary is *wp{wp}us.lex*. Or, *wp{wp}uk.lex* is the United Kingdom dictionary file, and *wp{wp}fr.lex* is the French dictionary file.

 The main dictionary is fairly comprehensive. In the U.S. main dictionary, for example, it includes some technical terms, such as "endocrinology", and some proper nouns, such as "John" and "Smith". But, a main dictionary by no means contains every word in the language. Therefore, the Speller gives you the opportunity during a spell-check to add words. The words are added to a separate dictionary, called a *supplementary dictionary*. For instance, you may wish to add your company's name or certain technical words used in your business. Once you add them, the Speller will recognize these words every time you spell-check. The supplementary dictionary works in conjunction with the main dictionary, and is stored in a file named *wp{wp}xx.sup*, where again, *xx* is a language code.

Spell-Checking a Document

 Whenever you use the Speller, a Speller window appears near the bottom of the screen.

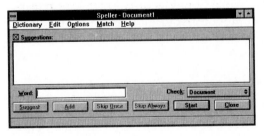

 Notice that the Speller window has some of the same elements as the WordPerfect window, including a menu bar and resizing buttons. It also has a check box, a text box, a pop-up list box, and command buttons, as dialog boxes do.

The default Speller option is to spell-check an entire document. The Speller checks not only the main text, but also any headers, footers, footnotes, endnotes, figure captions, or text boxes in that document—looking for words that don't appear in the main or supplementary dictionaries. (You can also specify that the spell-check only cover parts of your document—such as the main text. You'll learn how to do this in the "Checking Part of a Document" section, later in this chapter.) In addition to checking your spellings against its dictionaries, the Speller also looks for words containing numbers, two occurrences of the same word in a row, such as "the the", and for certain capitalization errors. To perform a spell-check, follow these steps:

1. Make sure the document you want to check is on screen.

2. Choose Tools, Speller. The Speller window appears. The option "Document" is automatically selected on the Check pop-up list box. This signifies that WordPerfect will spell-check the entire document.

3. Choose Start. The Speller checks each word to the end of the document.

    When a word in your document is not found in the main or supplementary dictionary, the Speller stops. The word is highlighted in reverse video and listed as not found at the bottom of the speller window, as "tenty" is in Figure 9-1. If the Suggestions check box is turned on, as is the case in Figure 9-1, suggested replacements are provided for the misspelled word in the Suggestions list box. No suggestions are offered if the check box is off. (Turning off the Suggestions check box before you begin a spell-check makes the spell-checking process quicker because you edit the words yourself rather than waiting for the Speller to offer potential replacements.)

4. Choose one of the Speller's suggested replacements or choose another option from the Speller window (your choices at this stage will be detailed in the next section).

    Or, you can temporarily switch to the document window. Click anywhere in the document workspace; edit the misspelled word yourself (and any other text); click in the Speller window to make

9

the Speller active again; and choose <u>R</u>esume to continue the spell-check from the insertion point's location forward.

5. The Speller continues checking words until the entire document is checked and you respond to each occurrence of a word not found in the dictionary. Then, a Speller dialog box appears to inform you that the spell-check is complete.

6. Choose OK from the dialog box.

7. Choose <u>C</u>lose to close the Speller window. You can also close the window by double-clicking the Speller control-menu box or pressing (ALT) + (F4).

Or, you can keep the Speller window open on screen if you plan to perform another spell-check momentarily. Click in the document workspace to make the document window active, edit the current document or open another document, and then click in the Speller window when you're ready to perform another spell-check.

shortcut (CTRL) + (F1) *is the shortcut for* <u>T</u>ools, <u>S</u>peller.

Figure 9-1. *The Speller suggests replacements for "tenty"*

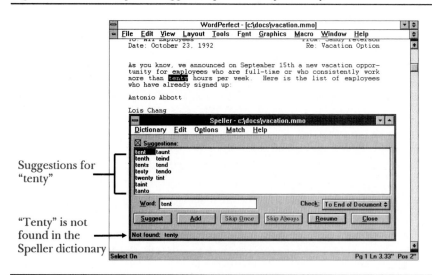

Suggestions for "tenty"

"Tenty" is not found in the Speller dictionary

Once a spell-check is complete and words have been corrected, you can't undo the changes. Therefore, it's a good idea to save a document before you perform a spell-check on it.

Keep in mind that the Speller and the Speller's main dictionary need to be installed properly before you can use them. (Installation procedures are provided in Appendix A.) Once the Speller and main dictionary are installed, they are stored in the same directory where other shared WordPerfect products are stored, *c:\wpc* (unless you store it in another directory).

The Speller program is a file named *spwin.exe*. If WordPerfect cannot locate the Speller when you choose <u>T</u>ools, <u>S</u>peller, it displays a dialog box with the message "Unable to locate Speller". In that event, type the full path for the Speller. For instance, if the speller has been installed in the directory *c:\wpc*, then type **c:\wpc\spwin.exe** and choose <u>R</u>un to load the Speller and display the Speller window.

The main dictionary is *wp{wp}xx.lex*, where *xx* is the language code, as previously described. If WordPerfect cannot locate the main dictionary, a dialog box appears for you to type the full path for the main dictionary. For instance, if the main dictionary is the U.S. English version and has been installed in the directory *c:\wpc*, type **c:\wpc\wp{wp}us.lex** and choose OK. (You can avoid this problem in the future by specifying where the main dictionary is located with <u>F</u>ile, Pre<u>f</u>erences, <u>L</u>ocation of Files, as described in Chapter 17.)

Responding to the Speller

How you respond to the Speller in step 4 of the previous procedure depends on the word that is highlighted as not found in the Speller's dictionaries. When the word is misspelled and the Speller gives the appropriate replacement in the Su<u>g</u>gestions list box, simply select (highlight) the word and choose <u>R</u>eplace.

shortcut *If you double-click a replacement word in the Su<u>g</u>gestions list box, that is equivalent to selecting the word and choosing <u>R</u>eplace.*

9

If the Su<u>g</u>gestions check box is off, choose the <u>S</u>uggest command button so that the Speller provides a list of possible replacements.

When the word is misspelled but the Speller has not suggested the appropriate replacement, type the correct replacement into the W̲ord text box and choose R̲eplace. A second alternative is to type a word pattern into the W̲ord text box using wildcard characters and then choose S̲uggest. This elicits new suggestions from which you can select a replacement. In a *word pattern,* the question mark (?) represents one character, while the asterisk (*) represents any number of characters (zero or more). So, for instance, typing "hippo*" will help if you can't remember how to spell "hippopotamus". Use "r?p?t?tion" when you can't remember the first three vowels in the word "repetition". A third alternative is to type into the W̲ord text box how a word sounds and then choose S̲uggest. This elicits other suggestions. For instance, typing "sinomon" will help you discover how to spell "cinnamon". And "fobea" will lead to several suggestions, including "phobia".

When the Speller stops at a word that is correctly spelled (but not in one of the Speller's dictionaries), you can choose Skip O̲nce to pass over that particular instance of the word. You can also Choose Skip A̲lways to pass over the word every time it occurs during the spell-check you're currently performing. A third alternative is to choose A̲dd to insert that word into your supplementary dictionary, so that the Speller recognizes it as a correctly spelled word in every spell-check from then on. (However, note that words added to the supplementary dictionary are never provided when the Speller lists suggested replacement words.) This last alternative is useful, for instance, when you wish to add your own name or your company's name to the supplementary dictionary.

During a spell-check, the Speller also checks for two words in a row, such as "the the". If it finds back-to-back occurrences of a word, the Speller dialog box appears.

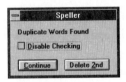

You can choose from this dialog box to: C̲ontinue, which leaves both words as they are in the document; or Delete 2̲nd, in which the second occurrence of the word is deleted. Moreover, if you wish to have the Speller ignore duplicate words for the remainder of the spell-check, select Disable Checking to turn on this check box before you choose Continue or Delete 2nd.

The Speller also checks for irregular capitalization, which is unusual instances of upper- and lowercase in the first three letters of a word (or in all the letters if there are three or fewer letters in the word). Table 9-1 shows examples of the five types of capitalization errors and how the Speller would correct them when instructed to do so. If the Speller finds irregular capitalization, a Speller dialog box appears.

You can choose from this dialog box to: Continue, which leaves the capitalization as it is; or Replace, in which the Speller corrects the word according to the pattern shown in Table 9-1. Moreover, if you wish to have the Speller ignore irregular capitalization for the remainder of the spell-check, select Disable Checking to turn on this check box before you choose Continue or Replace.

Table 9-1. *The Speller Can Find and Correct a Capitalization Error*

Irregular Capitalization	Speller Correction
WOrd	Word
wOrd	Word
wORD	WORD
woRd	word
iT	It

9

Checking Part of a Document

Unless you specify otherwise, the Speller will check an entire document. The option "Document" will automatically display on the Check pop-up list box when you first open the Speller window.

You can instead spell-check just a section of text. To do so, select the text before you choose Tools, Speller. When the Speller window opens, the option "Selected Text" will automatically appear on the Check pop-up list box. Proceed with the spell-check as usual. Only the selected text will be spell-checked.

You can also spell-check a word, a page, or to the end of a specified section of your text. To see your options for spell-checking parts of a document, position the insertion point, choose Tools, Speller to open the Speller, and then choose the option you want from the Check pop-up list box. The other options include:

- *Word* or *Page* spell-checks the word or page where the insertion point is located.

- *End of Page, Document,* or *Selection* spell-checks from the insertion point to the end of the page or document, or to the end of the text originally selected.

Finally, you can spell-check a header, footer, footnote, endnote, graphics caption, or text box independent of the main text of your document. To do so, open the Speller after displaying the text of the header or footer or footnote (and so on) on screen.

The Speller Menu Bar

The Speller window contains a menu bar listing five menus with features for changing the way the Speller operates or assisting you in using the Speller.

The first menu, Dictionary, lets you specify a different main or supplementary dictionary. After you open the Speller, but before you begin a spell-check, specify which dictionary you want the Speller to use for that spell-check. A different main dictionary can be one you purchased in a different language, such as *wp{wp}fr.lex* if you purchased the French language module from WordPerfect Corporation. The name of the dictionary will be listed in the documentation that comes with the dictionary. (More information on working in another language is provided farther on in this chapter.) A different supplementary dictionary can be one that you created. (See more on supplementary dictionaries in the next section.) WordPerfect 5.0 and 5.1 for DOS dictionaries can also be used with the WordPerfect for Windows Speller.

The second menu on the Speller menu bar is Edit. The items on the Edit menu pertain only to the contents of the Word text box. Before or during a spell-check, you can Cut and Copy text from the text box into the Clipboard. Conversely, you can Paste text from the Clipboard into the text box. Select All selects the entire contents of the text box. Undo reverses the last change made in the text box.

The next menu, Options, determines certain aspects of how the Speller will operate. Before you begin a spell-check, you can change any of these options. The options will stay in effect until you close the Speller window. The next time you open the Speller, the Speller's default settings are reinstated. The options include:

- *Words with Numbers*   When this item is off (no check mark next to the menu item), the Speller ignores words with numbers in them. When this item is on, which is the default setting, the Speller checks words containing numbers.

- *Duplicate Words*   When this item is off (no check mark next to the menu item), the Speller always ignores duplicate words like "the the". When this item is on, which is the default setting, the Speller notifies you if the same word is used twice in a row.

- *Irregular Capitalization*   When this item is off (no check mark next to the menu item), the Speller ignores instances of irregular capitalization. When this item is on, which is the default setting, the Speller looks at the first three letters of words (or all of them if the word has three or fewer letters) to check for capitalization errors. Table 9-1 shows examples of the five types of errors and how the Speller would correct them.

- *Move to Bottom*   Choose this item to move the Speller window to the bottom of the screen, in order to see more of your document while spell-checking.

9

The Match menu inserts wildcard characters into the Word text box when you are typing a word pattern such as "hippo*" or "r?p?t?tion". These wildcard characters can be typed from the keyboard using a question mark (?) to represent one character, or an asterisk (*) to represent multiple characters. (If you're unsure of how to do this, refer to the "Responding to the Speller" section earlier in this chapter.) If you forget which symbol to use, you can instead choose 1 Character or Multiple Characters, and the question mark or asterisk will be inserted into the Word text box for you.

The Help menu, the last item on the Speller menu bar, provides assistance on using the Speller just like the Help menu of the WordPerfect menu bar provides assistance on using WordPerfect. See Appendix C for detailed information on using the WordPerfect Help feature. The Speller Help feature works in the same way.

Working with Supplementary Dictionaries

Technically, when you use the Add option to add a word to the supplementary dictionary during a spell-check, WordPerfect places that word in the computer's memory (RAM) until the spell-check is complete. Then, all the words in memory are copied to *wp{wp}xx.sup*, such as to *wp{wp}us.sup* when using the U.S. English dictionaries. There may be instances when you try to add a word to the supplementary dictionary and WordPerfect prompts "Dictionary Full". If this happens, end the spell-check by closing the Speller window. The words will be copied to the supplementary dictionary. Then, to spell-check the remainder of the document, open the Speller window and either choose To End of Document from the Check pop-up list box in the Speller window or select the remainder of text and choose Selected Text from the Check pop-up list box. (Later in this chapter you'll learn how to use the Speller Utility if you amass more words in your supplementary dictionary than the computer's memory can hold.)

You can add words to the supplementary dictionary not only during a spell-check, but independent of a spell-check. You can also delete words from the supplementary dictionary, which you will do if you accidentally select the Add option when the Speller is highlighting a word that is misspelled. To add or delete words, open the supplementary dictionary file just as you would a document. The file *wp{wp}xx.sup* is usually in the same directory as the main dictionary which, unless changed, is stored in *c:\wpc*. So, for instance, when using the U.S. English version of WordPerfect, open *c:\wpc\wp{wp}us.sup*.

Once you open the supplementary dictionary, you'll notice that all the words in it are alphabetized, and that each word is on its own line in lowercase. To remove a word, select the word and the hard return that follows it, and press (DEL). To add a word, position the insertion point at the beginning of the line where the word should appear, type the word, and then press (ENTER) to insert a hard return. Once you've edited the supplementary dictionary, save and close the file.

caution *Do not try this method with the main dictionary. Also, do not try this with the supplementary dictionary if it has been compressed. See the section later in this chapter on the Speller Utility for information regarding ways to add or delete words from the main or from supplementary dictionaries that have been compressed.*

You can also create and use supplementary dictionaries other than *wp{wp}xx.sup*. Separate supplementary dictionaries are convenient if you work with different types of documents. For instance, you can create one to spell-check legal documents in which you store correct spellings of legal terms, and create another to spell-check personal documents in which you store correct names of friends and family or towns where they live. To create a new supplementary dictionary, start with a clear document window. Type each word on a separate line. Then save this file using a name that reminds you of its contents, such as *legal.sup*. Save this file in the same location as *wp{wp}xx.sup*, which is usually *c:\wpc*. Then, when you're ready to use another supplementary dictionary, choose Dictionary, Supplementary from the Speller's menu bar and type in the name, such as *legal.sup*, before you begin the spell-check.

Understanding the Speller's Limitations

Keep in mind that using the Speller is no substitute for a final proofreading because it cannot catch grammatical errors. For instance, it cannot check for homonyms such as "no" and "know" or "see" and "sea". So, for example, suppose one sentence in your document reads:

```
I hope to sea you soon.
```

9

WordPerfect won't pause during the spell-check, even though the sentence should read "*see* you soon".

Nor can WordPerfect figure out whether a sentence makes sense. For instance, suppose your document contained the following sentence:

```
We hope to distribute bonus cheeks by Friday.
```

Since "cheeks" is a word found in the dictionary, WordPerfect won't pause during the spell-check to alert you to this problem, even though the sentence should read ". . . bonus *checks* by Friday".

Hands-on Exercise: Use the Speller

 Let's spell-check the document named *vacation.mmo,* which you created in Chapter 6. Open this file. It is a one-page memorandum, so the result will be the same whether you spell-check the document or a page.

To make the spell-check more interesting, purposely misspell some words:

- Near the top of the memo, remove the "i" in "Option".
- In the first full paragraph, remove the "w" in "twenty".
- In the last paragraph, remove the "w" in "wish".

Then begin the spell-check, by following these steps:

1. Choose Tools, Speller or press (CTRL) + (F1).
2. If the Suggestions check box is off, choose Suggestions to turn it on.
3. Choose Start to begin the spell-check. Or press (ENTER), since the Start command button is preselected.

    The Speller highlights "opton" and offers suggestions; the suggested replacement word, "option", is preselected.
4. Double-click "option". Or, choose Replace. Or press (ENTER), since the Replace command button is preselected. The word is replaced.

The Speller continues, stopping to highlight "tenty" and offer suggestions.

5. Select (highlight) the word "twenty", and then double-click or choose <u>R</u>eplace. The word is replaced, and the Speller continues, stopping to highlight "Abbott".

6. Choose Skip <u>O</u>nce or choose Skip A<u>l</u>ways (in this case each gives you the same results since the proper name "Abbott" appears only once in the document anyway). "Abbott" is left intact, and the Speller highlights "Chang".

7. Choose Skip <u>O</u>nce. The Speller highlights "Fingerman".

8. Choose Skip <u>O</u>nce. The Speller highlights "McClintock". Suppose that Paul McClintock's name appears frequently in documents that you type. It makes sense, therefore, to add his name to the supplementary dictionary.

9. Choose <u>A</u>dd. "McClintock" remains intact, and is added to the supplementary dictionary. The Speller continues, stopping to highlight "ish". The appropriate replacement is not among those suggested.

10. Choose <u>W</u>ord, type **wish** in the <u>W</u>ord text box, and choose <u>R</u>eplace. The Speller continues, stopping to highlight "30th".

11. Choose Skip <u>O</u>nce. A dialog box appears indicating that the spell-check has been completed.

12. Choose OK and then choose <u>C</u>lose to close the Speller window.

The Speller Utility

WordPerfect provides a separate application that can help you manage the words in the Speller dictionary. You can add or delete words, display words in the common word list, or check to see if a word is in the main dictionary. You can also create your own dictionary.

One of the important features of the Speller Utility is the ability to transfer the words you created during a spell-check from the supplementary dictionary

9

to the main dictionary. In general, this will be necessary only if you compile so many words in the supplementary dictionary that, when you attempt to add another word, the message "Dictionary Full" appears on screen during a spell-check. You could add these supplementary words to the main dictionary and then begin a new supplementary dictionary.

If you are under a time constraint, don't use the Speller Utility. Adding or deleting just a few words from the dictionary can take several or many minutes. Also you want to make sure that you don't accidentally erase part of the dictionary when shuffling words. In general, you will rarely (if ever) need to use the utility.

The Speller Utility is a non-Windows application and cannot be accessed directly from within WordPerfect. Instead, you can switch from WordPerfect into the File Manager, an application that lets you organize files (described in Chapter 16), and then load the Speller Utility, which is a file named *spell.exe.* (You must install the Speller Utility before you can use it; see Appendix A if you haven't yet installed utility files.)

To run the Speller Utility, follow these steps:

1. In WordPerfect, Choose File, File Manager. In moments, the File Manager will appear on screen.

2. Choose File, Run.

3. Type **c:\wpc\spell.exe** if the Speller Utility was installed in *c:\wpc.* (It is typically installed along with the Speller.) Or, type in another path.

In a few moments, you'll see the Speller Utility main menu, as shown in Figure 9-2. This Speller Utility is identical to the one packaged with Word-Perfect 5.1 for DOS. Notice that the upper right corner in Figure 9-2 says "WP{WP}US.LEX". This means that the menu items listed currently pertain to the main U.S. English dictionary. (If the main dictionary is not stored in the same directory as WordPerfect, a message displays asking whether you wish to create *wp{wp}us.lex.* In that case, choose "No" by typing **n**, and then enter the complete path where the main dictionary can be found—usually *c:\wpc\wp{wp}us.lex.* Then the Speller Utility main menu will appear.)

Figure 9-2.   *Speller Utility main menu*

```
┌─Spell — WordPerfect Speller Utility                        WP{WP}US.LEX─┐
│0 - Exit                                                                 │
│1 - Change/Create Dictionary                                             │
│2 - Add Words to Dictionary                                              │
│3 - Delete Words from Dictionary                                         │
│4 - Optimize Dictionary                                                  │
│5 - Display Common Word List                                             │
│6 - Check Location of a Word                                             │
│7 - Look Up                                                              │
│8 - Phonetic Look Up                                                     │
│9 - Convert 4.2 Dictionary to 5.1                                        │
│A - Combine Other 5.0 or 5.1 Dictionary                                  │
│B - Compress/Expand Supplemental Dictionary                             │
│C - Extract Added Words from Wordlist-based Dictionary                   │
│                                                                         │
│Selection:                                                               │
│                                                                         │
│                                                                         │
│                                                                         │
└─────────────────────────────────────────────────────────────────────────┘
```

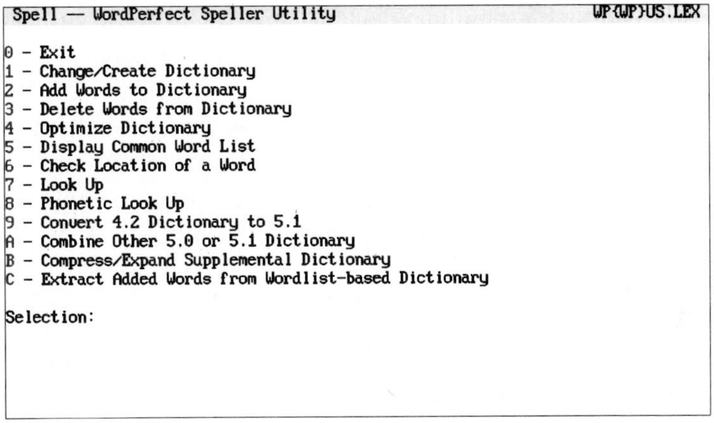

The options on the Speller Utility main menu are described below. When you wish to backtrack and return to the main menu after selecting an option, press (F1).

- *Exit (0)* returns you to the File Manager after you've finished using the Speller Utility. Exit the File Manager by choosing F̲ile, E̲xit or pressing (ALT) + (F4), or double-clicking the File Manager application control-menu box. You are returned to WordPerfect.

- *Change/Create Dictionary (1)* switches you from *wp{wp}us.lex* (assuming the U.S. English dictionary) to another dictionary. If the filename of that dictionary is not found on disk, WordPerfect asks whether you wish to create a new dictionary with the name indicated. Type **y** for "Yes" to create it, or type **n** for "No" and then type in the dictionary's full path. Whatever dictionary you specify, the name appears in the upper right corner on screen. This dictionary becomes the current dictionary, the one that the remaining menu items on the Speller Utility will address.

9

- *Add Words to Dictionary (2)* allows you to add words to the compressed portion of the current dictionary. (If the current dictionary is a main dictionary such as *wp{wp}us.lex,* the words will be added to the common word list.) You can add words either by typing the words from the keyboard (pressing (ENTER) after each word) or by transferring them from a file where you already typed the words.

   This option lets you transfer words from your supplementary dictionary (such as *wp{wp}us.sup*) into the main dictionary. Afterward, you would return to WordPerfect and erase the file *wp{wp}us.sup;* WordPerfect would create a new supplementary dictionary the next time you chose <u>A</u>dd during a spell-check.

- *Delete Words from Dictionary (3)* works just like adding words but is used for deleting words.

- *Optimize Dictionary (4)* is used after you've created a dictionary, to *compress* the dictionary. This reduces the amount of disk space required to store the file and makes the dictionary run faster.

- *Display Common Word List (5)* shows the common word list screen by screen. The common word list is part of the main dictionary.

- *Check Location of a Word (6)* allows you to determine whether a word is in the dictionary, and, if so, whether it is in the common word list or the main word list. (This option can be used for the main dictionary only.)

- *Look Up (7)* enables you to look up words in the current dictionary by specifying a word pattern. Use a question mark (?) to represent one character, and the asterisk (*) to represent multiple characters. A list of suggestions that meet the word pattern will be displayed.

- *Phonetic Look Up (8)* enables you to look up words based on a sound pattern, such as "sinomon" to find "cinnamon".

- *Convert 4.2 Dictionary to 5.1 (9)* provides the ability to convert a dictionary you created using WordPerfect version 4.2 for DOS format into 5.1 format. (WordPerfect 5.1 for DOS and WordPerfect 5.0 for DOS dictionaries can be used in WordPerfect for Windows without modification.)

- *Combine Other 5.0 or 5.1 Dictionary (A)* allows you to combine several dictionaries into one. This is especially useful if you often use two languages in your documents and want a dictionary that contains words in both languages.

- *Compress/Expand Supplementary Dictionary (B)* allows you to compress a supplementary dictionary to reduce the amount of disk space required to store the file. Also, if you compress a supplementary dictionary, words in that dictionary will never be ignored if the computer's memory is insufficient. Moreover, words in that dictionary will appear as suggestions during a spell-check. You can also expand a supplementary dictionary—convenient when you wish to open it and edit it just like you would a standard document.

- *Extract Added Words from Wordlist-based Dictionary (C)* lets you change from a word-list dictionary to an *algorithmic* dictionary that uses specific rules rather than word lists to check spelling. Not all of WordPerfect's foreign language dictionaries are algorithmic when first released, but they will become available later on. An algorithmic dictionary can find phonetic matches, and therefore can find more misspelled words than word-list dictionaries. However, algorithmic dictionaries cannot be modified like word-list dictionaries can.

   This option lets you extract words that you previously added to the word-list dictionary when you wish to switch over to using the algorithmic dictionary. When you select this option, the Speller Utility asks you for the name of your word-list dictionary, your algorithmic dictionary, and your supplementary dictionary (where non-matching words will be placed). The Speller Utility then spell-checks the words in the word-list dictionary based on the algorithmic dictionary and adds to the supplementary dictionary any words that are not recognized by the algorithmic dictionary.

The Thesaurus

The Thesaurus is a stand-alone application, separate from WordPerfect, that can provide synonyms and antonyms for over 10,000 words. A *synonym* has the same meaning as the word you're looking up; for instance, a synonym for the word "dark" is "unlit". An *antonym* has the opposite meaning; for instance, an antonym for the word "dark" is "light". The Thesaurus can help you learn the meaning of a word or find another one that fits in better.

Whenever you use the Thesaurus, a Thesaurus window appears near the bottom of the screen.

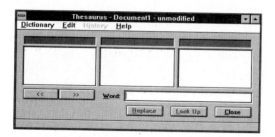

This window has some of the same elements as the WordPerfect window, including a menu bar and resizing buttons. It has list boxes, a text box, and command buttons just as a dialog box does.

Looking Up One Word

Any word that can be looked up in the Thesaurus window is called a *headword*. Synonyms and antonyms for that headword are called *references*. Synonyms are listed first, organized into nouns (n), verbs (v), and adjectives (a). Antonyms (ant) are listed last. To use the Thesaurus, follow these steps:

1. Position the insertion point in the word you wish to look up.

2. Choose Tools, Thesaurus. If the word is a headword, the Thesaurus window appears and references are provided. In Figure 9-3, for instance, the headword is "wish". It is highlighted in the document, appears in the Word text box, and also appears above the first list box. Synonyms and antonyms appear in the list box itself.

    If the word is not a headword, the Thesaurus appears without references, and a message at the bottom of the Thesaurus window indicates that the word is not found. An example is the word "telephone", shown in Figure 9-4.

Figure 9-3. *Thesaurus showing references for the headword "wish"*

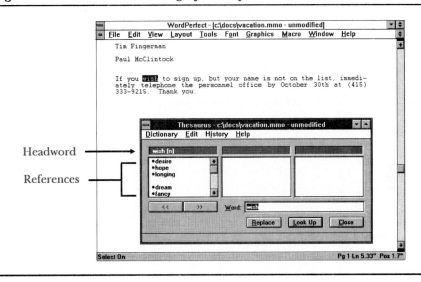

Headword

References

Figure 9-4. *Thesaurus indicating that "telephone" is not a headword*

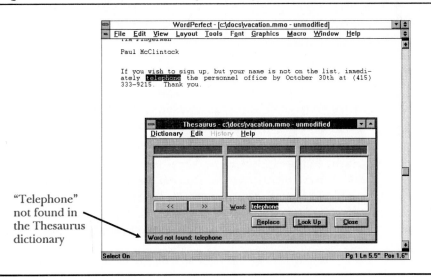

"Telephone"
not found in
the Thesaurus
dictionary

9

If the Thesaurus brings up no references, try again with a new word, by typing that new word into the Word text box and choosing Look Up. If you like you can skip to step 4 to close the Thesaurus.

3. Select (highlight) a reference. (If the number of references is too great to fit in the list box, a vertical scroll bar appears, and you must scroll in order to see the additional references.)

4. Choose Replace to insert the selected reference in place of the original word. The Thesaurus window closes.

    You can also choose Close to close the Thesaurus window without substituting a reference for the original word. Or close the window by double-clicking the Thesaurus control-menu box or by pressing (ALT) + (F4).

    Or, you can temporarily switch to the document window without closing the Thesaurus. Click anywhere in the document workspace; edit text and perform other tasks in your document; click in the Thesaurus window to make the Thesaurus active again; and then continue using the Thesaurus.

shortcut (ALT) + (F1) *is the shortcut for* Tools, Thesaurus.

Keep in mind that the Thesaurus and the Thesaurus dictionary, which is used to provide reference words, need to be installed properly before you can use them. (Installation procedures are provided in Appendix A.) Once the Thesaurus and Thesaurus dictionary are installed, they are stored in the same directory where other shared WordPerfect products are stored— *c:\wpc* (unless you store them in another directory).

The Thesaurus program is stored in a file named *thwin.exe*. If WordPerfect cannot locate the Thesaurus program when you choose Tools, Thesaurus, it displays a dialog box with the message "Unable to locate Thesaurus". In that event, type the full path for the Thesaurus. For instance, if the Thesaurus has been installed in the directory *c:\wpc*, type **c:\wpc\thwin.exe** and choose Run to load the Thesaurus and display the Thesaurus window.

The dictionary is stored in *wp{wp}xx.ths,* where *xx* is the language code, as previously described. If WordPerfect cannot locate the dictionary, a dialog box appears for you to type the full path for the dictionary. For instance, if the dictionary is the U.S. English version and has been installed in the directory *c:\wpc,* then type **c:\wpc\wp{wp}us.ths** and choose OK. (You can avoid this problem in the future by specifying where the dictionary is located with File, Preferences, Location of Files, as described in Chapter 17.)

Looking Up Multiple Words

You can look up additional words once the Thesaurus window is open. Any reference that is preceded by a bullet is actually another headword. For instance, all the references shown in the first list box in Figure 9-3 are also headwords that can be looked up separately. To look up a reference that is also a headword, double-click the reference. Three things happen:

- A hand pointer is placed next to that reference.
- The reference becomes a new headword and appears at the top of the next list box.
- New references are displayed underneath the new headword.

Or, select (highlight) the reference and choose Look Up to look up another reference.

You can use the Thesaurus this way to look up a whole series of words. Figure 9-5, for instance, shows three lists of words. Only three can be shown in the Thesaurus window at the same time, but you can continue to look up more words, and then use the arrow buttons (located below the first list box) to move left and right through the list boxes, bringing ones that were off screen back on screen.

You can look up another word not listed as a reference by typing it into the Word text box and choosing Look Up. Any previously occupied list boxes will clear, and references for the new word will appear in the first list box. (Rather than type a word into the Word text box, you can insert a word into it using the Edit or History menu on the Thesaurus menu bar, as described next.)

9

Figure 9-5.   *Thesaurus showing references for three headwords at once*

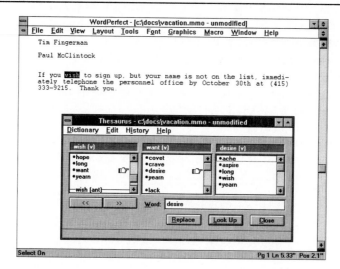

The Thesaurus Menu Bar

The Thesaurus window contains a menu bar listing four menus with features for changing the way the Thesaurus operates, or for assisting you in using the Thesaurus.

The first menu, Dictionary, lets you indicate a different dictionary file to be used by the Thesaurus. While WordPerfect comes with only one copy of the Thesaurus dictionary, you can buy additional copies in other languages—as part of language modules—from WordPerfect Corporation. (More information on working in another language is provided later in this chapter.)

The second menu on the Thesaurus menu bar is Edit. The items on the Edit menu pertain only to the contents of the Word text box. You can Cut and Copy text from the Word text box into the Clipboard. Conversely, you can Paste text from the Clipboard into the text box. Select All selects the entire contents of the text box. Undo reverses the last change made in the text box.

The History menu displays the last words you looked up in the Thesaurus since the Thesaurus window was opened. When you select one of the words, it's as if you typed that word into the Word text box and chose Look Up; previously occupied list boxes will clear, and references for the new word will appear in the first list box.

The Help menu, the last item on the Thesaurus menu bar, provides assistance on using the Thesaurus, just like the Help menu of the WordPerfect menu bar provides assistance on using WordPerfect. See Appendix C for more information on using the WordPerfect Help feature. The Thesaurus Help feature works in the same way.

Hands-on Exercise: Use the Thesaurus

 For the document on screen, *vacation.mmo,* suppose you want to find an alternative for the word "wish". Follow these steps:

1. Position the insertion point anywhere within the word "wish" near the bottom of the memorandum.

2. Choose Tools, Thesaurus or press (ALT) + (F1).

3. Since the word is a headword, the Thesaurus window appears with a list of references, as shown in Figure 9-3.

4. Scroll down in the list box until you view the synonyms for "wish" that are verbs. These are indicated under the heading that reads "wish (v)".

5. Double-click on the reference "want". The second list box is now occupied with references for "want".

6. In the second list box, double-click on the reference "desire". Now, all three list boxes are occupied.

7. Select (highlight) "want", which appears in the first list box.

8. Choose Replace. The selected reference "want" replaces the original word "wish" in the document. The Thesaurus window closes.

9

Using the Speller or Thesaurus for a Document in Another Language

WordPerfect for Windows comes with language module files for only one language. For instance, if you purchased WordPerfect in the United States, it is the U.S. English Language Module that is used whenever you use the Speller or Thesaurus.

If you create documents in different languages, you may want to purchase additional language modules, which allow you to work in another language when using the Speller and Thesaurus. Once you purchase a language module, be sure to install it. (Refer to Appendix A for information on using the Install program to install a language module.) You should install the language module in the same directory where the Speller and Thesaurus dictionaries for the current language module are located (which is usually the same directory where the WordPerfect program files are located).

Once a new language module is installed, it is ready to use in a Word-Perfect document. To tell WordPerfect to use a different language module, you have several options. First, you can open the Speller or Thesaurus window, and then choose Dictionary to specify the name of the new Speller or Thesaurus dictionary. The new dictionary will be used until you change it or close the Speller or Thesaurus window.

Instead of changing the dictionary in the Speller or Thesaurus window, another option allows you to insert a language code into the document itself. This is especially useful in a document containing text in two or more languages. You can insert a language code in each location where the language changes. To insert a language code in your document:

1. Position the insertion point where you want to specify that a new language begins. Or, select the text that is in another language.

2. Choose Tools, Language. A Language dialog box appears, with the current language listed at the top, as in this example:

3. Select another language from the Current Language list box. Or, if you install the language module for a language that is not on the list, select Other from the list box, and then type the appropriate two-letter language code (found in your language module documentation) in the Other text box.

4. Choose OK.

For a language change at the insertion point, WordPerfect inserts a single code. The code indicates the corresponding language module's two-letter code, such as [Lang:ES] to switch to Spanish as the current language or [Lang:DK] to switch to Danish as the current language. The language code is shown when you switch to the reveal codes workspace.

For a language change restricted to selected text, WordPerfect inserts two language codes. At the beginning of the selected text, a code is inserted to indicate a change to a new language. At the end of the selected text, a code is inserted to return to the original language.

When WordPerfect encounters a language code, it uses the corresponding language module's Speller (for both spell-checking and for hyphenating the document) and Thesaurus. Moreover, the language code also affects the Sort feature—WordPerfect uses the guidelines for that language's alphabet when sorting text. Finally, the language code affects the Date feature—WordPerfect inserts the date in your document the way dates are written in that language.

9

Word Counting

When working on a term paper or magazine article, you may need to know how many words the document contains. WordPerfect can provide you with that information, either for the entire document or for a section of text. For an entire document, open the document on screen and choose Tools, Word Count. To count words in only a section of text, select the text on screen and then choose Tools, Word Count. WordPerfect begins counting. In moments, the total number of words (excluding numerals) is displayed, like this:

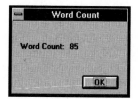

Choose OK to return to your document.

Quick Reference

- To spell-check a document, choose $\underline{T}$ools, $\underline{S}$peller or press $\boxed{\text{CTRL}}$ + $\boxed{\text{F1}}$. The Speller window is displayed. Then choose S$\underline{t}$art. You can also spell-check a section of text by selecting the text before displaying the Speller window.

- To respond when the Speller highlights a word not found in the main or supplementary dictionary, you can select from a list of suggested alternatives and choose $\underline{R}$eplace. Or choose Skip $\underline{O}$nce or Skip A$\underline{l}$ways to have the Speller pass over the word. You can also choose $\underline{A}$dd to add the highlighted word to your own supplementary dictionary so that, from that point on, the Speller will recognize it.

- To check for grammatical errors, don't rely on the Speller. The Speller checks for misspellings but is no substitute for a final proofreading.

- To look up synonyms or antonyms for a word, position the insertion point and choose $\underline{T}$ools, $\underline{T}$hesaurus or press $\boxed{\text{ALT}}$ + $\boxed{\text{F1}}$. Using the Thesaurus, you can acquire a better understanding of a word's meaning or find an appropriate substitute.

- To use the Speller or Thesaurus dictionaries of another language, choose $\underline{T}$ools, $\underline{L}$anguage to insert a language code in the document. Or, you can change the dictionary in the Speller or Thesaurus window by choosing $\underline{D}$ictionary.

- To count the number of words in your document, choose $\underline{T}$ools, $\underline{W}$ord Count.

9

10

Taking Advantage of Button Bars and Multiple Windows

This chapter discusses two options for working with WordPerfect that you simply can't ignore if you want to become a sophisticated WordPerfect user. The first is the Button Bar feature. Available only if you use a mouse, button bars provide shortcuts for accessing features and commands. Use a pre-defined button bar or create your own that you customize to help with tasks that you perform often.

The second option discussed in this chapter is how to take advantage of the fact that WordPerfect is a Windows application. You can resize and move a document window with your mouse or your keyboard. You can also open additional document windows and work with as many as nine at the same time. For instance, type an outline in one document window, and then refer to it as you write a report in a second document window. Reserve a third document window for typing random thoughts. Copy a paragraph from a fourth document window into the second. It's like having many separate documents on screen at once. Moreover, you can resize and move the

WordPerfect application window, so that you can work with multiple applications at the same time.

Displaying and Using a Button Bar

Button bars provide quick access to menu commands and macros with your mouse. They contain a series of buttons, which are rectangular with a drop shadow to resemble three-dimensional push buttons, similar to command buttons in a dialog box. Each button can have text and/or a picture on its face to indicate the command it performs. None of the buttons has mnemonic letters in the text; therefore you cannot choose a button on the button bar with your keyboard as you can in a dialog box—you must use your mouse. WordPerfect offers several predefined button bars, or you can create your own, as many as you want.

To view a predefined button bar, choose View, Button Bar. A button bar appears just below the menu bar on screen, slightly reducing the size of the document window. Figure 10-1 shows you how WordPerfect's main button bar appears on screen. This is the button bar that is displayed by default until you select a different one. The button bar remains on screen for the rest of the working session and every time thereafter when you load WordPerfect until you choose to hide it. To hide the button bar, choose View, Button Bar again to turn the feature off.

Once you display a button bar on screen, you can use its buttons instead of the corresponding commands on the menu bar. For instance, the first button in the main button bar shown in Figure 10-1 is the Close button. Click this button as a shortcut for File, Close. The last button is the Speller button. Click this button as a shortcut for Tools, Speller. The main button bar provides shortcuts for accessing the following commonly used features: Close, Open, Save, Print, Cut, Copy, Paste, Search, Font, and Speller. Each button is a shortcut using the mouse, just as a key combination such as (CTRL) + (F4) is a shortcut using the keyboard.

Just like on the menu bar, any buttons currently unavailable on the button bar are dimmed to a light shade of gray. For instance, notice that Cut and Copy are two of the buttons that are faded in Figure 10-1 because no text is

Figure 10-1.   *Main button bar near the top of the WordPerfect window*

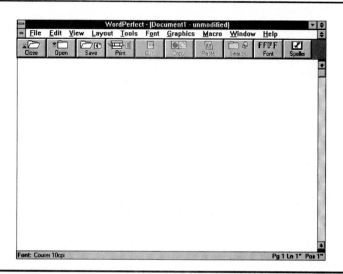

available for you to Cut or Copy from. If you select text, these buttons will be ready for you to use and no longer dim.

You have several options for how a button bar displays on screen. WordPerfect's initial setting is that the button bar appears near the top of the WordPerfect window, with each button showing both a caption (text) and a picture. You may or may not find this distracting. You can change both the position of the button bar and its style—whether to display text and/or pictures on the face of each button. To do so, choose View, Button Bar Setup, Options. The Button Bar Options dialog box appears:

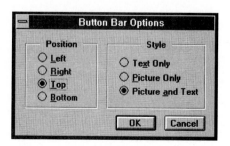

10

Choose a Position option and a Style option. Then choose OK. The change will take effect immediately, and WordPerfect will retain the new settings until you change them again. Figure 10-2 shows several different position and style selections. Notice that when you choose to display only text, each button is smaller, and therefore more can fit on the button bar. This is useful when you create a button bar that contains more than the ten buttons on the main button bar.

Selecting a Different Button Bar

As a default setting, WordPerfect assumes you wish to view the main button bar, the one displayed in Figures 10-1 and 10-2. However, you can choose from other button bars instead.

All of the button bars in WordPerfect are saved in files with the extension *.wwb* (which stands for WordPerfect for Windows Button Bar). The filename of the main button bar is *wp{wp}.wwb*.

Another predefined button bar is named Tables, with the filename *tables.wwb*; Tables is convenient for working with the Tables feature (which is discussed in Chapter 11):

You can select to view the other predefined button bar instead of the main one, or you can select one that you created yourself. To select another button bar, follow these steps:

1. Choose View, Button Bar Setup, Select. A Select Button Bar dialog box appears, as shown in Figure 10-3.

2. Select (highlight) one of the button bar filenames listed in the Files list box.

3. Choose Select.

shortcut *Double-clicking a button bar filename in the Files list box is a shortcut for selecting a filename and then choosing Select.*

Figure 10-2. *Examples of different position and style options for a button bar*

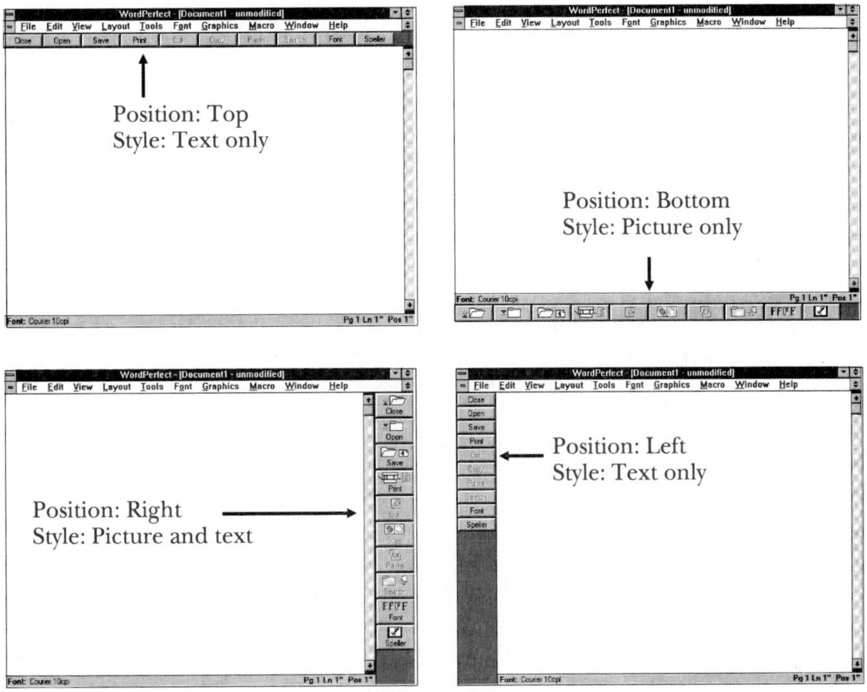

If the button bar file you want to select is not listed because it is in a directory other than that shown in the Select Button Bar dialog box, you must type in the button bar's full path. You can also change to the directory that contains the button bar file you want in order to select it. (Do this by double-clicking on the directory you want from the Directories list box in the Select Button Bar dialog box.) WordPerfect assumes that button bars are saved to and recalled from the button bar directory specified when you select File, Preferences, Location of Files, as described in Chapter 17. This directory is usually *c:\wpwin\macros*.

Once a new button bar is selected, WordPerfect remembers and displays that button bar every time you choose View, Button Bar to turn on the feature, until you select a different button bar.

10

Figure 10-3.   *Select Button Bar dialog box*

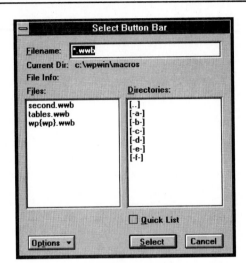

WordPerfect has three other predefined button bars that you cannot select to display in a document window. They appear only when you are using the feature that each is associated with: when you create an equation with the Equation Editor (see Chapter 12), edit a graphics figure box (see Chapter 12), or use the Print Preview feature (see Chapter 16).

Constructing a Button Bar

You can create your own button bar, containing buttons for the commands and macros you use most often. You can also edit a button bar; either your own or a predefined one.

Creating a New Button Bar

A button bar can contain as many buttons as you want. If you add too many buttons to fit on screen, arrows appear at the edge of the button bar so that you can scroll to those buttons that are not visible.

Perhaps a better strategy than creating an enormously large button bar is to create many, smaller ones. Each button bar can serve for a specific type of task. For instance, create one button bar to help produce your company's monthly newsletter. Create another to handle shortcuts when inserting graphics images into your documents. Create a third one specifically for the legal documents that you type.

To create a new button bar, follow these steps:

1. Choose <u>V</u>iew, Button Bar <u>S</u>etup, <u>N</u>ew. A blank button bar and the Edit Button Bar dialog box appear, as shown in Figure 10-4. The mouse pointer's graphical image will now change on screen as follows: it changes to an arrow inside the dialog box; it changes to a "button hand" (a hand holding a button) when positioned in the empty button bar or in the menu bar; and it changes to a "prevent pointer" (a circle with a slash through it) in an area on screen where you cannot select a feature for the button bar.

2. To add a button to the button bar, choose its corresponding command from the menu bar as you normally would. For instance, using a mouse, click <u>T</u>ools, <u>S</u>peller to choose the Speller. Then, click F<u>o</u>nt, <u>S</u>ize, <u>E</u>xtra Large to choose the Extra Large size attribute. Then click F<u>o</u>nt, <u>B</u>old to choose the Bold attribute. As a result, these three buttons will appear on the button bar:

Once you click outside of the Edit Button Bar dialog box so that the document window is active instead of the dialog box, you can also add a button using the keyboard. You can choose a command from the menu bar using mnemonic keys. For instance, choose <u>T</u>ools, <u>T</u>hesaurus by pressing (ALT) + (T), (T) to add the Thesaurus button. Or, you can press the command's corresponding shortcut key. For instance, press (ALT) + (F1) to add the Thesaurus button. (Refer back to Table 2-1 in Chapter 2, or to the command card at the back of this book, for a list of shortcut keys.)

10

3. If you want to delete a button, click the button and drag it off the button bar.

4. If you want to move a button, click the button and drag it to a new position on the button bar.

5. If you want to add a button for a previously created macro, choose <u>A</u>ssign Macro to Button from the Edit Button Bar dialog box, select the macro's filename from the new dialog box that appears, and then choose <u>A</u>ssign. (See Chapter 15 for more on macros.)

6. When you are done, choose OK from the Edit Button Bar dialog box. WordPerfect displays the Save Button Bar dialog box.

7. Type a name for the button bar (eight characters or less) and choose <u>S</u>ave. When WordPerfect saves the file, the extension *.wwb* is automatically assigned to the filename.

Figure 10-4.   *Creating a new button bar*

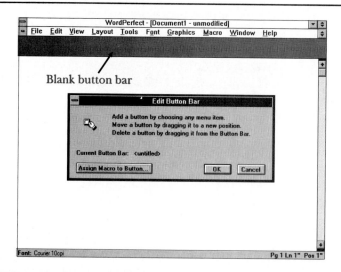

Editing a Button Bar

You can edit any of the button bars, whether predefined or one that you created. To edit an existing button bar, follow these steps:

1. Make sure that the button bar you wish to edit appears on screen.

2. Choose View, Button Bar Setup, Edit. The Edit Button Bar dialog box appears. Inside the dialog box the filename of the button bar that you are about to edit is shown next to the item "Current Button Bar".

3. Add a button to the button bar by choosing a command from the menu bar with the mouse or the keyboard—just as you did when creating a new button bar. Delete a button by clicking and dragging it off the button bar. Move a button by clicking and dragging it to a new position on the button bar. Add a button for a macro by choosing Assign Macro to Button, selecting a macro filename, and choosing Assign.

4. When you are done, choose OK from the Edit Button Bar dialog box.

You may wish to edit a button bar but retain the original version as well. For instance, suppose you create a button bar for your business documents. Now, you want to create a new button bar for your personal documents that will contain almost the same buttons. You can copy a button bar and then edit the copy. Make sure that the button bar you wish to copy appears on screen. Choose View, Button Bar Setup, Save As. Type in a new name where the copy will be stored and choose Save. The button bar has now been copied. Next, select the copy so that it is displayed on screen. The copy is ready to be edited and arranged any way you like; the original button bar is maintained just as it was.

Working with Document Windows

As discussed previously in this book, the Windows environment means that you work with WordPerfect in a rectangular area called a window. There

10

are actually two windows that are opened on screen when you initially load WordPerfect. First, the WordPerfect application window appears. Second, an empty document window appears inside the application window, and is given the name Document1. Document1 becomes the *active* document window, the one you are working in. The title bar of this active window is shaded. You have the ability to change the size or location of a document window. Moreover, you can open additional document windows.

Maximizing, Restoring, and Minimizing a Document Window

You can specify three predefined sizes for a document window. First, you can *maximize* a document window to fill the entire WordPerfect application window. The Document1 window is always maximized when you first load WordPerfect.

Second, you can *restore* a document window. It shrinks to a medium-sized window (neither maximized nor minimized) within WordPerfect, as shown in Figure 10-5. When a document window is medium-sized its elements are clearly distinguished from the WordPerfect application window. It no longer shares the application window's title bar, but has its own title bar instead. Notice in Figure 10-5, for instance, that the application window has a title bar that reads "WordPerfect", while the document window has a title bar that reads "Document1 - unmodified". Also in a medium-sized document window, the application control-menu box is clearly distinguished from the document control-menu box. And, the application resizing buttons are clearly distinguished from the document resizing buttons.

Third, you can *minimize* a document window. It shrinks to the size of an icon within WordPerfect. You don't see the contents of the document window, but the window is still open. The icon's caption lists the contents of the title bar, such as "Document1 - unmodified" in Figure 10-6. The advantage of minimizing a document window is that it clears the WordPerfect application window but is available whenever you need it. Keep in mind, however, that a minimized window still occupies computer memory.

A quick way to maximize, restore, or minimize a document window uses your mouse and the document window's resizing buttons. In a maximized

Figure 10-5. *A medium-sized document window inside the WordPerfect application window*

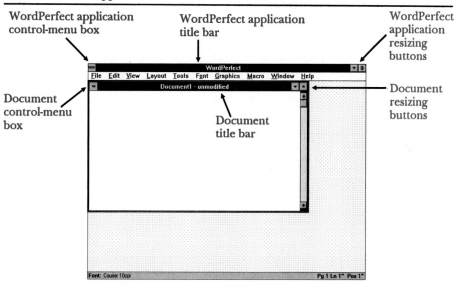

WordPerfect application control-menu box

WordPerfect application title bar

WordPerfect application resizing buttons

Document control-menu box

Document title bar

Document resizing buttons

Figure 10-6. *A minimized document window inside the WordPerfect application window*

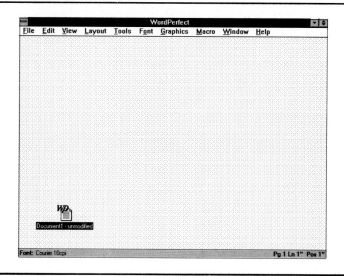

10

document window, the restore button appears on the same line as the menu bar and just below the WordPerfect application resizing buttons.

Document restore button

You click the document restore button to return it to a medium-sized window.

caution *When a document window is maximized, the document window restore button and WordPerfect application window restore button are near each other. Make sure not to get them confused. The document window restore button is below the application window restore button.*

In a medium-sized document window, the restore button disappears and is replaced by the minimize and maximize buttons, as shown here:

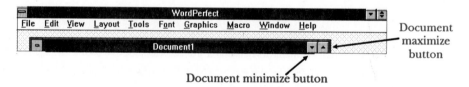

Document maximize button

Document minimize button

Click one of these buttons in a document window to minimize or maximize it.

In a minimized document window, the window is reduced so that you cannot see any resizing buttons. Double-click the icon of a document window to restore it to a medium-sized window.

You can also restore, maximize, or minimize a document window by relying on the document control-menu box. (This is your only option if you don't use a mouse.) Click the document control-menu box or press (ALT) + (-) to display the Control menu for the active document window, shown here:

Then, choose either Restore, Minimize, or Maximize.

caution *When a document window is maximized, the document control-menu box and the WordPerfect application control-menu box are near each other. Make sure not to get them confused. The document control-menu box is below and slightly smaller than the application control-menu box.*

Sizing a Document Window Manually

In addition to shrinking or enlarging a window to one of the predefined sizes, you can establish your own window size. Mouse users can use the document window's frame to resize the window. Simply follow these steps:

1. Point to any portion of the frame. The mouse pointer changes to a vertical two-headed arrow if you pointed to the top or bottom edge of the frame. It changes to a horizontal two-headed arrow if you pointed to the left or right edge. It changes to a diagonal two-headed arrow if you pointed to a corner.

2. Click and drag the mouse. A box outline shows the change to the size of the window. If you pointed to the top or bottom edge, the height of the window changes; if you pointed to one of the side edges, the width is changed. Here's an example:

10

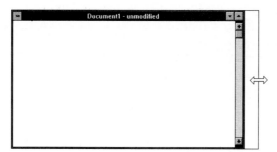

If you pointed to a corner, both height and width change. Here's an example:

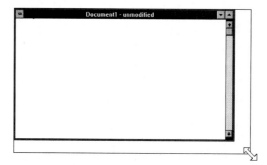

3. When the window is the size you want it to be, release the mouse button. Or, to cancel the resizing, press (ESC) before you release the mouse button.

You can also adjust the window size with the document control-menu box. Click the document control-menu box or press (ALT) + (-) to display the Control menu for the active document window. Choose Size. The mouse pointer changes to a four-headed arrow. Next, use the arrow keys to resize the window. A box outline shows the change. When the window is the size you want it to be, press (ENTER). Or, press (ESC) before you press (ENTER) to cancel the resizing.

Keep in mind that a document window that has been maximized or minimized cannot be resized. You must restore it to a medium-sized window first, and then resize it manually.

Also, keep in mind that once you manually change the size of a window, the window returns to that size when you maximize or minimize the window and then restore it.

Moving a Document Window

The same procedure you learned about in Chapter 2 for moving dialog boxes also applies for any window that contains a title bar, including a document window. With your mouse, click the window's title bar and drag the window. A box outline of the window moves with the pointer. When the outline is positioned where you want the window to be, release the mouse button. Or, press (ESC) before releasing the mouse button to cancel the move.

You can also move a document window using its control-menu box. Click the document control-menu box or press (ALT) + (-) to display the Control menu for the active document window. Choose <u>M</u>ove. The pointer changes to a four-headed arrow. Use the arrow keys to move the window. A box outline shows the change. When the outline is where you want the window to be, press (ENTER). Or, press (ESC) before pressing (ENTER) to cancel the move.

Keep in mind that a document window that has been maximized cannot be moved. You must restore it to a medium-sized window first, and then move it manually.

Working with Multiple Document Windows

You can open additional document windows at any time. Each can contain a different document. As long as your computer has sufficient memory, you can work with as many as nine open document windows in WordPerfect at one time. The more documents you have open at once, the more computer memory you use.

10

Opening Additional Document Windows

You have two options for opening a new document window in Word-Perfect:

- To open a new document window that is empty, use the New feature. Choose File, New. The empty document window is opened on screen, and given a new name, such as Document2. Choose File, New again and you'll create Document3, and so on. The most recently opened empty document window becomes the active one.

- To open a new document window and simultaneously recall an existing file into that window, use the Open feature. Choose File, Open and specify a filename. If the active document window is occupied (even with just one character), the file you specified is recalled into a new document window. The new document window becomes the active one. (If the active document window is empty, the file is recalled into the empty window.)

shortcut   (SHIFT) + (F4) *is the shortcut for* File, New. (F4) *is the shortcut for* File, Open.

Every new document window operates just like the Document1 window, but independently. You can type, edit, and use all the features from the menu bar in a new document window. When more than one document window is open, keystrokes and menu bar selections apply to the *active* window only. Thus, when multiple document windows are open, make sure that the correct document window is the active one before you begin typing, editing, or using the menu bar.

You can type different text into each document window. Or, you can open the same document into two separate windows, which is handy for viewing two sections of a long document at the same time. However, the second time you open the document, a dialog box will appear informing you that the document is already in use and that the second window will have a "read-only" status, meaning that you can view the document in the second window, but cannot edit and then resave it under the same filename. You will want to restrict your editing to the first document window. Or, if you edit the same document in the second window, you must save it under a different filename.

When you're ready to close a document window, you use the Close feature. As described in Chapter 4, two methods to do so are to choose File, Close or to double-click the document control-menu box.

WordPerfect gives you the opportunity to resave a document that has been modified since it was last saved. Then, if only one document window is open, the document will close and an empty Document1 window will become the active window displayed on screen. Or, if multiple document windows are open, both the document and the document window will close and one of the currently open document windows will become the active window displayed on screen.

shortcut CTRL + F4 *is the shortcut for* File, Close. CTRL + SHIFT + F4 *is the shortcut for closing a document without saving it and without closing the document window; the document window is cleared.*

You can also close all document windows in the same command when you use the Exit feature. As described in Chapter 1, two methods to do so are to choose File, Exit or to double-click the WordPerfect application control-menu box. WordPerfect gives you the opportunity to resave any documents in open document windows that have been modified since they were last saved. The document windows are closed and WordPerfect is exited.

Switching Between Document Windows

When two or more document windows are open at the same time, only one document window can be active. The active window will always be on screen, overlapping any other windows that may also be on screen. If the active window is maximized on screen, it completely hides all the other open windows behind it.

Whether you see one or many open document windows on screen, you can display a list of the open document windows. Choose Windows. The Windows drop-down menu appears, listing at the bottom the document windows that are open. The document window that is currently active is preceded by a check mark. As an example, suppose you proceed as follows:

1. Type text into the Document1 window.

2. Open *vacation.mmo* into a second window.

3. Open *smith01.ltr* into a third window.

4. Use the <u>F</u>ile, <u>N</u>ew command to open a fourth window.

In that case, four open windows will be listed when you choose <u>W</u>indows:

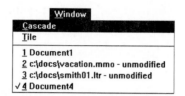

The check mark beside Document4 indicates that this document is the active document window, the one in which you are currently typing and editing text.

To switch between open document windows, you have three alternatives:

- Choose <u>W</u>indows and then choose the name of the document to which you want to switch.

- Press (CTRL) + (F6) to select the next window, or (CTRL) + (SHIFT) + (F6) to select the previous window without displaying the Windows drop-down menu.

- Click the document window you wish to select, which is possible only if at least a corner of the window you wish to select is displayed on screen. (When a window is maximized so that the others are totally hidden behind it, you cannot use this method.)

The document window you select becomes the active one: its title bar becomes shaded, and the window itself moves in front of all the other open document windows, overlapping the other document windows. If it is maximized, it completely hides the other open windows.

caution *The menu bar is shared by all the document windows. If several windows are open on screen at once, make sure that the correct document window is active before you use the menu bar to perform tasks such as closing a document or editing text in a document.*

Because it is so easy to switch between open windows, it is simple to transfer text back and forth between windows via the Clipboard. As described in Chapter 8, the Clipboard is an area in memory where text and graphics can be stored, and then inserted in other places in that document. The same procedure you learned in Chapter 8 for transferring information *within* a document also applies *between* documents. For instance, select text in one document and then choose Edit, Cut, to place that text into the Clipboard. Next, switch to a second document window using any of the three methods just described. Position the insertion point, and choose Edit, Paste to insert the Clipboard contents into the second document. The procedure to transfer information becomes especially easy if you tile or cascade the windows, as described next.

Tiling and Cascading

When you have two or more document windows open, you can manually resize and move them so that you can view them all at once. However, it's easier to let WordPerfect do it for you. You can have WordPerfect *tile* your windows, in which case they are arranged edge to edge so that you can see the contents of each window. You can also have WordPerfect *cascade* your windows, or line them up like cards in a stack with just the title bars showing. Here's how to use the Tile and Cascade features.

- *Tiling* When you choose Window, Tile, the Tile feature arranges the windows so that you can see them all. This makes it more convenient to work with several documents at once. The active window is placed at the top of the screen, and the others are tiled in the order that they were opened. The active window is always placed at the top, but exactly how the document windows are sized depends on the number of document windows currently open. With three or less, the windows fill the width of the WordPerfect window, as shown in Figure 10-7. With four or more, some or all of the windows fill only a tiny portion of the screen, as shown in Figure 10-8, and are often too tiny to realistically work with until you resize them.

10

- *Cascading* When you choose Window, Cascade, the Cascade feature arranges the windows in a stack so that they overlap, with their title bars showing. The active window is placed on top. Cascading is handy when you wish to see which documents are currently open. (It is all too easy to "lose" a document because it has become hidden behind one or two others.) An example of cascaded windows is shown in Figure 10-9.

After you choose Tile or Cascade, you can switch between the windows quickly. For instance, click another tiled document to make it active. You can also press (CTRL) + (F6) or (CTRL) + (SHIFT) + (F6) when viewing cascaded windows to place the next or previous document window at the top of the stack. You can also resize any or all of the document windows manually, or minimize some. You can maximize one window, but when you maximize one, they all become maximized and are hidden behind the active window. Or close some and open additional ones, and then tile or cascade the windows again. In Figure 10-10, for example, five windows were cascaded. Then, two were

Figure 10-7. *Three windows are tiled with Document1 active*

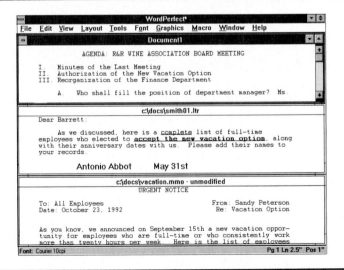

Figure 10-8. *Five windows are tiled with Document5 active*

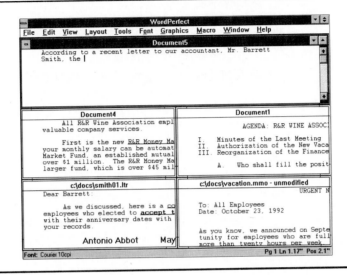

Figure 10-9. *Five windows are cascaded with Document5 active*

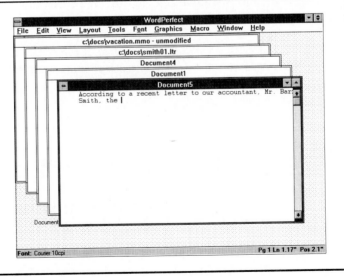

10

Figure 10-10. *A convenient arrangement of windows when working with five documents at once*

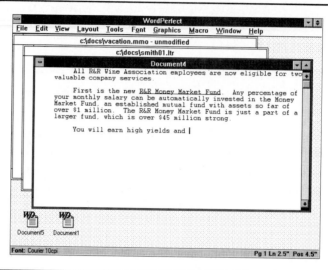

minimized and one was enlarged slightly. With this arrangement, you can quickly switch back and forth between documents.

note *Keep in mind that when a window is maximized, it completely overlaps all the other windows. You will be able to see other windows that are open only if you: restore the maximized window to a medium-sized window; switch to another window; or tile or cascade all the document windows.*

Working with the WordPerfect Application Window

In the Windows environment, not only can you work with multiple document windows, but you can work with multiple application windows at the same time. For instance, you can load WordPerfect, switch back to Windows' Program Manager, load Lotus 1-2-3 for Windows, and then switch back and forth between them. You can size or move the WordPerfect application window, or switch to another application.

Sizing and Moving the WordPerfect Application Window

You size and move the WordPerfect application window with its resizing buttons and control-menu box in the same manner as you size and move a document window. (See the discussion earlier in this chapter.) Just make sure to use the WordPerfect application window resizing buttons and control-menu box, and not the document window ones. Remember that when a document window is maximized, the WordPerfect application window's resizing and control-menu boxes are on the very top line in the application window. Moreover, if you are using a keyboard to size or move the Word-Perfect application window, access the application window's control-menu box by pressing (ALT) + (SPACEBAR), as opposed to a document window's control-menu box, which is accessed by pressing (ALT) + (-).

Keep in mind that when the WordPerfect application window is maximized, as is the case when you first load WordPerfect, you cannot move the application window, resize it manually, or see any other applications that are running until you restore it to a medium-sized window.

Switching Between Application Windows

The method for switching between the WordPerfect application window and other application windows is quite different than switching between document windows within WordPerfect. To switch to another application, one method is to use the application control-menu box:

1. Click the application control-menu box or press (ALT) + (SPACEBAR) to display the application's Control menu, as shown here:

10

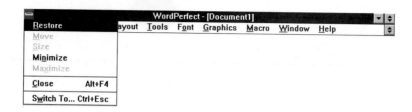

2. Choose S<u>w</u>itch To to display a Task List dialog box such as this:

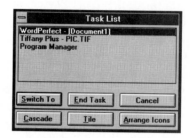

This is a dialog box associated with Windows, not WordPerfect. All the applications currently running are listed. (If you loaded Windows and WordPerfect, only two applications are listed, Word-Perfect and Windows' Program Manager. The preceding Task List shows three applications running.)

3. Select (highlight) the application you wish to switch to.

4. Choose S<u>w</u>itch To.

shortcut (CTRL) + (ESC) *is the shortcut for choosing S<u>w</u>itch To from the application control-menu box.* (ALT) + (TAB) *is the shortcut for switching to the application window that was active most recently.*

Another method for switching between application windows is to click the application window you wish to select, which is possible only if at least a corner of the window you wish to select is displayed on screen. (When an application window is maximized so that the others are totally hidden behind it, as is the case when you first load WordPerfect, you cannot use this method.)

The Task List dialog box also offers other options for working with multiple application windows. For example, you can tile or cascade application windows, just as you can tile and cascade document windows.

Be sure to see your Windows manual for more details on working with multiple applications. (Your ability to work with multiple applications may be limited based on the processor and amount of memory in your computer and whether the applications that you're switching between are all Windows applications or not.)

Working with Dialog Boxes and Special Windows

Even if you don't work with multiple document windows in WordPerfect or with multiple application windows, you are constantly working with dialog boxes. Dialog boxes are windows with limited capabilities. They have title bars and control-menu boxes, and can therefore be moved like a document window. This is convenient if a dialog box is overlapping a section of your document that you wish to reference. Most dialog boxes cannot be resized, and must be closed before you can continue to work in the document workspace.

A few dialog boxes, however, can be resized, which is convenient when you want to see more than what the small-sized box would otherwise display. For instance, you can maximize the View dialog box to see more of the contents of a document that you are viewing. (See Chapter 16 for more on the View feature.) Dialog boxes that can be resized have resizing buttons, and can also be resized using the control-menu boxes.

A few dialog boxes can remain on screen as you switch back and forth between them and the document window. You can press (CTRL) + (W), for instance, to display the WordPerfect Characters dialog box, and then switch back and forth between it and the document window as you insert special characters into your text. When a dialog box is active, its title bar is shaded and the document window's title bar is dimmed. When you switch, the dialog box's title bar is dimmed, while the document window's title bar is shaded.

The method for switching between the document window and a dialog box is to click in the window or dialog box. Or, using your keyboard, you can

10

press (ALT) + (F6) or (ALT) + (SHIFT) + (F6) to switch to the next or previous window using the keyboard. (If you are in a special window that is comprised of panes, such as the Equation Editor window, click in a pane to switch to it. Or press (F6) or (SHIFT) + (F6) to switch to the next or previous pane.)

Some dialog boxes are, in actuality, application windows. Therefore, they can not only be moved, resized, and kept on screen as you switch back to the document window, but can stay open and behind the scenes while you work in a WordPerfect document window. This is the case for related WordPerfect products, such as the Thesaurus, Speller, File Manager, and WordPerfect for Windows Help. These are stand-alone applications, separate from Word-Perfect even though they can display in a WordPerfect document window.

If you plan to use a related application frequently throughout a Word-Perfect work session, save time by leaving it open. For instance, suppose you plan to spell-check a number of documents in one session. You can choose Tools, Speller to display the Speller window in a WordPerfect document window. After performing a spell-check on the first document, you can minimize the Speller by clicking the Speller's minimize button. The Speller is minimized and disappears behind the WordPerfect application window. Later, when you're ready to use the Speller again, you can switch back to the Speller window. One method to do so would be to press (CTRL) + (ESC) to display the Task List, and then select the Speller. Now, the Speller reappears in a document window. Perform another spell-check and then again minimize the Speller window. Repeat this procedure, and close the Speller window only after performing a spell-check on the last document.

Quick Reference

- To view the button bar, choose View, Button Bar. Buttons on a button bar are shortcuts for accessing commands. To hide the button bar, choose View, Button Bar again. You must have a mouse to use a button bar.

- To select a different button bar, choose View, Button Bar Setup. WordPerfect provides several predefined button bars to choose from, or you can select one that you created.

- To create a button bar customized for your needs, choose View, Button Bar Setup, Create. Add a feature to the button bar by choosing from the menu bar. Delete a button by clicking and dragging it off the button bar. Move a button by clicking and dragging it to a new position on the button bar. Add a button for a macro by choosing Assign Macro to Button, selecting a macro filename, and choosing Assign.

- To restore, maximize, or minimize a document window, click the corresponding document window resizing button. With your keyboard press ALT + - and choose either Restore, Minimize, or Maximize.

- To move a window, it must first be restored to a medium-sized window. Then, click and drag the window's title bar. Using your keyboard, press ALT + - and choose Move, and then reposition the window with the arrow keys.

- To open a new empty document window, choose File, New. If the active document window is occupied, you can open a new document window and recall an existing file into the new window by choosing File, Open.

- To switch between document windows, choose Windows and then select the name of the document you wish to switch to. Or press CTRL + F6, or click the document window you wish to switch to.

- To view all the open document windows at once, choose Windows. Then, choose Tile to arrange them so that you can see them all, or choose Cascade to arrange them in a stack with their title bars showing.

- To switch between the WordPerfect application window, Windows' Program Manager, and other applications that are currently running, display the Task List by clicking the application control-menu box or pressing ALT + SPACEBAR and then choosing Switch To. Or, press CTRL + ESC to display the Task List. Then, select the application you wish to switch to.

10

11

Creating Tables and Columns

It is common practice to rely on tab stops when you want to format text into columns. But, tabular columns are difficult to manage when you type entries that are longer than one line—and it is even more difficult to add, delete, or edit tabular columns once the text has been typed.

With WordPerfect, you don't need to use tabs to type multiple-line entries. Two WordPerfect features make it easier: the Tables feature lets you create a grid of rows and columns for typing text and the Columns feature lets you calculate the proper column spacing between columns and wrap text independently in each column. Using either Tables or Columns, you can edit the text in one column without causing the other columns to become misaligned. Both features are described in this chapter.

Creating a Table Structure

Use the Tables feature to type text into multiple columns when you want related column entries to remain together, side by side on the page. Tables are perfect for typing a wide range of documents, such as address lists, inventory lists, charts, scripts, financial statements, or fill-in-the-blank forms. A table can be created anywhere in a document, except within a newspaper or parallel column. (However, a table can be created in a graphics box, and the graphics box can be placed in a newspaper or parallel column.)

When you work with the Tables feature, you create a structure of columns and rows. The *columns* run vertically. You can have a maximum of 32 columns, labeled alphabetically starting with A, B, C, all the way through Z, and then continuing with AA, AB, AC, and through to AF. The *rows* run horizontally. You can have as many as 32,765 rows, labeled numerically starting with 1, 2, 3, and so on. The small rectangle at each intersection of a column and row is called a *cell*. You can type one column entry in each of these cells. WordPerfect identifies a specific cell with its column letter first, and its row number second; this identification is referred to as a *cell address*. Here's an example with a table containing three columns and three rows:

	Column A	Column B	Column C
Row 1 →	Cell A1		Cell C1
Row 2 →		Cell B2	
Row 3 →	Cell A3		Cell C3

Graphics lines are automatically drawn between each column and row to give you a table grid. When you print a table, the graphics lines will print as well—provided that your printer supports graphics. If you like you can remove or alter the lines.

There are three ways to create a new table structure: using the menu bar, using the button bar, and using the ruler. In each case, WordPerfect assumes that you want evenly sized columns that fit within the boundaries of the current margin settings. Later in this chapter, you'll learn how to change these settings to vary column widths. You'll also learn how to convert a set of previously created tabular columns or parallel columns into a table.

Constructing a Table with the Menu Bar

Follow these steps to create a table grid using the menu bar:

1. Position the insertion point where you want the table to appear.

2. Choose Layout, Tables, Create. The Create Table dialog box appears, as shown here:

3. Type the number of columns you want in the Columns text box.

4. Type the number of rows you want in the Rows text box.

5. Choose OK.

shortcut (CTRL) + (F9) *is the shortcut for* Layout, Tables.

Constructing a Table with the Button Bar

As described in Chapter 10, WordPerfect's Button Bar feature provides shortcuts for accessing features using your mouse. Because the Tables feature is so widely used, one of WordPerfect's predefined button bars is designed specifically for creating or editing tables. Use that predefined button bar, which is named Tables, to create a table. Follow these steps:

1. If the button bar is not currently displayed on screen, choose View, Button Bar. When the button bar appears, you can change to the Tables button bar by choosing View, Button Bar Setup, Select, and selecting *tables.wwb*.

2. Position the insertion point where you want the table to appear.

3. Click the first button on the button bar, marked "Table". The Create Table dialog box appears.

4. Type the number of columns you want in the <u>C</u>olumns text box.

5. Type the number of rows you want in the <u>R</u>ows text box.

6. Choose OK.

You can then continue to display the Tables button bar on screen as you use it to edit the table.

Constructing a Table with the Ruler

As described in Chapter 6, the ruler is a quick way for mouse users to execute layout changes in a document. One button on the ruler is designed for creating a table. The maximum size for a table you can create using the ruler is 32 columns by 45 rows. Use the ruler to create a table grid by following these steps:

1. If the ruler is not currently displayed on screen, choose <u>V</u>iew, <u>R</u>uler.

2. Position the insertion point where you want the table to appear.

3. Click and hold the Tables button, which is the fourth button from the right. A grid pattern appears, as shown here:

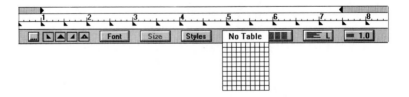

4. Drag the mouse until the size of the table you want is filled in on the grid pattern. Here's an example of a seven column by six row ("7x6") table:

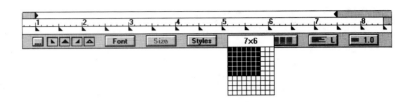

The maximum size is 32 columns by 45 rows.

5. Release the mouse button.

shortcut *Double-clicking the Tables button on the ruler is equivalent to choosing Layout, Tables, Create on the menu bar. The Create Table dialog box appears.*

Constructing a Table from Tabular or Parallel Columns

In addition to creating a brand-new table, you can also convert existing tabular columns (described in Chapter 6) or parallel columns (described later in this chapter) into a table structure. For instance, you may have begun an address list using tabular columns, only to realize that the process could be simpler within a table. To convert tabular or parallel columns into a table, follow these steps:

1. Select the tabular or parallel columns that you wish to convert.

2. Choose Layout, Tables, Create. The Convert Table dialog box appears, as shown here:

3. Select Tabular Column or Parallel Column, and choose OK.

When converting tabular columns, tab settings determine the cell widths, and hard returns define the rows. When converting parallel columns, the column margins determine the cell widths, and hard returns define the rows. The text of each column is automatically inserted into the table structure.

Typing Text in a Table

After you create a table structure, the insertion point sits in cell Al, and the right side of the status line contains a "Cell" indicator such as this:

```
Cell A1 Pg 1 Ln 1.14" Pos 1.12"
```

The "Cell" indicator lets you know the cell address where the insertion point currently resides.

Think of each cell as a narrow version of the document workspace. When you begin typing into a cell, word wrap maintains your text within the width boundaries of the cell. Press (ENTER) in a cell only when you wish to end a paragraph, end a short line of text, or insert a blank line of text within a cell—just as when you type in a document. You can type as many lines in a cell as will fit on one page; the row height will automatically expand to accommodate the text, as shown here:

one line	one line	Notice how the entire row expanded in height because this column entry is seven lines long.	

Be careful not to press (ENTER) after typing a cell entry unless you wish to expand the height of the row by an extra line.

Once you finish typing within a cell and your insertion point is at the end of the cell, press (↓) to move to the next cell down in the same column. Press (→) or (TAB) to move to the next cell to the right in the same row. If your insertion point is in the last cell for a particular row, (→) or (TAB) moves the insertion point to the first cell in the next row.

You can enter text into cells in any order. For instance, Figure 11-1 shows an example of a completed table. You could fill out this table by typing the name, background information, and telephone number across row 1, and then moving on to row 2, row 3, and so on. You could also type all the names in the cells in column A, then type all the background information in column B, and then type all the phone numbers in column C.

There are a variety of ways to move the insertion point within and between cells. With a mouse, click in the cell that you want to move to. With the keyboard, either use the arrow keys, or use any of the shortcut keys given in Table 11-1.

You can also use the Go To feature to move quickly to a specific part of a table. When the insertion point is placed within a table, choose Edit, Go To or press (CTRL) + (G) to display the Go To dialog box. From the Position pop-up list box, you can then select to go to the top or bottom of the current cell, to the first or last cell in the table, to the top or bottom cell of the current column,

Figure 11-1. *List of managers created with the Tables feature*

R&R WINE ASSOCIATION: LIST OF MANAGERS

Lonnie Chang	Director of the Public Relations Department since 4/12/83.	(415) 333-4109
Tim Hader	Distribution Manager, West Coast Region, since 6/1/87. Stationed in Oakland, California.	(415) 549-1101
Paula Garcia	Distribution Manager, East Coast Region, since 12/2/82. Stationed in New York City.	(212) 484-1119
P.J. McClintock	Assistant to the President since 5/13/86.	(415) 333-4401
Sandy Peterson	President since 3/2/82.	(415) 333-4400
John Samsone	Director, Office of Administration, since 3/2/82.	(415) 333-9215

Table 11-1.   *Shortcut Keys for Moving the Insertion Point Within and Between*
Cells in a Table

Key Combination	Moves Insertion Point To
(HOME)	Beginning of line in current cell
(END)	End of line in current cell
(ALT) + (HOME)	Top of current cell
(ALT) + (END)	Bottom of current cell
(HOME), (HOME)	First cell in a row
(END), (END)	Last cell in a row
(ALT) + (↑)	Next cell up
(ALT) + (↓)	Next cell down
(ALT) + (←) or (SHIFT) + (TAB)	Previous cell
(ALT) + (→) or (TAB)	Next cell

to the first or last column, or to a specific cell. To move the insertion point
to a specific cell, choose Go To Cell and then type the column letter and row
number, such as C1 or E5, into the Go To Cell number box. (Chapter 3
discusses how to use the Go To feature when the insertion point is not located
in a table.)

If your table has more than one page, WordPerfect will insert page breaks
automatically for you. A page break is inserted between rows so that a row is
not split between pages. If you wish to create a page break before a page is
full, press (CTRL) + (ENTER); a page break will occur above the current cell, at
the row boundary. This is referred to as a *hard row*. A [Hrd Row] code is
inserted.

Selecting Text in a Table

Just as in a document, you select the text in a table that you wish to edit.
There are a variety of methods for selecting text in a table. The following tells
you how to select text in cells, columns, and rows.

- To select text within a cell without affecting the table structure, place the insertion point in the cell and select as you would in a document. (See Chapter 3 for information on selecting text in a document.)

- To select text that is both inside and outside a table, select as you would in a document. For instance, to select text from the insertion point to the end of the document, click and drag through the table to the end of the document or press (SHIFT) + (CTRL) + (END). (See Chapter 3 for more information.)

- To select whole cells, rows, or columns with a mouse—in order to edit both the text and the table structure—use the options shown in Table 11-2. The mouse pointer changes from an I-beam to an up arrow when you point to the top border of a cell, or to a left arrow when you point to the left border of a cell.

- To select whole cells, rows, or columns with the keyboard, use the options shown in Table 11-3. The current cell, row, or column is defined as the one where the insertion point is currently located.

- To cancel a selection, click the mouse button or press an arrow key, just as you would in a document.

Table 11-2. *Mouse Shortcuts for Selecting in a Table*

Selection	Mouse Action
Cell	Display up arrow at the top border or left arrow at the left border of the cell and click
Column	Display up arrow at the top border of any cell in the column and double-click
Row	Display left arrow at the left border of any cell in the row and double-click
Table	Display up arrow at the top border or left arrow at the left border of any cell and triple-click

Table 11-3.   *Keyboard Shortcuts for Selecting in a Table*

Selection	Key Combination
Current cell	(SHIFT) + (F8)
Current cell to next cell, row, or column (and can extend outside the table)	(SHIFT) + (F8), (SHIFT) + arrow key
Current cell to next cell, row, or column (in the table only)	(ALT) + (SHIFT) + arrow key
Current cell to beginning of row	(SHIFT) + (HOME), (SHIFT) + (HOME)
Current cell to end of row	(SHIFT) + (END), (SHIFT) + (END)
Current cell to beginning and end of row (entire row)	(SHIFT) + (F8), (CTRL) + (←) or (→)
Current cell to beginning and end of column (entire column)	(SHIFT) + (F8), (CTRL) + (↑) or (↓)

When you select cells within a table, the entire area of all the cells is highlighted, as shown here:

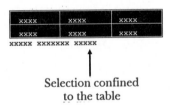

Selection confined
to the table

On the other hand, when you make a selection that focuses on text rather than the table structure, and extends outside the table, only the text—and not the table structure—is highlighted, as shown here:

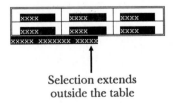

Selection extends
outside the table

11

Such a selection is useful, for instance, when you delete text both in the table and outside the table, without affecting the table structure.

Editing the Table Structure

WordPerfect offers a variety of methods for editing the table structure as well as the contents of the table.

Deleting Columns or Rows

To delete columns at the right end of the table, or rows at the bottom of the table, follow these steps:

1. Place the insertion point anywhere inside the table.
2. Choose Layout, Tables, Options, or click the Tbl Opts button on the Tables button bar. The Table Options dialog box appears, as shown in Figure 11-2.
3. Choose Columns or Rows, and type in the new number. As an example, suppose a table contains four columns and two rows and you wish to delete one column and one row. Choose Columns and type **3**. Then choose Rows and type **1**.
4. Choose OK. The contents are deleted along with the rows and/or columns.

An alternative is to delete particular rows or columns—not just those at the right-most or bottom-most edge of the table. When you wish to delete specific columns or rows, follow these steps:

1. To delete specific columns, position the insertion point in the left-most column you want to delete, or select the columns.

    To delete specific rows, position the insertion point in the top-most row you want to delete, or select the rows.
2. Choose Layout, Tables, Delete, or select the Tbl Del button on the Tables button bar. A Delete Columns/Rows dialog box appears.

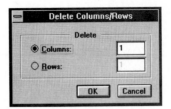

3. Select the Columns or Rows option.

4. Type the number of columns or rows into the corresponding number box and choose OK. Or, if you had selected columns or rows in step 1, simply click OK.

shortcut (ALT) + (DEL) *is a shortcut for deleting a single row where the insertion point is located.*

There is another method for deleting columns or rows in which you decide whether to delete only the contents or both the contents and the structure.

Figure 11-2.   *Table Options dialog box*

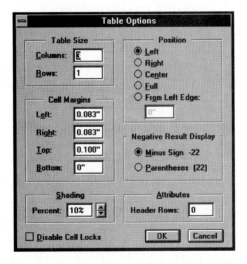

11

1. Select the column(s) or row(s) you wish to delete.

2. Press (BACKSPACE) or (DEL). A Delete Row or Delete Column dialog box appears. Here's an example when deleting rows:

3. Select Column(s) or Rows(s) to delete the structure as well as the contents. You can also select Contents (text only) to erase the text only and leave the structure intact. Then choose OK.

Inserting Columns or Rows

To insert columns at the right end of the table, or rows at the bottom of the table, follow these steps:

1. Place the insertion point anywhere inside the table.

2. Choose Layout, Tables, Options, or click the Tbl Opts button on the Tables button bar. The Table Options dialog box appears, as shown in Figure 11-2.

3. Choose Columns or Rows, and type in the new number. As an example, suppose a table contains eight columns and eight rows and you wish to add one column and one row. Choose Columns and type **9**. Then choose Rows and type **9**.

4. Choose OK. WordPerfect replicates the structure of the last column when you add columns, and replicates the structure of the bottom row when you add rows.

You also have the option of inserting rows or columns at a particular location in the table, (not just at the right-most or bottom-most end of the table). To insert a row or column in the middle of a table, follow these steps:

1. To insert columns, position the insertion point in the column to the right of where you want to insert new columns.

   To insert rows, position the insertion point in the row below where you want to insert new rows.

2. Choose Layout, Tables, Insert, or select the Tbl Insert button on the Tables button bar. An Insert Columns/Rows dialog box appears, as shown here:

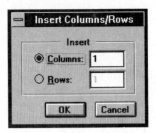

3. Select the Columns or Rows option.

4. Type the number of columns or rows into the corresponding number box and choose OK. WordPerfect replicates the structure of the column or row where the insertion point was located.

shortcut (ALT) + (INS) *is a shortcut for inserting a single row above where the insertion point currently resides.* (ALT) + (SHIFT) + (INS) *inserts a row below the current location of the insertion point.*

Keep in mind when inserting a column that left and right margins are a limiting factor. WordPerfect will attempt to insert a column of the same size as the column where the insertion point is located or, if that's not possible, a narrower column. If the entire space between the margins is occupied, however, then rather than insert a new column, WordPerfect will split the current column in half.

Cutting or Copying Rows and Columns

You cut or copy text within one cell in much the same way as you cut or copy text in a document. You can also cut or copy cells, rows, or columns by

11

selecting the cells, rows, or columns and choosing Edit, Cut or Edit, Copy. The Table Cut/Copy dialog box appears, as shown here:

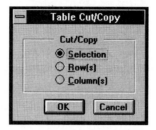

If you select Selection and choose OK, the text alone, without the structure, will be cut or copied into the Clipboard. Then, when you place the insertion point in a cell, row, or column and choose Edit, Paste, WordPerfect adds the contents of the Clipboard—or just the text—to what is already in the cell, row, or column.

If you select Column(s) or Row(s) and choose OK, the text and structure both are cut or copied into the Clipboard. Then, when you place the insertion point in a table and choose Edit, Paste, WordPerfect adds columns from the Clipboard to the left of the insertion point or adds rows above the insertion point.

Adjusting Column Widths

You can widen or reduce the width of columns in several ways. One method uses the Format Column dialog box, as shown in these steps:

1. Position the insertion point in the column you wish to change, or select the columns.

2. Choose Layout, Tables, Column, or click the Tbl Col button on the Tables button bar. The Format Column dialog box appears.

3. Choose Column Width, type in a new measurement, and choose OK.

When a column is widened, the whole table expands until the right margin is reached. If the table extends fully from the left to the right margin, then for every increase in the width of a column, WordPerfect decreases the largest column to the right by a corresponding amount. When a column is reduced in width, the entire table is reduced in width (unless you set the table to extend across the full width of the page on the Table Options dialog box, as described later in this chapter).

The other option for adjusting column widths is with the ruler. Choose View, Ruler if the ruler is not already displayed on screen. When the insertion point is in a table, arrowheads pointing downward on the ruler represent *table column markers*.

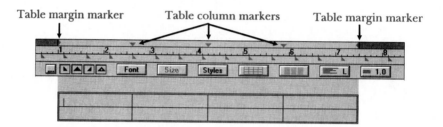

Click and drag a table column marker to widen or reduce a column. When you do, the width of the table is unaffected but the width of each column to the right is changed. You can also hold down (SHIFT) while you drag a marker to have only that marker move. Hold down (CTRL) while you drag a marker, and the whole table changes in size so that all the markers to the right retain their original widths. You can also change the width of the first or last column by dragging the left or right table margin marker.

Adjusting the Row Height

Rows in WordPerfect are fluid; a row will expand in height to accommodate both lines of text that you type in and a change in the height of the characters (such as when you change the font to a larger type size). You can make the row layout less fluid, for instance to create and complete fill-in-the-blank forms or a calendar, by using options that limit the amount of text you can have in each row.

11

Position the insertion point in a row or select rows. Then, choose Layout, Tables, Row or click the Tbl Row button on the Tables button bar. The Format Row dialog box appears as shown here:

Select from the options presented and choose OK. The Single Line option allows only one line of text to be typed and displayed per row, while Multi Line is the initial setting, which allows for as many lines in a row as you type. (If a row has multiple lines with text on each line and you change to the Single Line option, only the first line of text appears in the table. The other lines of text will reappear only if you switch back to the Multi Line option.) Auto Row Height will adjust the height of each row based on the size of the characters, while Fixed Row Height allows you to specify a height for each row, regardless of the font size of the text. The measurement in the Fixed Line Height number box when you first display the dialog box is the current row height.

Joining or Splitting Cells

You can combine, or *join*, multiple cells into one cell by selecting the cells you wish to combine and choosing Layout, Tables, Join. Or, click the Tbl Join button on the Tables button bar. If the cells contain text, WordPerfect replaces column delineations with hard tabs and row delineations with hard returns.

Conversely, you can break one cell into many cells by positioning the insertion point in the cell you wish to *split* and choosing Layout, Tables, Split. Or, click Tbl Split on the Tables button bar. From the dialog box that appears, select Column(s) or Row(s) and type a number that represents the number of columns or rows you wish to create from the cell. Then choose OK. WordPerfect attempts to split a cell by modeling it after existing columns or rows. Selecting multiple cells before you split it means each cell will be split into the number of columns or rows you specify.

Figure 11-3 shows an invoice created by first creating a table of six columns and 25 rows, and then joining some cells (to create the large area below "SHIPPING ADDRESS", for example) and splitting others. (Line styles, described next, were also changed for some of the cells, and some of the cells were shaded, which you'll learn how to do later in this chapter.)

Changing the Line Style

You can change the *line style,* or the appearance of the lines that make up the table grid. The default setting for a table is to have outside borders of double lines, and inside borders of single lines.

You can change the line style of the top, bottom, left, or right borders for a single cell. Or, if you select a group of cells, columns, or rows, you can change the top, bottom, left, or right borders, the inside border, or the outside border for the selected cells all at once.

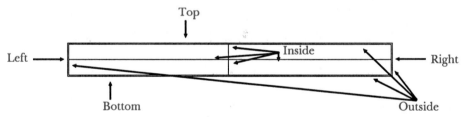

Position the insertion point in a cell or select multiple cells. Then choose Layout, Tables, Lines, or click Tbl Lines on the Tables button bar. The Table Lines dialog box appears, as shown here:

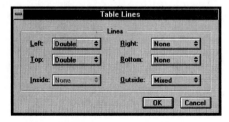

11

Figure 11-3. *An invoice created by joining certain cells in a table and splitting others*

SHIPPING ADDRESS		INVOICE NUMBER			
		ACCOUNT #			
		DATE			
BILLING ADDRESS		TERMS			
		SHIPPING/HANDLING			

ITEM #	DESCRIPTION	SHIP DATE	QTY	PRICE	TOTAL

METHOD OF PAYMENT					
		SUBTOTAL			
		SALES TAX			
		AMOUNT DUE			

The current line styles are shown for each border. ("Mixed" signifies that a border for a group of cells is currently a mixture of different line styles.) Select a border that you wish to change, and choose from the pop-up list box. Your choices are: <u>N</u>one (no line), <u>S</u>ingle, <u>D</u>ouble, D<u>a</u>shed, D<u>o</u>tted, <u>T</u>hick, and <u>E</u>xtra Thick. Then choose OK.

note *Because no space exists between borders, a border line may become thicker than you desired. For instance, if you choose a single line for both the right border of one cell and for the left border of the next cell to the right, the border line will be double the usual thickness. To set a single-line border, set one of these borders to "single line" and the other to "none".*

Deleting a Table

When you create a table grid, a table definition code is inserted into the text. It indicates the table number (used if you create lists of tables, as described in Chapter 15), the number of columns in the table, and the width of each column. Here's an example of a table definition code for the first table in a document containing three columns, each 2.17 inches in width:

```
[Tbl Def:I;3,2.17",2.17",2.17"]
```

To view this code, press <u>V</u>iew, Reveal <u>C</u>odes, which switches you to the reveal codes workspace. (You will see other codes as well: [Row] and [Cell] codes reserve space for each row and column, and the [Tbl Off] code marks the end of the table.)

One way you can delete a table's structure, a table's contents, or both, is by deleting the table's definition code. Position the insertion point on the table definition code, and press (DEL). A Delete Table dialog box appears with three selection options: <u>E</u>ntire Table, <u>C</u>ontents, and <u>T</u>able Structure. Choose <u>E</u>ntire Table and press OK to delete the entire table including both the structure (the grid) and the text within the table. Choose <u>C</u>ontents (text only) and press OK to delete the text; the table structure remains. Choose <u>T</u>able Structure (leave text) and press OK to delete the table structure but not the text; the text remains, and is formatted into tabular columns.

Another method to delete a table is to select all the cells in the table and press (DEL) or (BACKSPACE). The Delete Table dialog box appears, with the same three selection options: Entire Table, Contents, and Table Structure.

If you make a selection that includes the entire table and also extends outside the table, then when you press (DEL) or (BACKSPACE), the whole table (structure and text) is deleted immediately.

Formatting in a Table

Just as you do in the document workspace, you can format text within a cell using features such as Indent, Center, or Flush Right. (Keep in mind, however, that because (TAB) moves the insertion point to the next cell when in tables, you must press the key sequence (CTRL) + (TAB) to insert a hard tab, such as for indenting the first line of a paragraph. Similarly, press (CTRL) + (SHIFT) + (TAB) to insert a margin release code.) You can also use font and font attributes in a cell. For instance, press (CTRL) + (B) within a cell, and text that you type will be boldfaced until you press (CTRL) + (B) to turn off boldface in that cell. Or you can select the text and then press (CTRL) + (B).

Another way to change the format in tables is to use commands on the Tables menu, which can apply to the entire table, a column or group of columns, or particular cells.

Options for Formatting a Table

You can make changes to the entire table by positioning the insertion point anywhere in the table and choosing Layout, Tables, Options or clicking the Tbl Opts button on the Tables button bar. The Table Options dialog box appears. (Refer to Figure 11-2.) Your format options in the Table Options dialog box are as follows:

- *Table Size* This option sets up the number of columns and rows that will comprise the table (discussed previously).

- *Cell Margins*   This option determines how much white space to have between the text of each cell and the left, right, top, and bottom borders of that cell. The effect of cell margin changes will not show in the document workspace, but will appear on the printed page (or when using the Print Preview feature).

- *Shading*   This option specifies the amount and degree of gray shading in a table. The higher the percentage, the darker the shading, so 10 percent is faint shading and 100 percent is black. Your printer may or may not be able to print cells with shading.

  This option affects only those cells for which you turn on shading in the Format Cell dialog box (which is described shortly).

- *Disable Cell Locks*   This option turns on or off the ability to lock cells. It is useful to lock cells that contain information you don't want to be accidentally erased by you or someone else who edits the table. An example of a cell that you may wish to lock is one that contains a formula.

  This option affects only those cells that you lock using the Format Cell dialog box (which is described shortly). Because cells are locked individually, you can turn this option on to temporarily unlock all the cells in the table without permanently unlocking each locked cell. When you turn this option off again to reinstate the cell locks, only those cells locked before you turned the option on will be locked.

- *Position*   This option establishes the horizontal position of your table on the page. This option allows you to place the table in relation to the left margin, the right margin, centered between left and right margins, extending across the full width between the left and right margins, or at a specific measurement from the left edge of the page (the default setting).

- *Negative Result Display*   This option indicates to WordPerfect how negative math results will be displayed—whether to show the negative results of calculations preceded by a minus sign (the default setting) or displayed in parentheses. The ability to perform math in tables is described farther on in this chapter.

- *Attributes*   This option designates specific rows that will be repeated at the top of every page if the table extends beyond one page. For example, suppose you type a table similar to that shown in Figure 11-1, but the table extends for five pages. In the cells across the very first row of the table, you could type the headers **Name**, **Position**, and **Phone Number**. Then, in the Table Options dialog box, choose Attributes and type **1** into the Header Rows number box; the headers will be repeated as the top row on every page. The default setting is 0, which means no header rows.

Options for Formatting a Column

You can format all the cells in one or more columns in a simple command. First position the insertion point in the column you wish to reformat or select a group of columns. Then, choose Layout, Tables, Column, or click the Tbl Col button on the Tables button bar. The Format Column dialog box appears, as shown in Figure 11-4.

Figure 11-4.   *Format Column dialog box*

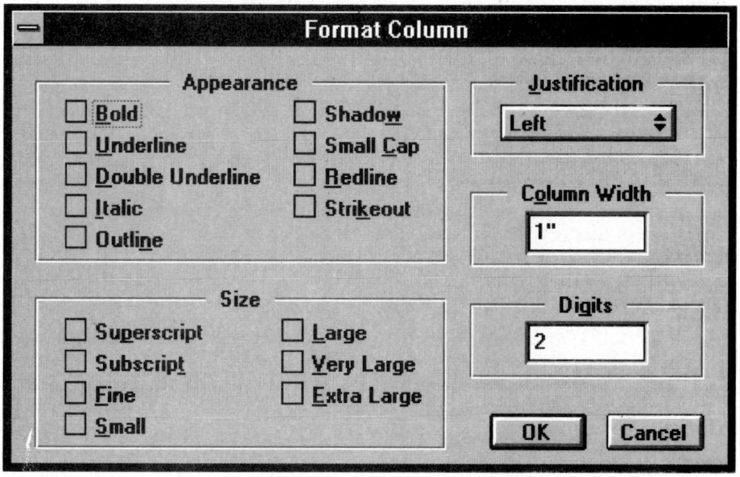

Your options for effecting changes in columns are as follows:

- *Appearance* and *Size*   These options turn on or off appearance and size attributes for text in the column(s). When you first display the Format Column dialog box, an X in a check box means the attribute is currently turned on for the column(s). Shading in a check box means that the attribute is turned on for some, but not all of the columns you are about to format.

- *Justification*   This option specifies whether text in the columns is left-justified, fully justified, centered, right-justified, or decimal aligned.

- *Column Width*   This option sets the width of the column(s), as discussed previously.

- *Digits*   This option determines how many digits will appear after the decimal for calculated results when performing math in a table.

Options for Formatting a Cell

Position the insertion point in the cell you wish to reformat or select a group of cells. Then, choose Layout, Tables, Cell, or click the Tbl Cell button on the Tables button bar. The Format Cell dialog box appears, as shown in Figure 11-5.

Your options are as follows:

- *Appearance* and *Size*   These options turn on or off appearance and size attributes for text in the cell(s). When you first display the Format Cell dialog box, an X in a check box means that the attribute is currently turned on for the cell(s). Shading in a check box means that the attribute is turned on for some, but not all, of the columns you are about to format. An appearance or size change made for a cell overrides a setting of the same type for the column where the cell is located, and thus the Use Column Size and Appearance check box is turned off.

- *Justification* This option determines whether text in the cell(s) is left-justified, fully justified, centered, right-justified, or decimal aligned. A justification change made for a cell overrides the justification setting for the column where the cell is located, and thus the Use Column Justification check box is turned off.

- *Alignment* This option aligns text in a cell vertically at the top, bottom, or center of the cell(s). The result is displayed at the printer, but not in the document workspace.

- *Shading* This option turns shading on or off for the cell(s). The degree of shading is specified in the Table Options dialog box, as previously described.

- *Lock* This option turns the Lock feature on or off for the cell(s). When you lock a cell, the insertion point is not allowed in that cell. This lets you protect the contents of a cell from accidental changes.

- *Ignore Cell When Calculating* This option determines whether or not the contents of the cell(s) are taken into account when math is performed in the table.

Figure 11-5. *Format Cell dialog box*

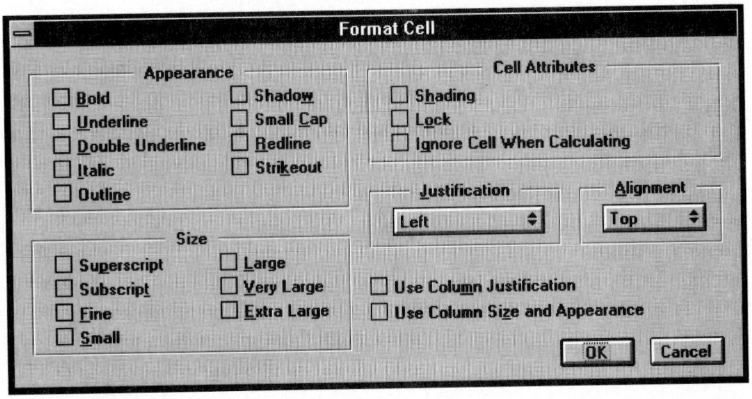

Performing Math in a Table

If you have created a table using the Tables feature, you can perform a variety of mathematical calculations within the table. An example of a table before and after WordPerfect calculations is shown in Figure 11-6.

Before calculating in a table, construct a table and insert the text and the known values. You then insert a *formula* anywhere you wish to calculate a result. A formula can contain numbers, cell addresses (such as B4 or C1), parentheses (to change the order of calculations; otherwise WordPerfect calculates formulas from left to right), and the following math operators:

+   Addition
–   Subtraction
∗   Multiplication
/   Division

Here are some examples of formulas (note that there are no spaces between the operators and the values):

a1*2	Multiplies the value in cell A1 by 2
a1–a2	Subtracts the value of A2 from A1
a1+a2/3	Adds the values in cells A1 and A2, and divides the result by 3
a1+(a2/3	Adds the value of A1 to the result of dividing A2 by 3

You can also insert an abbreviated formula, called a *function*, into a cell. The function must be inserted on its own in a cell, unaccompanied by values, cell addresses, or any other characters. There are three functions:

Function Symbol	Function Name	Function Description
+	Subtotal	Adds all the numbers directly above the function in the same column and produces a subtotal
=	Total	Adds the subtotals directly above the function in the same column and produces a total
*	Grand total	Adds the totals directly above the function in the same column and produces a grand total

Figure 11-6. *Table math used to calculate yearly totals and yearly increases*

Before table math

R&R WINE ASSOCIATION TWO YEAR SALES COMPARISON (in thousands of cases)			
CATEGORY	JANUARY 1993	JANUARY 1992	INCREASE
Cabernet	233.8	130.1	
Chardonnay	444.5	343.2	
Chenin Blanc	220.3	222.3	
Pinot Noir	410.5	512.8	
Sauvignon	960.5	745.4	
Total			

After table math

R&R WINE ASSOCIATION TWO YEAR SALES COMPARISON (in thousands of cases)			
CATEGORY	JANUARY 1993	JANUARY 1992	INCREASE
Cabernet	233.8	130.1	103.70
Chardonnay	444.5	343.2	101.30
Chenin Blanc	220.3	222.3	-2.00
Pinot Noir	410.5	512.8	-102.30
Sauvignon	960.5	745.4	215.10
Total	2,269.60	1,953.80	315.80

Figure 11-7 shows an example of where subtotal and total functions could be used.

Insert a formula or function into a cell with these steps:

1. Position the insertion point in the cell where you want to calculate the results of a formula.

2. Choose <u>L</u>ayout, <u>T</u>ables, <u>F</u>ormula, or select the Tbl Form button. (You may need to scroll in the Tables button bar to view this button.) The Tables Formula dialog box appears, as shown here:

3. Type a formula or function in the <u>F</u>ormula text box.

4. Choose OK.

The result of the formula (or function) is shown in the cell. The formula itself is displayed on the left side of the status line, preceded by an equal sign, when the insertion point is in that cell. For instance, suppose you insert the formula **b2–b3** in a cell. The left side of the status line when the insertion point is in that cell will read

```
=b2-b3
```

If you insert the subtotal function, the left side of the status line will read

```
=+
```

To change a formula, repeat steps 1 and 2 in the preceding list and then change the formula in the <u>F</u>ormula text box. To delete a formula, select the cell containing the formula and press (BACKSPACE) or (DEL).

So that you don't have to repeat a formula, you can copy a formula to another cell. You can also copy formulas down in a column or across in a row.

Figure 11-7. *Values can be added in columns using subtotal and total functions*

R&R WINE ASSOCIATION REGIONAL SALES (in thousands of cases)			
REGION	JANUARY 1993	JANUARY 1992	JANUARY 1991
Eastern U.S.	33.8	23.9	30.8
Central U.S.	44.5	42.5	44.9
Western U.S.	20.3	14.7	20.4
United States			
Eastern Europe	5.1	16.1	15.0
Western Europe	25.4	20.2	5.4
Europe			
Total			

Place total function here

Place subtotal function here

All cell addresses in a formula are relative to the formula's location. For example, suppose that in cell B1, you insert the formula **a1+15**. WordPerfect thinks of that formula as "cell to the left" plus 15. Here's what you'll get, therefore, if you copy the formula to the next row:

	Column A	Column B Formula	Column B Results
Row 1	100	a1+15	115
Row 2	950	a2+15 ⎦ copied	965

To copy a formula into another cell, follow these steps:

1. Position the insertion point in the cell containing the formula you want to copy.

2. Choose Layout, Tables, Formula or select the Tbl Form button.

3. Select To Cell and type in the cell address to which you want to copy the formula. (WordPerfect suggests the current cell.)

   If you want to copy the formula down, select Down and type the number of rows you want to copy it down to.

   To copy the formula to the right, select Right and type the number of columns you want to copy the formula right to.

4. Choose OK.

Here are some pointers when using math in tables:

- If you change any values on which a formula relies, the formulas will not automatically recalculate. You *must recalculate* the table. To do so, position the insertion point inside the table and choose Layout, Tables, Calculate, or select Tbl Calc from the Tables button bar. It's a good idea to recalculate a table before you save or print a file, to make sure that the calculations are current.

- If a cell has more than one line, WordPerfect will use the number closest to the bottom of a cell in calculations. It is therefore a good idea to enter only one number in each cell. Also keep in mind that if the line contains numbers as well as other characters, the other characters will be ignored in a calculation. For instance, if a cell contains "50#2", the number 502 is used. If a cell contains "15 bottles in 2 cases", the number 152 is used.

- If a cell in a table contains numbers that you don't wish to be part of calculations, make sure to ask WordPerfect to ignore that cell when calculated. In Figure 11-6, for instance, the cells containing "January 1993" and "January 1992" must be ignored or else the 1993 and 1992 will be included in the subtotal. Simply turn on the Ignore Cell When Calculating option in the Format Cell dialog box, as discussed earlier.

- You may wish to lock cells that contain formulas so that the insertion point cannot move to those cells. As a result, the formulas cannot accidentally be changed. A formula in a locked cell is still calculated. You lock a cell in the Format Cell dialog box, as discussed earlier.

- You can format numbers to align at a decimal point, as shown in Figures 11-6 and 11-7, using the Justification option in the Format

11

Column or Format Cell dialog box. You can also determine how many digits are placed to the right of the decimal point using the Digits option in the Format Column dialog box. Moreover, you can specify how negative results are shown using the Negative Result Display option in the Table Options dialog box.

Defining and Turning On Columns

In addition to the Tables feature, WordPerfect offers another feature for aligning text into columns. With the Columns feature, you can create as few as 2 and as many as 24 columns. There are two basic types of columns that you can select from: newspaper columns and parallel columns. In newspaper columns, text runs down the page in one column, and then starts at the top of the next column, as in a magazine or newspaper or brochure. In parallel columns, column entries are held together side by side across the page. Text runs across the rows, as in, for example, a script, or inventory list, or chart. You can also select parallel block protect columns, which are identical to parallel columns except that column entries are protected from being split by a page break.

The flow of text in both types of columns is shown in Figure 11-8. The newspaper column is one that the Tables feature cannot emulate. However, parallel columns and the Tables feature can both be used for the same types of documents. You may wish to try both, and see which you prefer—although you may quickly discover that tables are much easier to edit, and decide to use columns only when your document needs to be in newspaper style.

There are two ways to create columns: using the menu bar, or using the ruler.

Creating Columns with the Menu Bar

When creating columns, you must specify the number of columns you desire and where you want the left and right margins of each column. If you

Figure 11-8.   *How text flows for different types of columns*

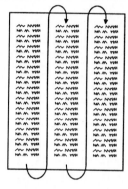

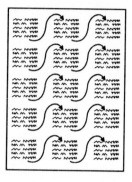

Newspaper columns

Parallel or parallel block
protect columns

want columns of equal width, WordPerfect can calculate the column margins automatically. To define columns, follow these steps:

1. Position the insertion point where you want columns to begin.

2. Choose Layout, Columns, Define. The Define Columns dialog box appears, as shown in Figure 11-9.

   This dialog box shows the initial settings for columns. Unless you have already defined columns, you'll have these settings: two columns, newspaper type, extending from the left to the right margins across the full page with .5 inch of gutter space between the columns.

3. To change the number of columns, type a new entry into the Number of Columns text box.

4. To change the type of columns, select Newspaper, Parallel, or Parallel Block Protect.

5. If you want evenly spaced columns, but wish to change the gutter space between columns on the page, select Distance Between Col-

11

Figure 11-9. *Define Columns dialog box*

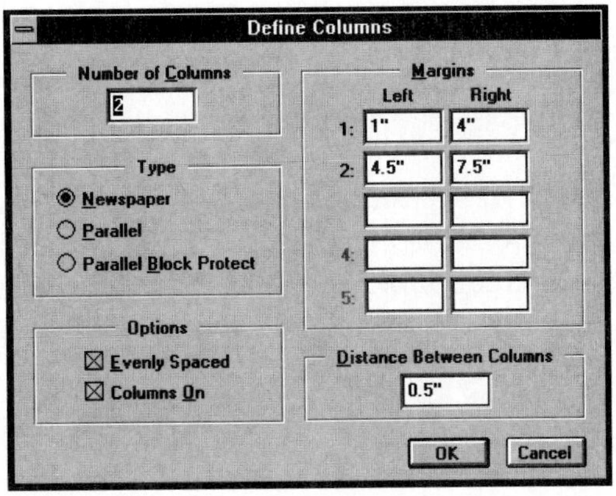

Define Columns

Number of Columns
2

Type
● Newspaper
○ Parallel
○ Parallel Block Protect

Options
☒ Evenly Spaced
☒ Columns On

Margins

	Left	Right
1:	1"	4"
2:	4.5"	7.5"
4:		
5:		

Distance Between Columns
0.5"

OK   Cancel

umns and type in a new measurement. And, make sure that the Evenly Spaced check box is turned on.

If you want to set your own margin settings in each column, type in new left and right measurements for each column in the Margins number boxes. (You are not limited to the current left/right margins across the full page when setting your own column margins. For instance, even when the left margin of the page starts at 1 inch, you can start the left margin of the first column at .5 inch.)

If you set your own column margins, be sure not to overlap columns and be sure to leave some space between columns so that the columns are easy to read. For instance, if you wish to create two columns and the first has left/right margins of 1 inch and 3.5 inches, you must make sure that the second column starts after position 3.6"; somewhere between position 3.8" and 4.1" would be best to ensure sufficient gutter space between columns for easy reading.

6. If you want to turn columns on as soon as you close the dialog box, make sure that the Columns On check box is turned on.

7. Choose OK.

shortcut (ALT) + (SHIFT) + (F9) *is the shortcut for* Layout, Columns.

A column definition code is inserted in the text, which indicates the type, number, and margins of each column. For instance, if you set two newspaper columns, one with margins of 1 inch and 4 inches and the other with margins of 4.5 inches and 7.5 inches, the code would be

```
[Col Def:Newspaper;2;1",4",4.5",7.5"]
```

Moreover, if the Columns On check box was turned on, the code [Col On] is inserted to turn columns on, and the status line displays a new indicator, the Column indicator. This indicates the column where the insertion point currently resides. For instance, at the top of the document, the status line would read

```
Col 1 Pg 1 Ln 1" Pos 1"
```

If the Columns On check box was turned off, you can turn columns on at any time in your text by choosing Layout, Columns, Columns On. You must turn columns on for the column definition to take effect.

Creating Columns with the Ruler

As described in Chapter 6, the ruler is a quick way for mouse users to execute layout changes in a document. One button on the ruler is designed for creating columns. You can choose from two to five columns. They will be evenly spaced and newspaper type. Use the ruler to create columns with these steps:

1. If the ruler is not currently displayed on screen, choose View, Ruler.

2. Position the insertion point where you want the column format to begin.

3. Click and hold the Columns button, which is the third button from the right. A drop-down menu displays with options for you to select two, three, four, or five newspaper columns.

4. Drag the mouse to select from two to five newspaper columns. (Columns created using the ruler will be evenly spaced.)

5. Release the mouse button.

A column definition code and a column on code are inserted, such as,

```
[Col Def:Newspaper;2;1",4",4.5",7.5"] [Col On]
```

The status line displays a Column indicator.

shortcut *Double-clicking the Columns button on the ruler is equivalent to choosing Layout, Columns, Define on the menu bar. The Define Columns dialog box appears.*

Typing Text in Columns

How you type text into columns depends on whether you're using newspaper or parallel columns.

Newspaper Columns

When typing in newspaper columns, enter text as if typing a regular document. Word wrap will ensure that the text remains within the boundaries of the first column. When you reach the bottom of the page, a soft page code [SPg] is inserted. The insertion point moves to the top of the next column automatically. When you reach the bottom of the last column on the page, a soft page code is again inserted, but this time a single line appears on screen to signify a soft page break, and the insertion point jumps to the beginning of the first column on a new page.

You can also end a column before it is full by creating a manual page break. Follow these steps:

1. Position the insertion point where you want the page break to occur.
2. Select Layout, Page, Page Break.

shortcut (CTRL) + (ENTER) *is the shortcut for Layout, Page, Page Break.*

This forces an end to that column, just as it forces an end to a page when you're typing a normal document without columns. A hard page code [HPg] is inserted in the text and the insertion point moves up to the top of the next column. Or, if you create a manual page break when the insertion point is in the last column on the page, a double line is inserted to signify a hard page break, and the insertion point jumps to the first column on a new page.

With the Columns feature, the standard typing features work within each individual column. For instance, you can press (TAB) to indent the first line in a paragraph within a column. Or, with the insertion point at the left margin of a column, press (SHIFT) + (F7) to center a short line of text over that column. Or press (ALT) + (F7) to align a short line of text at the right margin of the column. Figure 11-10 shows an example of text typed into three columns with the first line of each paragraph indented and headings centered.

After typing text into columns, turn off the Columns feature if you wish to type additional text that you don't want formatted into columns. To do so, position the insertion point where you want the column layout to stop, and choose Layout, Columns, Columns Off. A [Col Off] code is inserted in the text, and the insertion point moves to the left margin of a blank line.

Parallel and Parallel Block Protect Columns

Unlike with newspaper columns, when typing into parallel or parallel block protect columns, you must insert a page break after each parallel column entry. The quick method is to press (CTRL) + (ENTER). A hard page code [HPg] is inserted in the text, and the insertion point moves across to the next column, where you type the next entry and press (CTRL) + (ENTER) again to continue. So, in parallel columns, you type each group across the row before moving to the next group. Thus, the entries are typed row by row.

First parallel column
in a group

Last parallel column in a
group is about to be typed

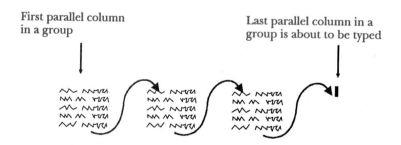

Figure 11-10. *A newsletter created with newspaper columns*

R&R WINE ASSOCIATION
EMPLOYEE NEWS

NEW SERVICE

All R&R Wine Association employees are now eligible for two valuable company services.

First is the new R&R Money Market Fund. Any percentage of your monthly salary can be automatically invested in the Money Market Fund, an established mutual fund with assets so far of over $1 million. The R&R Money Market Fund is just a part of a larger fund, which is over $45 million strong.

You will earn high yields and enjoy a variety of extras. These include free check writing on your account. The service is unlimited; write as many checks as you need. In addition, there's free reinvestment of your dividends so that your earnings grow faster.

The R&R Money Market Fund is professionally managed by The Thomas Corporation, one of the nation's leading mutual fund companies.

Second, and as a complimentary feature, we now offer a financial planning service, free to all employees. You'll learn how to minimize taxes, what to do about life insurance, and how to handle emergency needs. You'll also be advised on pension plan options.

Why do we offer the Money Market Fund? So that your investments are wise ones, so that you get long-term profit from your earnings at R&R.

Why do we offer the FREE financial planning service? For the same reasons.

To find out more about the benefits of joining our company's Money Market Fund, call Karl Nottings at (415) 666-9444. He's also the person you'll want to speak with about setting up an appointment for any of your financial planning needs!

WORLD OF WINES

In our last newsletter, we completed a five-part series on wines produced in the United States. Next month, we begin a new series on the wines of Europe. Our first nation in Europe? By popular request, it will be France.

France is most often considered the greatest wine-producing country in the world. The variety of wines grown here is absolutely amazing: the sparkling wines of Champagne, the red wines of Bordeaux, the red and white wines of Burgundy, the sweet wines of Barsac--just to name a few!

You'll learn about all the French wines we ship around the country in our next edition of R&R Wine News.

-- Lini Snyder

When you complete the last column of a related group and press (CTRL) + (ENTER), the insertion point inserts a blank line and moves to the left margin of what will be the next row of parallel columns.

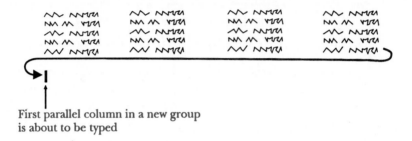

First parallel column in a new group
is about to be typed

You can produce results such as shown in Figure 11-11. Behind the scenes, a variety of codes are inserted when you create parallel columns: [Col On]

Figure 11-11.   *A list of managers created with parallel block protect columns*

R&R WINE ASSOCIATION: LIST OF MANAGERS

```
Lonnie Chang        Director of the Public        (415) 333-4109
                    Relations Department
                    since 4/12/83.

Tim Hader           Distribution Manager,         (415) 549-1101
                    West Coast Region, since
                    6/1/87.  Stationed in
                    Oakland, California.

Paula Garcia        Distribution Manager,         (212) 484-1119
                    East Coast Region, since
                    12/2/82.  Stationed in
                    New York City.

P.J. McClintock     Assistant to the             (415) 333-4401
                    President since 5/13/86.

Sandy Peterson      President since 3/2/82.       (415) 333-4400

John Samsone        Director, Office of          (415) 333-9215
                    Administration, since
                    3/2/82.
```

and [Col Off] codes around each row of entries for parallel columns, and also [BlockPro:On] and [BlockPro:Off] codes around each row for parallel block protect columns.

Moving Between and Editing Columns

To move between columns with your mouse, click in the next column you wish to move to. With the keyboard, you can use the arrow keys. Or a quick method for jumping between columns involves the (ALT) key. Press (ALT) + (←) to move one column to the left, and (ALT) + (→) to move one column to the right.

You can also use the Go To feature to move quickly in and between columns. When the insertion point is placed within a column, choose Edit, Go To or press (CTRL) + (G) to display the Go To dialog box. From the Position pop-up list box, you can then select to go to the top or bottom of the current column, to the first or last column, or to the previous or next column. (Chapter 3 discusses how to use the Go To feature when the insertion point is not located in a column.)

You can redefine your columns—changing the column width, the number of columns, or the distance between columns. Position the insertion point in the first paragraph where the column layout takes effect and choose Layout, Columns, Define to return to the Define Columns dialog box and enter the new measurements. when you choose OK, the [Col Def:] code will be revised and the columns will be reformatted automatically. (However, if the Auto Code Placement feature is off and you wish to redefine your columns, you must position the insertion point more precisely. Reveal codes and place the insertion point just to the right of the [Col Def:] code before you choose Layout, Columns, Define. (See Chapter 17 for more on the Auto Code Placement feature.)

You can also use the ruler to change the column widths. Position the insertion point in the first paragraph where the column layout takes effect. When the insertion point is within a column format, arrowheads pointing in opposite directions on the ruler represent column margin markers, and the gray area between the arrowheads represents the gutter space between columns.

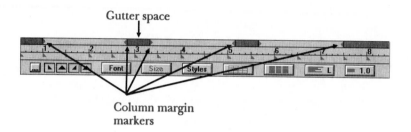

To change a column's width, click and drag a column margin marker to a new position. To move column margins, click and drag the gutter space (gray area) to a new position. To delete a margin, drag the gray area below the ruler and release the mouse button.

When editing in columns, WordPerfect responds more slowly than when editing normal text. This is because continually adjusting the columnar text each time you revise places a heavy burden on WordPerfect. If you are planning extensive editing within columns, you can speed up WordPerfect by turning off the Side-by-Side Columns Display feature, effectively requesting WordPerfect to stop the side-by-side display of columns. Each column would appear on a separate page, with a single line separating them, and Word-Perfect wouldn't take so long to process each of your edits.

Once you revise the columns, you can again choose to display columns side by side. The Side-by-Side Columns Display feature is accessed when you choose File, Preferences, Display as described in Chapter 17.

With newspaper columns, you also have the flexibility to type text first and then format it into columns later. For instance, you can define columns but not turn them on. Type the text. Next, position the insertion point at the top of the text and choose Layout, Columns, Columns On to insert a [Col On] code that turns on the column definition that you previously defined. The text below the [Col On] code is reformatted into columns. You may have text at the bottom of a document that you don't want formatted into columns. In that case, select the text that should be formatted into columns before choosing Layout, Columns, Columns On. Columns are turned on at the start of the text with a [Col On] code and turned off at the end of the selected text

11

with a [Col Off] code. Typing and editing the text first and then formatting into columns later is often an easier and faster method of creating newspaper columns.

Because columns are narrower than a full page of text, uneven spacing in lines is a common problem. For this reason, you might find that hyphenation is useful in columns. An effective way to work with hyphenation is to turn it on after you type the columns.

To add a professional look to your columns, you may wish to place graphics lines between columns or graphics boxes inside columns. See Chapter 12 for a discussion of how to employ the Graphics feature. If you want the graphics between columns, make sure that the insertion point is to the right of the [Col On] code before attempting to insert the graphics.

Quick Reference

- To create a table, choose Layout, Tables, Create and specify the number of columns and rows. You can also click and drag the Tables button on the ruler, or display the Tables button bar, and choose the Table button. The Tables button bar offers shortcuts for choosing table commands.

- To type text into a table, position the insertion point in a cell and begin typing. Word wrap will keep the text within the column's width boundary, and the row boundary will automatically expand to accommodate your text.

- To change the appearance of lines in the table structure, position the insertion point in the cell you wish to change, or select a cell. Then, choose Layout, Tables, Lines. You can choose not to display lines or to display lines of various widths. Your printer must support graphics to be able to print lines in a table.

- To insert or delete rows at the bottom of a table, or to insert or delete columns at the right edge of a table, place the insertion point in the table and choose Layout, Tables, Options. Next, choose Columns or Rows, and type in the new number. You can also insert or delete specific rows or columns with Layout, Tables, Insert or Layout, Tables, Delete.

- To change the width of a table column, position the insertion point in the column and choose Layout, Tables, Columns, Column Width. You can also move the corresponding table column marker on the ruler.

- To use the Table math feature, position the insertion point in a cell where you want to calculate a result and choose Layout, Tables, Formula. Then type a formula into the cell.

- To define the layout of columns, choose Layout, Columns, Define. You can work with newspaper columns or with parallel or with parallel block protect columns. Once columns have been defined, you must turn on columns before the column definition takes effect.

12

Using Graphics and Typesetting in Desktop Publishing

With the advent of desktop publishing, computers have created a publishing revolution. *Desktop publishing* is the ability to control the publishing process for a document using the computer equipment that sits on your desk. WordPerfect's desktop publishing abilities will interest you if, instead of sending your text to designers, typesetters, and printers, you aspire to produce professional-looking newsletters, business reports, brochures, company publications, or manuals on your own.

You learned in Chapter 5 one aspect of desktop publishing—the ability to access fancy fonts and font attributes in your text. This chapter describes some of the other sophisticated features WordPerfect offers for desktop publishing. You'll learn how to insert graphics images into your documents so that you can merge pictures with text. You'll learn how to insert lines in your text—either graphically or by using the Line Draw feature. And, you'll learn how to use some typesetting features to refine how text appears on the page.

Be aware that the graphics and typesetting features available to you depend on the capabilities of your printer. PostScript and laser printers usually offer the most features for desktop publishing; they can produce printed documents of nearly typeset quality and can print good-quality graphics.

About Graphics Boxes and Graphics Images

WordPerfect lets you insert graphics boxes into your text. A *graphics box* is a rectangular-shaped area on screen that can be filled with either a graphics image, with text that you want set off from the body of your document, or with an equation. You can also leave the graphics box empty—for those times, for example, when you will print out the document and paste a photograph or other graphic into the space set aside for your art.

There are five different types of graphics boxes to choose from: figure, text, equation, table, or user. Each type is numbered separately. For instance, if you insert two figure boxes and five text boxes in your document, the figures are numbered as "figure 1" and "figure 2", while the text boxes are numbered 1 through 5.

Generally, you use the five different types of graphics boxes according to what you intend to insert into them. This table tells you which graphics box is usually used for a specific type of image.

Box Type	Contents
Figure	Graphic image—such as picture, diagram, chart
Text	Text—such as a quote, headline, sidebar
Equation	Equation
Table	Text formatted into a table
User	Blank space, or contents of your choice

If you want all the boxes in your document to be numbered sequentially, you could use only one type of graphics box for an entire document—regardless of the contents of each box. You don't have to follow the rules just given if you don't want to. However, if you do choose to use graphics boxes according to the list just given, they let you treat each type of artwork consistently by virtue of their initial settings.

The initial settings for how the five box types appear on the printed page all differ. For example, the initial setting for border style, or how the borders of the art will look, is single-line border for figure boxes, thick top and bottom borders for text and table boxes, and no borders at all for equation and user boxes. Another initial setting is gray shading: text boxes contain ten percent gray shading, while the others contain no shading. The initial settings produce the kind of printed results shown in Figure 12-1. You can change the initial

Figure 12-1. *Initial settings depend on the graphics box type*

Figure box has a single-line border

Wines	East	West
1993	899	566
1992	500	951
1991	338	540

Table box has thick top and bottom borders

```
"Believe it or not," she
said, "every time I drink
a glass of red wine, I
have nightmares!"
```

Text box has gray shading, and thick top and bottom borders

$$T = \sum \frac{P_i}{(1+i)_i}$$

Equation box has no borders

User box has no borders

settings for any of the graphics box types as described in the "Changing the Box Appearance Options" section later in this chapter.

The most common reason for using a graphics box is for placing graphic images into your text. Where do you find a graphics image to insert into a graphics box? WordPerfect Corporation includes 36 graphics images with WordPerfect so that you can start using graphics right away. Each image has the filename extension *.wpg*, which stands for WordPerfect graphic. Figure 12-2 illustrates all 36 images. Because each one is in WPG format, it is ready to be inserted into a graphics box at any time. (You must have installed the graphics files when you installed WordPerfect to have them available. The graphics files are stored in the graphics directory, which is *c:\wpwin\graphics* unless you installed WordPerfect to a different directory. If you have not yet installed the graphics files, see Appendix A.)

Figure 12-2.   *The 36 graphics images packaged with WordPerfect*

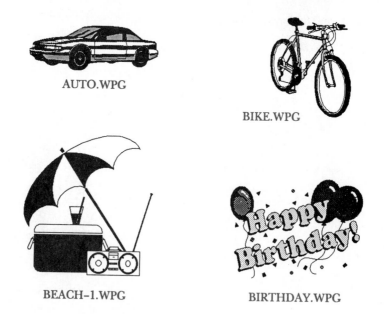

AUTO.WPG

BIKE.WPG

BEACH–1.WPG

BIRTHDAY.WPG

Figure 12-2. *The 36 graphics images packaged with WordPerfect (continued)*

BKGRND–2.WPG

CHECKMAR.WPG

BLUERIBN.WPG

COMPUTR.WPG

BOOKWORM.WPG

BORD–2.WPG

DAISIES.WPG

12

Figure 12-2.   *The 36 graphics images packaged with WordPerfect (continued)*

DEGREE.WPG

GOLF–DGN.WPG

DESK–W.WPG

GUITAR–2.WPG

DRAMA.WPG

HARVEST.WPG

DUCKLING.WPG

JET–2.WPG

FATPENCIL.WPG

LAW.WPG

Figure 12-2. *The 36 graphics images packaged with WordPerfect (continued)*

12

MANUFACT.WPG

PIANO.WPG

MAP–WORL.WPG

MBA.WPG

QUIET.WPG

OWL–WISE.WPG

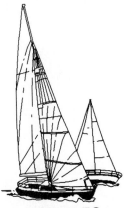

SAIL–BT.WPG

Figure 12-2.   *The 36 graphics images packaged with WordPerfect (continued)*

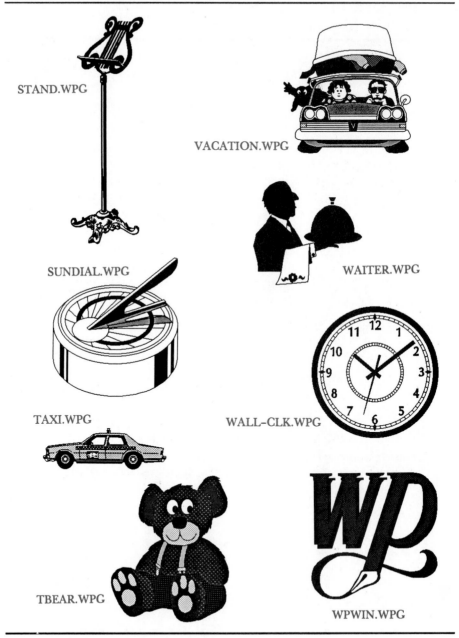

STAND.WPG

VACATION.WPG

SUNDIAL.WPG

WAITER.WPG

TAXI.WPG

WALL–CLK.WPG

TBEAR.WPG

WPWIN.WPG

In addition to these 36 graphics images, you can insert into a graphics box any of the graphics images packaged with earlier versions of WordPerfect, including 5.1 for DOS or 5.0 for DOS.

A WordPerfect graphics box also accepts images from other sources. You can use *clip art* (ready-made) images from other manufacturers. You can use images that have been created using another program (such as Windows Paint) and saved into the Windows Clipboard.

Moreover, you can use images that have been created using another program and saved on disk into a format that WordPerfect supports. Table 12-1 lists the graphics formats that WordPerfect supports, as well as some of the graphics programs that can create each format. As an example, create a pie chart in Lotus 1-2-3 and save it to disk in Lotus's PIC format. Or, create a bar graph in Harvard Graphics and save it in CGM format. Or, draw a diagram in AutoCAD and save it in HPGL format. Then, switch to Word-Perfect and retrieve that pie chart, bar graph, or diagram into a graphics box. When it is inserted, the graphic is converted into WPG format. (If your graphics application is not listed in Table 12-1, you may still be able to capture the contents of the screen to the Clipboard using (PRINT SCREEN); see your Windows manual for details.) The procedure to retrieve a graphic image into a graphics box is described next.

Creating Figure Boxes

WordPerfect assumes you wish to retrieve a graphics image into a figure box. As a result, WordPerfect automatically opens the *Figure Editor,* which is a feature that lets you retrieve and edit a graphics image. Follow these steps to create a figure box and retrieve a graphics image into that box:

1. Position the insertion point where you want the graphics box to appear.

2. Choose Graphics, Figure, Create. This opens the Figure Editor.

3. Choose File, Retrieve. The Retrieve Figure dialog box appears (for the graphics directory, assuming that you installed the WordPerfect graphics files).

Table 12-1. *Graphics Formats Supported by WordPerfect*

WordPerfect-Supported Graphics Format	Graphics Programs to Use
Windows (3.*x*) and OS/2 Presentation Manager Bitmap (BMP)	Windows and OS/2 applications
Computer Graphics MetaFile (CGM)	Arts & Letters, CorelDRAW, Freelance Plus, Graphwriter, Harvard Graphics, PicturePaks, DrawPerfect, PlanPerfect, (for versions of PlanPerfect before 4.0, obtain the graphics driver META.SYS from WordPerfect Corporation), Pixie, Lotus 1-2-3, Designer, Graph Plus
Dr. Halo PIC (DHP)	Dr. Halo II, III
AutoCAD (DXF)	AutoCAD, AutoSketch
PostScript and Encapsulated PostScript (EPS)	Adobe Illustrator, Harvard Graphics, Quattro, ChemText, GRAFPLUS, Designer, Graph Plus
GEM Draw (GEM)	GEM Draw
Hewlett-Packard Graphics Language Plotter File (HPGL)	Anvil-5000, AutoCAD, IBM CBDS, IBM CATIA, IBM GPG, AutoSketch, SlideWrite Plus, Microsoft Chart, Harvard Graphics, VersaCAD, IBM CADAM, IBM GDDM, Graph-in-the-box, DiagramMaster, ChartMaster, CCS Designer, SignMaster, Diagraph, Generic CAD, Chemfile, Easyflow, Windows Draw, VP Graphics, Schema, Mirage, GRAFPLUS, Designer 1.2, DrawPerfect, Graph Plus, Graphics Editor 200, Microsoft Excel, SAS/Graph, Schema, SignMaster
GEM Paint (IMG)	GEM SCAN, DFI Handy Scanner, Boeing Graph, GEM Paint, EnerGraphics

Table 12-1. *Graphics Formats Supported by WordPerfect (continued)*

WordPerfect-Supported Graphics Format	Graphics Programs to Use
Microsoft Windows (2.*x*) Paint (MSP)	Windows Paint
PC Paintbrush (PCX)	CorelDRAW, PC Paintbrush, SlideWrite Plus, HP Graphics Gallery, HP Scanning Gallery, PicturePaks, PFS:First Publisher, Pizazz, Lotus 1-2-3, Designer, Graph Plus
Lotus 1-2-3 PIC (PIC)	Symphony, VP Planner, SuperCalc 4, Words & Figures, Lotus 1-2-3, Quattro, Reflex, Paradox
Macintosh Paint (PNTG)	Macintosh Paint
PC Paint Plus (PPIC)	PC Paint Plus
Tagged Image File (TIFF)	GEM SCAN, DFI Handy Scanner, GEM Paint, EnerGraphics, SlideWrite Plus, CIES (Compuscan), HP Graphics Gallery, HP Scanning Gallery, VGA Paint, Scan Man, GeniScan, Pizazz, Designer, Graph Plus, CorelDRAW
Windows Metafile (WMF)	Windows Applications
WordPerfect Graphics (WPG)	PicturePaks, VGA Paint, Hotshot, Hijaak, DrawPerfect, CorelDRAW

Note: Some programs can be saved in more than one graphics format.

4. Type or select the name of a graphics file you wish to recall and choose <u>R</u>etrieve.

   If the graphics file is in WPG format, it is inserted into the box. If the graphics file is in a format supported by WordPerfect (see Table 12-1), it is converted into WPG format and inserted into the box. (If the graphics file is in a format not supported by WordPerfect, a message will appear indicating the incorrect format. That graphics file cannot be retrieved unless converted to a WordPerfect-supported format.)

5. If you wish, you can edit the figure. (More on the Figure Editor later in this chapter.)

6. Choose File, Close, or press (CTRL) + (F4).

Another method of creating a figure box bypasses the Figure Editor entirely and is a quicker method for creating a figure box containing an image. Follow these steps:

1. Position the insertion point where you want the graphics box to appear.

2. Choose Graphics, Figure, Retrieve. The Retrieve Figure dialog box appears for the graphics directory.

3. Type or select the name of a graphics file you wish to recall and choose Retrieve.

shortcut (F11) *is the shortcut for* Graphics, Figure, Retrieve.

A third method applies only if you created a graphics image in another graphics program (such as Windows Paintbrush) and saved that image into the Clipboard. Position the insertion point where you want the graphics image to appear in your WordPerfect document and choose Edit, Paste. Since the Clipboard contains a graphics image, it is automatically inserted into a figure box. (See Chapter 8 for more on the Clipboard.)

Creating Text Boxes

WordPerfect assumes you wish to type text into a text box, and so automatically opens the *Text Editor*, which is a feature that lets you type and edit text. Follow these steps to create a text box:

1. Position the insertion point where you want the graphics box to appear.

2. Choose Graphics, Text Box, Create. This opens the Text Editor.

3. Type the text you want to appear in the text box, just as you would in the document workspace. You can use the Columns or Tables features (see Chapter 11), choose a different font or font attribute, or use other editing and formatting features in a text box.

    You can also choose File, Retrieve and recall a file (no longer than one page) into the text box.

    Text will wrap according to the current width of the box, which when you first create a text box is half the width between margins.

4. If you wish, you can rotate the text (more on the Text Editor later in this chapter).

5. Choose Close, or press (CTRL) + (F4).

shortcut (ALT) + (F11) *is the shortcut for Graphics, Text Box, Create.*

Creating Equation Boxes

WordPerfect assumes you wish to insert an equation into an equation box, and so automatically opens the *Equation Editor*, which is a feature that lets you insert and edit equations. Follow these steps to create an equation box:

1. Position the insertion point where you want the graphics box to appear.

2. Choose Graphics, Equation, Create. This opens the Equation Editor.

3. Type the equation (more on the Equation Editor later in this chapter).

    You can also choose File, Retrieve and recall a file into the Equation box.

4. Choose Close, or press (CTRL) + (F4).

Creating Table or User Boxes

In a table or user box, you can specify what the contents will be—either a graphics image, text, or an equation—based on which editor you select. Follow these steps:

1. Position the insertion point where you want the box to appear.

2. Choose Graphics, Table Box, Create or Graphics, User Box, Create. The Select Editor dialog box appears:

3. Select the editor based on the type of art you plan to put in that box. That is, select Figure Editor to insert a graphics image into the box. Select Text Editor to type text. Select Equation Editor to insert an equation.

4. Retrieve the image, type the text, or create the equation you wish to insert in the box.

5. Choose Close, or press (CTRL) + (F4).

Viewing a Graphics Box On Screen

How a graphics box is positioned in your document when you first create it depends on the type of box. For figure, text, table, and user boxes, the box takes up half the available width between margins on the page, and is placed on the line below the insertion point. It aligns at the right margin, and existing text aligns against the left margin, on the left side of the image. (The only way to place text on both sides of a box is to format the text into columns and place the box between them.) For equation boxes, the box takes up the full width between margins and is placed on the line above the insertion point. A box's position and size can be changed, as described later in this chapter in the "Changing the Box Position and Size" section.

What you see on screen when you create a graphics box depends on the status of the View Graphics feature. When the feature is off—meaning that there is no check mark next to the View, Graphics command—a box outline appears. The box type and number is indicated in the upper left corner inside the box. If you choose View, Graphics to turn the feature on, the border style and contents of the box will display on screen, just as it will appear on the printed page. Examples of graphics boxes when the View Graphics feature is off and on are shown in Figure 12-3. Turning View Graphics off will allow WordPerfect to run faster, and is therefore a good idea when working in a long document or where multiple graphics boxes are inserted in the same document.

A hidden code indicates the box type, the box number, the name of the graphics file if one was retrieved, and a caption code [Box Number], if that box has a caption. (The procedure to insert a caption is described next.) The code is placed at the insertion point for a figure, text, table, and user box. It is placed at the beginning of the paragraph where the insertion point is located for the equation box. (The Anchor To command determines where the code is placed, as described in the section "Changing the Box Position and Size" later on in this chapter.) So, suppose you just defined your first figure in a document, which contains a graphics image named *auto.wpg*. The code inserted is [Figure:1;auto.wpg]. If you just defined your first text box, the code inserted is [Text:1;;]. If the text box had a caption, the code would be [Text:1;;[Box Number]].

You can delete a graphics box by revealing codes and then deleting the graphics box code. You can also select the box and press (DEL).

Inserting a Box Caption and Renumbering a Box

You can create a caption for any graphics box in your document, which can include the box number (such as "Figure 1"), a description of the box's

Figure 12-3.   *A Graphics box can be displayed either revealing or hiding its contents*

View Graphics is turned off

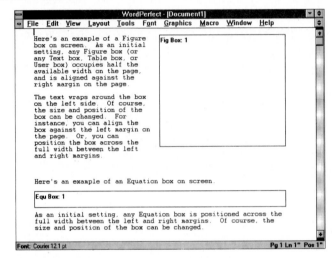

View Graphics is turned on

12

contents (such as "Map of the Region"), or a combination of both. A caption is *not* automatically inserted for you. You must open and close the Caption Editor for each graphics box for which you want to display and print a caption. To open the Caption Editor and create a new caption or edit an existing caption, follow these steps:

1. Choose Graphics and the type of box you wish to edit (such as Figure), Caption. A dialog box appears, such as the Edit Figure Caption dialog box for a figure box:

2. WordPerfect will assume that you wish to edit the caption for the next box forward from the insertion point's location. Choose OK. Or, if you want to edit a different box caption, type in its graphics box number and choose OK.

Mouse users have an alternate method of viewing the Caption Editor. Follow these steps:

1. Position the mouse pointer inside the graphics box for which you want to create or edit a caption.
2. Click the *right* mouse button.
3. Choose Edit Caption.

Figure 12-4 shows an example of the Caption Editor on screen. Three command buttons appear just below the menu bar, and a caption appears in the caption workspace. The first time you display the Caption Editor, the default caption is always automatically inserted. In Figure 12-4, the default caption is for the first figure box in a document. Here is the default caption setting for each of the different box types:

Box Type	Default Caption Numbering and Style
Figure	Figure 1
Text	1
Equation	(1)
Table	Table I
User	1

WordPerfect will insert each of your captions in this style, and in boldface, unless you change the default caption settings for a particular box type, as described later in the "Changing the Box Appearance Options" section.

The default caption that WordPerfect automatically inserts in the Caption Editor is actually the code [Box Num], and not text at all. For instance, if you reveal codes when viewing the Caption Editor screen shown in Figure 12-4, you'll discover that the "Figure 1" is not text, but rather the code [Box Num].

With the Caption Editor shown you have these choices when deciding on the content and display of the caption:

- Accept the default caption by simply choosing <u>C</u>lose.

Figure 12-4.   *Caption Editor for "Figure 1"*

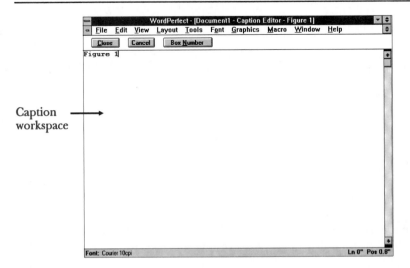

12

- Edit the caption and then choose <u>C</u>lose. You can, for example, add text to the caption that describes the contents of the box. Or you can change the font or font attribute used to print the caption. You can also remove the default caption with the (BACKSPACE) or (DEL) key and type a caption that contains no box number. (Remember when you're typing that the text of the caption remains within the boundaries established by the width of the box.) To insert the code [Box Num], thereby reinserting the default caption, choose Box <u>N</u>umber.

- Delete the caption and/or delete everything in the caption workspace. After deleting, choose <u>C</u>lose. In this way, you remove a caption from the graphics box.

Where the caption appears in relation to the box depends on another setting. Here is the default caption position setting for each of the different box types:

Box Type	Default Caption Position
Figure	Below the box and outside its border
Text	Below the box and outside its border
Equation	Right of the equation and inside the box border
Table	Above the box and outside its border
User	Below the box and outside its border

WordPerfect will insert each of your captions in this location, unless you change the default caption position, as described later in the "Changing the Box Appearance Options" section. Here's an example of a figure caption with the default caption numbering style and the default caption position:

Figure 1

The caption will print in the current text. You can change the font for a single caption in the Caption Editor. Or, you can change the font for all captions in a document by changing the Document Initial Font (see Chapter 5 for more information).

All graphics boxes are numbered consecutively in a document according to the box type. So the caption for the first figure box will be "Figure 1", and the caption for the second figure box will be "Figure 2". However, you can start numbering anew anywhere in the text. For instance, you can insert five figures in a document, (numbered 1 through 5), and then add a later figure and number it 1 (instead of 6). You may want to do this to restart the numbering because you're beginning a new section in your document.

To start numbering with a new number, position the insertion point where you want the new number to take effect, such as before the position where you will create your next box. Then, choose Graphics, the type of box you wish to renumber (such as Figure), New Number. A dialog box appears requesting a new number. Type a new number and choose OK. A code is inserted in the text, such as [New Fig Num:1]. All graphics boxes of the same type located forward from the code will be renumbered accordingly. For instance the figure box following a [New Fig Num:1] code will be numbered as "Figure 1", the next figure box as "Figure 2", and so on.

Changing the Box Position and Size

You can change the location and size of a graphics box using either of two options. First, you can manipulate the box on screen with your mouse. You can also open the Box Position and Size dialog box.

Using the Mouse

With your mouse, you can change the location or size of a graphics box visually right on screen. Follow these steps:

1. Position the mouse pointer inside the graphics box.

2. Click the *left* mouse button to select the box. An outline with sizing handles appears around the graphics box, as shown in this example:

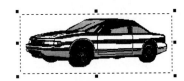

The handles on the top and bottom are the *vertical sizing* handles, those on the sides are the *horizontal sizing* handles, and there are four *corner sizing* handles.

Or, if the Wrap Text Around Box option (described in the next section) is off, then you must click the *right* mouse button and choose Select Box to select the box.

3. To move the box, position the mouse pointer in the graphics box so that the pointer appears as a four-headed arrow.

   To change either the length or width of the box, position the mouse pointer on one of the graphics box's horizontal or vertical sizing handles so that the pointer appears as a two-headed arrow.

   To change *both* the length and width of the box, position the mouse pointer on one of the graphics box's corner sizing handles so that the pointer appears as a diagonal two-headed arrow.

4. Click and drag; this moves the outline on screen.

5. When the outline is moved or sized so that the graphics box appears as you want it to, release the mouse button.

6. Click anywhere in the document window that is outside the box to unselect the box.

Using the Box Position and Size Dialog Box

The Box Position and Size dialog box allows you to change the location and size of the box with precise measurements, rather than using your mouse to drag it visually. The dialog box also lets you change several other characteristics of the box, such as how the box is anchored to the text. There are several ways to display the Box Position and Size dialog box. To use your keyboard, follow these steps:

1. Choose Graphics, the type of box you wish to position and size (such as Figure), Position. A dialog box appears.

2. Type in the number of the box you wish to move or size if different from the number suggested by WordPerfect, and choose OK.

To use your mouse, follow these steps:

1. Position the mouse pointer inside the graphics box you wish to edit.

2. Click the *right* mouse button.

3. Choose Box Position.

shortcut *Pressing* (SHIFT) *while double-clicking a graphics box (with the left mouse button) is equivalent to clicking the right mouse button and choosing Position.*

You can also display the Box Position and Size dialog box when you are working with the Figure, Text, or Equation Editor by choosing the Box Position option from inside the Editor.

An example of the Box Position and Size dialog box is shown in Figure 12-5. It lets you specify box type, what you'd like to anchor text to, vertical and horizontal positioning, size, and how you'd like word wrap to work.

Box Type

Setting the box type is useful if you change your mind once a box has been created. Changing the box type will not change the position, size, or contents of the box, but instead changes the box's appearance to conform to other boxes of that type.

Anchor To

Anchoring text determines how the box is positioned and how it moves with the text if you edit it later. You have three options:

*   *Page* The Page option anchors the box to a fixed position on a page; the graphics box code is placed one line above the top of the box.

Figure 12-5.   *Box Position and Size dialog box*

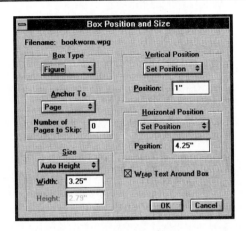

WordPerfect's initial setting for figure, text, table, and user boxes is that they are anchored to a page. (WordPerfect's initial setting for equation boxes anchors them to a specific paragraph.) For a box anchored to the page, you can specify the Number of Pages to Skip if you want the box to appear beyond the insertion point. For instance, if the insertion point is on page 1 and you want the graphics box to appear on page 2, type 1 as the number of pages to skip.

- *Paragraph*   The Paragraph option anchors the box to a specific paragraph; the graphics box code is placed at the beginning of that paragraph. Should you edit your document later, the graphics box will move with the paragraph. If, however, the paragraph is so close to the bottom of the page that the graphics box won't fit on the page, the box is placed at the top of the next page. WordPerfect anchors equation boxes to a paragraph as its initial setting.

- *Character*   The Character option anchors the box to a character to its left on the line; the graphics box code is placed at the insertion point. The box is treated like a single character in the line, so if you later edit the line, the location of the box will readjust (or even wrap down to the next line like a character would). You can, for example, anchor a box to a tab stop.

Several types of anchoring positions are shown in Figure 12-6.

Vertical Position

The vertical position of the box depends on how the box is anchored. Choose Vertical Position.

For a box anchored to a page, select Top or Bottom to position the box at the top or bottom on the page. Select Center to position the box centered vertically between the top and bottom margins. Select Set Position to indicate how much space you want from the top of the page to your graphics box. Select Full Page to fill the entire page area with the box.

For a box anchored to a paragraph, indicate in the Position number box how much space you want from the top of the paragraph to your graphics box. A value of **0** means the top of the box will be aligned with the top of the first line of the paragraph.

For a box anchored to a character, choose Vertical Position and select Top, Center, or Bottom to align the top, center, or bottom of the box to the *baseline* of the line on which the box is located. Select Baseline to align the baseline of the last line of text inside the box with the baseline of the line on which the box is located.

Horizontal Position

The horizontal position of the box also depends on how the box is anchored. Choose Horizontal Position.

For a box anchored to a page, you can position the box relative to margins: select Margin Left or Margin Right to position the box at the left or right margin; select Margin Center to position the box centered horizontally between the left and right margins; or select Margin Full to fill the entire area between the left and right margins. You can also position the box relative to columns that you defined on the page: select Column Left or Column Right to position the box at the left or right of the column(s); select Column Center to position the box centered horizontally within the column(s); or select Column Full to fill the entire area of the column(s). You must specify the column number in the Columns box, and can indicate not only one column, but also a range of columns. For instance, type **1-3** to position a graphics box

Figure 12-6.   *Graphics boxes can be anchored to the page, the paragraph,*
or specific characters

Text box anchored
to the page

R&R WINE ASSOCIATION

NEW SERVICE OFFERED

All R&R Wine Association employees are now eligible for two valuable company services.   First is the new <u>R&R Money Market Fund.</u> Any percentage of your monthly salary can be automatically invested in the Money Market Fund, an established mutual fund with assets so far of over $1 million. The R&R Money Market Fund is just a part of a larger fund, which is over $45 million strong. You will earn high yields and enjoy a variety of extras. These include free check writing on your account. The service is unlimited; write as many checks as you need. In addition, there's free reinvestment of your dividends so that your earnings grow faster. The R&R Money Market Fund is professionally managed by The Thomas Corporation, one of the nation's leading mutual fund companies.

Figure box anchored
to the paragraph

A wise investment!

Second, and as a complimentary feature, we now offer a <u>financial planning service,</u> free to all employees. You'll learn how to minimize taxes, what to do about life insurance, and how to handle emergency needs. You'll also be advised on pension plan options.

Why do we offer the Money Market Fund? So that your investments are wise ones, so that you get long-term profit from your earnings at R&R. Why do we offer the FREE financial planning service? For the same reasons. To find out more about the benefits of joining the Money Market Fund, call:

User boxes anchored to
characters (tab stops)

☑   Karl at (415) 666-9444   ☑   Tina at (212) 444-8222

☑   Scott at (312) 555-1444

They're also the people you'll want to speak with about setting up an appointment for any of your financial planning needs.

relative to columns 1, 2, and 3. Or you can choose <u>S</u>et Position to indicate how much space you want from the left edge of the page to your graphic box.

For a box anchored to a paragraph, you can position the box relative to margins: select Margin Left or Margin Right to position the box at the left or right margin of the paragraph; select Margin Center to position the box centered horizontally between the left and right margins; or select Margin Full to fill the entire area between the left and right margins. Or you can choose Set Position to indicate how much space you want from the left edge of the page to your graphic box.

For a box anchored to a character, you cannot choose a horizontal position. The box is positioned just after the character to its left.

Size

When first created, a graphics box is sized as follows: Width is one half the available space between left and right margins for all but equation boxes—for these, width is the full available space between left and right margins. Height is determined by the type and contents of the graphics box. For a graphics image, for instance, the height is adjusted to maintain the relative proportions of the image's height to width.

Choose Size. Then you can select Auto Width to specify a height for the box and let WordPerfect calculate the corresponding width. Select Auto Height to specify a width for the box and let WordPerfect calculate the corresponding height. Select Set Both to specify your own measurements. Select Auto Both to restore the original dimensions of a graphics image or equation.

Wrap Text Around Box

If turned on, the Wrap Text Around Box option wraps text to the next line when it encounters a graphics box, rather than continue across the line and on top of the box. If turned off, text is printed on top of the box.

Turning off this feature allows you to overlay text or graphics images, or combine text and graphics in the same box. For instance, create a user box containing the fancy border in the file named *bord-2.wpg*. Turn off the Wrap Text Around Box feature and then type text inside the border to get results like those shown in Figure 12-7. (The Advance feature is also handy for positioning text inside graphics boxes, or for overlaying one graphic image on top of another. The Advance feature is discussed in Chapter 7.)

You can also use this option to align text up against the edge of an image. Insert the graphics image into a box without borders, such as a user box. Turn off the Wrap Text Around Box feature and then type the text, pressing (ENTER) where you want text to be wrapped down to the next line. You can get a result like this:

There is also a brand new sales incentive to consider!! The person with the most sales during March will receive two round-trip tickets to Hawaii plus seven nights at the lovely Mai Tai Resort Hotel. Be sure to jot down your total sales figures and send them to John Pinor by the end of April so that you, too, can be included in this exciting Hawaii drawing. Bon Voyage!!!

Figure 12-7.   *Text typed inside a graphics box when the Wrap Text Around Box feature is turned off*

R&R WINE ASSOCIATION

FIRST ANNUAL AWARDS BANQUET

December 19th, 6:00 pm

Helen and Isaac's Restaurant
7th & West Side Drive

Changing the Box Appearance Options

As previously described, each box type has default settings for how it will appear in your document. These default settings are provided in Table 12-2. To change one or more settings for a particular box type, position the insertion point where you want the change to take effect. Next, choose Graphics and the type of box you wish to change default options for (such as Figure), Options. A dialog box appears, such as the Figure Options dialog box shown in Figure 12-8 for figure boxes. The appearance options that you can alter are discussed next.

Border Styles

All four borders of a graphics box are set with Border Styles. The choices are None, Single, Double, Dashed, Dotted, Thick, or Extra Thick. If you choose thick or extra thick lines for two adjacent borders and thinner lines for the two other borders, you can create a three-dimensional effect, as shown here:

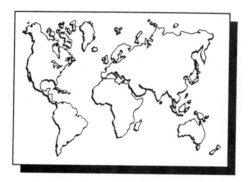

Gray Shading

Shading inside the box is determined by the Gray Shading option. A value of 0 percent represents no shading and 100 percent represents black. Your printer must support shading for this option to have an effect.

Printers with PostScript capabilities can produce text with white letters on a black background if you specify a Gray Shading of 100 percent and then choose Font, Color and set the color of text at the printer to white. (See Chapter 5 for more on the Color feature.)

Table 12-2. *Default Settings for the Five Types of Graphics Boxes*

	Figure	**Text**	**Equation**	**Table**	**User**
Border Style					
Left	Single	None	None	None	None
Right	Single	None	None	None	None
Top	Single	Thick	None	Thick	None
Bottom	Single	Thick	None	Thick	None
Gray Shading					
(Percent of black)	0%	10%	0%	0%	0%
Outside Border Space (in inches)					
Left	0.167	0.167	0.083	0.167	0.167
Right	0.167	0.167	0.083	0.167	0.167
Top	0.167	0.167	0.083	0.167	0.167
Bottom	0.167	0.167	0.083	0.167	0.167
Inside Border Space (in inches)					
Left	0	0.167	0.083	0.167	0
Right	0	0.167	0.083	0.167	0
Top	0	0.167	0.083	0.167	0
Bottom	0	0.167	0.083	0.167	0
Caption Numbering Method					
First Level	Numbers	Numbers	Numbers	Roman	Numbers
Second Level	Off	Off	Off	Off	Off
Caption Style					
Boldface	Figure 1	1	(1)	Table I	1
Caption Position					
	Below Box, Outside	Below Box, Outside	Right, Inside	Above Box, Outside	Below Box, Outside
Minimum Offset from Paragraph (in inches)					
	0	0	0	0	0

Figure 12-8.   *Figure Options dialog box*

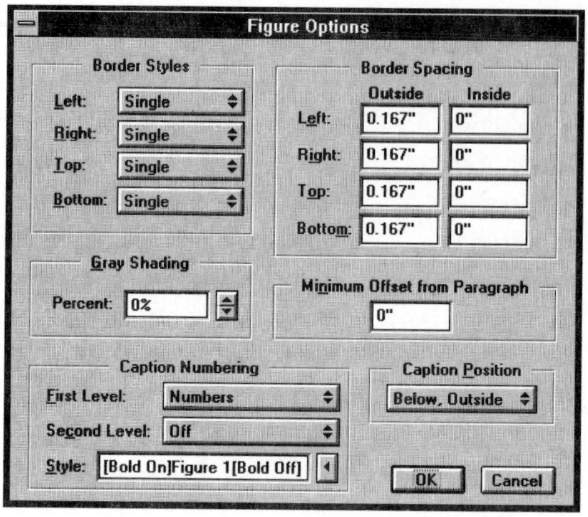

Caption Numbering

You can alter the caption numbering and the caption style with the Caption Numbering option. As previously mentioned, each box type has a default caption numbering system, such as "Figure 1" for a figure, or "Table I" for a table, or "(1)" for an equation.

You have four numbering choices: Off, Numbers (Arabic), Letters, or Roman Numerals. These choices are available for first-level and second-level captions (if you want the number for each box to have both a first and second level). Letters and Roman numerals are displayed in uppercase for first-level numbers and lowercase for second-level numbers. For instance, to number figures as "Figure A", "Figure B", "Figure C", and so on, select letters for the first level and select "off" for the second level. To number figures as "Figure 1a", "Figure 1b", "Figure 1c", and so on—perhaps for the first chapter of a book—select numbers for the first level and letters for the second level.

The numbers and text you type into the Style text box dictate what the default caption will contain in relation to the numbering selection. Type **1** when defining the style wherever you want the first-level number to appear, and type **2** where you want the second-level number to appear. For instance, type the style for a figure as **Figure #1-2**. If you had selected numbers for the first-level numbering and letters for the second-level numbering, this translates to figure captions as follows: "Figure #1-a", "Figure #1-b", "Figure #1-c", and so on. You can also change the font attribute of the caption by choosing Bold, Italics, Underline, or Small Caps from a pop-up list by clicking the button with an arrowhead located to the right of the Style text box.

Caption Position

You can determine the location of the caption relative to the box with the Caption Position option. This is pertinent only for those boxes in which a caption has been inserted. In equation boxes, the caption can be placed Below, Above, on the Left, or on the Right side, within the border of the box. In figure, text, table, and user boxes, the caption can be placed Above or Below the box, and Outside or Inside the border of the box.

Border Spacing

You can set the amount of space you desire between the borders (Left, Right, Top, Bottom) of your box and the text outside the box in the Outside Border Spacing column. Set the amount of space you desire between the borders of your box and the text or image inside the box in the Inside Border Spacing column.

Minimum Offset from Paragraph

When a box is anchored to a paragraph, you can determine the minimum distance that it can be positioned from the top of a paragraph with the Minimum Offset from Paragraph option. WordPerfect will try to keep the paragraph and box on the same page. This option comes into play only when the paragraph is too close to the bottom edge of the page for the box to fit on the same page.

Changing the Box Contents: Figure, Text, and Equation Editors

You can alter the contents of a graphics box by using the Figure, Text, or Equation Editor. When you first create a graphics box, you can display the Editor on screen. You can use it then or when you edit a previously created graphics box. To view the Editor for a graphics box that you created earlier, follow these steps:

1. Choose Graphics, the type of box you wish to edit (such as Figure), Edit.

2. Type in the figure number you wish to edit if different from the number suggested by WordPerfect, and choose OK.

shortcut (SHIFT) + (F11) *is a shortcut for* Graphics, Figure, Edit. (ALT) + (SHIFT) + (F11) *is the shortcut for* Graphics, Text box, Edit.

Mouse users can edit a graphics box by following these steps:

1. Position the mouse pointer inside the graphics box you wish to edit.

2. Click the *right* mouse button.

3. Choose to edit the box. For instance, for a figure box, choose the option Edit Figure. Or, for a user box, choose the option Edit User box.

shortcut *Double-clicking a graphics box (with the left mouse button) is equivalent to positioning the mouse pointer, clicking the right mouse button, and choosing the* Edit *option.*

When you choose to edit a graphics box, either the Figure, Text, or Equation Editor will appear—depending on the box's contents.

Figure Editor

Figure 12-9 shows an example of the Figure Editor screen. The example is for a box containing the graphics file named *bookworm.wpg*. The Figure

12

Figure 12-9. *Figure Editor screen*

Editor's title bar lists the current document as well as the name of the graphics file. Five menu names appear on the menu bar: <u>F</u>ile, <u>E</u>dit, <u>V</u>iew, <u>W</u>indow, and <u>H</u>elp. A button bar appears on the left side. It is an alternative to selecting commonly used commands from the menu bar.

The commands for the first three of the Figure Editor menus are provided below. (The last two menus are the same as on the menu bar in the document workspace.) Keep in mind that the button bar can be used as an alternative for selecting certain commands.

File Menu Commands

The File menu commands enable you to open and save graphics files, set box defaults, and close the Figure Editor.

Retrieve Use the <u>R</u>etrieve command to recall a graphic image. If an image is already in a graphics box, the new graphics image will replace the existing one.

Save As You can save a graphics image into the WordPerfect graphics format using the <u>S</u>ave As command. This is useful when you've recalled an image that had been originally saved in another format, and you plan to use that image in WordPerfect in the future. By saving the file, you save it into WPG format.

Graphic on Disk   Save a graphics file separately, rather than along with the document, using the Graphic on Disk command. When the document is printed, WordPerfect looks for the graphics file in the graphics directory. The Graphic on Disk command is useful for conserving space when you want to repeat the same image numerous times in a document. It is also convenient when you predict that an image (such as a chart) may change before the document is printed, and you wish to use the updated version when printing. Moreover, use this command when you wish to include a graphics image in a style. (Styles are discussed in Chapter 15.) You can include a graphics image in a style only when its graphics file is saved separately.

Box Position   The Box Position command simply opens the Box Position and Size dialog box. See "Changing the Box Position and Size" earlier in this chapter for more information.

Cancel   The Cancel command aborts the Figure Editor, closing it without saving the changes you may have made since you opened it. If you haven't yet retrieved a file, Cancel closes the editor without creating a figure box.

Close   Close the Figure Editor and save the changes using the Close command. A figure box is inserted into the text of your document, whether you have retrieved a graphics file or not.

Edit Menu Commands

The Edit menu commands change the appearance of the graphics image.

Move   Move the image *within the boundaries of the box* by selecting the Move command and then clicking and dragging with your mouse to where you want the image moved. The Pos X and Pos Y numbers on the status line record the horizontal and vertical distance, respectively, that the image is moved from its original position (which has Pos X and Pos Y values of 0). Using your keyboard, press the (↑), (↓), (←), or (→) key to move the image by the percentage shown in the lower right corner on the status line. Then select

12

Mo<u>v</u>e again to turn this command off. (You can also move an image a specific distance using the <u>E</u>dit All option, covered shortly.)

Rotate   When you select the <u>R</u>otate command, an upside-down "T" axis appears. You use this to turn the image in a circle. Click and drag the right end of the axis in a circle to rotate the image. You can also rotate the image by clicking a location—the right end of the axis points to where you clicked. Select <u>R</u>otate again to turn this menu item off. (You can rotate an image a certain number of degrees using the <u>E</u>dit All option, covered shortly.) Here's an example after the image in Figure 12-9 is rotated:

shortcut Press (CTRL) + (←) *to move the figure counterclockwise and* (CTRL) + (→) *to move the figure clockwise by the percentage shown in the lower right corner of the status line.*

Scale   <u>S</u>cale, <u>E</u>nlarge Area allows you to use the mouse to "zoom in" on a portion of the image; click and hold the mouse to select one corner of the area, and then drag to the opposite corner. <u>S</u>cale, Enlarge % increases the size of the figure by the percentage in the lower right corner on screen. <u>S</u>cale, Re<u>d</u>uce % decreases the size of the figure by the percentage shown in the lower right corner of the status line. <u>R</u>eset Size returns the image to its original scale and position. (You can also scale an image a certain amount using the <u>E</u>dit All option, discussed shortly.) Here's an example after enlarging the face of the image in Figure 12-9:

shortcut   *Press* (CTRL) + (↑) *to enlarge the figure and* (CTRL) + (↓) *to reduce the figure by the percentage shown in the lower right corner of the status line.*

Mirror   Flip the image on its vertical axis when you select <u>M</u>irror. For instance, if the image is an arrow pointing to the right, the mirror image is an arrow pointing to the left. You can select <u>M</u>irror again to turn this menu item off. Here's a mirror image of the picture in Figure 12-9:

Invert   Display the complementary colors of the image using the <u>I</u>nvert command. Select <u>I</u>nvert again to turn this menu item off. This item has no effect on black-and-white images.

Outline   Display the image as a line drawing using the <u>O</u>utline command. All colors are changed to white, so that it becomes a black-and-white image. You can select <u>O</u>utline again to turn this menu item off. This item has no effect on images that are already black and white.

Black and White   Display the contents of your box as a black-and-white image using the <u>B</u>lack and White command. All colors are changed to black. Select <u>B</u>lack and White again to turn this command off.

Edit All   The Edit All dialog box that opens when you select the <u>E</u>dit All command lets you edit the various aspects of the graphics image all at one time.

- Move the image by entering horizontal and vertical measurements, where positive numbers move the image up and to the right, and negative numbers move the image down and to the left. The measurements are in relation to the image's original position (which has Pos X and Pos Y values of 0).

- Scale the image by entering horizontal (scale X) and vertical (scale Y) percentages. The percentages are in relation to the image's original size. For instance, enter **50** for scale X, and the image becomes half as wide as its original size. Enter **200** for scale Y, and the image becomes twice as tall as its original size.

- Rotate the image counterclockwise by entering a number of degrees. The image will move that number of degrees from its original orientation.

- Choose to mirror, outline, invert the image, or change it to black and white, or any combination of these.

- Apply all the editing changes to the image while the dialog box remains open by choosing Apply. This makes it easy to continue editing the image if you don't like the results, without having to exit the Edit All dialog box and then choosing Edit All again.

Reset All　　To return the image to its original appearance, select the Reset All command. The image will look as it did when you first recalled it into the graphics box.

note　　*Press* (INS) *to change the percentage shown in the lower right corner of the status line in the Figure Editor. Your options are 1%, 5%, 10%, or 25%. The percentage you select determines the percent change when you use shortcut keys* (↑), (↓), (←) *or* (→) *to move, rotate, or scale the image, and also the percent change when you choose Scale, Enlarge % or Scale, Reduce %.*

View Menu Commands

The View menu commands show or hide the Figure Editor's button bar.

Button Bar　　Turn on or off the display of the Figure Editor button bar by selecting the Button Bar command.

Button Bar Setup　　Edit the Figure Editor button bar or change its position or style when you select the Button Bar Setup command.

See Chapter 10 for more on displaying, using, and changing the setup for button bars.

Text Editor

Figure 12-10 shows an example of the Text Editor screen containing text. The text that appears in the workspace remains within the boundaries established by the width of the box. Four buttons appear just below the menu bar: Close, Cancel, Box Position, and Rotate.

Box Position   This button opens the Box Position and Size dialog box. See "Changing the Box Position and Size" for more information.

Rotate   This button opens the Rotate Text dialog box. You can choose to rotate the text 90 degrees, 180 degrees (where the text is printed upside down), or 270 degrees inside the box. Keep in mind, however, that not all printers can rotate the text. For instance, many laser printers can rotate only 0 or 90 degrees, and some cannot print some text with no rotation and other text with a rotation on the same page.

Figure 12-10.   *Text Editor screen*

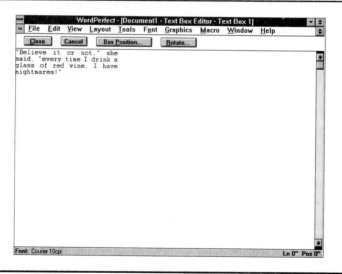

Cancel   This button aborts the Text Editor, closing it without saving the changes you may have made since you opened it. If you haven't yet typed text, Cancel closes the editor without creating a text box.

Close   This button closes the Text Editor and saves the changes. A text box is inserted into the text of your document, whether you have typed text or not.

Equation Editor

Figure 12-11 shows an example of the Equation Editor screen. Used to create, align, and edit an equation, the Equation Editor will make you an expert at formatting equations into boxes, but will do no calculations.

The top of the editor contains a menu bar with features for creating equations. Use the Equation Editor button bar, just below the menu bar, for easy access to commonly used features. The largest portion of the Equation Editor is split into three separate panes, which are described briefly here.

Editing Pane

The editing pane is the top right pane, where you type the equation text. You can type numbers, letters, and the following operators and symbols directly into the pane:

+	Plus	=	Equal to	?		,
−	Minus	>	Greater than	.		;
*	Multiply	<	Less than	|		:
/	Divide	!	Not	@		

Special symbols such as ' " { } ( ) have certain meanings and can be entered either from the keyboard or from the equation palette. Special characters such as Greek symbols or arrows can be entered either by pressing (CTRL) + (W) to display the WordPerfect Characters dialog box or from the equation palette.

Equation Palette

The equation palette is the tall pane on the left, where you choose commands, symbols, or functions for insertion as part of an equation into the

Figure 12-11.   ***Equation Editor screen***

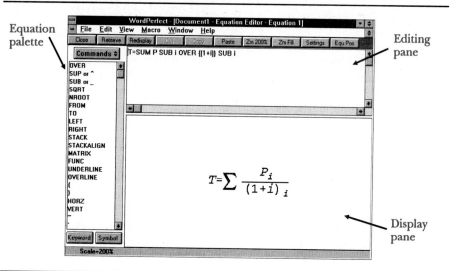

editing pane. When you first enter the Equation Editor, the heading "Commands" is displayed, to indicate that the menu of Commands is on screen. Table 12-3 provides a list of the most commonly used commands, and Figure 12-12 shows examples of the proper syntax for many of these commands in creating equations.

To move from the editing pane to the equation palette, click on that pane, or press F6 to move from one pane to the next. Then use the mouse or the arrow keys to select a command; the command's meaning and syntax are displayed at the bottom of the screen. Next, double-click the command or press ENTER to insert your selection. (Some commands can be inserted into an equation either as a keyword or symbol; in that case, you can choose the Keyword or Symbol command button at the bottom of the equation palette.) You can also choose to display other commands or functions in the equation palette by selecting from the Commands pop-up list box located at the top of the equation palette pane.

12

Table 12-3. *Commonly Used Commands in the Equation Palette*

Command	Use of Command in Equation
{ and }	Signals the start and end of a group
~	Indicates that a space should be printed
'	Indicates that a thin space should be printed
\	Signals that the next operator or command be treated as characters rather than as an equation operator or command
BOLD	Signals that the next character or group be boldface
BINOM	Creates a binomial, placing the first character that follows on top, the second character on the bottom, and enclosing the binomial in parentheses
FROM and TO	Signals the start and end limits for operators. The FROM symbol is placed on the bottom and the TO symbol placed on the top of the operator
ITAL	Signals that the next character or group be italicized
OVER	Creates fractions, placing one character or group over another and separating them with a horizontal line
SQRT	Creates the square root of the character or group that follows
SUP or ^	Signals that the next character or group should be superscripted
SUB or _	Signals that the next character or group should be subscripted

Display Pane

The display pane is the bottom right pane, where you preview how the equation will print. To preview an equation, choose View, Redisplay (or press (CTRL) + (F3)). You must choose View, Redisplay every time you edit the equation or the display pane will not redraw the equation. The equation will appear magnified in the display pane and the percent in the lower left corner

Figure 12-12.   *Sample equations created with the Equation Editor*

```
{av + ax} TIMES 2 OVER {n - ax}
```

$$av + axx \dfrac{2}{n-ax}$$

```
av ~+ ~{ax TIMES 2} OVER n ~- ~ax
```

$$av + \dfrac{ax \times 2}{n} - ax$$

```
x = {-a PLUSMINUS SQRT {c^3^2 - SQRT {b^3-b^2}}} OVER a^4
```

$$x = \dfrac{-a \pm \sqrt{c^{3^2} - \sqrt{b^3 - b^2}}}{a^4}$$

```
T = SUM P SUB i OVER {{(1 + I)} SUB i
```

$$T = \sum \dfrac{P_i}{(1+I)_i}$$

```
B(f) = INT SUB{-INF} SUP{INF} alpha (t) e SUP{beta}
```

$$B(f) = \int_{-\infty}^{\infty} \alpha(t)\, e^{\beta}$$

of the screen indicates the viewing magnification. For instance, "200%" means that the equation is being displayed at two times its size when printed. You can also use the <u>V</u>iew menu to change the size of your equation in the display pane.

If you receive an error message after redisplaying an equation, you have some kind of syntax error. The insertion point relocates in the editing pane next to the error. You must correct the error before displaying the equation.

Creating Graphics Lines

In addition to graphics boxes, graphics lines—also referred to as *rules*—can be inserted into a document. The lines can be horizontal or vertical and of any thickness or shading. You can use graphics lines, for example, to separate headings from text, to separate columns, or to border a page. Figure 12-13 shows an example of a thick horizontal line below an address (effective for creating letterhead) and two, thinner vertical lines separating columns. Your printer must support graphics in order to print these lines.

Inserting Horizontal Lines

When you insert a horizontal line in your text, WordPerfect initially assumes that you want a line that is: .013 inch thick; black; positioned at the baseline of the line where the insertion point is currently located; and full, meaning it extends from the left to the right margin. To insert such a horizontal graphics line in your document, follow these steps:

1. Position the insertion point where you want the line to appear.

2. Choose <u>G</u>raphics, <u>L</u>ine, <u>H</u>orizontal. A Create Horizontal Line dialog box appears with the initial settings displayed, as shown here:

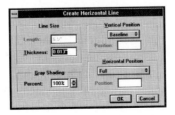

3. Choose OK.

shortcut (CTRL) + (F11) *is the shortcut for* <u>G</u>raphics, <u>L</u>ine, <u>H</u>orizontal.

Figure 12-13.   *Graphics lines in a printed document*

R&R WINE ASSOCIATION
3345 Whitmore Drive, #505
San Francisco, CA 94123

NEW SERVICE

All R&R Wine Association employees are now eligible for two valuable company services.

First is the new *R&R Money Market Fund*. Any percentage of your monthly salary can be automatically invested in the Money Market Fund, an established mutual fund with assets so far of over $1 million. The R&R Money Market Fund is just a part of a larger fund, which is over $45 million strong.

You will earn high yields and enjoy a variety of extras. These include free check writing on your account. The service is unlimited; write as many checks as you need. In addition, there's free reinvestment of your dividends so that your earnings grow faster.

The R&R Money Market Fund is professionally managed by The Thomas Corporation, one of the nation's leading mutual fund companies.

Second, and as a complimentary feature, we now offer a *financial planning service*, free to all employees. You'll learn how to minimize taxes, what to do about life insurance, and how to handle emergency needs. You'll also be advised on pension plan options.

Why do we offer the Money Market Fund? So that your investments are wise ones, so that you get long-term profits from your earnings.

Why do we offer the FREE financial planning service? For the same reasons.

To find out more about the benefits of joining our company's Money Market Fund, call Karl Nottings at (415) 666-9444. He's also the person you'll want to speak with about setting up an appointment for any of your financial needs!

WORLD OF WINES

In our last newsletter, we completed a five-part series on wines produced in the United States. Next month, we begin a new series on the wines of Europe. Our first nation in Europe? By popular request, it will be France.

France is most often considered the greatest wine-producing country in the world. The variety of wines grown here is absolutely amazing: the sparkling wines of Champagne, the red wines of Bordeaux, the red and white wines of Burgundy, the sweet wines of Barsac--just to name a few!

You'll learn about all the French wines we ship around the country in our next edition of R&R Wine News.

-- Lini Snyder

WordPerfect inserts a code into the text, such as: [HLine:Full,Baseline,6.5",0.013",100%]. To erase the line, you can reveal codes and delete the horizontal line code. Or, you can position the mouse pointer on the graphics line until the pointer changes to an arrow, click once, and then press (BACKSPACE).

You can change any of the horizontal line settings when you first display the Create Horizontal Line dialog box, before choosing OK. The five settings are explained here:

- *Horizontal Position*   Set the horizontal position of the line with the Horizontal Position option. Select Full to begin at the left margin and extend the line to the right margin. Select Left or Right to position the line against the left or right margin. Select Center to center the line between the margins. Choose Specify to indicate how much space you want from the left edge of the page to the start of the graphics line.

- *Length*   Set the length of the line using the Length option. If the horizontal position is set to Full, then the length of the line is automatically calculated as the distance between the left and right margins and cannot be changed. If the horizontal position is set to Left or Right, the length of the line is initially set as the distance from the insertion point to that margin, but can be changed. If the horizontal position is set to Center, the length of the line is automatically calculated as the distance between the left and right margins, but can be changed. If the horizontal position is set to Specify, enter a length measurement of your own.

- *Vertical Position*   Set the vertical position of the line using the Vertical Position option. Select Baseline to align the bottom edge of the graphics line with the baseline of the text line where the [HLine:] code is inserted. Select Specify to indicate how much space you want from the top edge of the page to the graphics line.

- *Thickness*   Set the thickness of the line with the Thickness option. If you enter a large measurement, then you will be actually defining a shaded rectangle, which expands upward if the vertical position is set to Baseline, or expands downward if the vertical position is set to Specify.

- *Gray Shading*   The Gray Shading option lets you set the intensity of shading, where 100 percent is black. The lower the percentage entered, the lighter the gray shading.

Inserting Vertical Lines

When you insert a vertical line in your text, WordPerfect initially assumes that you want a line that is: .013 inch in thickness; black; positioned at the left margin; and full page, meaning it extends from the top to the bottom margin. To insert such a vertical graphics line in your document, follow these steps:

1. Position the insertion point on the page where you want the graphics line to appear.

2. Choose Graphics, Line, Vertical. A Create Vertical Line dialog box appears with the initial settings displayed, as shown here:

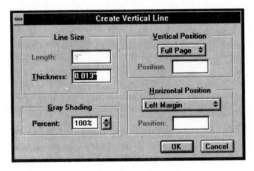

3. Choose OK.

shortcut (CTRL) + (SHIFT) + (F11) *is the shortcut for* Graphics, Line, Vertical.

WordPerfect inserts a code into the text, such as: [VLine:Left Margin,Full Page,9",0.013",100%]. To erase the line, delete the hidden code. Or, you can position the mouse pointer on the graphics line until the pointer changes to an arrow, click once, and then press (BACKSPACE).

You can change any of the vertical line settings when you first display the Create Vertical Line dialog box, before choosing OK. These five settings are explained here:

- *Vertical Position* Set the vertical position of the line with the Vertical Position option. Select Full Page to extend the line from the top to the bottom margin. Select Top or Bottom to position the line against the top or bottom margin. Select Center to position the line centered between the top and bottom margins. Select <u>S</u>pecify to indicate how much space you want from the top of the page to the start of the graphics line.

- *<u>L</u>ength*   Use the <u>L</u>ength option to set the length of the line. If the vertical position is set to <u>F</u>ull Page, then the length of line is automatically calculated as the distance between the top and bottom margin and cannot be changed. If the vertical position is set to <u>T</u>op or <u>B</u>ottom, the length of the line is initially set as the distance from the insertion point to that margin, but can be changed. If the vertical position is set to <u>C</u>enter, then the length of line is automatically calculated as the distance between the top and bottom margins, but can be changed. If the vertical position is set to <u>S</u>pecify, enter a length measurement of your own.

- *Horizontal Position*   Set the horizontal position of the line with the <u>H</u>orizontal Position option. Select <u>L</u>eft Margin or <u>R</u>ight Margin to position the line slightly to the left of the left margin or slightly to the right of the right margin. Select <u>B</u>etween Columns to indicate a column number—the line will be positioned to the *right* of that column. Select <u>S</u>pecify to indicate how much space you want from the left edge of the page to the graphics line.

- *<u>T</u>hickness*   Set the thickness of the line with the <u>T</u>hickness option. If you enter a large measurement, you will be actually defining a shaded rectangle, which will expand to the right.

- *<u>G</u>ray Shading*   The <u>G</u>ray Shading option lets you set the intensity of shading, where 100 percent is black. The lower the percentage entered, the lighter the gray shading.

Editing Horizontal or Vertical Lines

You have two ways to edit a graphics line that you already created. You can manipulate the line right on screen with your mouse or you can open the Edit Horizontal Line or Edit Vertical Line dialog box.

Using the Mouse

To change the location or size of a graphics line on screen with your mouse, follow these steps:

1. Position the mouse pointer on the graphics line until the pointer changes from an I-beam to an arrow.

2. Click the *left* mouse button to select the line. An outline with sizing handles appears around the graphics line, as shown in this example for a horizontal line.

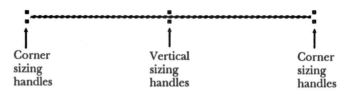

Corner	Vertical	Corner
sizing	sizing	sizing
handles	handles	handles

3. To move the line, position the mouse pointer on the graphics line until the pointer changes to a four-headed arrow.

   To change either the length or thickness of the line, position the mouse pointer on one of the graphics line's horizontal or vertical sizing handles. (When a line is narrow, either the horizontal or vertical sizing handles will not appear.)

   To change both the length and thickness of the line, position the mouse pointer on one of the graphics line's corner sizing handles.

4. Click and drag; this moves the outline on screen.

5. When the outline is positioned and sized just as you want the graphics line to appear, release the mouse button.

6. Click anywhere in the document window off the line to unselect the line.

Using the Edit Horizontal Line or Edit Vertical Line Dialog Box

You can also change the settings for an already created graphics line by displaying the Edit Horizontal Line or Edit Vertical Line dialog box, (which contains the exact same items as the Create Horizontal Line and Create Vertical Line dialog boxes). You can display the Edit Horizontal Line or Edit Vertical Line dialog box in one of two ways. First, you can choose Graphics, Line, and then Edit Horizontal or Edit Vertical. WordPerfect searches backward from the insertion point for a horizontal or vertical line code, and displays the corresponding dialog box. (WordPerfect searches forward for the line code only after no such code is found backward in the text.) The second method lets you use a mouse. Follow these steps:

1. Position the mouse pointer on the graphics line you wish to edit so that the mouse pointer changes from an I-beam to an arrow.

2. Click the *right* mouse button.

3. Choose Edit Horizontal Line or Edit Vertical Line.

shortcut Double-clicking a graphics line (with the left mouse button) is equivalent to clicking the right mouse button and choosing Edit Horizontal Line or Edit Vertical Line.

Once the dialog box appears, change any of the items and choose OK.

Working with Line Draw

Besides the Graphics Lines feature, another feature lets you insert lines in your document: the Line Draw feature lets you create simple drawings that contain straight lines and sharp corners—such as organizational charts, graphs, borders, and works of art. You cannot change a line's gray shading or control a line's thickness with precision in Line Draw as you can with

Figure 12-14.   *Drawing created on screen using the Line Draw feature*

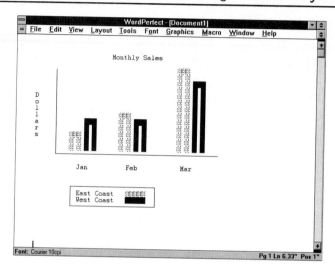

Graphics Lines, but Line Draw is invaluable if you don't have access to more complex drawing programs.

You will want to use Line Draw if:

- Your printer does not support graphics but can print WordPerfect characters used in the Line Draw feature.

- You wish to create a simple line drawing and don't have access to a more sophisticated drawing program.

- You wish to edit a previously created line drawing.

An example of what you can produce with Line Draw is shown in Figure 12-14.

To use Line Draw, position the insertion point on the line where you want the line or drawing to begin, and choose **T**ools, **L**ine Draw.

shortcut (CTRL) + (D) *is the shortcut for* **T**ools, **L**ine Draw.

Figure 12-15. *Line Draw dialog box and workspace*

Line draw workspace

12

The screen automatically switches to Draft mode and a Line Draw dialog box appears at the bottom of the screen, as shown in Figure 12-15. You have these options:

- *Characters* Select from any of the 10 preset line characters. Or choose Character and then type a character that you wish to use into the Character text box. (If the character you wish to draw with is a special character not found on the keyboard, press (CTRL) + (W) and insert a special character into the Character text box; see Chapter 5 for more on special characters.)

- *Mode* Choose Draw to draw with the selected character. Choose Move to move the insertion point to another location before continuing to draw. Choose Erase to erase a line.

Once you've selected a character and a mode, use (↓), (↑), (←), and (→) to draw, move, or erase one character at a time. To work more quickly, follow these quick key combinations:

Key Combination	Moves Insertion Point To
(HOME)	Left margin
(END)	Right margin
(CTRL) + (←)	Left margin (or any line that crosses its path before reaching the margin)
(CTRL) + (→)	Right margin (or any line that crosses its path before reaching the margin)
(CTRL) + (↑)	Top margin (or any line that crosses its path before reaching the margin)
(CTRL) + (↓)	Bottom margin (or any line that crosses its path before reaching the margin)

You cannot use your mouse to move the insertion point or to draw when using Line Draw.

As you draw using single or double lines, tiny arrows appear at the end of the line. These will print out as half-lines. If you want to extend a half-line to a full line, when the Line Draw dialog box is on screen, position the insertion point on the arrow and press (ALT) + (END). You can erase the half-line when you switch to Erase mode.

You can type the text first and then use the Line Draw feature to create lines. However, be careful because Line Draw works in Typeover mode; if you accidentally draw over text, the text will be overwritten by the line. You can instead open Line Draw to draw the lines, then close Line Draw, and then type the text. Before typing, press the (INS) key to switch into Typeover mode. This will ensure that you won't disfigure the drawing when typing text.

Be aware that Line Draw should be used only when the alignment of text is set to left justification. (See Chapter 6.) And, make sure to select a monospaced (non-proportionally spaced) font. (See Chapter 5.)

Typesetting

WordPerfect offers the ability to refine the spacing between characters and between lines of text with the Typesetting feature. To institute a typesetting change, position the insertion point and choose Layout, Typesetting. The Typesetting dialog box shown in Figure 12-16 appears. Each item is explained

Figure 12-16. *Typesetting dialog box*

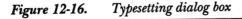

here. Keep in mind that these items are available to you only if your printer supports them.

Word Spacing and Letterspacing

Adjust the spacing between words with the Word Spacing option. The initial setting is WordPerfect Optimal, which is the optimal spacing according to WordPerfect Corporation. Other options include Normal and Percent of Optimal. Normal is the spacing chosen by the font manufacturer (in monospaced fonts, Normal and WordPerfect Optimal are the same). Percent of Optimal allows you to set your own spacing. You can indicate a percentage, where 100 percent is comparable to WordPerfect Optimal, numbers less than 100 percent reduce the space, and numbers greater than 100 percent increase the space. Or, indicate an exact pitch in the Set Pitch number box, such as 10 characters per inch, and this is then converted by WordPerfect as a percentage of the optimal setting based on the current font.

Adjust the spacing between letters with the Letterspacing option. It has the same menu items as the Word Spacing option except that Normal and WordPerfect Optimal are always identical.

Here's an example when the font size and then the letterspacing was changed for the second line of a heading:

R&R Wine
⌐ Association

100% Optimal

R&R Wine
⌐ A s s o c i a t i o n

200% Optimal

Once you change the Word Spacing or Letterspacing setting, a code is inserted that lists the word spacing first and the letterspacing second, such as [Word/Ltr Spacing:Optimal, 200% of Optimal]. This code takes effect from its location forward, to the end of the document or until another [Word/Ltr Spacing:] code is encountered.

Word Spacing Justification Limits

Change how WordPerfect justifies text with the Word Spacing Justification Limits option. If your document is set for full justification, WordPerfect assumes that the space between words can be compressed by 60 percent or expanded by 400 percent to produce an even right margin. When these compression and expansion limits are reached, then and only then will WordPerfect adjust spacing between characters. However, if your printer supports it, you can change these limits in a document to fine-tune how justification operates. Increase the 60 percent if the words are too compressed. Decrease the 400 percent if the words are spaced too far apart.

Underline

With the Underline option, you determine whether or not spaces and tabs are underscored along with text where the Underline feature has been turned on in your document. (Chapter 5 discusses the Underline feature.)

For instance, here's how Underline operates by default, where spaces are underlined and tabs are not underlined:

Jackie Johnson   Jim Berg
Cynthia Camp   Jack Allens
Otto Sprat   Lisa Craig

Here's what happens if you decide to turn on underlining for both spaces and tabs:

Jackie Johnson   Jim Berg
Cynthia Camp   Jack Allens
Otto Sprat   Lisa Craig

Or, here's what happens when you turn off underlining for both spaces and tabs:

Jackie Johnson   Jim Berg
Cynthia Camp   Jack Allens
Otto Sprat   Lisa Craig

Once you change the Underline setting, a code is inserted that lists each setting if it is on. For instance, [Underln:Spaces, Tabs] means that both are turned on, while [Underln:] means both are turned off. This code takes effect from its location forward, to the end of the document or until another code of the same type is encountered.

Line Height Adjustment

With the Line Height Adjustment option, you can add to the vertical space (or *leading*) assigned to lines that end with soft return [SRt] codes separately from those that end with hard return [HRt] codes. In this way, you can have different vertical spacing for lines within paragraphs and for the lines that separate paragraphs, such as is often found in a newsletter.

Once you change the Line Height Adjustment, a code is inserted that lists the adjustment for lines ending with [SRt] first, and for lines ending with [HRt] second, such as [Line Height Adj: 0",0.05"]. This code takes effect from its location forward, to the end of the document or until another [Line Height Adj:] code is encountered. (Leading is usually measured in points. You can enter your numbers using points by typing the measurement followed by a "p", such as **3p** to add 3 points to the line height. In WordPerfect, 72 points equal one inch. For more on the Units of Measure feature, refer to the File, Preferences, Display command discussed in Chapter 17.)

Kerning

You can adjust the spacing between letter pairs with the Kerning option. *Kerning* means to bring together two letters with a disproportionately large space between them. Kerning is commonly used to eliminate excessive white space between letters in headings or other large-sized fonts that would otherwise have excessive space between them because of their slant and shape. Examples are the "A" and "V" in "BRAVE" or the "L" and "T" in "WILTED". Once these letters are brought slightly closer together, the entire word becomes easier to read.

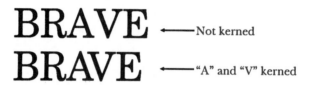

If the printer and font you use support kerning, then you can turn on Automatic Kerning where you want kerning to begin. A [Kern:On] code is inserted. Specific letter pairs, that have been predefined, are adjusted to the end of the document or until you turn off kerning and a [Kern:Off] code is inserted. The kerning is shown only at the printer or when you use the Print Preview feature to preview the text before printing.

You can also manually kern a pair of letters. Place the insertion point between the pair of letters you wish to kern and choose Manual Kerning. You can specify whether you are using inches, points, centimeters, or 1200ths of an inch. Then, specify a kerning amount, where negative numbers decrease the spacing and positive numbers increase the spacing between the letter pair. To move the character located to the right of the insertion point closer to the left, click the down arrow on the increment box or press ⊥ repeatedly. To move the character farther to the right, click the up arrow on the increment box or press ↑ repeatedly. Then choose OK. An Advance code is inserted to reposition the characters. For insance, [AdvLft:0.013] means that the character has been positioned .013 inch to the left.

First Baseline at Top Margin

WordPerfect normally aligns the *top* of the first line of text with the top margin on the page so that no text prints in the top margin. As a result, the baseline of the first text line is below the top margin. Consequently, the baseline will vary when the font is altered in the text, resulting in problems when you wish to place characters precisely on the page relative to the first baseline. With the First Baseline at Top Margin option, you can make sure that the baseline remains constant. (This is useful when you are placing text on the page with the Advance feature; see Chapter 7 for more details.)

For the First Baseline at Top Margin feature to work properly, make sure to position the insertion point either at the top of the document or in the Document Initial Codes workspace before turning it on or off.

Also, you must set the Line Height feature to a fixed setting. (See Chapter 7 for more details on the Document Initial Codes and Line Height features.)

When you turn the First Baseline at Top Margin feature on, a [BLine:On] code is inserted that takes effect from that location to the end of the document or to where you turn off the feature and a [BLine:Off] code is inserted.

Printer Command

With the Printer Command option, you can enter a string of printer codes or download a file that is sent directly to the printer during printing. Because WordPerfect can access all the features on most printers, this option is rarely used.

Quick Reference

- To insert a graphics box into your document, choose Graphics. Then, choose the type of box you wish to insert—either Figure, Text Box, Equation, Table Box, or User Box—and choose Create. You can insert a graphics image, text, or an equation into a graphics box. Thirty-six graphics images are packaged with WordPerfect, or you can create a graphic image using a graphics program.

Quick Reference *(continued)*

- To insert a caption for a graphics box in the text, you must display the Caption Editor for that graphics box. Choose <u>G</u>raphics, the type of box you wish to create a caption for, <u>C</u>aption. Then, type in the number for that box.

- To change a graphics box's position or size, click and drag the box to a new position, or click and drag a size handle to resize the box. You can also move or size a box using the Box Position and Size dialog box.

- To change the appearance for a box type, choose <u>G</u>raphics, the type of box you wish to change, <u>O</u>ptions. You can alter the default settings for borders, gray shading, and the caption numbering and style for a box type.

- To change the contents of a particular graphics box, you must display the Figure Editor, Text Editor, or Equation Editor for that box. Choose <u>G</u>raphics, the type of box you wish to edit, <u>E</u>dit. Then, type in the number for that box. The contents of the box determines which type of Editor appears. When a box contains graphics, the Figure Editor offers various features for moving, rotating, and scaling the graphics image inside the box.

- To create a graphics line, choose <u>G</u>raphics, <u>L</u>ine. Then choose either <u>H</u>orizontal or <u>V</u>ertical. You can edit the length and thickness of graphics lines with your mouse by clicking and dragging the line, or you can use the Edit Horizontal Line or Edit Vertical Line dialog box.

- To use the Line Draw feature, choose <u>T</u>ools, <u>L</u>ine Draw, or press CTRL + D. You can choose different draw characters and then use the arrow keys to create simple drawings like a bar graph or organizational chart.

- To refine the spacing in your text, choose <u>L</u>ayout, Typesettin<u>g</u>. The Typesetting feature enables you to change elements such as word spacing, letter spacing, and word spacing and justification limits, and to kern letter pairs.

13

Numbering Footnotes, Endnotes, Outlines, Paragraphs, and Lines

When you'd like to insert footnotes and endnotes in your text, you can let WordPerfect do the work of numbering them in sequential order and positioning them correctly on the page. You can also let WordPerfect number outlines, paragraphs, or lines on the page so that the numbers will be inserted automatically.

What the Footnote, Endnote, Outline, Paragraph Numbering, and Line Numbering features have in common is that WordPerfect makes sure that the items that result from use of these features—such as footnotes or outlines—are *always* numbered properly. Insert a footnote and all subsequent footnotes are renumbered to accommodate the insertion. Delete an outline entry and all subsequent entries are renumbered to accommodate the deletion. Move a paragraph in the text and all the following paragraphs are renumbered accordingly. These numbering features are covered in this chapter.

Working with Footnotes and Endnotes

Legal documents, research articles, and academic papers are commonly peppered with footnotes or endnotes. A *footnote* is a source citation or a supplement to the text. A footnote number is inserted in the main text, and the footnote itself is placed at the bottom of the page. An *endnote* is like a footnote except that the endnote's text is placed at a location other than at the bottom of the page—such as compiled with other endnotes at the end of the document.

WordPerfect automatically numbers footnotes and endnotes for you. Footnotes and endnotes are numbered separately so you can include both in a single document. Each footnote or endnote can run from one line to thousands of lines long.

For footnotes, WordPerfect automatically allows enough room on a page to accommodate the footnote text, readjusting the main text on a page as necessary. A sample of footnotes at the bottom of a printed page is shown in Figure 13-1. Notice that each footnote number in the main text is a superscript number. The footnote itself is separated from the main text by a two-inch-long line, and each footnote number is superscript and placed five spaces from the left margin. This is the default format for footnotes (which can be changed, as described later in this chapter).

For endnotes, WordPerfect places them at the end of the document or at another location if you so specify. A sample of endnotes on the last page of a printed document is shown in Figure 13-2. Notice that, just as with footnotes, an endnote number in the main text is superscript. In the endnote itself, endnote numbers are not superscript, but rather positioned on the baseline, flush at the left margin, and followed by a period. This is the default format for endnotes (which can be changed, as described later in this chapter).

Inserting Footnotes and Endnotes

You create footnotes and endnotes in basically the same way. Follow these steps:

1. Position the insertion point in the main text where you want the footnote or endnote number to appear.

Figure 13-1. ***Footnotes on a page in a printed document***

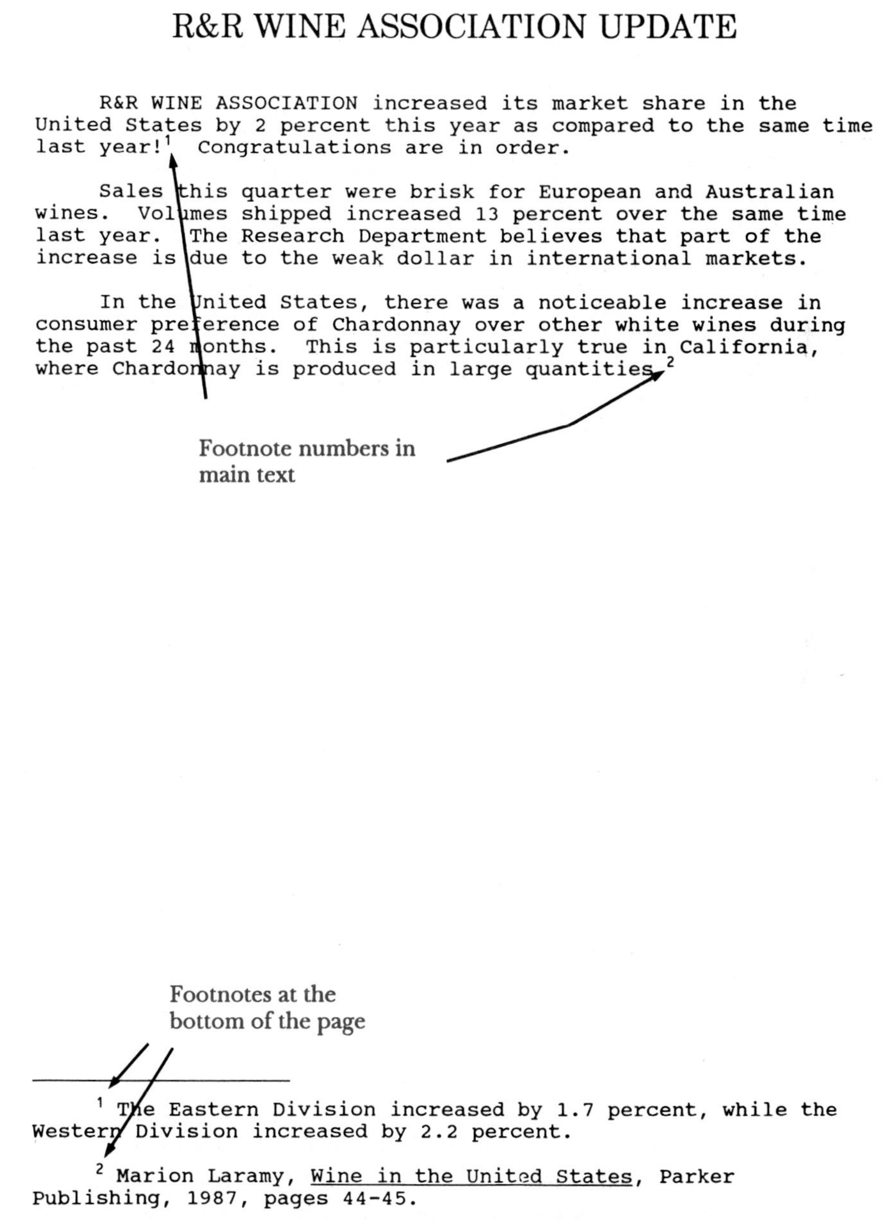

R&R WINE ASSOCIATION UPDATE

R&R WINE ASSOCIATION increased its market share in the United States by 2 percent this year as compared to the same time last year![1] Congratulations are in order.

Sales this quarter were brisk for European and Australian wines. Volumes shipped increased 13 percent over the same time last year. The Research Department believes that part of the increase is due to the weak dollar in international markets.

In the United States, there was a noticeable increase in consumer preference of Chardonnay over other white wines during the past 24 months. This is particularly true in California, where Chardonnay is produced in large quantities.[2]

Footnote numbers in
main text

Footnotes at the
bottom of the page

[1] The Eastern Division increased by 1.7 percent, while the Western Division increased by 2.2 percent.

[2] Marion Laramy, <u>Wine in the United States</u>, Parker Publishing, 1987, pages 44-45.

Figure 13-2.   ***Endnotes on the last page of a printed document***

Endnote number in main text

```
Overall, the economy is expected to follow the pattern previously
stated.  It is predicted that similar growth trends will continue
over the next five years.⁴  For more detailed information than
has been provided in this report, refer to the R&R Wine
Association's budget projections.  Otto has that information, and
plans to distribute the projections at next week's marketing
meeting.
```

```
1. These projections are based on data from ABC Data
Incorporated, a research company based in Philadelphia,
Pennsylvania.

2. The Eastern Division increased by 1.7 percent, while the
Western Division increased by 2.2 percent.

3. Marion Laramy, Wine in the United States, Parker Publishing,
1987, pages 44-45.

4. These projections are based on a report from XYZ Company, our
consultant in Salt Lake City, Utah.
```

Endnotes at the end of the document

2. Choose Layout, Footnote or Endnote, Create. A footnote or endnote workspace appears on screen, temporarily overlapping the
   document workspace. An example of the workspace for footnote 1
   is shown in Figure 13-3. Four buttons appear just below the menu
   bar: Close, Note Number, Previous, and Next. The number of the
   note that you are creating is inserted as the first character in the
   note. That number is actually a [Note Num] code.

3. With the insertion point just to the right of the note number, press
   the (SPACEBAR) or press the (TAB) key, or use the Indent feature (press
   (F7))—depending on how you want the text aligned in relation to the
   note number.

4. Type in the text of the note. You can type and edit the text as you
   normally would, using all the editing and formatting features available. For instance, you can change the font, change the justification,

or underline certain words for the text of that particular note. (The current font for that note is displayed on the status line at the bottom of the workspace.)

5. If you accidentally erase the note number while typing and editing the text, select Note Number to reinsert it.

6. Choose Close or press (CTRL) + (F4) to save your changes and return to the main text of your document.

In your document, a footnote or endnote number appears. It is super-scripted on the screen (and, as a result, may show uneven line spacing on that line; the printed result should not have uneven line spacing). If you open the reveal codes workspace, you'll find that this note number is actually a code. The code contains the first portion of the note's text. For instance, for the first footnote, as shown in Figure 13-1, the code is [Footnote:1;[Note Num] The Eastern Division incre ...]. The "[Note Num]" within the footnote code represents the footnote number that appears in the main text.

Figure 13-3.   *Workspace for footnote number 1*

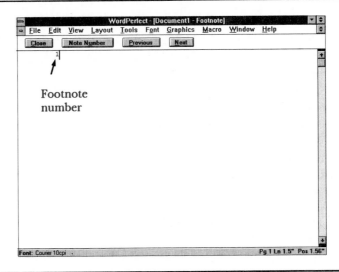

You can insert a new footnote or endnote anywhere in a document, at any time, and WordPerfect will automatically renumber subsequent footnotes or endnotes for you.

The text of footnotes and endnotes appears on the printed page but is *not* visible in the document workspace. To review the contents of a note before printing, you can reveal codes to view up to the first 25 characters. Or, you can edit the note (described soon) to review the text of the entire footnote. You can also see how your footnotes or endnotes will appear on the printed page by previewing the document on screen using the Print Preview feature, as described in Chapter 16.

note *If you ever choose to create a footnote or endnote by mistake, choose Close to exit the footnote or endnote workspace and then delete the note number in the document.*

Changing the Font or Layout of Footnotes and Endnotes

As previously mentioned, you can insert a font or layout code into the footnote or endnote workspace when typing the text of an individual footnote or endnote. The change you specify is used for that particular note, instead of the current font or layout settings in the main text of the document.

If you wish to change the current font or layout settings for *all* footnotes or endnotes, placing font and layout codes in each footnote or endnote workspace is time-consuming. There are quicker methods.

To change the font, choose a new Document Initial Font (see Chapter 5). This changes the font for the entire document, including the main text as well as footnotes and endnotes (and also other elements, such as captions in graphics boxes). Moreover, you can still make the font for the main text different from the footnotes/endnotes by inserting a font code at the top of the document. As a result, the footnotes/endnotes use one font (the Document Initial Font), and the main text uses another font (governed by the font code inserted at the top of the document). Another way to change the font is when you change footnote and endnote options, described later in this chapter.

To change a layout setting, such as margins or justification, insert the layout code in the Document Initial Codes workspace (see Chapter 7). This changes the layout for the entire document, including the main text as well as elements such as footnotes and endnotes. Moreover, you can still make the layout for the main text different from the footnotes/endnotes by inserting layout codes at the top of the document. For instance, change left/right margins on the Document Initial Codes workspace to **2"**, and then insert a left/right margin code at the top of the document to **1"**. The footnotes/endnotes use the 2-inch margins, and the main text uses the 1-inch margins.

13

Deleting Footnotes and Endnotes

A footnote can be deleted either in the document workspace or the reveal codes workspace by deleting the footnote code—use either the (DEL) or (BACKSPACE) key to erase the note number in the text. For instance, position the insertion point just to the right of the note number in the text and press (BACKSPACE). In the document workspace, WordPerfect will display a dialog box asking you to verify that you wish to delete the footnote. When reveal codes is open, WordPerfect will not prompt to verify the deletion, but will delete the footnote immediately.

An endnote can be deleted with (DEL) or (BACKSPACE) as well, but only when the reveal codes workspace is open.

If you accidentally delete a footnote or endnote, use the Undelete or Undo feature to restore it (see Chapter 3).

Editing Footnotes and Endnotes

You can edit the text or numbering of notes, or change the location of the compiled endnotes.

Altering the Text

You can edit or review the text of footnotes or endnotes any time after creating them. Follow these steps:

1. Choose Layout, Footnote or Endnote, Edit; a dialog box appears. When editing a footnote, this will be the Edit Footnote dialog box, as shown here:

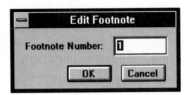

WordPerfect suggests that you wish to edit the next note forward in the text from the insertion point.

2. Type in the number of the note you want to edit if different from WordPerfect's suggestion and choose OK.

3. Edit the text in the footnote or endnote workspace.

4. To save your changes and return to the main text of your document, choose Close or press (CTRL) + (F4).

Instead, you can choose to browse through and edit other footnotes or endnotes that you have previously created, by choosing Previous or Next. The note you edit is saved, and the previous or next note of the same type is displayed. For instance, if you are editing footnote 2 and choose Next, footnote 2 will be saved, and footnote 3 will appear on screen. If you are editing endnote 5 and choose Previous, endnote 5 will be saved, and endnote 4 will appear.

Renumbering Footnotes and Endnotes

When working with footnotes or endnotes, you may wish to specify a new starting number. This is useful when you want one document's numbering to begin where another's has left off—such as when you split a long chapter into two separate documents.

To indicate a new starting number, position the insertion point in the text before the footnote or endnote you wish to renumber and choose Layout, Footnote or Endnote, New Number. A dialog box appears for you to type in a new number. When you type in the number and press OK, a code is inserted at that location. For instance, if you reset footnotes to begin at number 30, the code inserted is [New Ftn Num:30]. All footnotes following the code would be renumbered sequentially: 30, 31, 32, 33, and so on. If you reset endnotes to begin at number 100, the code inserted is [New End Num:100].

Choosing the Placement of Endnotes

WordPerfect reserves space at the end of a document for any endnotes you create. The endnotes are placed just below the main text. If you want the endnotes to begin on a separate page, insert a hard page break at the end of the document (by pressing (CTRL) + (ENTER) at the end of the document).

If you want endnotes printed someplace other than the last page, you can specify the location by inserting an Endnote Placement code in the text. Position the insertion point where you wish endnotes to appear in the text when printed. This location must be beyond the last endnote you want compiled at that location. For instance, if you've created endnotes on pages 1 through 6, then the insertion point must be positioned after the last endnote on page 6 in order for all those endnotes to be compiled where you specify. Any endnote numbers that are farther forward in the text will be compiled at the end of the document or at the location of the next Endnote Placement code.

Once the insertion point is positioned, choose Layout, Endnote, Placement. The Endnote Placement dialog box appears, as shown here:

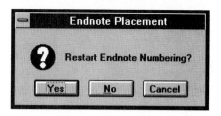

Here WordPerfect asks whether you wish to restart endnote numbering at 1 for all endnotes that follow the current position of the insertion point. Choose Yes to begin renumbering, or choose No to continue consecutive endnote numbering. (Choose Cancel to abort the Endnote Placement command.) WordPerfect inserts an [Endnote Placement] code in the text, followed by an [HPg] code so that additional text starts at the top of the next page. And, if you elected to restart endnote numbering for endnotes below the code, WordPerfect inserts a third code, [New End Num:1], which dictates that the next endnote will be renumbered to start at number 1. Wherever the Endnote Placement code is inserted, a special comment displays on screen to remind you that endnotes will be located here when printed, like this:

> **Endnote Placement**
> It is not known how much space endnotes will occupy here.
> Generate to determine.

If you wish, you can determine how much vertical space the endnotes will take up by choosing **T**ools, **G**enerate. Then, choose **Y**es to begin the generation of endnotes (as well as any Tables, Indexes, or Cross-References, features described in Chapter 15). In moments, the special comment on screen will display, as shown here:

> **Endnote Placement**

The comment appears in the document workspace as only one line in length, but you can use this comment to determine how much space is required to print the endnotes. You would position the insertion point just above the comment, check the Ln indicator on the status line, press ⟶ to position the insertion point on the other side of the comment, and again check the Ln indicator. The difference in the line measurement is the amount of space that will be occupied by the compiled endnotes when the page is printed. For instance, if the status line reads Ln 2" above the comment and Ln 7" below the comment, this indicates that the endnotes will occupy 5 inches of vertical space on the page.

Changing Footnote and Endnote Options

You can also alter the defaults that control how footnotes and endnotes will appear on the printed page. For instance, you can change the spacing within notes to double-spacing; or, instead of using Arabic numerals to reference a footnote in the main text, you can use letters or other characters, such as the asterisk (*).

To change footnote or endnote options, position the insertion point where you want the new options to take effect. For example, place the insertion point on page 2 to alter an option starting on that page. Place the insertion point in the Document Initial Codes workspace (described in Chapter 7) to alter an option starting at the top of the document. Then, choose Layout, Footnote or Endnote, Options. The Footnote Options dialog box is shown in Figure 13-4, while the Endnote Options dialog box is shown in Figure 13-5. Make your selections, as described next, and then choose OK. For footnotes, a [Ftn Opt] code is inserted that will affect all footnotes beyond that code. For endnotes, the code is [End Opt].

Keep in mind that the font or font attribute in effect wherever a [Ftn Opt] or [End Opt] code is inserted will also become the font for all footnotes or endnotes that follow the code. For instance, if a [Ftn Opt] code is placed within text where italics is in effect, the fonts that follow are printed as italicized text. Therefore, you can use a [Ftn Opt] or [End Opt] code as a way to change the footnote or endnote font.

13

Figure 13-4. Footnote Options dialog box

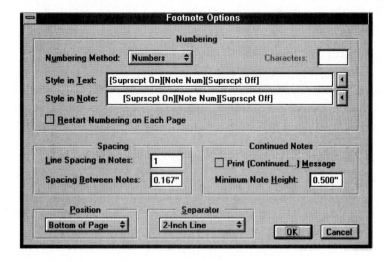

Figure 13-5.   *Endnote Options dialog box*

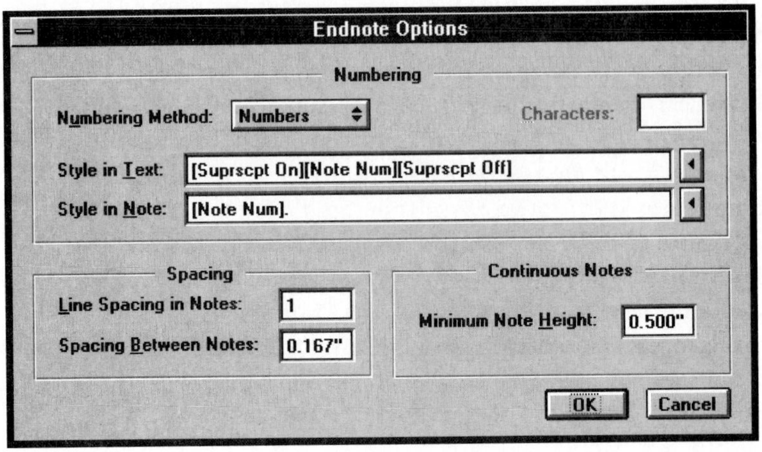

Options for Both Footnotes and Endnotes

The following six options are available for footnotes in the Footnote Options dialog box and for endnotes in the Endnote Options dialog box.

Numbering Method

You can choose the type of number (or letter or symbol) representing footnotes in the text using the Numbering Method option. This option is preset for Arabic numbers (1, 2, 3...). You have two other choices. Select Letters to number footnotes or endnotes with lowercase letters (a, b, c...). Select Characters and then type as many as five characters that you wish to use. (To type a special character not found on the keyboard, such as †, press (CTRL) + (W) and choose a special character, as described in Chapter 5.)

When you type in characters, each one is used once, then twice, then three times, and so on until it is used 15 times. Then the cycle begins again. For instance, if you use an asterisk (type *) as the character, then the first note will be marked with one asterisk (*), the second with two asterisks (**), and so on. If you use an asterisk and a dagger (type *†), the first note will be marked with one asterisk (*), the second with one dagger (†), the third with two asterisks (**), the fourth with two daggers (††), the fifth with three asterisks (***) and so on.

When typing the characters, make sure not to insert spaces between them—for instance, type ***†** and not *** †**—or the space will be considered one of the characters.

Style in Text

You can set the style for the note numbers in the main text by using the Style in Text option. As shown in the Style in Text box in Figures 13-4 and 13-5, this option is preset as:

```
[Suprscpt On] [Note Num] [SuprScpt Off]
```

This means that the note number (Note Num) in the main text is super-scripted. You can select a different style; for example, you can remove the superscript by deleting the superscript codes. You can also insert underline or boldface or other attributes. Select different attributes by clicking the arrowhead button located at the end of the Style in Text text box and then making a selection from the pop-up list that appears.

Style in Note

Set the style for the note numbers in the notes with the Style in Note option. This option is preset for footnotes as:

```
        [Suprscpt On] [Note Num] [Suprscpt Off]
```

This means note numbers are superscripted and get a five-space indent. This option is preset for endnotes as:

```
[Note Num] .
```

This means the note number is simply followed by a period, without any indentation or superscript. You can select a different style. For instance, you can remove the superscript by deleting the superscript codes, or you can insert underline or boldface or other attributes. Select different attributes by clicking the arrowhead button located next to the Style in Note text box and then making a selection from the pop-up list that displays.

Line Spacing in Notes

Use the Line Spacing in Notes option to set the line spacing within a note. This option is preset to single-spacing. To change this, you can type **.5** for half-spacing, **2** for double-spacing, and so on.

Spacing Between Notes

Determine how much line spacing there will be between notes that appear on the same page with the Spacing Between Notes option. This option is preset at .167 inch so that there is one blank line, one-sixth of an inch in height, between each footnote or endnote. You can change that setting; for instance, enter **.2** inch for slightly more space between notes.

Minimum Note Height

If a note too long to fit on one page must be split among several pages, you can use the Minimum Note Height option to determine the minimum number of text lines to be kept together in the footnote text. This option is preset to keep .5 inch of a long note on a page before continuing the note on the next page. If WordPerfect has insufficient room to print the text of a note on one page, it will keep the first .5 inch on the first page and print the rest on the next page. You can increase or decrease this setting.

Options for Footnotes Only

Four additional options for altering the appearance of notes are available just for footnotes. These options are found in the Footnote Options dialog box.

Restart Numbering on Each Page

Initially, the Restart Numbering on Each Page option is turned off so that notes are numbered sequentially throughout a document. If you wish the numbering to restart at 1 on every page, turn this option on.

Print (Continued...) Message

Initially, the Print (Continued...) Message option is turned off so that no message is printed if a footnote is too long to fit on a page and must be split between two pages. If you like, turn this option on so that a "(Continued...)"

message prints at the end of the footnote on the first page and at the beginning of where it continues on the next page.

Position

You can set where on the page footnotes will print with the <u>P</u>osition option. This option is preset to <u>B</u>ottom of Page, which causes footnotes to print at the bottom of the page, regardless of whether the main text fills the page. If you like, you can instead have footnotes appear just below the main text on partially filled pages by choosing <u>A</u>fter text.

Separator

Choose whether or not you want a separator line between the main text and the footnotes using the <u>S</u>eparator option. This option is preset for a 2-inch separator line. Other options include having no line, or a line that extends from the left margin to the right margin.

Numbering Paragraphs and Outlines

WordPerfect offers a numbering method for paragraphs or outlines. You can number your paragraphs or outline entries on your own—inserting characters such as I., II., A., 1., and so on. However, if you take advantage of WordPerfect's Paragraph Numbering and Outline features, the whole job will be a lot easier because the numbers automatically update if you rearrange your document—whether you move, add, or delete paragraphs or outline entries.

Paragraph Numbering

WordPerfect's default for the group of characters used when inserting a paragraph number (or when typing outline entries) is referred to as the *Outline format.* There are eight levels in this format. Each level has a different style of numbering. For instance, the first level is an uppercase Roman numeral followed by a period. The second level is uppercase letters followed by a period. The third level is Arabic numbers followed by a period. The following lists all the styles for the eight levels in the Outline format:

Level	Style
1	I. II. III. ...
2	A. B. C. ...
3	1. 2. 3. ...
4	a. b. c. ...
5	(1) (2) (3)...
6	(a) (b) (c)...
7	i) ii) iii)...
8	a) b) c)...

With the Paragraph Numbering feature, paragraph numbers are inserted one by one into a document as you type. This feature is best used for inserting the occasional paragraph number or for a short list of numbered paragraphs, as in Figure 13-6. Notice in Figure 13-6 that only the first level of the Outline format is used.

Figure 13-6.   *Paragraph numbering with the Outline format*

R&R WINE ASSOCIATION UPDATE

I. R&R WINE ASSOCIATION increased its market share in the United States by 2 percent this year as compared to the same time last year! Congratulations are in order.

II. Sales this quarter were brisk for European and Australian wines. Volumes shipped increased 13 percent over the same time last year. The Research Department believes that part of the increase is due to the weak dollar in international markets.

III. In the United States, there was a noticeable increase in consumer preference of Chardonnay over other white wines during the past 24 months. This is particularly true in California, where Chardonnay is produced in large quantities.

Level-one paragraph numbers

You can insert a paragraph number in two ways. First, you can insert it with an *auto* (automatic) numbering level. This means WordPerfect will insert the level number based on how many times you tab before requesting the number. At the left margin, a first-level number will appear. At the next tab stop, a second-level number will appear. At the next tab stop, a third-level number will appear, and so on for the eight levels.

Second, you can insert a paragraph number with a *manual* numbering level. You can indicate the level independent of the number's relation to tab stops. For instance, suppose you want to number a group of paragraphs with Arabic numerals—1., 2., 3., and so on—which corresponds to the third level. But, you want the numbers to appear at the left margin. In that case, manually indicate that the paragraph numbers should each be fixed at level 3.

To work with paragraph numbering, follow these steps each time you're ready to insert a paragraph number:

1. Position the insertion point where you want a paragraph number to appear.

2. Choose Tools, Outline, Paragraph Number. The Paragraph Numbering dialog box displays, as shown here:

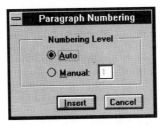

3. If you want the level of the paragraph number to be based on the insertion point's tab stop location, maintain Auto as the selected option.

   If you want to specify the numbering level, select Manual, and then type a number into the number box to dictate the type of numbering you want (use the list of levels given earlier as a reference).

4. Choose Insert.

≡shortcut≡ (ALT) + (F5) *is the shortcut for Tools, Outline, Paragraph Number.*

The paragraph number appears in the document workspace. This paragraph number is actually a code. When an auto paragraph number is inserted, it reads [Par Num:Auto]. When a manual paragraph number is inserted, the numbering level is displayed in the code, such as [Par Num:3] or [Par Num:5]. Of course, the codes are shown only when you open the reveal codes workspace.

Once you have inserted a paragraph number, you can press the (SPACEBAR) to separate the paragraph number from the paragraph you are about to type. Or, press (TAB) to indent the first line. Or, press (F7) to insert an indent code so that the entire paragraph will be indented at the next tab stop (as shown in the example in Figure 13-6). Then type the text of the paragraph.

The level of an auto paragraph number is flexible. If you later insert or delete tabs or indents in front of the paragraph number, the number level will change. For instance, position the insertion point to the left of a paragraph number at the first level and press (TAB); the number moves to the next tab stop and increases to the second level. Press (TAB) again and the number will move to the next tab stop and increase to the third level.

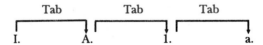

Press (SHIFT) + (TAB) (or press (BACKSPACE) to delete the tab code) to decrease the level.

On the other hand, the level of a manual paragraph number is fixed. Press (TAB) to move the number to the next tab stop, and the number remains at the level you set it at.

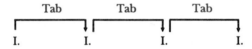

Whether you use an auto or manual paragraph number, the number itself will change if you later edit your text and add, delete, or move paragraph numbers. The numbers remain in sequential order. For instance, suppose you edit Figure 13-6 by deleting the first paragraph number along with its associated text. The paragraphs will automatically renumber to reflect the editing change, as shown in Figure 13-7. Now what was numbered as paragraph II. in Figure 13-6 is renumbered as paragraph I. in Figure 13-7.

Refer to Chapter 15 if you plan to insert numerous paragraph numbers with the Paragraph Numbering feature. You'll learn to create a macro as a handy shortcut for inserting paragraph numbers into your text. Also consider inserting the paragraph numbers with the Outline feature, described next.

13

Outlining

Like the Paragraph Numbering feature, the Outline feature inserts paragraph numbers, and also uses the Outline format for the default characters used for numbering. But, rather than insert the paragraph numbers one by

Figure 13-7.   *After editing, an outline is automatically renumbered*

R&R WINE ASSOCIATION UPDATE

I.   Sales this quarter were brisk for European and Australian wines. Volumes shipped increased 13 percent over the same time last year. The Research Department believes that part of the increase is due to the weak dollar in international markets.

II.   In the United States, there was a noticeable increase in consumer preference of Chardonnay over other white wines during the past 24 months. This is particularly true in California, where Chardonnay is produced in large quantities.

Figure 13-8.   *An outline using the Outline format*

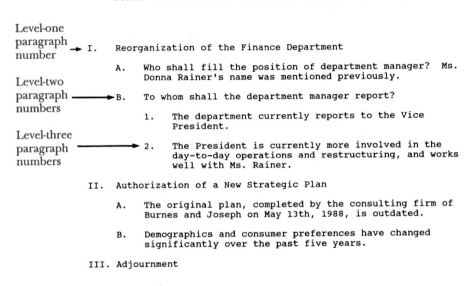

AGENDA
R&R WINE ASSOCIATION BOARD MEETING

Level-one
paragraph → I.   Reorganization of the Finance Department
number

                A.   Who shall fill the position of department manager? Ms.
Level-two   Donna Rainer's name was mentioned previously.
paragraph ──────→ B.   To whom shall the department manager report?
numbers
                    1.   The department currently reports to the Vice
                          President.
Level-three
paragraph ──────────→ 2.   The President is currently more involved in the
numbers   day-to-day operations and restructuring, and works
                            well with Ms. Rainer.

        II.   Authorization of a New Strategic Plan

                A.   The original plan, completed by the consulting firm of
                      Burnes and Joseph on May 13th, 1988, is outdated.

                B.   Demographics and consumer preferences have changed
                      significantly over the past five years.

        III. Adjournment

one, you can switch into Outline mode, and then insert a number every time you tap the (ENTER) key. The Outline feature is best used for inserting frequent paragraph numbers, such as in the outline shown in Figure 13-8.

Although you can create an outline without using the Outline feature, it is much easier to keep outline entries numbered properly with it. (You could use the Paragraph Numbering feature later to add individual entries to an outline.) The Outline feature also has the advantage of offering attributes to help you edit the outline easily.

Follow these steps to use the Outline feature:

1. Choose Tools, Outline, Outline On. The message "Outline" appears in the lower left corner on the status line, reminding you that the feature is now activated; you are in Outline mode.

2. Press (ENTER) to move down a line and insert a first-level paragraph number. (If you press (ENTER) a second time, you can insert a blank line and move the paragraph number down another line.)

3. If you want to change a number to the next level paragraph number (such as from the first to the second level) press the (TAB) key. To change to the previous level (such as from the second to the first level) press (SHIFT) + (TAB).

4. Press the (SPACEBAR) or press (CTRL) + (TAB) or use the Indent feature (press (F7))—depending on how you want the text aligned in relation to the number. (In Outline mode, pressing (TAB) after inserting a paragraph number will change text to the next outline level. Therefore, if you wish text to stay at the current outline level but want to insert a tab code so that the line of text you are about to type is indented, you must press (CTRL) + (TAB) instead.)

5. Type the text.

6. Press (ENTER) to insert another paragraph number. WordPerfect inserts the new number at the level of the last paragraph number you inserted. For instance, if you just typed text for a second-level paragraph number (such as A.), then another second-level paragraph number appears (such as B.).

7. Repeat the previous steps, beginning at step 3, until the outline is finished.

8. Choose Tools, Outline, Outline Off. The message "Outline" disappears.

As with the Paragraph Numbering feature, the Outline feature ensures that all outline entries are numbered in sequential order. When you edit the outline, WordPerfect renumbers it to reflect the changes.

Unlike with the Paragraph Numbering feature, however, you have no choice between auto and manual when using the Outline feature. An auto paragraph number is *always* inserted, which is actually a [Par Num:Auto] code, the identical code used for automatic numbering with the Paragraph Numbering feature. If you later insert or delete tabs or indentation just before the paragraph number, the number level will change. For instance, position the insertion point to the left of a first-level paragraph number and press (TAB); the number moves to the next tab stop and increases to the second level. Press (TAB) again and the number will move to the next tab stop and increase to the third level. Press (SHIFT) + (TAB) (or press (BACKSPACE) to delete the tab code) to decrease the level.

In addition to [Par Num:Auto] codes, outline codes are inserted with the Outline feature. An [Outline On] code is inserted at the top of the outline, wherever you turned on the feature, and an [Outline Off] code is inserted at the bottom of the outline, wherever you turned off the feature. These codes mark the boundaries of the outline. To return to Outline mode for the same outline, simply position the insertion point between the On and Off outline codes. "Outline" will again display on the status line, and when you press (ENTER), a paragraph number will again appear.

Moving the Insertion Point

Four key combinations are shortcuts to help you move the insertion point quickly in Outline mode.

Movement	Key Combination
To the next paragraph number	(ALT) + (→)
To the previous paragraph number	(ALT) + (←)
To the next paragraph number of the same level	(ALT) + (↓)
To the previous paragraph number of the same level	(ALT) + (↑)

Moving, Copying, and Deleting a Family

In Outline mode, you can easily move, copy, or delete a family. An outline *family* consists of the paragraph number and text on the line where the insertion point is located plus any subordinate (lower) outline entries. For instance, suppose that the insertion point in Figure 13-8 is on the line that reads "B. To whom shall the department manager report?". In that case, here's the family:

```
B. To whom shall the department manager report?

   1. The department currently reports to the Vice
      President.

   2. The President is currently more involved in the
      day-to-day operations and restructuring, and works
      well with Ms. Rainer.
```

If the insertion point in Figure 13-8 is on the line that reads "I. Reorganization of the Finance Department", then this is the family:

```
I. Reorganization of the Finance Department

   A. Who shall fill the position of department manager? Ms.
      Donna Rainer's name was mentioned previously.

   B. To whom shall the department manager report?

      1. The department currently reports to the Vice
         President.

      2. The President is currently more involved in the
         day-to-day operations and restructuring, and works
         well with Ms. Rainer.
```

When in Outline mode, you can move, copy, or delete entire outline families in one command. Follow these steps:

1. Position the insertion point on the first line in the family.
2. Choose <u>T</u>ools, <u>O</u>utline, and then <u>M</u>ove Family or <u>C</u>opy Family or <u>D</u>elete Family.

13

If you choose Move Family, the family is selected (highlighted) on screen. An example is shown in Figure 13-9.

Use the arrow keys to move the family. The ⬆ and ⬇ keys reposition the entire family to a different location within the outline, above or below other outline entries. Here the family in Figure 13-9 is moved up one entry:

```
I.    Reorganization of the Finance Department

      A.    To whom shall the department manager report?

            1.   The department currently reports to the Vice
                 President.

            2.   The President is currently more involved in the
                 day-to-day operations and restructuring, and works
                 well with Ms. Rainer.

      B.    Who shall fill the position of department manager?  Ms.
            Donna Rainer's name was mentioned previously.

II.   Authorization of a New Strategic Plan
```

The ⬅ and ➡ keys increase or decrease the numbering level of the family (but cannot do so by more than one level difference from the level of the line preceding the family). Here the family in Figure 13-9 is increased by one level:

```
I.    Reorganization of the Finance Department

      A.    Who shall fill the position of department manager?  Ms.
            Donna Rainer's name was mentioned previously.

            1.   To whom shall the department manager report?

                 a.   The department currently reports to the Vice
                      President.

                 b.   The President is currently more involved in
                      the day-to-day operations and restructuring,
                      and works well with Ms. Rainer.

II.   Authorization of a New Strategic Plan
```

Press (HOME), ⬆ or (HOME), ⬇ to move the family to the very top or bottom of the outline. After the family is relocated, press (ENTER) to make the move permanent.

If you choose Copy Family, a copy of the family appears on screen just below the original family, and is highlighted. Use the arrow keys as just described to relocate the copy, and then press (ENTER) to insert the copy in the outline.

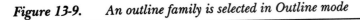

Figure 13-9.   *An outline family is selected in Outline mode*

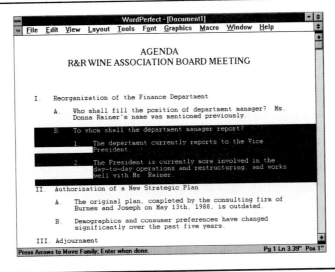

13

If you choose <u>D</u>elete Family, the family is selected (highlighted) and a dialog box appears; choose <u>Y</u>es to erase the family from the outline, or choose <u>N</u>o to abort the delete command.

Defining a New Paragraph Number or Outline Format

You can customize the Paragraph Numbering and Outline features to your needs. Position the insertion point in your text where you want the changes to take effect, and choose <u>T</u>ools, <u>O</u>utline, <u>D</u>efine. A Define Paragraph Numbering dialog box appears, as shown in Figure 13-10. Make your selections (described below) and then choose OK.

An automatic Paragraph Number Definition code is inserted in your document: [Par Num Def:]. This code takes effect for all paragraph numbering and outlining from that point forward in the text.

shortcut (ALT) + (SHIFT) + (F5) *is the shortcut for* <u>T</u>ools, <u>O</u>utline, <u>D</u>efine.

Figure 13-10.   *Define Paragraph Numbering dialog box*

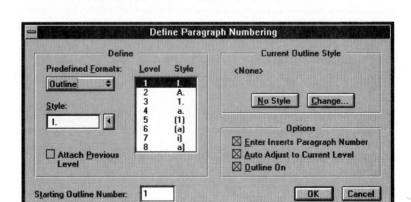

There are four categories of options you can choose from in the Define Paragraph Numbering dialog box.

Define

Use the options in the Define group box to change the numbering style for paragraph numbers. WordPerfect offers four predefined formats to choose from: Outline (the default format), Paragraph, Legal, and Bullets. All four formats are shown in Figure 13-11. Figure 13-12 shows an example of a section of an outline using the last three of these different formats. You can define a new numbering style before or after creating an outline or inserting paragraph numbers; just make sure to position the insertion point before the paragraph numbers you wish to affect.

As another option, you can select the user-defined format to create your own numbering format. You can then specify the numbering style for each level. Select a level from the Level list box, and then either type a character into the Style text box or choose the arrowhead button next to the Style text box and choose a style from the pop-up list that displays. Repeat for all levels you wish to define. If you turn on the Attach Previous Level check box, a

Figure 13-11. *Four predefined formats for paragraph numbering and outlining*

Outline Format					**Legal Format**			
Level	*Style*				*Level*	*Style*		
1	I.	II.	III. ...		1	1	2 ...	3 ...
2	A.	B.	C. ...		2	1.1	2.1 ...	3.1 ...
3	1.	2.	3. ...		3	1.1.1	2.1.1 ...	3.1.1.
4	a.	b.	c. ...		4	1.1.1.1	...	
5	(1)	(2)	(3) ...		5	1.1.1.1.1		
6	(a)	(b)	(c) ...		6	1.1.1.1.1.1		
7	i)	ii)	iii) ...		7	1.1.1.1.1.1.1		
8	a)	b)	c) ...		8	1.1.1.1.1.1.1.1		

Paragraph Format					**Bullets Format**		
Level	*Style*				*Level*	*Style*	
1	1.	2.	3. ...		1	●	(Bullet)
2	a.	b.	c. ...		2	○	(Hollow bullet)
3	i.	ii.	iii. ...		3	–	(Minus sign)
4	(1)	(2)	(3) ...		4	■	(Square bullet)
5	(a)	(b)	(c) ...		5	*	(Asterisk)
6	(i)	(ii)	(iii) ...		6	+	(Plus)
7	1)	2)	3) ...		7	●	(Small bullet)
8	a)	b)	c) ...		8	x	(Lowercase x)

paragraph number is connected to the previous level (as is the case, for instance, with levels 2 through 8 of the Legal format).

Starting Outline Number

You can specify different paragraph numbers with the Starting Outline Number option. For instance, you can create two or more independent outlines in the same document that are numbered sequentially. Or, you can create two outlines in different documents that are numbered sequentially. Indicate the new starting number using Arabic numbers, and separate each level by a period.

Figure 13-12.   ***Example of the same outline using three different formats***

Paragraph format

    1.   Reorganization of the Finance Department

        a.   Who shall fill the position of department manager? Ms. Donna Rainer's name was mentioned previously.

            i.   To whom shall the department manager report?

                (1)   The department currently reports to the Vice President.

                (2)   The President is currently more involved in the day-to-day operations and restructuring, and works well with Ms. Rainer.

    2.   Authorization of a New Strategic Plan

Legal format

    1   Reorganization of the Finance Department

    1.1 Who shall fill the position of department manager? Ms. Donna Rainer's name was mentioned previously.

        1.1.1   To whom shall the department manager report?

           1.1.1.1   The department currently reports to the Vice President.

           1.1.1.2   The President is currently more involved in the day-to-day operations and restructuring, and works well with Ms. Rainer.

    2   Authorization of a New Strategic Plan

Bullets format

    •   Reorganization of the Finance Department

      o   Who shall fill the position of department manager? Ms. Donna Rainer's name was mentioned previously.

         –   To whom shall the department manager report?

            ■   The department currently reports to the Vice President.

            ■   The President is currently more involved in the day-to-day operations and restructuring, and works well with Ms. Rainer.

    •   Authorization of a New Strategic Plan

As an example, suppose you type an outline using the Outline format for numbering, with outline entries I to XI. In a separate document, you wish to begin an outline where the outline in the first document left off, with entry XII (the Roman numeral for 12). Before beginning the second outline, display the Define Paragraph Numbering dialog box and set the Starting Outline Number to 12. The next level-one paragraph number will be XII, rather than I. Or, if you set the Starting Outline Number to 7.3, the next level-one paragraph number will be XII, and the next level-two paragraph number will be c.

13

Options

Use the three items in the Options group box to change how the Outline feature operates.

By default, pressing the (ENTER) key while in Outline mode inserts a paragraph number. Turn off the Enter Inserts Paragraph Number check box to be able to press (ENTER) in Outline mode without inserting a paragraph number. If Enter Inserts Paragraph Number is off, you must use the Paragraph Numbering feature to insert a paragraph number.

Also by default, the paragraph number inserted will be at the same level as the paragraph number inserted just before. Turn off the Auto Adjust to Current Level check box to insert each new outline number as a first-level paragraph number. Then use the (TAB) key if you wish, to change a paragraph number to the next level.

Finally, Outline mode is normally turned on after you make selections from the Define Paragraph Numbering dialog box and choose OK. Turn off the Outline On check box if you don't want to turn on Outline mode. In that case, you must turn on the Outline feature manually by choosing Tools, Outline, Outline On.

Current Outline Style

The Current Outline Style option combines the Outline feature with the Styles feature (discussed in Chapter 15). You can define a highly sophisticated style—which is a combination of codes and text—for each level of an outline. For instance, you can create an outline style for the first level that automatically turns on boldface, inserts a paragraph number, turns off boldface, and inserts an indent code. Create an outline style for the second level that turns on underlining, inserts a paragraph number, turns off underlining, and inserts an indent code.

An outline style saves time when creating an outline or when numbering paragraphs because you have fewer keystrokes to type. For instance, you don't need to press (F7) after each number to insert an indent code; the style does it for you. Moreover, an outline style can ensure not only that the paragraph numbers are in sequential order, but that the format of each outline entry or paragraph is consistent.

As a default, no outline style is used; this is indicated by the message "<None>" under the heading Current Outline Style in Figure 13-10. To select an outline style, choose the Change command button from the Define Paragraph Numbering dialog box. An Outline Styles dialog box appears, displaying a list of preexisting outline styles (these may be outline styles you previously created and/or outline styles that you installed when you installed WordPerfect). Select a style and choose Select; the style's name now appears under the heading Current Outline Style. Paragraph numbers that you insert will now be formatted according to the outline style in effect.

In the Outline Styles dialog box, you can also create or edit outline styles, or retrieve or save a group of outline styles. The procedure is the same as described in Chapter 15, which describes the Styles feature when not pertaining to outlines, except that when creating an outline style, you specify the text and codes associated with each level of the style. An outline style is therefore like eight separate styles, one for each level in an outline.

Numbering Lines at the Printer

WordPerfect offers another numbering feature that can automatically number lines on a page. With the Line Numbering feature, numbers are positioned at or near the left margin of the page. An example is shown in Figure 13-13. Line numbering comes in handy in documents that will be discussed by a group. You can call attention to a specific section of text, as in "please turn your attention to lines 5 through 8". Or, line numbering might prove useful when editing documents for which you have a line limit. Line numbering is also commonly used in legal documents and can be used to create the same effect as legal pleading paper.

13

Figure 13-13.   *Line numbering on a printed page*

```
1    R&R WINE ASSOCIATION increased its market share in the United

2    States by 2 percent this year as compared to the same time last

3    year!  Congratulations are in order.

4

5    Sales this quarter were brisk for European and Australian wines.

6    Volumes shipped increased 13 percent over the same time last

7    year.  The Research Department believes that part of the increase

8    is due to the weak dollar in international markets.

9

10   In the United States, there was a noticeable increase in consumer

11   preference of Chardonnay over other white wines during the past

12   24 months.  This is particularly true in California, where

13   Chardonnay is produced in large quantities.
```

To use the Line Numbering feature, follow these steps:

1. Position the insertion point where you want line numbering to begin or end.

2. Choose Layout, Line, Numbering. The Line Numbering dialog box appears, as shown here:

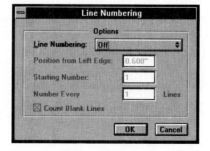

3. Select Continuous from the Line Numbering pop-up list box to number the lines consecutively, regardless of page breaks.

   Select Restart Each Page to number the lines separately on each page. On every new page, the numbering is restarted.

   If line numbering had previously been turned on, select Off to turn off line numbering for the rest of the document.

4. Change any other option in the dialog box, as described next.

5. Choose OK.

A [Ln Num:On] code is inserted into the text when you turn the feature on, and a [Ln Num:Off] code is inserted when you turn the feature off. Other options in the Line Numbering dialog box include:

- *Position from Left Edge*   This option determines where the page numbers are printed, as measured from the left edge of the page.

- *Starting Number*   This option determines whether numbering starts with 1 or with another number.

- *Number Every*   This option determines whether a number is printed on every line or in other increments. For instance, an entry of **2** will number lines 2, 4, 6, and so on.

- *Count Blank Lines*   This option determines whether or not blank lines are included in the line count.

Line numbers appear on the printed page but not in the document workspace. The line numbers will display on screen, however, when you use the Print Preview feature, as described in Chapter 16.

Be aware that line numbering is dependent on the line-spacing selection. For instance, when a document is double-spaced, then line numbers are double-spaced also (as in Figure 13-13), unless you change the Number Every box in the Line Numbering dialog box.

If you want line numbering to extend to the last line on a page, then either text or hard returns must occupy each line. Thus, if text only occupies half the page, continue to press (ENTER) to insert [HRt] codes down to the bottom of the page.

You can use the Line Numbering feature to create legal pleading paper. Then, to create the line or double-line down the page that is usually part of the pleading paper layout, you can use the Graphics Lines feature, as described in Chapter 12. Also refer to the discussion of the Styles feature in Chapter 15; WordPerfect provides a predefined style for pleading paper.

13

Quick Reference

- To insert a footnote or endnote, choose Layout, Footnote or Endnote, Create. To delete a footnote or endnote, erase the note number in the main text. The remaining notes are renumbered automatically.

- To specify that endnotes are printed at a location other than at the end of the document, position the insertion point at another location and choose Layout, Endnote, Placement.

- To change the options for how footnotes or endnotes are printed and the style with which they are numbered, choose Layout, Footnote or Endnote, Options.

- To insert a paragraph number, choose Tools, Outline, Paragraph Number, or press (ALT) + (F5). Then indicate whether you wish to use automatic or manual numbering.

- To turn on Outline mode, choose Tools, Outline, Outline On. Now, a paragraph number will appear every time you press the (ENTER) key, and its level will change when you press (TAB) or (SHIFT) + (TAB).

- To change the default numbering style for paragraph numbers or to change how the Outline feature operates, choose Tools, Outline, Define.

- To number lines near the left margin of your document, choose Layout, Line, Numbering. You can specify continual numbering, or you can restart numbering on every page.

14

Merging and Sorting

Merging is the process of combining information from different sources to produce a new document. You can produce contracts, memos, or phone lists. You can create personalized letters and envelopes for mass mailings.

For instance, suppose you write the same letter to 50 people. Rather than type each letter separately, you can type the letter once, and with the Merge feature personalize it 50 times, creating 50 letters each having different addresses and salutations. Then, you can type an envelope form, and with the Merge feature personalize it 50 times, creating 50 addressed envelopes. You can type a label form and rely on Merge to create 50 labels. You'll learn in this chapter how the Merge feature produces repetitive documents quickly and easily.

You'll also learn about the Sort feature, with which WordPerfect rearranges documents alphabetically or numerically. You can sort lines, paragraphs, rows in a table, or merge records. You can also have WordPerfect select lines, paragraphs, rows, or merge records that meet your specifications.

Merges Using the Keyboard

The main source for any type of the merge is called a *primary file*. The primary file controls the merge. It contains the text that stays the same in every document. And it contains special *merge codes* that tell WordPerfect where to insert information imported from another source—information that personalizes the final document. This other source can be the keyboard.

Merging by inputting with the keyboard is convenient when the primary file is a form or memorandum, where the basic structure of the text stays the same, but specific information changes every time you complete the form or memorandum. The procedure resembles a fill-in-the-blanks process. For instance, if you worked in the personnel office at the R&R Wine Association (and your name was Cynthia Allen), you might find yourself frequently sending out a memo such as the one shown in Figure 14-1. The circled copy represents the type of information that changes from memo to memo. The other information stays the same every time.

Figure 14-1 is a perfect application for a merge with the keyboard. You have two tasks. First, you create the primary file containing the text that stays the same. Then, every time you wish to produce a memorandum, perform a merge.

Creating a Primary File

You begin a primary file just as you begin any other document: just start typing on a new, blank screen. You can format the primary file—changing margins, tabs, spacing, fonts, and so forth—just as you would any standard document.

Wherever the memo will be personalized, you must insert a merge code. The type of merge code you insert is called an input code, because it tells WordPerfect to pause during the merge for input. To insert an input code, follow these steps:

1. Position the insertion point where you want to personalize the text during each merge.

Figure 14-1. *The results of a merge using the keyboard*

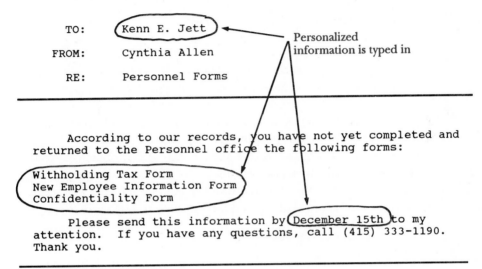

MEMORANDUM FROM THE OFFICE OF PERSONNEL

TO: Kenn E. Jett — Personalized information is typed in

FROM: Cynthia Allen

RE: Personnel Forms

According to our records, you have not yet completed and returned to the Personnel office the following forms:

Withholding Tax Form
New Employee Information Form
Confidentiality Form

Please send this information by December 15th to my attention. If you have any questions, call (415) 333-1190. Thank you.

2. Choose <u>T</u>ools, <u>M</u>erge, <u>I</u>nput. The Insert Merge Code dialog box appears, as shown here:

3. Type a message that will be placed on screen during the merge to remind you what personalized information you will type. For instance, type **Employee's Name** to correspond to the location where you will type a name during the merge. Or, type **Due Date** to correspond to the location where you will type a date during the

merge. Leave the Enter Message text box blank if you prefer no message.

4. Choose OK.

shortcut (CTRL) + (F12) *is the shortcut for* *Tools*, *Merge*.

The primary file for the R&R Wine Association's Office of Personnel memo, which contains three input codes, is shown in Figure 14-2. (Most memorandums also contain the date. You can insert a fourth input code wherever you wish to insert the date in the memorandum during the merge. Or, as you will see shortly, there's another merge code that can insert the current date automatically during the merge.)

Unlike most codes in WordPerfect, merge codes appear on the document workspace—though in a different form than in the reveal codes workspace. Suppose you typed the message **Employee's Name**. This will appear in the document workspace (and indeed does appear in Figure 14-2):

`{INPUT}Employee's Name~`

Figure 14-2.   *Primary file for a merge using the keyboard*

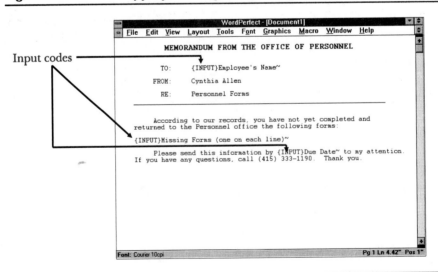

The merge code is enclosed in curly brackets, is followed by the message, and ends with a tilde (˜).

note *Merge codes occupy space in the document workspace, but not on the printed page. You can request that the document workspace hide merge codes with the Files, Preferences, Display command (see Chapter 17) so that you can predict how the text will lay out on the page once the merge is performed. However, when you're first creating a primary file, be sure to keep the merge codes displayed.*

After you've typed a primary file, be sure to check carefully for grammatical, punctuation, and spelling errors. Otherwise, every mistake you make will appear every time you use the primary file to produce a new document. Also check the location and syntax of your merge codes carefully. There must be a tilde (˜) following an {INPUT} code, either directly after the code or directly after the message if you include one, as in:

{INPUT} ~

or

{INPUT} *message~*

Once the primary file is complete, save it on disk. You will want to identify this file as a primary file containing merge codes, and not as a standard document. One good method for doing so is to choose a descriptive filename. For instance, use the letters "pf" or "pri" in the filename extension, such as in *memoform.pf* or *memo.pri*.

Performing the Merge

After you have stored a primary file on disk, you can initiate a merge at any time. Open a new, blank document workspace and then follow these steps:

1. Choose Tools, Merge, Merge. The Merge dialog box appears, as shown here:

14

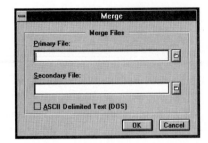

2. In the <u>P</u>rimary File text box, type the name of the primary file. If you can't remember the name, click the file button just to the right of the text box so that you can browse through your list of files and select the primary file that you want.

3. Choose OK.

The primary file will appear on screen, and the following message will display at the bottom of the screen, on the status line, to remind you that you have initiated a merge:

```
- Merging -
```

WordPerfect will have already located and erased the first {INPUT} code. The insertion will be positioned at that location. If you had typed a message when inserting that input code in the primary file, a Merge Message dialog box containing the message will also appear at the bottom of the screen, as shown in Figure 14-3. Type in the appropriate information, (in this case, the employee's name to whom the memo is addressed), where the merge has paused.

When you are done typing the information in that first location in the document, choose <u>T</u>ools, <u>M</u>erge, <u>E</u>nd Field to continue on with the merge.

 (**ALT**) + (**ENTER**) *is the shortcut for* <u>*T*</u>*ools,* <u>*M*</u>*erge,* <u>*E*</u>*nd Field.*

Now, the insertion point jumps to the next {INPUT} code in the text, erases the code, and pauses for you to type the personalized information appropriate for this new location. When you are done typing, again press (**ALT**) + (**ENTER**); the insertion point jumps to the next {INPUT} code. Continue

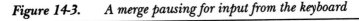

Figure 14-3. *A merge pausing for input from the keyboard*

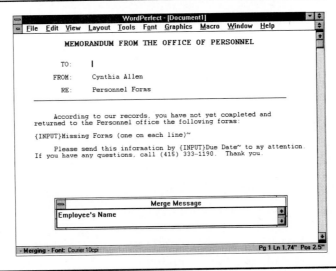

until you fill in the last blank holding an {INPUT} code. Then, press (ALT) + (ENTER) once more to end the merge process.

After the merge, you are ready to print out the document, save it, edit it, or perform any combination of these actions. You can then close the file and, on a blank document workspace, start the merge process over again to create another personalized memorandum.

If you wish, you can be reminded of how to continue when a merge is paused for input. Include this reminder as part of each input code's message. For instance, when creating the primary file shown in Figure 14-2, rather than insert the first input code to read "{INPUT}Employee's Name~", insert a longer message so that the code reads "{INPUT}Type Employee's Name; Press (ALT) + (ENTER) to continue~". Here's what will appear during the merge when WordPerfect pauses:

This is especially useful when you are designing a fill-in-the-blanks form or memorandum that will be completed by someone who is not familiar with the Merge feature.

Merges Using a File

A primary file can be merged not only by inputting with the keyboard, but also from a different source. In a merge, the information that personalizes the final document can come from another file, which is called the *secondary file*.

Merging with a file is convenient when you compile information in a list—such as names and addresses, or products and product descriptions—and want to create a document for each name or product in the list. For instance, suppose you wish to send a bimonthly letter to each person on the R&R Wine Association's wine-tasting committee.

Because you will be sending periodic mailings, your secondary file, or the one holding the information to be inserted into the primary file, will consist of names and addresses. The secondary file becomes a database—a collection of information separated into records. Each record in a database is like a card in a card file, containing the information for one person.

It is usual to create the secondary file first, so that you know what information is available to be input into a document. Then, you create the primary file containing the text of the document and merge codes. When you initiate the merge, the primary and secondary files are combined. The result of this merge is the final ouput—a letter personalized for each record in the secondary file. A visual example of what a merge with a file accomplishes is shown in Figure 14-4.

Creating a Secondary File

Figure 14-5 shows the proper format for a secondary file. This is not standard text but rather a strict format for the information that personalizes each record. Remember that a secondary file's information is organized into records (a record is one whole set of related information, such as one

Figure 14-4. *The results of merging a primary and secondary file*

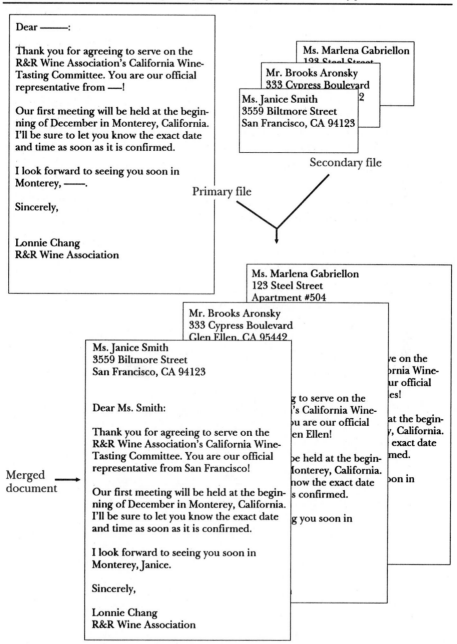

committee member's name and address). The end of a record is denoted with an {END RECORD} merge code and is followed by a hard page break. (As noted in Chapter 7, a hard page break appears in the document workspace as a double line and in the reveal codes workspace as the code [HPg].)

Notice in Figure 14-5 that there are three records. Each record contains information about one particular person. If you use this secondary file in a merge, the result will be three separate letters.

Records are broken into separate units, called fields. A *field* is one piece of information in a record, such as one committee member's first name. The field may be as short as one character, or any number of lines long. Each field is separated by an {END FIELD} merge code. In Figure 14-5, there are seven fields in each record. The fields are numbered consecutively.

Begin in a new, clear document workspace. Create a secondary file by following these steps:

1. Type in the text of the first field.

2. Choose <u>T</u>ools, <u>M</u>erge, <u>E</u>nd Field. An {END FIELD} code is inserted. A hard return code is also inserted so that the insertion point is positioned on the next line.

3. Type the next field.

4. Choose <u>T</u>ools, <u>M</u>erge, <u>E</u>nd Field.

5. Repeat steps 3 and 4 until the first record is completed.

6. Choose <u>T</u>ools, <u>M</u>erge, End <u>R</u>ecord. An {END RECORD} code is inserted. A hard page code is also inserted so that the insertion point is positioned on the next page.

7. Repeat steps 1 through 6 for all the remaining records.

shortcut   (ALT) + (ENTER) *is the shortcut for* <u>T</u>ools, <u>M</u>erge, <u>E</u>nd Field. (ALT) + (SHIFT) + (ENTER) *is the shortcut for* <u>T</u>ools, <u>M</u>erge, <u>E</u>nd Record.

When you insert each {END FIELD} or {END RECORD} code, the field number where the insertion point is currently located displays on the left side of the status line at the bottom of the screen. This helps you keep track of the field number you're currently typing. You can press (CTRL) + (HOME) to move the insertion point to the top of the document and temporarily remove the

Figure 14-5. *Secondary file ready to be merged with primary file*

Ms.{END FIELD} ◄─────────── Field 1 in record 1
Janice{END FIELD}
Smith{END FIELD}
3559 Biltmore Street{END FIELD}
San Francisco{END FIELD}
CA{END FIELD}
94123{END FIELD} ◄─────────── Field 7 in record 1
{END RECORD}

Mr.{END FIELD} ◄─────────── Field 1 in record 2
Brooks{END FIELD}
Aronsky{END FIELD}
333 Cypress Boulevard{END FIELD}
Glen Ellen{END FIELD}
CA{END FIELD}
95442{END FIELD} ◄─────────── Field 7 in record 2
{END RECORD}

Ms.{END FIELD} ◄─────────── Field 1 in record 3
Marlena{END FIELD}
Gabriellon{END FIELD}
123 Steel Street
Apartment #504{END FIELD}
Los Angeles{END FIELD}
CA{END FIELD}
90068{END FIELD} ◄─────────── Field 7 in record 3
{END RECORD}

field number from the status line. When the insertion point again moves beyond one of these merge codes, the field number will appear again.

After typing all the records into a secondary file, save the information on disk with a name that reminds you that this is not a standard document, but rather a secondary file of information. One way to do this is to name a secondary file with a filename extension of "sf" or "sec" to remind you that this is a secondary file, as in *wtcomm.sf* or *wtcomm.sec* (for wine-tasting committee secondary file).

Creating a secondary file is a time-consuming process. But, once you create the secondary file, you'll never have to type those names and addresses again. You can just keep using the secondary file over and over. You can update the secondary file at any time by opening the file and adding additional records to it.

When creating a secondary file, it is critical to remember that each record *must* contain the same number of fields, and those fields *must* be listed in the same order. Notice in Figure 14-5, for example, that each record contains seven fields. In this set of records, the first field (referred to as field 1) always contains a title, such as "Mr." or "Ms.", field 2 always contains a first name, field 3 always contains a last name, field 4 always contains an address, and so on.

Even if you have no information for a field in a given record, you must still insert the code {END FIELD} to occupy a line, so that the record has the same number of fields as all the others. For instance, suppose that you didn't know Ms. Smith's first name when typing the first record in Figure 14-5. You would enter her record as

```
Ms.{END FIELD}
{END FIELD}
Smith{END FIELD}
3559 Biltmore Street{END FIELD}
San Francisco{END FIELD}
CA{END FIELD}
94123{END FIELD}
{END RECORD}
```

If you *forget* to insert an {END FIELD} to occupy the blank field 2, WordPerfect will assume that field 2 is Smith, field 3 is 3559 Biltmore, and so on, and you'd get awkward results in the final merged letter addressed to Ms. Smith. For example, instead of this,

```
Ms. Smith
3559 Biltmore Street
San Francisco, CA   94123
```

you could get the following awkward result as an address after a merge:

```
Ms. Smith 3559 Biltmore Street
San Francisco
CA, 94123
```

A field may, however, have a varying number of lines. As an example, notice in Figure 14-5 that the addresses in field 4 are each one line long for the first two records. But for the last record, field 4 contains a two-line address. This is permissible in WordPerfect; it is the {END FIELD} code, and *not any hard returns*, that defines the end of a field.

Another important consideration when creating a secondary file is how the information will be combined into your final, merged document. For instance, if a person's full name is used only in the address, it can be placed into one field in the secondary file, such as this:

```
Ms. Janice Smith{END FIELD}
```

However, suppose you wish to personalize the salutation in each letter with the person's first name, such as "Dear Janice", or by their last name, such as "Dear Ms. Smith". Give yourself greater flexibility by splitting each person's full name into three, smaller fields, as shown here:

```
Ms.{END FIELD}
Janice{END FIELD}
Smith{END FIELD}
```

Then, you can use each field separately in your merged document for both the address and the salutation. You can also create two fields, as shown here:

```
Ms. Janice Smith{END FIELD}
Janice{END FIELD}
```

Then you could use the first field above in the address, and the second field in the salutation. Both options work fine, so long as you create a primary file that corresponds to how you structured the secondary file.

Creating a Primary File

The primary file that will eventually be merged with a secondary file must contain merge codes that correspond to fields in the secondary file. The merge code you insert in the primary file is called a *field* code. The appearance of a field code is {FIELD}*n*~, where *n* represents a specific field number. An example of a primary file for a letter to be addressed to members of the wine-tasting committee and containing field codes is shown in Figure 14-6. The field numbers correspond to those in the secondary file. For example, notice the line "Dear {FIELD}1~ {FIELD3}~:" in Figure 14-6. If you refer back to Figure 14-5, you'll see that these fields correspond to a person's title and last name, and will thus result in "Dear Ms. Smith:" in the first merged letter, "Dear Mr. Aronsky:" in the second one, and so forth.

You create a primary file for a merge just as you begin any other document: simply begin typing on a new, blank screen. You can also format the primary file—changing margins, tabs, spacing, fonts, and so on—just as you would any standard document. However, keep in mind that any layout codes that you insert at the top of the document will be repeated in each letter, which can create a clutter of codes on each page of the merged result. You can avoid this problem by placing layout codes in the Document Initial Codes workspace (described in Chapter 7).

Wherever the document will be personalized, you must insert a merge code. The code you insert in this case is a *field code*, because it tells WordPerfect which field number to import into the merged document. To insert a field code, follow these steps:

1. Position the insertion point where you want to personalize the text.

2. Choose <u>T</u>ools, <u>M</u>erge, <u>F</u>ield. The Insert Merge Code dialog box appears, as shown here:

3. Type the field number that corresponds to the information you wish to insert.

4. Choose OK.

reminder $\boxed{\text{CTRL}} + \boxed{\text{F12}}$ *is the shortcut for* <u>T</u>*ools,* <u>M</u>*erge.*

You must know which field number corresponds to the information you wish to insert. One way to do this is to open the secondary file in one

Figure 14-6. *Primary file ready to be merged with secondary file*

Field codes

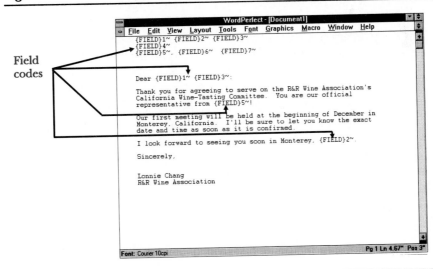

document workspace and then type the primary file in the other. Then, continually refer back to the secondary file as you type the primary file. You can also create a simple list of the fields. For example, for the secondary file displayed in Figure 14-5, you could devise the following list:

Field	Information
1	Title
2	First name
3	Last name
4	Street address
5	City
6	Two-letter state abbreviation
7	ZIP code

Place this list beside you, or in a second document workspace, so that you can refer to it as you create the primary file.

In the primary file, you can use as many {FIELD}n~ codes as you like and in any order. Notice in Figure 14-6, for example, that fields 1, 2, and 3 are each used twice. You don't even need to use all the fields contained in a secondary file. For instance, a secondary file might contain a company name in field 8 and a telephone number in field 9, but since neither of these is used in the primary file shown in Figure 14-6, the company name and telephone number codes would appear nowhere in the final merged document. They would appear in your secondary file but would be involved in a merge only when the primary file contained {FIELD}8~ or {FIELD}9~ codes.

Once you've typed a primary file, be sure to check carefully for grammatical, punctuation, and spelling errors; otherwise, every mistake you make will appear each time you use the primary file to produce a new document. Also check the location and syntax of your merge codes carefully. There must be a number and a tilde (~) following a {FIELD} code. Check also that the field numbers are correct.

After a primary file is complete, save it on disk. You will want to identify this file as a primary file containing merge codes, and not as a standard document. One good method for doing so is to choose a descriptive filename.

For instance, use the letters "pf" or "pri" in the filename extension, such as in *wtcomm1.pf* or *wtlet1.pri* (for wine-tasting committee letter 1).

Performing the Merge

Once you have stored a secondary and primary file on disk, you can initiate a merge at any time. Open a new, blank document workspace and then follow these steps:

1. Choose <u>T</u>ools, <u>M</u>erge, <u>M</u>erge to display the Merge dialog box.

2. In the <u>P</u>rimary File text box, type the name of the primary file. If you can't remember the name, click the file button just to the right of the text box so that you can browse through your list of files and select the primary file that you want.

3. In the <u>S</u>econdary File text box, type the name of the secondary file. If you can't remember the name, click the file button just to the right of the text box and browse through your file to find the secondary file you want.

4. Choose OK.

The merge happens on the screen while you wait. (To stop the merge from completing, you can press the (ESC) key.) WordPerfect automatically inserts a hard page code after it merges the primary file with each record. Thus, if you are merging a one-page primary file with ten records, Word-Perfect will assemble a document containing ten pages of text—each a separate letter.

When the merge is complete, the insertion point is located at the bottom of the document, displaying the letter for the last record in the secondary file. If you move up to the top of the document, you will see the letter for the first record. Continue to press (ALT) + (PGDN) or use the scroll bar to view the separate pages.

Now the merged document is ready for use. You can edit any of the letters and then either print them out or store them on disk. However, it is usually unnecessary to store the letters since you can easily produce an identical copy of the same letters at any time, simply by merging the primary and secondary files again. By printing out the merged document and not saving it, you reserve disk space for files that you cannot reproduce so easily.

Creating a Primary File for Mass Mailing Envelopes and Labels

Once you've used the Merge feature to create hundreds of personalized letters and have printed those letters, you can easily produce mailing labels or envelopes so that you can send out those letters. You do this by performing another merge.

You already have stored on disk a secondary file that contains names and addresses. What you must do now is create a new primary file, either for envelopes or labels, and then perform another merge. The primary file will contain layout codes and merge codes. The layout codes—such as paper size and margin changes—make sure that the merged result (such as the recipient's address) will print properly on the envelopes or labels. The merge codes—field codes—are what causes each address to be created.

Begin in a new, blank document workspace and create a primary file for envelopes or labels by following these steps:

1. Choose Layout, Document, Initial Codes. This displays the Document Initial Codes workspace, where you will insert the layout codes. By inserting the codes here, and not in the document workspace, the codes will not be repeated on every page in the merged document. (See Chapter 7 for more on the Document Initial Codes feature.)

2. Choose Layout, Page, Paper Size. The Paper Size dialog box appears for the current printer.

3. Select a paper definition for envelopes or labels from the Page Type list box.

4. Choose Select to insert the page size/type code for envelopes or labels at the top of the page and to return to the document workspace.

5. For envelopes only, change margins. For instance, when using an envelope with the return address preprinted and assuming the standard 9.5-by-4-inch size, try these margin settings: set the top at 2.5 inches; the bottom at .5 inch; the left at 4.5 inches; the right at .5 inch. (See Chapter 7 for more on margin settings for envelopes.)

6. Choose <u>C</u>lose to close the Document Initial Codes workspace.

═note═ If you haven't yet created a paper definition for envelopes or labels, refer to Chapter 7 for the procedure before proceeding with the steps just provided. You need to tell WordPerfect the proper paper size, paper type, and printing instructions for the envelopes or labels before you can actually print them on your printer.

Next, you are ready to insert the field codes for the envelopes or labels, using the <u>T</u>ools, <u>M</u>erge, <u>F</u>ield command as described previously. The field codes must be in correct order for the addresses to print properly. For instance, a primary file for envelopes or labels corresponding to the fields in the secondary file shown in Figure 14-5 will contain codes in the following format:

```
{FIELD}1~ {FIELD}2~ {FIELD}3~
{FIELD}4~
{FIELD}5~, {FIELD}6~ {FIELD}7~
```

For envelopes with preprinted return addresses and for labels, the only information visible in the primary file will be these field codes.

For envelopes without preprinted return addresses, you will want to include the return address at position .5" approximately and then the field codes farther down in the primary file and to the right—at position 4.5" approximately. Here's an example of how such a primary file will appear:

```
R&R Wine Association
3345 Whitmore Drive, #505
San Francisco, CA    94123



                        {FIELD}1~ {FIELD}2~ {FIELD}3~
                        {FIELD}4~
                        {FIELD}5~, {FIELD}6~ {FIELD}7~
```

Once the primary file for envelopes or labels is complete, save it using a name that reminds you that it is a primary file for envelopes, such as *env.pri*, or a primary file for labels, such as *labels.pri.*

Now, you are ready to merge this primary file with a secondary file whenever you need to produce envelopes or labels. After the merge (the procedure was previously described), you'll get results like the document shown in Figure 14-7. This is the merge result for printing on envelopes with preprinted return addresses. A page break is inserted between each address because, as you'll remember, WordPerfect inserts a hard page code after it merges the primary file with each record in the secondary file. Each page on screen represents a separate envelope or label at the printer. You are then ready to print the envelopes or labels.

Enhancing the Merge Process

You've thus far worked with four different merge codes. You learned about placing {INPUT}˜ codes in a primary file to merge with the keyboard.

Figure 14-7.   *Merged document ready to be printed onto envelopes*

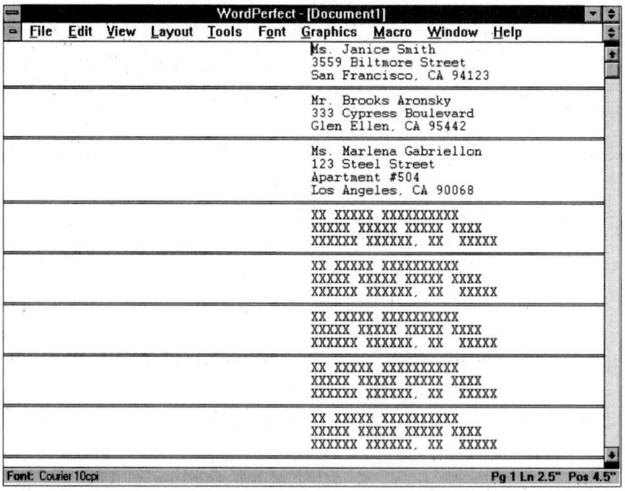

You learned about placing {FIELD}n~ codes in a primary file to merge with a file. And, you learned about placing {END FIELD} and {END RECORD} codes in a secondary file.

WordPerfect allows you some added flexibility in the merge process. You can combine {INPUT}~ and {FIELD}n~ codes in the same primary file. This lets you perform a merge with both the keyboard and a file. For instance, you can merge a primary and secondary file, but also have WordPerfect pause in the middle of every letter so that you can type in a few extra words from the keyboard. Figure 14-8 illustrates an example of a primary file combining input codes, field codes, and several other merge codes as well.

WordPerfect offers additional merge codes for even more flexibility. Merge codes are part of WordPerfect's sophisticated programming language. Many of the merge codes are quite complicated and used only by people with programming experience. But several of these additional merge codes are easy to use when you want to refine the merge process for specific needs. The most useful and most frequently used merge codes, or combination of merge codes, are described in the following sections. All are inserted into a primary or secondary file just as you'd insert the {INPUT}~ or {FIELD}n~ codes—that

Figure 14-8. *Primary file containing a variety of merge codes to enhance the merge process*

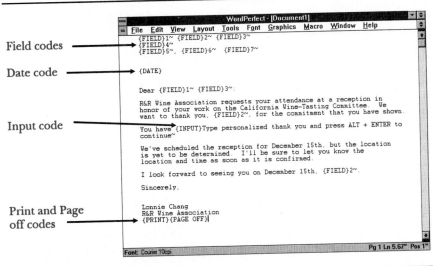

is, by positioning the insertion point, and choosing Tools, Merge. Then, you would choose a code from the menu that appears. If the code is not listed, choose Merge Codes from the menu to display a dialog box of additional merge codes that you can choose from.

{DATE}

WordPerfect inserts the current date into the merged document at the location of the {DATE} code (providing that your computer's clock has been set with the correct date). For example, in the primary file shown in Figure 14-8, a {DATE} code is inserted two lines above the salutation. After the merge, the current date would appear in each letter.

{PAGE OFF}

The {PAGE OFF} code suppresses the hard page code after each record is merged with the primary file. This is useful for creating a list from records in a secondary merge file. For instance, suppose you wish to create a document that lists the names of all the members of the wine-tasting committee at R&R Wine Association. You could create a primary file containing nothing except the following codes:

```
{FIELD}1~ {FIELD}2~ {FIELD}3~
{PAGE OFF}
```

The result after merging with the secondary file containing wine-tasting committee members would begin as follows:

```
Ms. Janice Smith
Mr. Brooks Aronsky
Ms. Marlena Gabriellon
```

{PRINT}{PAGE OFF}

You can merge directly to the printer, rather than into the document workspace, using the {PRINT}{PAGE OFF} code. Suppose your secondary file contained 500 records; if you were to merge into the document workspace, you'd have to wait for the merge on screen, and then you'd still have to print the 500-page document. Instead, print each letter as soon as it is merged.

To merge to the printer, insert the {PRINT}{PAGE OFF} combination at the bottom of the primary file, as shown in Figure 14-8. Before you merge, turn on your printer. When the merge begins, the {PRINT} command will cause a document to print that combines the primary file with the first record. The {PAGE OFF} command will suppress the hard page code so that you won't then print a blank page. Then, the merge will continue for the next record. No merged document is created on screen.

{NEXT RECORD}

Move to the next record in a secondary file with the {NEXT RECORD} code. You can insert this code during a merge. For instance, suppose you created a primary file containing an {INPUT}~ code as well as {FIELD}n~ codes, meaning that the merge will pull from both keyboard input and a file. During the merge, when WordPerfect pauses at the {INPUT}~ code, choose Tools, Merge, Next Record. The merge continues using the next record.

{IF NOT BLANK}n~ and {END IF}

You may allow for missing information using {IF NOT BLANK}n~ and {END IF}. For instance, suppose that you add an eighth field to the secondary file in Figure 14-5. Field 8 contains a person's company name. In some cases, you know the person's company name; in other cases, you don't. You'll get blank lines in addresses where field 8 is blank if you include the following in your primary file:

```
{FIELD}1~ {FIELD}2~ {FIELD}3~
{FIELD}8~
{FIELD}4~
{FIELD}5~, {FIELD}6~ {FIELD}7~
```

However, you typically don't want blank lines in a document. If you use the {IF NOT BLANK}n~ merge code, you can avoid a blank line in an address when field 8 is blank. WordPerfect checks the status of the field; if the field contains information, WordPerfect proceeds; otherwise, it skips to whatever follows the {END IF} code. To avoid blank lines, you would place codes in the primary file as shown here:

```
{FIELD}1~ {FIELD}2~ {FIELD}3~
{IF NOT BLANK}8~{FIELD}8~
{END IF}{FIELD}4~
{FIELD}5~, {FIELD}6~ {FIELD}7~
```

If field 8 contains a company name (that is, if it is not blank), the company name will be printed on a separate line. If field 8 is blank, then this entire line will be skipped.

{FIELD NAMES}

Reference fields with names rather than numbers by using the {FIELD NAMES} code. The first record in the secondary file must contain the {FIELD NAMES} merge code and be followed by the names you wish to assign to each field. Each name must be followed by a tilde (˜). Then, the code must end with an extra tilde and with the {END RECORD} merge code. Here's an example of how the first record would appear (when divided into separate lines) for the secondary file shown in Figure 14-5:

```
{FIELD NAMES}
Title~
First~
Last~
Street~
City~
State~
Zip~~
{END RECORD}
```

After using this code, you can create a primary file in which the field codes reference personalized information by field *names* rather than field *numbers*. For instance, you can include field codes such as {FIELD}Title˜ and {FIELD}Zip˜ instead of {FIELD}1˜ and {FIELD}7˜. Make sure to spell the field names exactly the same in the primary file as found in the first record of the secondary file.

Merging with Data from Other Applications

WordPerfect allows you to merge with files from other applications. First, you can use either primary or secondary files created in an earlier version of WordPerfect. WordPerfect 5.1 for DOS files can be used directly, with no conversion necessary. WordPerfect 5.0 or 4.2 for DOS files must be converted, so that the old merge codes in those files are converted to the new format. For instance, ^F1^ will be changed to {FIELD}1˜ in the primary file, or ^R will be changed to {END FIELD} in the secondary file. Open the old file in WordPerfect for Windows and choose Tools, Merge, Convert and then choose OK. The conversion takes only moments.

In addition, you can use data from another application—such as dBASE or Paradox—as a secondary file. The data must have been saved in ASCII delimited text format. Then, WordPerfect can use this data directly, with no conversion necessary. When you choose Tools, Merge, Merge to begin the merge and the Merge dialog box is on screen, type the name of a WordPerfect primary file in the Primary File text box, and type the name of an ASCII delimited text file in the Secondary File text box. Then, turn on the ASCII Delimited Text (DOS) check box. Once you choose OK to begin the merge, another dialog box will appear where you must indicate the *delimiters,* or the characters that mark the beginning and end of fields and records in the ASCII delimited file. For instance, in the following example, the comma is used as the delimiter to end each field, and the carriage return is used to end each record:

```
Janice,Smith,3559 Biltmore St.,San Francisco,CA,94123,
Brooks,Aronsky,333 Cypress Blvd.,Glen Ellen,CA,95442,
```

To insert a tab, line field, form feed, or carriage return as a delimiter, click the arrowhead button located at the right of each text box and choose from the pop-up menu that displays. Once you've indicated the delimiters, choose OK to begin the merge.

Sorting

WordPerfect offers some of the same capabilities as a traditional database manager. You can rearrange text in a specific order, either alphabetically or numerically—this is referred to as a *sort*. You can also isolate information that meets certain conditions, such as those names in a list that begin with the letter "P" or those lines that contain the name "San Francisco"—this is referred to as a *select*. You can even sort and select at the same time; for instance, you could select the names of people who live in San Francisco and sort those names alphabetically.

You can sort or select a document that is formatted into lines or paragraphs, merge records (in a secondary file), or the rows in a table (created when using the Tables feature, as described in Chapter 11). The following four types of documents are specifically defined for a sort:

- *Lines*   Each line that ends with a hard or soft return is considered to be a record. Within records, text typed at the left margin is in field 1. Text aligned on the next tab stop is in field 2. Text aligned on the next tab stop is in field 3, and so on. For instance, Figure 14-9 shows a document that is formatted into lines and could be sorted. Field 1 contains last names, field 2 contains first names, and field 3 contains cities.

- *Paragraphs*   Each paragraph that ends with at least two hard returns is considered to be a record. The paragraph can consist of multiple lines. A paragraph aligned at the left margin is in field 1. If it is aligned on the next tab stop, it is in field 2. Figure 14-10 shows an example of a part of a glossary which could be sorted by paragraphs.

Figure 14-9.   *Lines to be sorted*

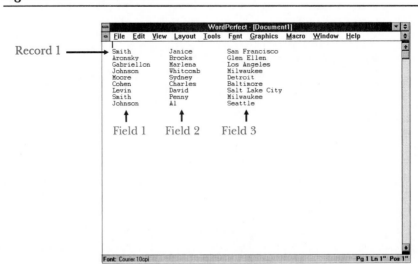

Figure 14-10. ***Paragraphs to be sorted***

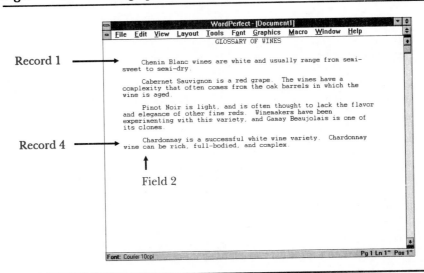

- *Merge Records* Each section in a secondary file that ends with an {END RECORD} code is a record. Within records, each item that ends with an {END FIELD} code is a field. A field can be comprised of multiple lines. An example of a secondary merge file that can be sorted is shown in Figure 14-5.

- *Table Rows* Each row in a table is a record. Within records, each cell is comparable to a field. A cell can be comprised of multiple lines. It is best to sort a table where the cells are arranged consistently, such as where there are the same number of cells in each row, as in the following example:

Smith	Janice	San Francisco	6/15/90
Aronksy	Brooks	Glen Ellen	7/18/92
Gabriellon	Marlena	Los Angeles	1/4/85

Record 1 → (first row)
Record 3 → (third row)

Cell (Field) 1   Cell (Field) 4

caution *Always save a copy of a document before attempting to sort it. You cannot undo a sort.*

Sorting with the Defaults

The default setting is to sort a list (lines) alphabetically in ascending order (A to Z) based on the text in field 1. For example, the list in Figure 14-9 would be sorted as follows:

Aronsky	Brooks	Glen Ellen
Cohen	Charles	Baltimore
Gabriellon	Marlena	Los Angeles
Johnson	Al	Seattle
Johnson	Whitcomb	Milwaukee
Levin	David	Salt Lake City
Moore	Sydney	Detroit
Smith	Janice	San Francisco
Smith	Penny	Milwaukee

Follow these steps to perform such a sort:

1. Display on screen the document containing the list to be sorted. If you want to sort only a portion of the document, select the text to be sorted.

2. Choose Tools, Sort. A Sort dialog box appears, as shown in Figure 14-11.

3. Choose OK.

shortcut (CTRL) + (SHIFT) + (F12) *is the shortcut for Tools, Sort.*

Changing the Sort

What if you wish to sort a list by the third column rather than the first column? Or in descending order (Z to A)? Or what if the document you wish to sort is organized not in lines but in paragraphs, or as a secondary merge

Figure 14-11. *Sort dialog box*

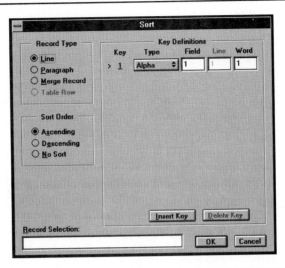

file, or as a table? Suppose you wish to select or extract only certain records from the document? If so, you must change the defaults in the Sort dialog box *before* choosing OK to begin the sort. The items in the Sort dialog box are described in the following sections:

Record Type

Specify the type of sort you desire from the Record Type group box. You can select a Line, Paragraph, or Merge Record sort. The Table Row sort is dimmed to gray, meaning that it cannot be selected, unless you position the insertion point *inside* a table and then choose Tools, Sort. When the Sort dialog box displays, the Table Row item is automatically selected.

Sort Order

Determine how the text will be rearranged by selecting from the Sort Order group box. You can choose Ascending order, which means A to Z for letters or smallest to largest for numbers. Choose Descending order, which means Z to A for letters or largest to smallest for numbers. Or choose the No Sort option to perform a record selection without rearranging the order of your records.

Key Definitions

Specify what word you wish to sort on using the options in the Key Definitions group box shown in Figure 14-11. A *key* is the specific item that you wish to sort on. For instance, the default for lines is to sort on the first word in field 1. The first word in field 1 is therefore automatically defined as a key. You can instead specify that the lines sort based on the first word in field 3. Or, you can specify that secondary merge files be sorted by ZIP codes (useful for bulk mailing discounts at the post office).

When sorting lines, you must define three aspects of a sort key:

- Whether it is *alphanumeric* (such as a last name or a ZIP code that is sorted character by character, as in 1, 19, 156, 2, 50) or *numeric* (such as a dollar amount, to be sorted in its entirety according to its value, as in 1, 2, 19, 50, 156).
- Which field the sort key is in.
- Which word is the sort key.

Paragraphs, merge records, and table rows can have multiple lines, so that you must define four aspects of the sort key:

- Whether it is alphanumeric or numeric.
- Which line the sort key is in.
- Which field the sort key is in (called a "cell" in tables).
- Which word is the sort key.

As an example, suppose that you wish to sort lines by city, which is field 3 in Figure 14-9. You would define key 1, which is the primary item you wish to sort, as follows:

Key	Type	Field	Word
1	Alpha	3	1

You can sort on more than one key. You can define a maximum of nine keys. To display another key that you wish to define, select the <u>I</u>nsert Key command button. (To erase the last key listed, select the Delete Key command button.) You can, for example, define two keys in a sort—key 1 could be last name and key 2 could be city. That way, if two people had the same last name, WordPerfect would perform a second-level sort for those two records by the city. The keys would be defined as follows:

Key	Type	Field	Word
1	Alpha	1	1

Key	Type	Field	Word
2	Alpha	3	1

14

Record Selection

Select records based on the statement you type into the Record Selection text box. For instance, you could select only those people in a list who resided in San Francisco. Or you could select only those records in a secondary merge file with a ZIP code of 94123. When you performed the sort, those records that met the statement's condition would remain on screen; the other records would disappear.

You specify a selection in relation to one or more keys that you previously defined in the Key Definitions group box. Type a selection statement where you reference the key(s) into the Record Selection text box. This statement is the criteria you wish to use to evaluate each record to determine if it will be a selected record. There are eight symbols you can use in the selection statements; they are shown in Table 14-1.

For instance, suppose you wish to select line items from the document in Figure 14-9, and you have already defined key 1 to be the last name and key 2 to be the city for the lines (records) in that document. To select only those lines in which the last name is Johnson, type this selection statement:

```
key1=Johnson
```

Instead, if you wish to select only those lines in which the city is Milwaukee, type this selection statement:

```
key2=Milwaukee
```

Table 14-1.   *Symbols Used in a Selection Statement*

Symbol	Meaning
=	Equal to
<>	Not equal to
>	Greater than
>=	Greater than or equal to
<	Less than
<=	Less than or equal to
+	OR (connects two key conditions together so that either condition can be true for a record to be selected)
*	AND (connects two key conditions together so that both must be true for a record to be selected)

As another example, suppose you wish to select those lines in which the city is Milwaukee and the last name is Johnson. Then, type this selection statement:

```
key1=Johnson * key2=Milwaukee
```

≡*caution*≡ *Make sure not to insert a space between "key" and the key number when inputting the selection statement. For instance, type* **key2** *and not* **key 2** *in the statement.*

You can also use "keyg" in a selection statement as a global key to represent any word on any line in any field in each record. For instance, to select records that contain the word "Brooks" anywhere in the record, type this selection statement:

```
keyg=Brooks
```

This is a shortcut, allowing you to skip the step of defining a key before it is used in a selection statement.

Quick Reference

- To merge with the keyboard, such as for completing a fill-in-the-blanks form, create a primary file containing the "form" and containing input codes that pause during the merge. Choose Tools, Merge, Input to insert each input code.

- To merge with a file, such as for a mass mailing, create a secondary file containing the database of names and addresses organized into fields and records. Press (ALT) + (ENTER) after typing the contents of each field, and (ALT) + (SHIFT) + (ENTER) after typing the contents of each record. Then, create a primary file containing the text of the document that stays the same and containing field codes that will import information from the secondary file during the merge. Chose Tools, Merge, Field to insert each field code.

- To initiate a merge, choose Tools, Merge, Merge. Indicate the name of a primary file, and, if merging with a file, also indicate the name of the secondary file. Then choose OK.

- To sort a document, choose Tools, Sort. You must specify whether you wish to sort a document formatted into lines or paragraphs, a secondary merge file containing records, or the rows in a table. Also specify the sort order, and specify a selection statement if you wish to select records during the sort.

14

15

Using Macros, Styles, and Long Document Features

Whenever you find yourself performing a task over and over again, you can use a macro or a style as a shortcut; you can turn an effort that would typically take many keystrokes or mouse movements into a task done with just a few. Macros and styles can increase your productivity.

Macros and styles are created and executed in completely different ways. In this chapter, you'll learn first how to work with macros. Next, you'll work with the Styles feature. You'll also learn about styles libraries, which are collections of styles stored in one place for easy access.

This chapter also describes special features for working with a lengthy document—whether a report, a thesis, or a book. You'll use WordPerfect to insert and update cross-references; generate tables of contents, lists, indexes, and tables of authorities automatically; and create a master document to manage all the text in a lengthy project.

Creating a Macro

A macro is comparable to the speed-dialing feature on a telephone. With speed dialing, the telephone stores a telephone number so that you simply press the pound sign (#) and one number instead of a seven- or ten-digit telephone number. Pressing # and 1 is much easier than dialing 415-555-1234.

Similarly, a *macro* is a group of keystrokes and/or commands that are bundled together and recorded for you. You execute a macro with just one simple action. You will want to create macros to help with repetitive tasks—sequences of keystrokes that you press often—just as you reserve speed dialing for telephone numbers you call often.

Preparing to Record a Macro

You must first select a task that would be a good candidate for a macro. Which task do you perform over and over again? Here are just a few suggestions for macros:

- Information that you type frequently is often easily made into a macro. For instance, you can create a macro that types your name, your company's name, your address, the closing of a letter, or the heading for a memorandum.

- If you spell-check every new document, you can create a macro that chooses Tools, Speller and then initiates a spell-check.

- If you work with the ruler and a button bar when formatting your text, you can create one macro that shows the ruler and button bar, and another macro that hides them. You can also create a macro that switches between two different button bars that you use frequently.

- If you work with several different directories when opening files, create a macro that chooses File, Open and displays the files for a specific directory.

- If you use the same footnote in different documents, you can create a macro that chooses Layout, Footnote, Create and then types the footnote text for you.

- If you change the layout (perhaps line spacing, margins, and tabs) on the Document Initial Codes workspace every time you write a certain kind of report, create a macro that chooses Layout, Document, Initial Codes and then makes the layout changes for you.

- If you typically print three copies of the memorandum that you write, create a macro that chooses File, Print, changes the number of copies in the Print dialog box to 3, initiates the printing, and then returns the number of copies to 1.

- If you forget to capitalize the first letter in names, titles, or headings, create a macro that uses the Select feature to highlight the letter to the right of the insertion point, chooses Edit, Convert Case, Uppercase to switch it to uppercase, turns off the Select feature, and moves the insertion point to the beginning of the next word. You can then use this macro for as many words in a row as necessary.

- If you tend to create misspellings because you transpose letters, such as "teh" when you meant to type "the", create a macro that fixes the typo by deleting the character to the left of the insertion point, moving the insertion point once to the left, and undeleting the character.

Once you decide what a macro should do for you, prepare to create the macro by first rehearsing—performing the steps without actually creating the macro. This lets you be sure about which steps you want to include before recording them.

Recording the Macro

After you know which steps will compose the macro, you must perform them again—this time to create the macro. WordPerfect will record the tasks as you perform them. Follow these steps:

1. Choose Macro, Record. The Record Macro dialog box appears.

2. In the Filename text box, type a name for the macro. You can type one to eight characters, including the letters "a" through "z" (upper- or lowercase makes no difference) and numbers 0 through 9. For

15

instance, type **rr** or **print3** or **spellall**. Once the macro is stored on disk, WordPerfect will automatically add the extension *.wcm* (which stands for WordPerfect Corporation macro) to the name, as in *rr.wcm*.

You can also press (CTRL) + a letter or number in the Filename text box. For instance, press (CTRL) + (1). WordPerfect will insert the name *ctrl1.wcm*.

Or, in the Filename text box, press (CTRL) + (SHIFT) + a letter or number. For instance, press (CTRL) + (SHIFT) + (P). WordPerfect will insert the name *ctrlsftp.wcm*.

3. If you want, type a description of the macro up to 68 characters in length, in the Descriptive Name text box. This descriptive name is used if you later assign the macro to the Macro menu, a procedure described soon.

4. If you want, type a longer description in the Abstract text box. This longer description can summarize the macro's contents, and is displayed when you are editing a macro and display its Document Summary.

5. Choose Record.

If a macro with the filename you specify already exists, Word-Perfect displays a dialog box where you can select Yes to replace the existing file with the new macro or No if you wish to return to the Record Macro dialog box and indicate a different filename.

Once you indicate a unique filename, the message "Recording Macro" displays at the left side on the status line. This message serves as a reminder that every task you perform from now on will be recorded—just as if you had turned on a tape recorder that records everything you say—until you stop the recording.

6. Perform the tasks to be accomplished just as you normally would. For example, type **R&R Wine Association** to create a macro that types the company name. To create a macro that spell-checks a document, choose Tools, Speller and press (ENTER) to initiate the spell-check.

Be aware that when recording a macro, your use of the mouse is somewhat limited, (this will be described shortly).

7. Choose <u>M</u>acro, <u>S</u>top to stop the recording once the complete macro has been recorded.

shortcut (CTRL) + (F10) *is the shortcut for* <u>M</u>acro, <u>R</u>ecord.
(CTRL) + (SHIFT) + (F10) *is the shortcut for* <u>M</u>acro, <u>S</u>top.

Naming the Macro Before Recording

When you name the macro just before the recording begins, keep in mind that using (CTRL) + a character or (CTRL) + (SHIFT) + a character creates a shortcut key for executing a macro. You simply press (CTRL) + the character or (CTRL) + (SHIFT) + the character (more on this shortly). Therefore, you may wish to reserve (CTRL) and (CTRL) + (SHIFT) for those macros that you use most often. However, don't name a macro with (CTRL) or (CTRL) + (SHIFT) if:

- *The macro could be destructive if executed accidentally.* For instance, if you create a macro that chooses <u>F</u>ile, <u>C</u>lose, <u>N</u>o—which closes the document on screen and clears it without saving changes to it—don't name it (CTRL) + a character or you're liable to lose an important document by accidentally executing the macro.

- *The key combination is already assigned to another task* (unless you want to change the assignment with the Keyboard Layout feature discussed in Chapter 17). For instance, don't name a macro (CTRL) + (P) because that key combination is already used as a shortcut for printing the full document (as you learned in Chapter 4). Key combinations that are predefined in WordPerfect for Windows, and that you won't want to use, include (CTRL) + the following letters: B, C, D, F, G, I, J, L, N, P, R, S, U, V, X, Z.

note *Those of you who are switching from WordPerfect for DOS are accustomed to naming macros with* (ALT) + *a character, so that you can then execute a macro, for example, by pressing* (ALT) + (A) *or* (ALT) + (X). *In WordPerfect for Windows, you must use* (CTRL) + *a character instead. The* (ALT) *key is reserved for selecting items from menus.*

15

Limited Use of the Mouse While Recording

When a macro is recording, the mouse pointer in the document work-space changes to a prevent symbol (a circle with a line through it) in the document workspace. This symbol serves to remind you that there are only certain tasks you can perform with your mouse. You can use your mouse to choose menu items, choose different document windows, and close documents. However, WordPerfect does not record the use of your mouse when you move the insertion point, scroll through the document or a list box, or select text. You must instead rely on the keyboard for performing these tasks. For instance, if you wish to move to the top of the document while recording a macro, press (CTRL) + (HOME) rather than using your mouse. If you wish to select several characters while recording a macro, press (SHIFT) + the arrow keys rather than clicking and dragging with the mouse. (Refer to Chapter 3 if you need to review the procedures for moving the insertion point and selecting text with the keyboard.)

Pausing or Stopping a Macro While Recording

What if you're not sure what key to press next while recording a macro? Choose Macro, Pause to temporarily stop recording the macro. Now, you can use WordPerfect to locate and experiment with a feature. When you are ready to continue recording the macro, choose Macro, Pause again—it's a toggle feature. (Note that the Pause feature interrupts the recording of a macro, but not the execution of a macro.)

What if you make a typing mistake while recording a macro? Choose Macro, Stop to stop recording the macro immediately. Then, begin the procedure all over again; that is, choose Macro, Record and indicate the same filename. A dialog box will display informing you that a macro by that name has already been created. Choose Yes to replace the existing macro with the one you are about to create. Now, record the macro correctly. (You can edit an existing macro by opening the file containing the macro on screen, making changes, and then saving and closing the document. However, you need to know something about the macro commands, which number over 600, to be able to edit a macro. A WordPerfect macros manual that lists all the commands can be purchased by calling WordPerfect Corporation. This manual is also valuable if you are interested in creating or editing sophisticated macros.)

Executing a Macro

When you execute a macro, you *play* the bundle of tasks that you previously recorded. There are many methods for playing a macro: you can use the Play Macro dialog box, use a key combination, assign a macro to the Macro menu, or assign it to a button bar. Each method is explained in the following sections.

Executing from the Play Macro Dialog Box

Any macro that you create can be played using the Play Macro dialog box by following these steps:

1. Choose Macro, Play. The Play Macro dialog box displays for the directory where macros are stored, as shown in Figure 15-1. (This directory is typically *c:\wpwin\macros*.) Only the macro files are shown in the Files list box, which are files with a *.wcm* extension.

15

Figure 15-1. *Play Macro dialog box*

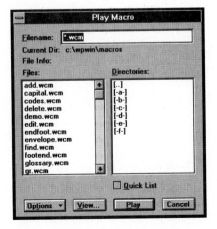

2. Type the filename of the macro you wish to play. (You can type the filename with or without the *.wcm* extension. For instance, you can type **rr.wcm** or you can type **rr** as a shortcut.) Or, select a macro file from the F_ile_s list box.

3. Choose P_la_y.

4. If the macro is found, it is executed. If the macro is not found, a dialog box appears, as shown here:

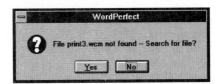

Choose Y_e_s to return to the Play Macro dialog box, so that you can search through the D_ir_ectories list box for the location of the macro you wish to execute. Choose N_o to cancel the macro execution.

shortcut (ALT) + (F10) *is the shortcut for* M_a_cro, P_la_y. *Also, double-clicking a filename in the Play Macro dialog box is the shortcut for selecting a filename and choosing* P_la_y.

The first time you play a macro after recording or editing it, WordPerfect pauses just before playing the macro. This gives WordPerfect an opportunity to compile the macro. Once compiled, WordPerfect does not need to recompile that macro again (unless you edit it). So, the next time you execute the macro, it will play immediately.

Sometimes a macro may not work properly when you first play it. Several things can go wrong. The task it is assigned to accomplish may be impossible to perform; for instance, the macro may be designed to open a document that doesn't exist. In that case, a dialog box indicates that there is an error. Choose OK to close the dialog box and stop the macro.

If the macro does not work properly because of a syntax error, a dialog box indicates the location of the syntax error. Choose C_a_ncel Compilation to close the dialog box and stop the macro. You can also choose C_o_ntinue Compilation to check for other errors that may be in the macro. The errors must be corrected before the macro can play. Trial and error is often a necessary part of getting a macro to work properly.

Executing with a Key Combination

If you named a macro with (CTRL) + a character or with (CTRL) + (SHIFT) + a character, then you assigned the macro to that key combination. You can therefore play that macro simply by pressing the appropriate key combination. For instance, suppose you created a macro that will print three copies of a document, and you named the macro just before recording it by pressing (CTRL) + (3). In that case, pressing (CTRL) + (3) executes the macro.

You can also play a macro after assigning it to a key combination that is not limited to (CTRL) + a character or to (CTRL) + (SHIFT) + a character, using the Keyboard Layout feature. (In fact, WordPerfect is packaged with a keyboard layout that contains over a dozen macros that are ready for use. You may find that some of the packaged macros fit your needs.) See Chapter 17 for more on the Keyboard Layout feature.

15

Executing from the Macro Menu

Once you assign a macro to the Macro menu, you can play the macro by selecting it just as you would select any other menu item. The macro will be listed at the bottom of the Macro menu. For instance, three macros have been assigned to the Macro menu in this example:

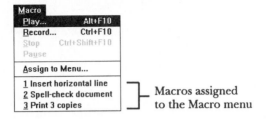

Macros assigned to the Macro menu

To play one of these three macros, you would simply choose its name (or corresponding number) from the Macro menu.

You can assign up to nine of the macros that you use most to the Macro menu. To assign a macro that you created earlier to the menu, follow these steps:

1. Choose Macro, Assign to Menu. The Assign Macro to Menu dialog box appears. Any macros that have already been added to the menu are listed. An example of this dialog box with three macros already added is shown in Figure 15-2.

2. Choose Insert. The Insert Macro Menu Item dialog box displays, as shown here:

3. Type the name of the macro in the Macro Name text box. Or, use the file button, located at the end of the Macro Name text box, to select a file. (If you gave the macro a descriptive name when you

Figure 15-2.   *Assign Macro to Menu dialog box*

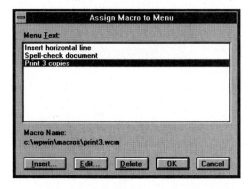

recorded it, the descriptive name displays automatically in the Menu Text text box.)

4. Type or edit the descriptive name in the Menu Text text box. Whatever is in the Menu Text box (up to 29 characters) is what will appear in the Macro menu to represent the macro. If the Menu Text box is blank, whatever is in the Macro Name text box is what will appear.

5. Choose OK to return to the Assign Macro to Menu dialog box.

6. Choose OK to return to the document workspace.

You can also edit or delete an item from the Macro menu. Choose Macro, Assign to Menu. The Assign Macro to Menu dialog box reappears. Be sure to select (highlight) the item in the Menu Text list box that you wish to edit or delete. Then, choose Edit to change the entry in the Macro Name or Menu Text boxes or choose Delete to erase the macro from the menu. (Note that the macro itself is not deleted—it is simply no longer listed in the Macro menu.)

Executing from the Button Bar

If you assign a macro to a button on a button bar, you can play the macro by selecting it like you select any other button on the button bar. To assign a macro on the button bar, follow these steps:

1. Display the button bar to which the macro will be assigned.

2. Choose View, Button Bar Setup, Edit. The Edit Button Bar dialog box displays.

3. Choose Assign Macro to Button. An Assign Macro to Button dialog box displays, listing the macros in *c:\wpwin\macros* (or another directory).

4. Select (highlight) a macro and choose Assign. A button appears on the button bar, displaying the name of the macro as well as a picture of an audio cassette, which is the picture used to represent a macro on all button bars.

5. Choose OK to close the Edit Button Bar dialog box.

When you assign a macro to a button bar, the Assign Macro to Button Bar dialog box includes a M̲acro on Disk check box. If you want the button to always use the current copy of the macro file on disk, make sure that this check box is on (which is the default setting). If the check box is turned off, a copy of the macro will be saved along with the button bar, and any changes you later make to the original macro file will not affect the button. In that case, you may wish to add a new button for the edited macro. (Refer to Chapter 10 for more details on the Button Bar feature.)

Creating a Style

While a macro is a time-saver for performing a series of commands, a style is a time-saver for formatting your text. A *style* is a combination of layout codes, and can also include text and graphic images. For instance, suppose that you produce newsletters once a month where you change top/bottom margins, type the newsletter's banner, and format the document into newspaper columns. You can create a style that groups all these formatting codes together. Or, suppose you apply Italic and Very Large size to all your headings. You can create a style that applies both font attributes at once. By using a style, you ensure consistency because you use the same style each time you do the newsletter or type a heading.

In one respect, styles are more limiting than macros. A style can be used only for formatting, while a macro can format a document and/or perform a variety of other tasks as well, such as printing a document, closing a document, or even executing a style.

In another respect, to format sections of text the same way, using styles can be more helpful over the course of a document than using macros. If you create a style to format section headings, for example, and then decide to format the headings differently, you can simply alter the style; all the headings will be updated to the new style without your having to change each heading.

When deciding on an appropriate candidate for a style, consider a document's design elements, such as the layout for the top of the document and the layout for headings, subheadings, paragraphs, long quotes, and so on. Decide which elements appear frequently, either in the same document or across different documents. You may want to create a style for only one particular element. Or you may decide to create many styles for all the different elements in a document.

There are two separate phases in creating a style for a document. First, you decide on the properties, or characteristics, best suited for the style. Then, you indicate the codes and text that will comprise the style.

Defining the Style Properties

When you define the properties of a style, you must define a style type. There are two types of styles:

- A *paired* type is comparable to a set of paired codes, (such as underline or bold codes). It is used for styles that have a beginning (on) and an end (off), affecting only a section of text. For example, use a paired type to format chapter headings or to format long quotes. Paired is the default setting.

- An *open* type is comparable to a single code, (such as a margin or justification code). It has only a beginning, and affects text from where the style is turned on to the end of the document. For example, use an open type to set the general format for a newsletter starting at the top of the document.

If you choose a paired type, you must also determine what the (ENTER) key will do after the style is created and once you turn on the paired style. You have three options for how you would like the (ENTER) key to function within paired styles: Hard Return, Style Off, and Style Off/On.

Hard Return causes no change in how the (ENTER) key normally functions. It inserts a hard return. The style remains on. Hard Return is the default setting.

Style Off causes the (ENTER) key to turn off the style. For example, use this option when creating a style for a heading or subheading.

Style Off/On causes the (ENTER) key to turn off the style and then turn it on again right away, to begin formatting a new section of text. For example, use this option when creating a style for a series of paragraphs, such as a series

15

of bulleted paragraphs. You could then press (ENTER) after typing each paragraph, which would turn the style off, and then immediately turn it on again for the next paragraph in the series.

Choose which attributes you'd like in a specific style with these steps:

1. When viewing a document in which you wish to create a certain style, choose Layout, Styles. The Styles dialog box displays. Any available styles are listed. An example of this dialog box with four styles listed is shown in Figure 15-3.

2. Choose Create. The Style Properties dialog box appears as shown here:

3. In the Name text box, type in a style name of 20 characters or less. You can include spaces in the name.

Figure 15-3.   *Styles dialog box*

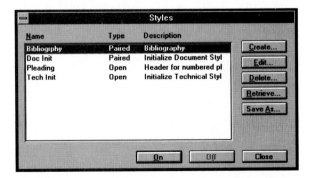

4. In the <u>D</u>escription text box, type in a description of what the style will accomplish. It will be displayed in the Styles dialog box, along-side the style name. Although typing a description is optional, it is useful to remind you of how the style affects text.

5. From the <u>T</u>ype pop-up list box, choose either <u>P</u>aired or <u>O</u>pen.

6. If you will be creating a paired style, choose an option from the <u>E</u>nter Key Inserts pop-up list box.

7. Choose OK.

shortcut (ALT) + (F8) *is the shortcut for <u>L</u>ayout, <u>S</u>tyles. Also, double-clicking the Styles button on the ruler is equivalent to choosing <u>L</u>ayout, <u>S</u>tyles.*

Immediately a Style Editor appears so that you can proceed with phase two: indicating the codes and text that will comprise the style.

15

Defining the Style Contents

The Style Editor is slightly different depending on whether you are creating an open or a paired style. Figure 15-4 shows a blank Style Editor for an open type of style. The title bar indicates the name of the style. Two buttons appear just below the menu bar: <u>C</u>lose, which closes the workspace and saves the changes, and <u>P</u>roperties, which redisplays the Style Properties dialog box for that style, to allow you to make changes. The reveal codes workspace is automatically open, so that you can see codes as you insert them to create the style.

Insert codes and text just as you would in the document workspace. For instance, suppose you are creating a style containing the masthead and layout for a newsletter. You could: choose <u>L</u>ayout, <u>M</u>argins and change left/right margins to .5 inch; choose <u>G</u>raphics, Text <u>B</u>ox and insert a text box containing the newsletter's masthead; choose <u>L</u>ayout, <u>C</u>olumns and establish three columns; and choose F<u>o</u>nt, F<u>o</u>nt and change the font. Layout codes are inserted, and Figure 15-5 shows the resulting style in the Style Editor. The masthead (contained in the text box) is displayed in the top area, and the codes are revealed in the bottom area.

Figure 15-6 shows a blank Style Editor for a paired type. The difference between the Style Editor for an open type and a paired type is that a comment

Figure 15-4.   *Style Editor before creating an open style*

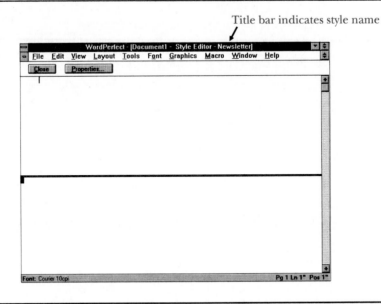

Figure 15-5.   *Example of an open style to format and set the banner for a
newsletter*

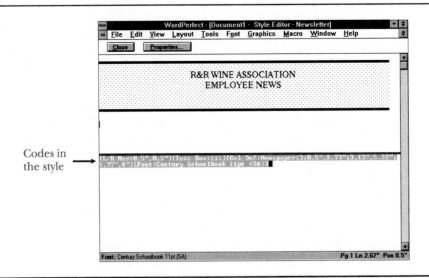

Figure 15-6. *Style Editor before creating a paired style*

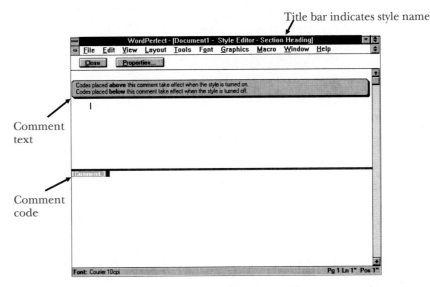

Title bar indicates style name

Comment text

Comment code

15

code displays for a paired type. This comment splits the Style Editor into an On section and an Off section. All text and codes inserted *before* the comment code are part of the style when it is turned on. All text and codes inserted *after* the comment code are part of the style when it is turned off.

For instance, suppose you are creating a style for section headings in a report. You could position the insertion point on the comment code and press (SHIFT) + (TAB) to create a margin release, press (CTRL) + (S) and choose Very Large to turn on Very Large size, and press (CTRL) + (I) to turn on Italic. Then, you could position the insertion point to the right of the comment code and press (CTRL) + (N) to turn off all attributes and press (ENTER) twice to insert hard returns. Figure 15-7 shows the resulting style in the Style Editor. (When using a paired code, such as [Italc On] and [Italc Off], you do not necessarily need to place the end (off) code in the Off section of the paired style; WordPerfect assumes that the attribute is to be turned off. However, the end codes were inserted in the example in Figure 15-7.)

Figure 15-7.   *Example of a paired style for a heading*

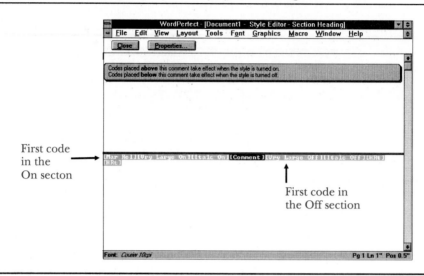

Once the style is created—as shown in the examples in Figure 15-5 and 15-7—choose Close to return to the Styles dialog box. Then, choose Close to return to the document workspace.

note   *Certain codes are not allowed in a style, including cross-reference codes, subdocument codes, and endnote placement codes. In addition, if you want to include a graphic image in a style, use the Graphic on Disk option when positioning the image in a graphics box.*

Using a Style

A style that you create becomes available for text within the document in which it was created. (As you will see shortly, you can use a style in other documents as well.) For an open style, you simply turn on the style. For a paired style, you must turn on the style and also turn it off again at the point where you wish the style to stop. You can use the Styles dialog box or the ruler to execute a style, as explained in the following sections.

Executing from the Styles Dialog Box

To apply an open style, or to apply a paired style to text yet to be typed, follow these steps:

1. Position the insertion point where you want the style to take effect.

2. Choose Layout, Styles. The Styles dialog box appears, displaying a list of available styles. (Refer back to Figure 15-3.)

3. If the style that you wish to turn on is listed, select (or highlight) that style and choose On.

    If the style you wish to turn on is not listed, you can choose Create to create a new style (as previously described) or retrieve a list of styles (to be described soon). Then, select the style and choose On.

4. Type the text to be affected by the style.

5. If the style is a paired type, you must remember to turn off the style. (Open styles are not turned off.) To turn off a paired style, choose Layout, Styles, Off. Or, if the properties of the style are such that the (ENTER) key will turn it off, simply press (ENTER).

reminder (ALT) + (F8) *is the shortcut for Layout, Styles.*

You can also apply a paired style to existing text, but to do so you must use the Select feature. Follow these steps:

1. Select the text.

2. Choose Layout, Styles. The Styles dialog box appears. (Refer back to Figure 15-3.)

3. Select (or highlight) the style you wish to apply to the selected text, and choose On.

4. Click the mouse or press an arrow key to turn off the Select feature.

When you turn on an open style, an Open Style code is inserted in the text. For example, if the style is named "newsletter", the code inserted is [Open Style:Newsletter]. Any text that you type following the code will be formatted according to the style named "newsletter".

When you turn on and then off a paired style, Style On and Off codes are inserted around the text affected by the style. For instance, if the style is named "section heading", the pair of codes surrounding the affected text are [Style On:Section Heading] and [Style Off:Section Heading].

A style code expands to show its contents when you choose <u>V</u>iew, Reveal <u>C</u>odes to show codes and when you position the insertion point on that code. This is convenient when you've previously inserted a style code into the text and now wish to identify the format dictated by that code.

For instance, here's what will display in the reveal codes workspace when the insertion point is just to the right on an Open Style code for the style named "newsletter":

```
[Open Style:Newsletter]
```

If you then position the insertion point on the Open Style code, here's what will be revealed:

```
[Open Style:Newsletter;[L/R Mar:0.5",0.5"][Text Box:1;;][Col Def:Newspaper;3;
0.5",2.73";3.13",5.37";5.77",8"][Font:Century Schoolbook 11pt <SA>]]
```

Should you later decide to cancel the effect of a style in your text, delete the Open Style code or Style On and Off codes. With the Style On and Off codes, you need to remove only one code of the pair; the other is erased automatically by WordPerfect.

Executing Styles from the Ruler

An alternative to using the Styles dialog box for turning a style on or off—but with the exact same effect—is to use the ruler. Using the ruler is quicker, and especially helpful if you're turning styles on and off frequently in a document. You must have a mouse to use the ruler. (For more information on the ruler, see Chapter 6.)

To display the ruler in your document, choose <u>V</u>iew, <u>R</u>uler. The ruler appears just below the menu bar and slightly reduces the size of the document workspace.

With the ruler displayed, apply an open style or apply a paired style to text yet to be typed by following these steps:

1. Position the insertion point where you want the style to take effect.

2. Click and hold the Styles button on the ruler. A list of available styles appears, such as in this example:

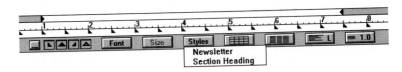

3. Drag the mouse to select the style you want, and release the mouse button.

4. Type the text.

5. If the style is a paired type, you must remember to turn off the style. Follow steps 2 and 3 above. Or, if the properties of the style are such that the (ENTER) key will turn it off, then simply press (ENTER).

To apply a paired style to existing text, you must first use the Select feature to select the text, and then click and drag the Styles button with your mouse to choose a style.

Editing or Deleting a Style

You can edit the format of a style in the Styles dialog box, but not in the document workspace. For instance, suppose that you decide to remove Italic as one of the attributes for section headings. You must choose <u>L</u>ayout, <u>S</u>tyles to return to the Styles dialog box (as shown in Figure 15-3). Then, position the insertion point on the name of the style you wish to edit and choose <u>E</u>dit.

15

You are immediately returned to the Style Editor for that style. Now, add or delete text or codes to alter the style. You can also alter the style properties by choosing Properties, and close the Style Editor by choosing Close.

When you edit a style that has already been turned on in a document, the results are truly amazing. The text governed by that style is immediately revised to reflect the editing changes. For example, if you remove Italic from the style named "section heading", any text containing italic between the [Style On:Section Heading] and [Style Off:Section Heading] codes will no longer be italicized.

You can also delete styles that you no longer use. Return to the Styles dialog box, position the insertion point on the name of the style you wish to erase, and choose Delete. You are presented with three options as to how the style will be deleted:

- *Leave Format Codes*   You delete the style from the Styles dialog box as well as style codes of the same name from the document, but leave the corresponding format codes in the document when you choose the Leave Format Codes option. All text that had been formatted by those style codes would continue to be formatted just as the style dictated. For instance, suppose your style was for left/right margins of .5 inch. The styles code would be deleted, but a margin code calling for left/right margins of .5 inch would be inserted in its place.

- *Delete Format Codes*   You delete the style from the Styles dialog box as well as style codes of the same name from the document when you choose the Delete Format Codes option. The formatting resulting from the style codes is also removed.

- *Delete Definition Only*   You delete the style from the Styles dialog box, but keep the style codes intact in the document by choosing the Delete Definition Only option. When WordPerfect encounters these style codes in the document, it re-creates the style in the Styles dialog box.

Managing Styles Between Documents

When Styles are first created, they are associated with a specific document. The styles are attached to that document when it is saved. The next time you retrieve that document and display the Styles dialog box, the styles you created will appear.

You can also save and retrieve a group of styles on their own, separate from the document in which the styles were created. In that way, you can apply styles created in one document to text in many different documents. For instance, you can apply the four styles you created for use in formatting your January newsletter in future newsletters.

To save a list of styles independently, return to the Styles dialog box where they were created and choose Save As. Now type in a filename, using the same rules for naming files as when storing a document on disk. A saved list of styles is referred to as a *styles library*.

It is a good idea to give a styles library a filename that reminds you of its contents, perhaps using an extension such as *.sty* or *.lib*. For instance, *newslets.sty*, could be a styles library that you use whenever you wish to produce a company newsletter.

To apply a styles library to another document, make sure that the other document is on screen. Return to the Styles dialog box, and choose Retrieve. Then type in or select the file containing the styles library that you wish to bring into the current document and choose Retrieve.

WordPerfect will check the current list of files. If no styles are listed, all the styles in the library are retrieved. If styles are listed, WordPerfect displays a dialog box notifying you that files already exist, and asking if you wish to replace the existing files. Choose Yes to retrieve all the styles; any existing styles with the same name as in the file you are retrieving will be replaced by the incoming style. Choose No to retrieve only those styles whose names do not match any existing style names.

You can designate a default styles library, one that should be automatically retrieved into *every* new document that you create. This is useful for styles that you may want to apply to all, or at least a majority, of your documents, regardless of type. For example, you may want all of your documents—whether reports, memos, or letters—to have headings that are bold and italic. Your default style library could contain such a style.

WordPerfect is packaged with a list of styles under the filename *library.sty*. Depending on how you installed WordPerfect, this list may have been designated as the default styles library (which explains why a list of files may appear the first time you display the Styles dialog box). You may wish to

15

examine each of the styles in *library.sty*, and decide whether any are appropriate for your needs. For instance, an open style named *pleading* can be used to create two vertical lines and numbers down the page to emulate pleading pages for law papers. You can edit some of the styles and delete others. If none meet your needs, you can designate a different styles library as the one to be attached to every new document. You can also choose to have no styles library. (You must have installed the style library file to have *library.sty* available.)

You designate, change, or remove a default styles library with the File, Preferences, Location of Files command, described in Chapter 17.

Working with Long Documents

WordPerfect offers several powerful features enabling you to manage the text in long documents. These include cross-references; tables, lists, and indexes; and master documents.

Cross-References

Suppose you insert the following phrase in your text: "For more on Chardonnay wines, refer to footnote 14, found on page 33". There are two *references* in this phrase—to a specific footnote and a specific page number. If you then edit your text so that footnotes or pages are renumbered, you must manually update the reference to Chardonnay wines. That's time-consuming.

Instead, employ the Cross-Reference feature. This feature will maintain accurate cross-references to a specific page number, graphics box, footnote, endnote, or paragraph number. The text or graphics to which you are referring is called a *target*. Should you later edit your document so that the target falls on a different page or so the number of the graphics box, footnote, endnote, or paragraph changes, all references will update automatically. There are two basic steps to using cross-references in WordPerfect: mark the cross-references, and then generate them.

Marking Cross-References

To mark a cross-reference, you must mark both the reference and its associated target. Follow these steps:

1. Position the insertion point within the referring text where you want the reference number to appear or, if no referring text exists, type it. For instance, type **For more on The R&R Wine Association, see page** and press the (SPACEBAR).

2. Choose Tools, Mark Text, Cross-Reference. A Mark Cross-Reference dialog box appears.

3. Select Reference and Target.

4. From the Tie Reference To pop-up list box, select a reference type (such as page number or footnote).

5. In the Target Name text box, type a name that will be used to link the reference to the target (for instance, R&R might be a good reference name for the R&R Wine Association cross-reference mentioned earlier).

6. Choose OK twice.

7. Position the insertion point in one of these places: within the text on the page (for a page reference); within the text of the note (for a footnote or endnote); or to the immediate right of the code (for a graphics box or paragraph number). Then, press (ENTER).

shortcut (F12) *is the shortcut for* Tools, Mark Text.

You are returned to your reference phrase in the text. That phrase now appears with the correct number; such as "For more on The R&R Wine Association, see page 23". But the reference number 23 is really a code. Reveal codes and you will view the following: "For more on The R&R Wine Association, see page [Ref(R&R):Pg 23]". This is a reference code, where the target name is "R&R" and the reference number is "Pg 23". The target, too, contains a code. For instance, beside the phrase "The R&R Wine Association" on page 23, you may find the code [Target(R&R)].

In some cases, you will choose not to mark a reference and target at the same time; you can mark each separately. You may wish to tie many references to the same target. For instance, your document may have three separate references to footnote 14.

Conversely, you may wish to tie one reference to multiple targets. For instance, you may include this statement: "R&R Wine Association has produced short-term, medium-term, and long-term budget projections, as provided on pages 15, 19, and 22". Those are instances where you must mark the references and targets separately.

To set up a cross-reference separately, place the insertion point within the referring text where you want the reference number to appear and choose Tools, Mark Text, Cross-Reference to display the Mark Cross-Reference dialog box. Select Reference and then specify what the reference will be tied to and a target name. When you choose OK to insert a reference code, a question mark (?) will appear instead of a reference number.

To set up a target separately, place the insertion point just after the target and choose Tools, Mark Text, Cross-Reference to display the Mark Cross-Reference dialog box. Select Target and then specify the same target name as for the corresponding reference. When you choose OK, a target code is inserted. Be sure to use the same target name for all reference codes and target codes that are linked together.

Generating Cross-References

It is critical after marking all your references and targets, and after editing your text, to generate the cross-references. This updates any cross-references that are not correct and inserts reference numbers in place of any question marks. To generate cross-references, follow these steps:

1. Choose Tools, Generate. A dialog box appears asking if you wish to generate not only cross-references, but also tables, indexes, lists, and endnote placements (see Chapter 13 for more on the Endnote Placement feature).

2. Choose Yes to continue or No to cancel the command.

shortcut (ALT) + (F12) *is the shortcut for Tools, Generate.*

Tables, Lists, and Indexes

In a dissertation, book, legal brief, or other long document, the document's author often prepares reference aids to help the reader easily find information in that document. WordPerfect offers assistance when you need to create reference aids, which include an index, a table of contents, or up to ten separate lists (of figures, illustrations, graphs, maps, and also of the captions for the graphics boxes inserted in your text). If you're creating a legal document, WordPerfect helps you create a table of authorities with up to 16 sections, each listing various cases, regulations, constitutional provisions, and so on. Best of all, if you let WordPerfect create these reference aids for you, WordPerfect will update them later when you edit your text.

The procedure for producing any of these reference aids involves the same three steps: mark the text that will be included, define the style of the reference aid, and generate.

Marking Text

You must insert codes around the specific text that you want incorporated in a reference aid. This is called *marking the text*. Suppose you want to mark a heading to be included in a table of contents. You would insert codes around this heading to mark it. Follow these steps to mark text:

1. Select the text. For instance, select the heading to be included in the table of contents, select the text that will be included in the index, or select the citation that will be included in the table of authorities.

2. Choose Tools, Mark Text.

3. Choose the option that corresponds to the reference aid for which you are marking text, which could be one of the following: Index; List; Table of Contents, Table of Authorities (ToA) Full Form; or ToA Short Form.

4. Respond to WordPerfect's prompts as to how the selected text should be treated (described in detail next).

reminder (F12) *is the shortcut for Tools, Mark Text.*

Marking Text for Lists   When you want the text you chose to be added to a list, WordPerfect asks you to specify which list the selected text should be marked for. List numbers 1 through 5 can represent any type of list that you choose. For instance, suppose you create one list of illustrations and another of maps. You could specify list number 1 for all text to be included in the list of illustrations. Then, specify list number 2 for all text to be included in the list of maps.

List numbers 6 through 10 are predefined, respectively, for figure captions, table captions, text box captions, user box captions, and equation captions. So, for instance, suppose you insert numerous figures with captions in your document. You don't have to mark any text for list 6 (the list predefined for figure captions).

Marking Text for a Table of Contents   When you want to mark text for entry into a table of contents, WordPerfect asks for the table of contents *level* for the selected text. A table of contents has a structure similar to an outline. You can choose from five different levels: level 1 text starts at the left margin, level 2 is indented one tab stop, and so on.

For instance, here's an example of a brief table of contents with three levels:

To produce this table of contents, chapter titles (such as "Introduction" and "Wine Sales") were marked in the text as table of contents level 1 entries, headings as level 2 entries, and subheadings as level 3 entries.

Marking Text for an Index   When you want to mark text to be an index entry, WordPerfect asks for the index heading and subheading for the selected text. WordPerfect always suggests the selected text as a heading; if you type in a different heading, WordPerfect suggests the selected text as a subheading.

As an example, you may want one entry in an index to appear as follows:

White Wines
      Chardonnay
      Chenin Blanc

When you select the text "White Wines" for entry into an index, you'll designate "White Wines" as a heading, without a subheading (for readers who are looking up the general category of White Wines). When you select the text "Chardonnay" or "Chenin Blanc" in the text, you'll want to specify "White Wines" as the heading, and designate the selected text as a subheading.

Instead of marking each phrase for an index entry individually, you can create a *concordance file,* which contains an alphabetical list of the principle words in a document that you want included in an index. In a clear document workspace, type the phrases, one on each line, and then save this document under a name that reminds you it's a concordance file. This saves you time because you don't have to mark the same index entry over and over again each time it occurs in your document. Just include that index entry once in the concordance file.

WordPerfect will ask for the name of the concordance file when you define the index (the procedure to define a reference aid follows). Then, when WordPerfect generates the index, it will search the document for those phrases contained in the concordance file and include the corresponding page numbers in the index. The phrases are assumed to be headings unless you mark those phrases in the concordance file—in the same way that you mark phrases in a document—as subheadings. Creating a concordance file does not mean you can't also mark phrases individually in the text—you still can. WordPerfect will compile both into an index when generated. But a concordance file does free you from having to mark the same phrase over and over again in the text.

15

Marking Text for a Table of Authorities For a table of authorities, which is a list of citations, the first time you select a citation, choose ToA F̲ull Form. WordPerfect prompts for that citation's section number. For instance, perhaps your table of authorities will have two sections, statutes and cases. Section 1 could be statutes, and section 2 could be cases. If the selected text is a citation to a case, you would specify section 2. Next, you must also specify the citation's *short form,* which will serve as a nickname for the citation for every other time it is mentioned in the text. Finally, the selected text will then be displayed on the screen. You can edit how it will appear in the table of authorities and then choose C̲lose.

After the first time you select a citation, the next time choose ToA S̲hort Form. WordPerfect prompts only for the short form.

Defining the Style and Location of the Reference Aid

Each time you mark text to be included in a reference aid, codes are placed beside that phrase. (Of course, those codes can be viewed only in the reveal codes workspace.) For a list or table of contents, a code pair is inserted. For instance, suppose you marked the heading "Sales Figures for the West Coast" as a level-2 entry in a table of contents. The heading would be surrounded with a pair of hidden codes as follows: [Mark:ToC,2]Sales Figures for the West Coast[EndMark:ToC,2]. For an index or table of authorities, a single code is inserted. For instance, suppose you marked the words "White Wines" as a heading. The code inserted is [Index:White Wines].

Your next step after marking text is to define the table, list, or index that you wish to create. Only one index or table of contents can be defined per document. However, since you can generate more than one list and multiple sections in a table of authorities in each document, every list and table of authorities section must be defined separately.

To define a reference aid, you must first position the insertion point where you want the reference aid to appear after it is generated. For a table or list, that is usually at the beginning of the document, before the main text. For an index, that is usually at the end of the document.

You will want the insertion point to be located on a separate page, so that the reference aid will be generated on a separate page. Thus, if the insertion point is at the top of the document, press (CTRL) + (ENTER) to insert a hard page break, and then move the insertion point back up to the top of the document, above the page break. If the insertion point is at the end of the document, press (CTRL) + (ENTER) and then keep the insertion point positioned below the hard page break.

Now you are ready to define the reference aid. Choose Tools, Define, and choose the option that corresponds to the reference aid you are defining: Index, List, Table of Contents, or Table of Authorities.

shortcut (SHIFT) + (F12) *is the shortcut for Tools, Define.*

For a list, specify the list number you are defining; for a table of authorities, specify the section number.

You must also determine how page numbers should appear for each list, for each level in a table of contents, and for the index. You can choose no page numbers, page numbers that follow the entries, page numbers that follow the entries in parentheses, page numbers that are positioned flush right on the line, or page numbers that are flush right on the line with dot leaders. With a table of contents, you must also specify how many levels should be generated and whether entries in the last level should be placed together on the same line and separated by semicolons—this is referred to as *wrapped format*. Examples of different page numbering styles are shown in Figure 15-8. In the Table of Contents, two styles are used: one style for levels 1 and 2, and a different style for level 3.

With an index, you also have the opportunity to indicate a filename for a concordance file that you may have created.

For a table of authorities, page numbers are always inserted flush right on a line. But, you can decide whether the page numbers should be preceded by dot leaders, the table should include underlining, and a blank line should be inserted between authorities.

Once you define a reference aid, a Definition Mark code is placed in the text. For instance, suppose you just defined list 1, where the numbering style will be flush right page numbers. Then the code inserted is [Def Mark:List,1:FlRgt]. If you defined section 3 of a Table of Authorities, then the code inserted is [Def Mark:ToA,3].

After you define all the reference aids for a particular document, and before you generate them, you may need to readjust page numbers. Placing a table or list at the beginning of the document causes the main text to begin

15

Figure 15-8.   *Examples of different page numbering styles*

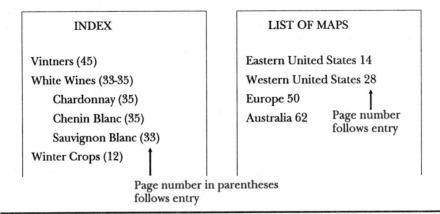

TABLE OF CONTENTS

Page number flush right with dot leaders

Page number follows entry

TABLE OF AUTHORITIES   Page number flush right

INDEX

Page number in parentheses follows entry

LIST OF MAPS

Page number follows entry

on a page other than page 1. For instance, suppose you place a Definition Mark code for a table of contents at the top of the document, followed by a page break, and then place a Definition Mark code for a list on the next page, which is also followed by a page break. The main text begins on page 3.

Typically, you will want the first page of the main text to be page 1. If that's the case, use the Page Numbering feature to renumber the first page of the main text as page 1. In other words, you would position the insertion point on the first page of the main text; choose Layout, Page, Numbering, New Page Number; type 1 to begin page numbering at number 1; and choose OK. (Refer to Chapter 7 for more complete information on the Page Numbering feature.)

(You may also wish to use the Page Numbering feature to change the numbering type of the pages containing the reference aids. For instance, you can renumber the page containing the table of contents as page 1 using lowercase Roman numerals, so that it appears as page i.)

Generating Reference Aids

After marking text and defining reference aids, the hard work is over. Your final task is to generate the reference aids. The procedure is the same as when generating cross-references, (as discussed in the "Generating Cross-References" section earlier in this chapter).

1. Choose Tools, Generate. A dialog box appears asking if you wish to generate not only tables, indexes, and lists, but also cross-references and endnote placements (see Chapter 13 for more on the Endnote Placement feature).

2. Choose Yes to continue or No to cancel the command.

reminder (ALT) + (F12) *is the shortcut for Tools, Generate.*

After the table, index, or list is generated, you can add finishing touches—a title, for example. Simply move the insertion point to the top of the page where a reference aid has been generated to type the title. If you later edit your document, such that text is shifted into different pages, remember to generate the reference aids again, simply by repeating steps 1 and 2 above. Page numbers will be updated in your tables, lists, and index.

Master Documents

If a document is extremely long, the Master Document feature lets you break your text into smaller parts. Each part of the long document is stored in a separate file and is referred to as a *subdocument*. The main document that links all the subdocuments together is referred to as the *master document*.

You can edit each subdocument separately, so that editing becomes more manageable. At the same time, you can expand the master document to work with all the subdocuments as a whole for tasks that require the documents be treated as one, such as for printing or generating a comprehensive table of contents, table of authorities, index, or list. And, all numbering features found in the subdocuments—such as footnotes, endnotes, paragraph numbering, automatic referencing, and page numbering—will operate consecutively when the subdocuments are linked to the master and the master document is expanded.

The master document is basically a small file consisting of text and links to each subdocument. Suppose, for instance, you are writing a book. Each chapter can be stored on disk as a separate subdocument, using filenames such as *chap1, chap2,* and so on. The master document may include a title page, reference aids such as a table of contents, an introduction, and links to each chapter.

To work with the Master Document feature, you can either type and save all the subdocuments on disk first, or you can create the master document first and then create the subdocuments later. When you're ready to create the master document, start typing in a clear document workspace just as you would to begin any document. When you're ready to create a link to a subdocument, follow these steps:

1. Position the insertion point in the master document where you want to insert a link to a subdocument.

2. Choose Tools, Master Document, Subdocument. An Include Subdocument dialog box appears.

3. Type in or select the name of the file to be linked to the master document.

4. Choose Insert.

A comment is inserted in the text. Repeat steps 1 through 4 until all subdocuments have been linked to the master. The master document may contain very little text—perhaps only a string of subdocument comments, one on each line. If you prefer, you can separate each subdocument comment with a hard page break (($\boxed{\text{CTRL}}$ + $\boxed{\text{ENTER}}$)) so that, when printed, each subdocument begins on a separate page. Figure 15-9 shows an example of a master document with links to four different subdocuments, each link placed on a separate page.

Each comment in a master document represents a subdocument code. For instance, if you reveal codes, you'll see the following for the first comment in Figure 15-9: [Subdoc: C:\DOCS\WINCHAP1]. It is this code that links the master to the subdocument named *winchap1*.

Save the file using a filename that will remind you that it is a master document. For example, name the master document *book.mas* or *winebook.mas* or *master.bk*.

When you're ready to print the document in its entirety, including all the subdocument text, you must *expand* the master document to retrieve all the

15

Figure 15-9.   *Example of a master document*

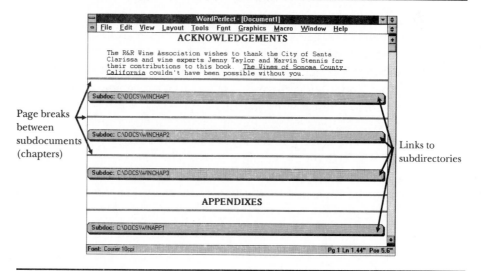

subdocuments into it. (You can also expand the master before generating a table, list, or index, but you don't have to; WordPerfect will do so automatically when you generate.) To expand the master document, choose Tools, Master Document, Expand Master. In moments, each subdocument is replaced by the text of the corresponding subdocument. The text of each subdocument will now be bordered by a *pair* of new comments. For instance, the comments around chapter 1 (called *winchap1* in Figure 15-9) will appear, as shown here:

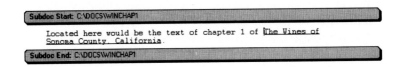

These comments represent two subdocument codes [Subdoc Start: C:\DOCS\WINCHAP1] and [Subdoc End: C:\DOCS\WINCHAP1].

(Should WordPerfect be unable to locate a subdocument on disk during the expansion process, it will ask whether you wish to continue. Choose Yes to do so, even though a certain subdocument cannot be expanded, or choose No to stop the expansion with that subdocument.)

After printing, you can again condense the master into its short form. To do so, choose Tools, Master Document, Condense Master. In case you edited any of the text of the subdocuments while the master was expanded, WordPerfect will display a dialog box asking whether you wish to save any changes made to all the subdocuments. Choose Yes if you made any editing changes in any of the subdocuments, in which case WordPerfect will ask whether you wish to replace the version of each separate subdocument on disk with the version on screen. Choose No if you made no changes to the subdocuments or don't wish to save any changes made. The master will then collapse into its short form. Remember to condense a master document again before resaving it on disk, so that the master takes up the least amount of space possible on disk.

Quick Reference

- To create a macro, choose Macro, Record and indicate a name for the macro. WordPerfect will record each command that you perform.

- To execute a macro, choose Macro, Play and indicate a macro name. You can also execute a macro with a key combination, by assigning it to the Macro menu, or by assigning it to a button bar.

- To create a style, choose Layout, Styles, Create and indicate a name for the style. Then, insert the text and formatting codes that will make up the style.

- To turn a style on or off, choose Layout, Styles. Select a style name and choose On or Off. You can also turn a style on or off from the ruler.

- To create a cross-reference, mark the reference and the target by choosing Tools, Mark Text, Cross-Reference. Generate all the cross-references by choosing Tools, Generate.

- To produce a reference aid (a table of contents, table of authorities, list, or index) mark all the entries to be included by selecting text and choosing Tools, Mark Text; define the reference aid by choosing Tools, Define; and then generate by choosing Tools, Generate.

- To split a long document into sections, create a master document with links to subdocuments. Establish a link in the master document by choosing Tools, Master Document, Subdocument. Expand a master document, so that subdocuments are retrieved into it, by choosing Tools, Master Document, Expand Master.

15

16

Managing Documents: At the Printer, on Disk, Across Applications

WordPerfect gives you special features for managing your documents; this chapter shows you how to use them. First you'll learn about advanced printing options—including how to preview a document before printing, how to select different printers, and how to redefine your printer so you can control how it works with WordPerfect and customize it to fit your needs.

Next, you'll learn how to maintain an orderly system for storing and handling the many files that you will quickly accumulate (or perhaps already have accumulated) on disk. You'll learn how to protect a file with a password so that only authorized people can open it, and you'll see how to create document summaries for your files. You'll also learn how to reorganize files already on disk, through deleting, renaming, or copying. You'll see how to create directories and use the Quick List feature to work with directories more easily.

The last section of this chapter describes how to transfer documents to and from WordPerfect. You'll learn how to convert text from other applications—such as MultiMate, Microsoft Word, or WordStar—into WordPerfect. Also, you'll learn how to copy text between applications, and to link a WordPerfect document to another file, such as a spreadsheet created in Lotus 1-2-3.

Previewing a Document Before Printing

The Print Preview feature is a convenient way to check the layout of your document before you actually print; it's especially handy for desktop publishing. WordPerfect displays the document's layout based on the printer you have selected to print it, and shows more features than those displayed in the document workspace, including headers, footers, page numbering, and footnotes.

You can see one or two full pages at a time, or zoom in for detail on a section of the page. Use this feature wisely, and you can save paper and time—by discovering layout mistakes before a document is actually printed.

To view your document, the document must be on screen. Position the insertion point on the first page you wish to preview and choose File, Print Preview.

shortcut (SHIFT) + (F5) *is the shortcut for* File, Print Preview.

Figure 16-1 shows an example of a full page of text in the Print Preview window. The title bar lists the name of the document currently being previewed. Just below the title bar, five menu names appear on a menu bar: File, View, Pages, Window, and Help. A predefined button bar also displays along the left side of the screen. Use this button bar as an alternative method for executing frequently used commands in the Print Preview window.

A status line appears at the bottom of the window. The status line indicates the scale of the document you are currently viewing. For instance, "100%" means the text in your document is being viewed at the actual size in which it will print. (The document in Figure 16-1 is shown at 65 percent of the size of the printed result.) The status line also indicates the page number you are currently viewing and the form (paper) size for that page.

Figure 16-1. *Full page of text displayed in the Print Preview window*

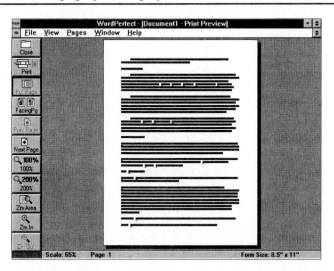

The commands available using the first three menus on the menu bar—File, View, and Pages—are described next. (The last two menus, Window and Help, are the same as on the menu bar in the document workspace.) Clicking a button on the button bar can be used as an alternative for selecting certain commands from the menu bar.

File Menu

From the File menu in the Print Preview window you can use the following commands.

Close   The Close command (or the Close button on the button bar) closes the Print Preview window and returns you to the document workspace. When you close the window, WordPerfect keeps track of the view and scale you had last selected, and duplicates this the next time you display the Print Preview window.

Print   The Print command (or the Print button on the button bar) closes the Print Preview window and displays the Print dialog box. (This is a shortcut

16

to choosing <u>C</u>lose to close the Print Preview window and then choosing the <u>F</u>ile, <u>P</u>rint command.)

View Menu

From the <u>V</u>iew menu in the Print Preview window, you have the following options.

100% or 200%   Choosing <u>1</u>00% lets you view the current page at its actual size. Choosing <u>2</u>00% lets you view it at twice its actual size. (You can also choose the 100% button and the 200% button on the button bar.)

Zoom Area   Choosing <u>Z</u>oom Area (or the Zm Area button on the button bar) allows you to magnify the view of a selected area in the document. Position the mouse pointer at the edge of the area you wish to view and drag the mouse to form a box outline. When you release the mouse button, the outlined area is resized to fill the Print Preview window. The mouse pointer changes to a four-headed arrow.

If you wish to select a different zoom area, first click once to view a miniature page, use the mouse to drag the box outline to another part of the page, and then release the mouse button to magnify the new zoom area.

Zoom to Full Width   Use Zoom to <u>F</u>ull Width to view the full width of the current page.

Zoom In   Zoom <u>I</u>n (or the Zm In button on the button bar) increases the viewing size by 25 percent, up to a magnification of 400 percent.

Zoom Out   Zoom <u>O</u>ut (or the Zm Out button on the button bar) decreases the viewing size by 25 percent, until the full page is displayed.

Button Bar   Use the <u>B</u>utton Bar option to display or hide the Print Preview button bar.

Button Bar Setup   The Button Bar <u>S</u>etup option lets you edit, change the position, or change the appearance of the Print Preview button bar. (See Chapter 10 for more information on working with button bars.)

Pages Menu

From the Pages menu on the Print Preview window, the following options are available.

Facing Pages   The Facing Pages command (or the Facing Pg button on the button bar) displays two consecutive pages from your document, with the even-numbered page on the left and the odd-numbered page on the right. (Page 1 has no facing page.)

Full Page   The Full Page command (or the Full Page button) displays a full view of the current page.

Go To Page   The Go To Page command makes a new page the current page, so that this new page can be viewed. Type in a page number in the Go To dialog box and choose OK.

Next Page or Previous Page   The Next Page and Previous Page commands display the following or preceding page (or facing pages). (You can also choose the Next Page button or the Prev Page button on the button bar.)

When you are viewing a page—in any mode except the Full Page view—you can view different parts of the page using the arrow keys or the scroll bars. You can also press (CTRL) + (PGUP) or (CTRL) + (PGDN) to move to the left or right of the page.

16

≡note≡ When WordPerfect is in the midst of redrawing the Print Preview window and you wish to stop the redrawing, press (ESC). Then, you can choose another menu item.

Controlling Print Jobs with the Print Manager

As described in Chapter 4, once you issue the Print command, WordPerfect displays the Current Print Job dialog box. Whenever this dialog box is on screen—while the document is being processed—you can stop the printing by choosing Cancel Print Job. If you do not stop the printing, the document processing is completed, and the print job is sent to the Print

Manager. The Print Manager, an application packaged with Windows, is started automatically to handle the printing. Once all jobs are printed, the Print Manager closes. Print Manager works behind the scenes.

(This discussion assumes that the Print Manager is enabled in Windows, so that you can continue working in WordPerfect while a document is being printed. If the Print Manager is disabled, you'll have to wait until a document finishes printing before you can continue working in WordPerfect. Should the Print Manager be disabled on your computer, you may wish to enable it using the Windows Control Panel, described in Chapter 17.)

Once a print job is sent to the Print Manager, you must use the Print Manager—and not WordPerfect—to pause, resume, or delete a print job. You use the Print Manager when a dialog box appears on screen with a message indicating that there is a printer problem, such as the dialog box shown here:

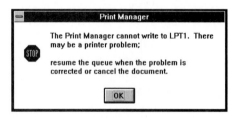

Moreover, you must use the Print Manager if you defined your printer so that paper is manually fed; the print job pauses for you to insert paper and waits for you to signal via the Print Manager that the printing should resume. You can also use the Print Manager to view the *print queue*—the list of print jobs in line, waiting to be printed.

Since the Print Manager is not part of WordPerfect, you must switch out of WordPerfect to use it. The procedure depends on whether the printing is local (meaning that the printer and computer are directly connected by a cable) or controlled by a network.

When your print job is local, you can quickly access the Print Manager.

From WordPerfect, follow these steps:

1. Click on the WordPerfect application control-menu box (the box in the upper left corner in the WordPerfect application window) or press (ALT) + (SPACEBAR) to display the Control menu.

2. Choose Switch To to display the Task List dialog box.

3. Select (highlight) Print Manager and choose Switch To. This displays the Print Manager. (If no print jobs are currently being processed, the Print Manager will not be loaded, and therefore will not be listed in the Task List dialog box.)

shortcut (CTRL) + (ESC) *is the shortcut for clicking on the WordPerfect application control-menu box and choosing Switch To.*

The Print Manager window is shown in Figure 16-2. Three buttons in the Print Manager window provide the basic control over documents in the print queue: Pause, Resume, and Delete.

Figure 16-2.   *Print Manager window displays the print queue*

16

Information
line ———➤

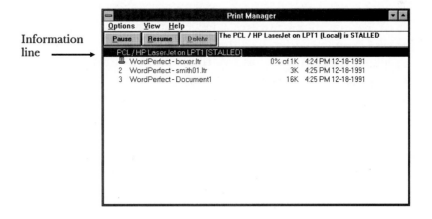

Just below these three buttons is the *information line,* which indicates the name of the printer, where the printer connects to your computer, and the current status of the printer. Below this line, the Print Manager displays the print queue, listing each print job's title, file size (in kilobytes or "K"), and the time and date you sent it to the Print Manager. Use the Print Manager as follows:

- To temporarily interrupt printing, select the information line and choose Pause.

- To resume printing, select the information line and choose Resume.

- To delete a print job from the print queue, select the print job, choose Delete and then choose OK.

- To delete all the print jobs in the print queue at once, double-click the Print Manager control-menu box or press (ALT) + (F4), and then choose OK. This closes the Print Manager window, thereby canceling all print jobs. You are returned to WordPerfect.

Once you're done using the Print Manager, return to WordPerfect (if you haven't closed the Print Manager window) by following the same three steps as previously described, except that in step 3 you select WordPerfect in the Task List dialog box and choose Switch To.

When a print job involves a network, the print job is sent to the network printer. You must then start the Print Manager from the Program Manager in Windows. You must also start the Print Manager from the Program Manager in Windows if no print jobs are currently being processed. (See your Windows manual for more information on network printing and additional information on the Print Manager.)

Working with Printers and Print Drivers

WordPerfect needs basic information about your printer in order to print your documents. It needs to know, for example, which plug the printer uses to attach to your computer and which sheet feeder the printer employs (if the printer is attached to one).

WordPerfect also needs to know which printer driver to use. As described in Chapter 4, a printer driver provides the computer codes that tell WordPerfect how to control the printer. You can use either of two different types of printer drivers: WordPerfect Corporation printer drivers, or Windows printer drivers.

Why use one type of printer driver over the other? Using a WordPerfect printer driver allows you to take full advantage of WordPerfect's features. You can establish different paper definitions, such as for special-size paper, envelopes, or labels. In the same print job, you can combine definitions—using both portrait and landscape printing, accessing different paper bins, and mixing different paper sizes. There are more printers supported with WordPerfect drivers (over 900), and you can use the same printer drivers as in WordPerfect 5.1 for DOS. Finally, printing will probably proceed faster with WordPerfect drivers than with Windows drivers. In most cases, you will want to use a WordPerfect printer driver.

Using a Windows printer driver allows you to use the same printer driver you already installed for other Windows applications. With color printers and a Windows printer driver that supports color, you can print any color graphics in color. You can also take advantage of Windows' system fonts, as well as soft fonts designed for Windows that you may have purchased, such as Bitstream Facelift for Windows or Adobe Type Manager for Windows. Finally, printers with LaserMaster cards and direct fax printing are only supported when you use a Windows printer driver.

You select a printer and printer driver directly in WordPerfect, which is described next. You can also edit the list of printers, adding or deleting printers from the list of those available.

Selecting a Printer

As described in Chapter 4, the current (or default) printer is the one set up to print. How WordPerfect formats text in your document depends on the current printer. You can view the name of the current printer at the top of the Print dialog box, which is displayed when you choose File, Print. When you save a document, the current printer's settings and formats are saved, too.

16

You need to know how to select a different printer as the current printer if you have more than one printer attached to your computer and want to switch between the two for printouts. For instance, you can select a low-resolution, fast-printing printer to print your draft documents, and a slower, high-resolution printer to print finals. You also need to know how to select a different printer if you have just one printer but wish to switch printer drivers (such as from a WordPerfect driver to a Windows driver).

To select a different printer, follow these steps:

1. Choose File, Select Printer. Or, if you're already displaying the Print dialog box, choose the Select command button. The Select Printer dialog box appears. The example shown in Figure 16-3 shows three printers listed.

2. Choose WordPerfect to work with a WordPerfect printer driver or choose Windows to work with a Windows printer driver. A list of printers set up for that printer driver displays.

3. Select the name of the printer you want to use. (If the printer you want to use is not listed, you must add a new printer; see the next section.)

4. Choose Select to make your selection the current printer.

When you select a new printer, that printer takes effect for the document currently on screen, and stays in effect permanently for that document as

Figure 16-3.   *Select Printer dialog box (WordPerfect printer driver)*

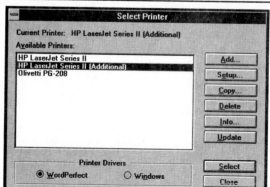

long as you save the document with the new printer selected. In addition, this new printer is now also in effect as the current printer for all *new* documents that you create until you select a new printer.

If you attempt to print a document on disk that has been formatted for a printer that is *not* the current printer, you will see a dialog box with the message "Document has not been formatted for current printer. Continue?". Choose Yes to print the document formatted for the current printer, which means that certain font codes and other printer-specific codes may be changed on the printout. Choose No to cancel the Print command.

Adding a Printer

WordPerfect printers are created during installation. When you installed WordPerfect, you probably also installed at least one printer file (with an *.all* extension). An *.all* file contains WordPerfect printer drivers for a number of printers. The *.all* files were used, in turn, to create the individual WordPerfect printer drivers (with a *.prs* extension) for each printer attached to your computer.

You will need to add a new printer if the one you wish to use isn't listed as an available printer in the Select Printer dialog box. (This assumes you wish to add a WordPerfect printer driver. For information on adding Windows printer drivers, see your Windows manual.) You can add a printer from an *.all* file or a *.prs* file.

To add a printer from an *.all* file, follow these steps:

1. Choose File, Select Printer. Or, if you're already displaying the Print dialog box, choose the Select command button. The Select Printer dialog box appears, as shown in Figure 16-3.

2. If the WordPerfect option at the bottom of the dialog box is not selected, choose WordPerfect to work with a WordPerfect printer driver.

3. Choose Add. The Add Printer dialog box appears.

4. If the Additional Printers (*.all) option at the bottom of the dialog box is not selected, choose Additional Printers (*.all). Now a list of printer drivers contained in all the *.all* files is displayed.

16

5. Select the printer in the Available Printers list box that you want to add, and choose Add. The Copy Printer dialog box appears.

    (If the name of the printer you want to add is not on the list, choose Change and specify a new directory where other *.all* files are located. If you still don't see the name of your printer, you must install additional *.all* files on your hard disk. Refer to Appendix A for instructions; you will want to repeat the installation procedure, for printers only.)

6. Choose OK to confirm the filename for the *.prs* file that WordPerfect is about to create, or specify a new filename and choose OK.

7. If a *.prs* file by that name has previously been installed, a message box appears. Choose Yes to overwrite the old *.prs* file, or choose No to return to the Copy Printer dialog box and specify a new filename.

To add a printer from a preexisting *.prs* file, repeat steps 1 through 3, and then choose Printer Files (*.prs) in step 4. A list of previously installed printers appears, from which you can select a printer. That printer will be added to the list of available printers.

Once you add a printer, it is available for your documents. However, before you select it, you may need to edit that printer's setup in order to specify a printer port or add fonts; the procedure is described next.

Editing the Printer Setup

You may need to change the setup of your printer after you add a new printer, or after you purchase additional print wheels, cartridges, soft fonts, or a new sheet feeder. During setup, you can also assign the printer a new name. Follow these steps:

1. Choose File, Select Printer. Or, if you're already displaying the Print dialog box, choose the Select command button. The Select Printer dialog box appears.

2. Choose WordPerfect to display available printers defined with a WordPerfect printer driver, or choose Windows for available printers defined with a Windows printer driver.

3. Select the printer you want to edit.

The options available to you at this point depend on whether you are editing a WordPerfect or Windows printer driver.

WordPerfect Printer Drivers

There are five command buttons in the Select Printer dialog box that pertain to editing available printers that use WordPerfect printer drivers: S_etup, _Copy, _Delete, _Info, and _Update.

Setup   The S_etup command lets you change settings for your printer. Choose S_etup and the Printer Setup dialog box appears for the printer you are editing. The example in Figure 16-4 shows the Printer Setup dialog box for the HP LaserJet Series II, with a printer driver in a file named *hplaseii.prs*. The options that you can change with the S_etup command are explained here:

- *_Name*   This option lets you determine a Name for your printer, which will appear in the Select Printer dialog box.

- *Path for _Downloadable Fonts and Printer Commands*   This option lets you indicate the directory where WordPerfect should look for soft font files and printer command files. (It is necessary to indicate a directory only if different from where the printer files are located.)

- *Initial _Font*   With the Initial _Font option, you specify the initial (default) font, the font assumed for all new documents you create using the printer. (As described in Chapter 5, you can later change the font within a particular document.)

- *Sheet Feeder*   Specify the type of sheet feeder used to feed paper into the printer, if your printer has one, with the _Sheet Feeder option. (For laser printers with a single paper bin, the single bin is not considered a sheet feeder.)

- *_Port*   Indicate the type and number of the port (plug) on the back of the computer to which the printer is attached with the _Port option. There are two different types of printer connections, those involving a parallel printer and those involving a serial printer. (Check your printer manual to discover which type of connection is correct for your printer. Parallel printers are the most common.)

16

LPT1 to LPT3 are for parallel printer connections. Generally, your printer is plugged into LPT1 if it is a parallel printer. COM1 to COM4 are for serial printers. File enables you to print to a file on disk, so that you can later print from a computer that does not have WordPerfect installed on it.

- *Network Printer*   Indicate whether or not your printer is attached through a network print queue with the Network Printer option.

- *Cartridges/Fonts*   Specify the cartridges, soft fonts, and print wheels you have purchased to use with your printer with the Cartridges/Fonts option. These are in addition to the printer's built-in fonts.

When you choose Cartridges/Fonts, a list of font sources appears for those that your printer supports; possibilities include built-in fonts, cartridges, soft fonts, and print wheels. Highlight the font source you wish to modify and choose Select.

Your task now is to indicate which of the listed cartridges, soft fonts, or print wheels are available for your printer. There are two ways to specify a

Figure 16-4.   *Printer Setup dialog box for the HP LaserJet Series II (WordPerfect printer driver)*

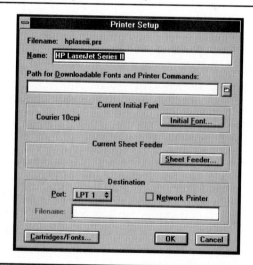

cartridge/font as being available: it is present when the print job begins, or it can be loaded/unloaded during the print job.

Mark a cartridge, print wheel, or soft font with an asterisk (*) to signify that it is always present when the print job begins. (Built-in fonts are automatically marked as present when the print job begins.) This means that the cartridge, print wheel, or soft font is ready for immediate use during a print job. Each time you mark with an asterisk, the "Available" column in the Cartridges and Fonts dialog box decreases. This keeps you from selecting more cartridges, fonts, and print wheels than your printer can accommodate. You can press the ⊙ key or double-click the left mouse button to mark with an asterisk.

Mark a soft font with a plus sign (+) to signify that the font can be loaded and unloaded during the print job. This is useful when your printer doesn't have sufficient memory to make all of the fonts always present when the print jobs begin. WordPerfect will instead load a font marked with a plus sign only when it is needed for a print job. When the print job is completed, Word-Perfect deletes the font from the printer's memory. You can press the ⊙ key or double-click the right mouse button to mark a font with a plus sign.

Keep in mind that if you mark any soft fonts with an asterisk, you must remember to initialize your printer every time you turn on your printer if you want any of the soft fonts ready for use. (See the next section for more on initializing your printer.) When you mark soft fonts with a plus sign, you don't need to initialize the printer, but printing a document with these fonts will take longer because WordPerfect must load the fonts before printing, and unload the fonts afterward.

Also keep in mind that when you mark soft fonts, whether with an asterisk or with a plus sign, you must also specify a path where these fonts are located. See the Path for Downloadable Fonts and Printer Commands option, discussed in the previous list.

note *Mark only those fonts for which you have purchased cartridges, print wheels, or soft fonts. Do not mark fonts that you do not have. WordPerfect can only access the font capabilities of your printer; it cannot expand those capabilities.*

Copy   The Copy command makes a copy of a printer listed in the Select Printer dialog box. Then you can modify the copy. In this way, you can quickly create a second listing for a printer that is similar to the first, but with some different settings, by changing the printer setup of the copy.

Delete   The Delete command deletes a printer from the list in the Select Printer dialog box. (This command does not erase the *.prs* file, however, so the printer can still be easily restored to the list with the Add command, explained earlier in this chapter.)

Info   The Info command displays information about the printer, such as the release date of the printer driver and special characteristics.

Update   The Update command upgrades the printer file, which is useful if you install a newer version of WordPerfect with changes to the *.all* file for the printer you are using.

Windows Printer Drivers

There are three command buttons in the Select Printer dialog box that pertain to editing the available printers that use Windows printer drivers: Setup, Initial Font, and Update.

Setup   The Setup command lets you change settings for your printer. When you use the command, a dialog box appears for the printer you are editing, as shown in the example in Figure 16-5. This looks slightly different from the dialog boxes you've seen thus far because it is a Windows dialog box, not a WordPerfect dialog box. The Setup options are briefly described here; see your Windows manual for more details.

- *Printer*   Specify the name of the printer with the Printer option.
- *Paper Source* and *Paper Size*   Indicate how the paper is fed into the printer (such as from a tray, bin feeder, or manually); and the size of the paper. (These are options that, when using a WordPerfect printer driver rather than a Windows driver, you specify in a paper definition, as described in Chapter 7.)
- *Memory*   Specify the amount of printer memory with the Memory option; use the default setting unless you have purchased additional memory for your printer.

- *Orientation*   Choose the paper orientation by selecting either the Po_rtrait or the _Landscape option. (Orientation is an option that, when using a WordPerfect printer driver, you specify in a paper definition. See Chapter 7 for more on paper orientation.)

- *Graphics Resolution*   Choose between _75, _150, or _300 dots per inch as the graphics resolution (if your printer supports different resolutions). The more dots per inch, the higher the resolution, and the slower the printing. (To access certain Windows fonts, you must select a higher resolution.)

- *Ca_rtridges* and _Fonts   Indicate the cartridges and soft fonts that you purchased and are available for your printer.

- _Help   Access on-line help for editing setup options with the _Help option.

- _About   Display the release date of the printer driver using the _About option.

Figure 16-5.   *PCL/HP LaserJet on LPT1 dialog box for the HP LaserJet Series II (Windows printer driver)*

16

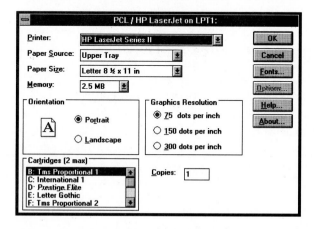

Initial Font The Initial Font command changes the font used in a document.

Update The Update command upgrades the printer file, which is useful if you install a newer version of the Windows printer driver.

Initializing a Printer

If you are using a WordPerfect printer driver with soft fonts marked as always present, you must *download* those soft fonts—or load the soft fonts into the printer's memory—every time you want to print a document that involves those soft fonts. Downloading the fonts into the printer is referred to as *initializing* the printer. To do this, turn on your printer and follow these steps:

1. Choose File, Print to display the Print dialog box.
2. Choose Initialize Printer.
3. Choose Yes to confirm that you want to begin the initialization process.

The soft fonts you specified as initially present (those marked with *) are downloaded. This may take a few moments to accomplish.

Working with Files on Disk

WordPerfect can help you manage your files and keep your hard disk neat and orderly and free of outdated files. The features for organizing and managing files on disk are described next: locking files with a password; getting a list of files; deleting, copying, and moving/renaming files; viewing files on disk; finding a file; and creating a document summary.

Locking a File with a Password

Some documents are confidential and meant to be read only by a specific group of individuals. When you find yourself typing a top-secret or personal document, WordPerfect lets you save that document with a password. Only those individuals who know the password can view, open, or print the contents of that file. To add a password, the file must be open in the document workspace. Then, follow these steps:

1. Choose File, Password. A Password dialog box appears with the message "Type Password for Document".

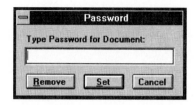

2. Type a password and choose Set. When you type the password, asterisks appear on screen instead of the characters you typed. A new message appears: "Re-Type Password to Confirm:"

3. Type the same password and again choose Set, to confirm that you typed the password exactly as you intended. (If the second attempt is different from the first, the message "Type Password for Document" reappears; you must repeat steps 2 and 3.)

4. Save your document.

After a file is locked with a password, WordPerfect will ask for that password whenever you try to view, open, retrieve, print, merge, or search that file. If you type the wrong password, the message "File is password-protected" will display, and you will be unable to work with that file.

16

≡*caution*≡ *Don't forget your password! If you do, you'll be locked out of your own file (unless you find a cryptologist who can unlock it.) Keep a written copy of each password somewhere (perhaps in your wallet), or use a password that you won't easily forget but that an office mate won't figure out (like your mother's birthday). Passwords are not case sensitive, so "june16" is treated the same as "JUNE16", for instance.*

You can change a file's password at any time. Open the file into the document workspace, and follow the same steps. Make sure to resave the document after changing the password so that the new password takes effect.

You can also remove a password. Again, the document must first be on screen. Then, choose File, Pass<u>w</u>ord, <u>R</u>emove. Make sure to resave the document so the removal of the password takes effect.

Getting a List of Files

You learned in Chapter 4 about dialog boxes where files are listed—such as the Open File dialog box, Retrieve File dialog box, and Save As dialog box. An example of the Open File dialog box is shown in Figure 16-6. The F<u>i</u>les list box on the left side displays a list of all the files in the current directory. *All* the files are listed whenever you first display the Open Files dialog box because the filename pattern *.* is displayed in the <u>F</u>ilename text box, as is the case in Figure 16-6.

In a filename pattern, an asterisk (*) is a wildcard that represents any number of characters and a question mark (?) represents one character. So, the *.* in the pattern represents all files, where the first asterisk (before the period) means any number of characters in the filename, and the second asterisk (after the period) means any number of characters in the filename extension.

When you're looking for or working with specific files, you can narrow down the list of files in a current directory by changing the filename pattern and choosing <u>O</u>pen. For instance, change the filename pattern in the <u>F</u>ilename text box to read !*.*, and choose <u>O</u>pen; only those files that begin

Figure 16-6.   *Open File dialog box*

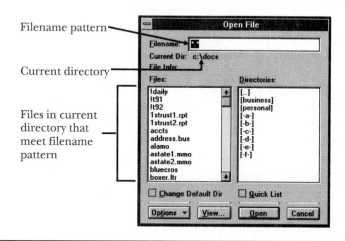

with the character ! will be listed. Or, change the filename pattern to read ***.mmo,** and choose Open; only those files with a *.mmo* filename extension are listed, which would include, for example, *astatel.mmo, astate2.mmo, financel.mmo,* and *vacation.mmo.* Or, change the filename pattern to read **astate?.mmo,** and only files such as *astatel.mmo* and *astate2.mmo* would be listed. This ability to choose which files to list is handy when you wish to look for or work with only a certain type of file defined by its filename.

Deleting, Copying, and Moving/Renaming a File

The ability to maintain your files is offered in the Open File or Retrieve File dialog box. Choose File, Open or File, Retrieve to display the dialog box, and then select (highlight) in the Files list box the file you wish to delete, copy, move, or rename. Next, choose the Options command button at the bottom of the dialog box and, from the pop-up list that appears, select either Delete, Copy, or Move/Rename.

The Delete option lets you erase the selected file. Choose <u>D</u>elete and the Delete File dialog box appears, as shown here:

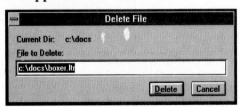

Choose <u>D</u>elete to delete the selected file, or type a different filename into the <u>F</u>ile to Delete text box and then choose <u>D</u>elete.

You can also delete multiple files simultaneously in the current directory by typing a filename pattern into the <u>F</u>ile to Delete text box, where an asterisk (*) represents any number of characters and a question mark (?) represents one character. So, for instance, type the filename pattern **letter?.*** to erase all files named *letter*, followed by one character, and any extension. This would include files such as *letter1.smi*, *letter8.tra*, and *letter9*. Type the filename pattern *****.ltr** to erase all files with a *.ltr* extension, including filenames such as *smith01.ltr*, *jones.ltr*, and *1154.ltr*. Type the filename pattern *****.*** to erase every file in the current directory.

≡caution≡ The <u>D</u>elete command removes a file permanently from disk. Delete a file only when you're certain that you will never again need to use or reference the file. Also, type a file pattern into the <u>F</u>ile to Delete text box only when you're certain that you will never again need to use any of the files with names that fit the pattern.

The <u>C</u>opy option lets you copy the selected file to another directory. Choose <u>C</u>opy and the Copy File dialog box appears, listing the selected file as the one to be copied, as shown here:

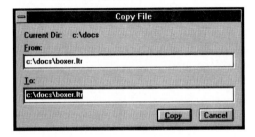

Type a path into the To text box; for example **c:\business\boxer.ltr** to copy *boxer.ltr* to the directory *c:\business*, or **a:\boxer.ltr** to copy *boxer.ltr* to the floppy disk in drive A, and choose Copy. (As a shortcut, you can leave out the filename. For instance, instead of typing **c:\business\boxer.ltr**, simply type **c:\business**. Wordperfect assumes you wish to copy the file using the same filename.) You can also copy a file into the same directory but with a different filename. Type the current directory but a new filename. For instance, type **c:\docs\smyth.ltr** to copy the contents of *boxer.ltr* into a new file named *smyth.ltr* in the same directory and choose Copy.

The Move/Rename option lets you move the selected file from one directory to another, or rename a file. Choose Move/Rename and the Move/Rename File dialog box appears listing the selected file as the one to be moved or renamed.

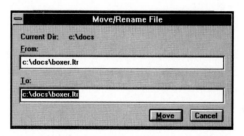

To move the file, type in the To text box the directory where you wish to move the file to, such as **c:\business** or **a:**. To rename the file, type the new filename, for example **smyth.ltr**, into the To text box. To move *and* rename the file in one command, type in the To text box both the new directory path and the new filename, such as **c:\business\smyth.ltr** or **a:\smyth.ltr**. Then choose Move.

Viewing a File on Disk

The View feature is a convenient way to check the contents of a file on disk before you delete, copy, move, or rename it. You can also use the View feature to verify that a file contains the document you wish to open before you actually open it.

The View feature is accessed from the Open File dialog box or the Retrieve File dialog box. In the dialog box, select (highlight) in the Files list

16

box the file you wish to view, and choose <u>V</u>iew. The Open File dialog box moves to the left to make way for a View window that displays the contents of the selected file. An example is shown in Figure 16-7.

You cannot make editing changes in the View window, but you can move through the entire document. Using your mouse, you can use the View window's scroll bar to scroll through the file. Using your keyboard, you can make the View window active by pressing (ALT) + (F6), and you can then scroll through the file using the arrow keys. You can also view a different file by switching back to the Open File dialog box and selecting a new filename; the View window will update to show that new file's contents. To close the View window when it is active, double-click the View control-menu box or press (ALT) + (F4).

Finding a File

No matter how diligent you are about assigning each file a unique filename, once numerous files are accumulated on disk, it becomes difficult

Figure 16-7.   *View window showing the contents of the file named* first

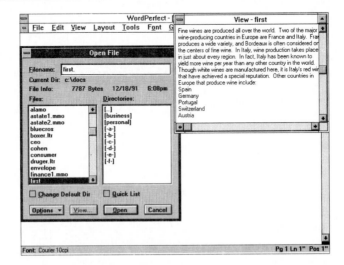

to remember which file contains which document. The Find feature can hunt down documents for you, either based on a file's *name* or a file's *contents*.

To initiate the Find feature, choose File, Open or File, Retrieve to display the Open File or Retrieve File dialog box. Then, choose the Options command button to display a pop-up list, and choose Find. The Find dialog box shown in Figure 16-8 appears.

Searching by Filenames

To search for a file according to its filename, choose Find Files from the Find dialog box. The Find Files dialog box appears, as shown here:

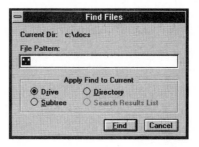

In the File Pattern text box, type a file pattern for the file that you are looking for. You can use the asterisk (*) to represent any number of charac-

16

Figure 16-8.   *Find dialog box*

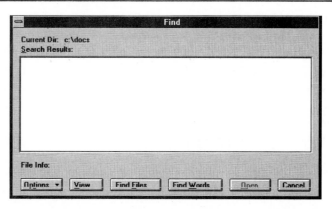

ters, and the question mark (?) to represent one character. For instance, type ***.ltr** to find all files with a *.ltr* file extension, such as *smith01.ltr* or *jones.ltr*. Then, indicate which of the following you want to search:

- *Directory*   Choose <u>D</u>irectory to search the current directory, which is the one listed at the top of the dialog box, such as *c:\docs*.

- *Subtree*   Choose <u>S</u>ubtree to search the current directory and all of its subdirectories, such as *c:\docs*, *c:\docs\business*, and *c:\docs\personal*.

- *Drive*   Choose D<u>r</u>ive to search all directories in the current drive, such as all the directories on drive C, including *c:*, *c:\docs* and all its subdirectories, *c:\wpwin* and all its subdirectories, and so on.

- *Search Results <u>L</u>ist*   Choose Search Results <u>L</u>ist to search all the files displayed in the <u>S</u>earch Results list box. (This option is available only after you have already undertaken a search and files are listed.)

Choose <u>F</u>ind to begin the search. Any files that match the file pattern are listed in the <u>S</u>earch Results list box.

Searching by File Contents

To search for a file according to its contents, choose Find <u>W</u>ords from the Find dialog box. The Find Words dialog box appears. In the <u>W</u>ord Pattern text box, type a word pattern for the word or words for which you want to search.

For a word pattern, you can use the asterisk (*) to represent any number of characters, and the question mark (?) to represent one character. Use a dash (-) to find files that do not contain the search word. For instance, the word pattern **wine*** will find documents that contain the words "wine", "wines", "winemaker", "winemakers", "winery", and "wineries", just to name a few. The word pattern **w?ne** will find documents that contain the words "wane" and "wine". The word pattern **–grapes** will find all documents that do not contain the word "grapes".

If the word pattern contains two or more words, you can separate the words by semicolons (;) or spaces to represent "and" and by commas to represent "or". If you type the words in quotation marks, the words are treated as a distinct phrase (group of words in succession) that must be located. For instance, the word pattern **wine;price** will locate files that contain both the word "wine" and the word "price". The pattern **wine, price** will locate files that contain either the word "wine" or the word "price". The pattern **"wine price"** will locate files that contain the phrase "wine price".

You can combine all these symbols in word patterns. For instance, the pattern **wine*;"Sonoma County";-Chardonnay** will locate files that: contain words such as "wine", "wines", "winegrower", "winery", and "wineries"; and contain the phrase "Sonoma County"; and do not contain the word "Chardonnay".

Once you type in a word pattern, indicate whether you want to search through the Directory, Subtree, Drive, or Search Results List. The search begins when you choose Find. Any files that contain text that matches the word pattern are listed in the Search Results list box.

Find Options

Once a list of files is displayed in the Search Results list box, you can then perform another search. Or, you can select (highlight) a file in the list and then choose one of the following: Options to display a pop-up list with items for copying, deleting, or moving/renaming the file; View to view the file's contents; or Open to open it into the document workspace.

16

Creating a Document Summary

The Document Summary feature attaches a summary form to a file. The form helps you keep track of the contents of or progress on a document and is often useful for billing purposes. It makes it possible to search for a file based on specific document summary categories, such as subject, author, or typist, when using the File Manager (the File Manager is described later in this chapter).

You can create a summary before or after you complete the document. Your insertion point can be located anywhere in the text. Choose Layout, Document, Summary and a Document Summary dialog box like the one shown in Figure 16-9 appears. The Creation Date and Revision Date text boxes are automatically filled in. The creation date is the date that the document summary was created, which is the current date if you are creating the document summary for the first time. The revision date is the date of the

Figure 16-9.   *Document Summary dialog box before entries are typed*

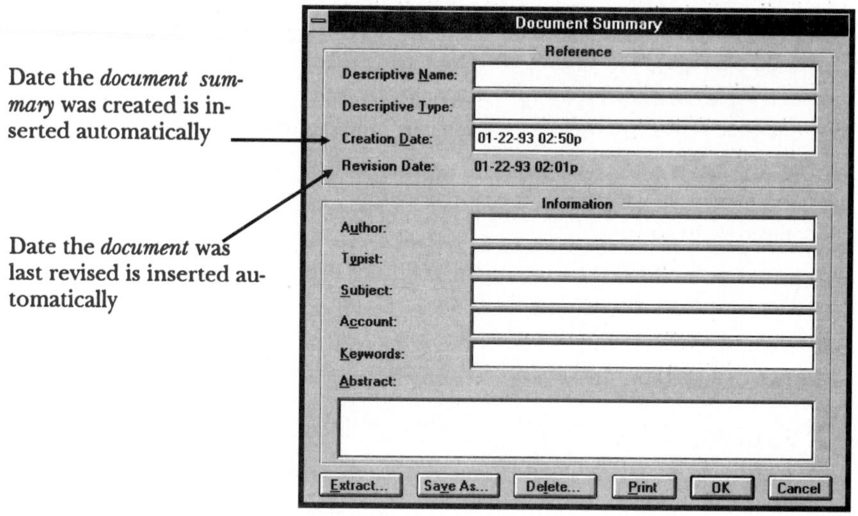

Date the *document summary* was created is inserted automatically

Date the *document* was last revised is inserted automatically

most recent revision of the document—you cannot change this date. (If the document has yet to be saved and edited, no revision date appears.)

Now you can type entries into those text boxes that you wish to complete in the document summary. You need not fill out all the items, but only those that will be useful for future reference. Items include:

- *Descriptive Name,* a detailed name that is longer than the filename
- *Descriptive Type,* an item for categorizing your documents, such as "memo" for a memorandum, or "report" for a report
- *Creation Date,* the date the summary was created (as previously discussed)
- *Author and Typist,* the author and typist of the document, who may or may not be the same individual
- *Subject,* the subject of the document

- *Account,* an additional text box to identify the document, such as with an account or client number

- *Keywords,* an additional text box to help identify the document by words that represent topics covered in the document

- *Abstract,* a brief summary of a document's contents

If your entries will duplicate most of the entries you made in the last document summary, instead of typing information, you can choose the Extract command button and then choose Yes. WordPerfect will automatically fill in the Author and Typist items with the entries you made in the most recent document summary that you created. WordPerfect will fill in the Abstract item with the first 400 characters of the document. Finally, WordPerfect will search for the text "RE:", and fill in the Subject item with the text immediately following the text, either the first 150 characters or the characters up to the first hard return, whichever comes first.

Once the document summary is complete, you can choose OK to save the summary and return to your document. You can view it anytime by returning to the Document Summary dialog box. You can also print or delete the summary by selecting the Print or Delete command button. Or, choose Save As to save a document summary as text into another file. This allows you to append a copy of some or all of your document summaries into one file, which is a convenient way of compiling a list of all the documents you authored or typed, or for compiling a list of all the documents you created for a particular client.

note   *You can also print a document summary from the Print dialog box. Choose File, Print, and either Multiple Pages or Document on Disk and choose Print. Then, if you turn on the Document Summary check box, the document summary will print along with any other pages that you specify.*

You can change the settings that determine how the Document Summary feature operates. For instance, you can have WordPerfect prompt you to create a document summary every time you save a new document. The File, Preferences, Document Summary command controls the changes, as described in Chapter 17.

Working with Directories

As you know, a hard disk can be divided into directories just like a file cabinet is organized into file drawers. You can organize your files into separate directories according to their contents, and maintain an efficient and orderly filing system. For instance, you will want to keep your document files separate from the WordPerfect program files (those files that make Word-Perfect run) and separate from program files for other applications.

WordPerfect offers special features for managing the directories that hold your files. These features are described next: changing the default directory, establishing a Quick List of directories, and using the File Manager to create and keep track of the contents of directories.

Changing the Default Directory

You learned in Chapter 4 that in WordPerfect, one directory is the default or current directory, which is the directory where WordPerfect assumes you wish to save files to and recall files from. This directory is displayed when you first open a dialog box that contains a directories list, such as the Open File, Retrieve, or Save As dialog box. In Figure 16-6, for instance, *c:\docs* is listed as the current directory.

You also learned in Chapter 4 how to use the File, Preferences, Location of Files command to designate one directory as the permanent default directory—the one that WordPerfect assumes each time when you first start up WordPerfect. For instance, you may have designated *c:\docs* as your permanent default. In that case, *c:\docs* is the directory that is always displayed as the current directory when you first start up WordPerfect. You also learned that, during a working session, you can change the current directory so that you can save files to and recall files from directories.

When you change the current directory, how long this change takes effect depends on the status of the Change Default Dir check box, a box that sits near the bottom of the Open File dialog box (or any other dialog box that contains a directories list).

When you change to a new directory and the Change Default Dir check box is on (the box is checked), the new directory becomes the default or current directory. It remains in effect until you change it or end your working session.

When you change to a new directory and the Change Default Dir check box is off (the box is unchecked), the change is only temporary. The default directory is unaffected.

For instance, suppose you choose File, Open to display the Open File dialog box and *c:\docs* is listed as the current directory. Then, suppose you change to *c:\docs\business* to search through that directory, and open a file from that directory. If the Change Default Dir check box was on, *c:\docs\business* is the new current directory. If the check box was off, *c:\docs* remains as the current directory.

Use the Change Default Dir check box strategically. For instance, you may wish to open files from various directories, and change the default directory every time. In that case, keep the Change Default Dir feature turned on. As another example, you may wish to change the default directory once, and then maintain the new default directory. In that case, turn on the Change Default Dir check box, select a new directory, and choose Open. The next time you display the Open File dialog box, you can turn this check box off.

Working with Quick Lists

16

If you have a large hard disk or work with a network, you probably have already created (or intend to create) separate directories for different types of files. For instance, you may have directories for program files, for example *c:\wpwin* for WordPerfect files, *c:\wpwin\macros* for WordPerfect macro files, and *c:\wpwin\printers* for WordPerfect printer files. Then, you may have one directory for all your word processing files, such as *c:\docs*, which is subdivided into personal and business files, *c:\docs\personal* and *c:\docs\business*. Then, perhaps your business files are subdivided further still.

Keeping track of the labyrinth of paths is difficult. Moreover, when you need access to a file, maneuvering through directories in the Open File, Retrieve, or Save As dialog box, or typing a path, is also difficult. The Quick List feature will make the process of working with directories a lot easier.

With the Quick List feature, you can create descriptive names to represent all the directories that you use frequently. For instance, suppose you save files most often to nine different directories. You can create a quick list as follows:

Quick List Name	Corresponding Directory Path
A: Drive (Floppy Disk)	a:\
Business Letters	c:\docs\business\ltrs
Business Reports	c:\docs\business\rpts
General Documents	c:\docs
Graphics Files	c:\wpwin\graphics
Magazine Articles	c:\docs\personal\mags
Personal Documents	c:\docs\personal
Spreadsheet Files	c:\123\data
WordPerfect Macros	c:\wpwin\macros

From then on, you can maneuver through directories in the Open File, Retrieve File, and Save As dialog boxes by their Quick List names, rather than their long and difficult path names. (The Change Default Dir check box, discussed in the previous section, still applies when you use the Quick List; the only difference is that the default directory is referred to by *name* rather than by directory path.)

When you installed WordPerfect, several Quick List items may have been set up for you, such as *c:\wpwin\graphics* for your graphics files directory and *c:\wpwin\macros* for a macro directory, and another for your document directory.

By default, the Quick List is off. To turn on the Quick List, open a dialog box that contains a directories list (such as the Open File, Retrieve, or Save As dialog box) and choose Quick List to place an X in the Quick List check box. The Directories list box is replaced by a Quick List, as shown in the Open File dialog box in Figure 16-10. You now have quicker and easier access to your files.

As long as the Quick List box is checked, the feature is turned on for all the dialog boxes that involve opening, retrieving, or saving files—for the current session and for all future WordPerfect sessions until you turn off the feature. To turn off the feature, choose Quick List again to uncheck the check box.

When the Quick List displays, you can alter items in the list. Choose Edit Quick List, a new command button that appears in the Open File dialog box whenever the Quick List feature is on. Now, you can delete, add, or edit a Quick List entry.

To delete a Quick List entry, select (highlight) the entry; its corresponding directory name appears at the bottom of the dialog box. Choose Delete.

Figure 16-10.   *Open File dialog box with the Quick List feature turned on*

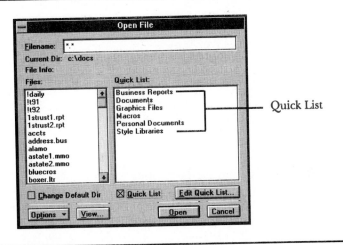

Quick List

To add a Quick List entry, choose <u>A</u>dd. An Add Quick List Item dialog box appears, as shown here:

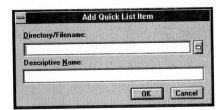

Type a directory name (such as **c:\docs\business**) in the <u>D</u>irectory/Filename text box or click on the file button, just to the right of this text box to select the appropriate directory. Then, type a descriptive name, which will appear on the Quick List, in the Descriptive <u>N</u>ame text box. Choose OK. The descriptive name appears as an entry in the Quick List.

You are not limited to adding a Quick List entry that represents a directory. A Quick List entry can represent a specific file, such as a file that you use often. Type the full path of the file, such as **c:\docs\business\accts.new**, into the <u>D</u>irectory/Filename text box. A Quick List entry can also represent a group of files. Type a filename pattern into the <u>D</u>irectory/Filename text box, where you use the asterisk (*) to represent any number of characters and the question mark (?) to represent any one character. For instance, type **c:\docs*.ltr** to represent files in the *c:\docs* directory with a *.ltr* extension.

To edit a Quick List entry, select (highlight) the entry; its corresponding directory name appears at the bottom of the dialog box. Choose Edit, and then make any changes on the Edit Quick List Item dialog box that appears.

Another method for creating and editing Quick List entries is with the File, Preferences, Location of Files command. See Chapter 17 for details.

Using the File Manager

The File Manager helps you organize and work with files stored on disk. It is a program that is packaged with, but separate from WordPerfect. You can run the File Manager without running WordPerfect, or you can access the File Manager from within WordPerfect. To start the File Manager from within WordPerfect, choose File, File Manager. After a few moments, the program is loaded, and appears on screen. Figure 16-11 shows how the File Manager window appears the first time you open it. (You can select various options to change the layout of the File Manager.)

The File Manager offers a number of features that are also available (although more limited) in WordPerfect—such as the ability to delete, copy, or rename files, or the ability to find files based on a filename or word pattern.

Three of the most important features of the File Manager—unavailable in WordPerfect and therefore of great interest to WordPerfect users—are the ability to create a directory, to get essential background information about your computer, and to start other applications.

The File Manager enables you to create new directories on your hard disk. To create a new directory, choose File, Create Directory, type a name for the directory (such as **c:\docs**, **c:\docs\business**, or **c:\work**) and choose Create. You can use this procedure to create directories for each type of document that you create, and then copy all pertinent files to the new directories that you created.

The File Manager provides background information on your computer system, your Windows program, your printers (using Windows printer driv-

Figure 16-11. *WordPerfect File Manager*

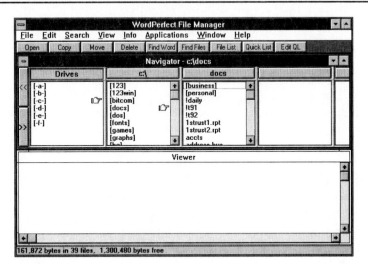

ers) and your disks. Choose Info, and then choose from: Disk Info, Printer Info, System Info, or Windows Info. You can ascertain how much space is still available on a floppy or hard disk for storing files, for example, or get information on the amount of free memory on your computer system. You can also choose Print Info Report to print out this information.

You can also start other applications from the File Manager. For instance, you can load a drawing program such as CorelDRAW, and then switch back and forth between CorelDRAW and WordPerfect. To load another application, choose File, Run. Then, type in the name of the executable file that controls the application you wish to load. (An executable file usually has an *.exe*, *.com*, or *.bat* extension.) Then choose Run to start up the application. The ability to work with multiple applications in Windows depends on the amount of memory and type of computer you have; see your Windows manual for details.

Use the File Manager's Help feature accessed by choosing Help, to discover more about how the File Manager operates. See Appendix C for instructions on how to use WordPerfect's Help feature, which works the same way.

16

When you're ready to return to WordPerfect, you can exit the File Manager window in a number of different ways: by choosing File, Exit; double-clicking the File Manager application control-menu box; or pressing (ALT) + (F4).

Sharing with Other Applications

WordPerfect 5.1—whether for Windows or for DOS—creates files in WP 5.1 format. Since they use the same file format, no conversion is necessary to use a file in either WordPerfect 5.1 for Windows or WordPerfect 5.1 for DOS.

Other applications, however, usually have a different format than WordPerfect 5.1. WordPerfect allows you to share with other applications by: converting files to/from other applications; transferring text to/from other application windows; and importing and linking spreadsheets.

Converting Files To and From WordPerfect

WordPerfect converts document files *on the fly*—meaning that a file is converted from another format into WP 5.1 format as you open it into the document workspace. You can convert files created by a wide variety of applications.

Conversely, you can convert a WordPerfect file into a variety of applications. The list of applications is updated regularly, and includes:

- Various versions of Ami Pro, MultiMate, Microsoft Word, DisplayWrite, OfficeWriter, WordStar, and XyWrite.

- ASCII Text (DOS) and ANSI Text (Windows) formats, which are the standards used by DOS and Windows applications, respectively. Files contain text, spaces, and carriage returns.

- ASCII Generic Word Processor (DOS) and ANSI Generic Word Processor (Windows) formats, which are similar to the previously mentioned formats but preserve more of the special formatting. These formats are more appropriate when you plan to use the converted file in another word processing program.

- Rich Text Format (RTF), a standard format in Windows applications, where fonts and many types of formatting (such as indents, tables, and font attributes) are preserved.

- WordPerfect 5.1, 5.0, and 4.2 formats, when you wish to edit or use files in these versions of WordPerfect. Unless you specify otherwise, WordPerfect for Windows saves files in WordPerfect 5.1 format. You may wish to save files into WordPerfect 5.0 or 4.2 format, for example, if you use WordPerfect 5.1 for Windows but the person across town who edits your documents uses WordPerfect 5.0 for DOS.

- ASCII Delimited Text (DOS) and ANSI Delimited Text (Windows), used to retrieve data from your DOS or Windows application (spreadsheet or database application that had been saved in this format) into a WordPerfect secondary merge file. Files contain delimiters, or characters, which mark the beginning and end of each field or record.

To convert a file into WP 5.1 format, follow these steps in WordPerfect:

1. Choose File, Open.

2. Type the name of the file you wish to convert and choose Open. A Convert File Format dialog box appears.

3. If the format that WordPerfect suggests you are converting from is the correct format, choose OK. The document is opened on screen.

   If the format is incorrect, select a different format from the pop-up list and choose OK. (Be sure to scroll to see the complete list.)

You can now edit the document as you would any other document in WordPerfect. Certain formatting features may not be common to WordPerfect and the other application. As a result, your document may not look the same after having been converted, and you may need to adjust the layout of the text.

You will want to save this converted document into WordPerfect 5.1 format if you wish to use it again in WordPerfect. Choose File, Save As, just as you do when saving a new document. Type in a new filename if you wish

16

to preserve the original file in the original format. Then, be sure to select WP 5.1 from the Format pop-up list box near the bottom of the Save As dialog box before you choose Save.

You can also convert a WordPerfect document to another format. To do so, the WordPerfect document you wish to convert must be in the document workspace. Then, follow these steps:

1. Choose File, Save As.
2. Type a name into the Filename text box.
3. Choose Format, and select the file format you want from the pop-up list that appears. (Be sure to scroll to see the complete list.)
4. Choose Save.

Transferring and Linking Information

Windows lets you work with many applications at one time. For instance, you can work with WordPerfect for Windows and with Lotus 1-2-3 for Windows simultaneously. This is because windows can *multitask*, which means that it can perform tasks in several applications simultaneously. Each application is in a separate window, and you can switch back and forth between different application windows, or you can resize the windows so they all appear on screen at the same time.

You can transfer information between applications via the Clipboard, which, as discussed in Chapter 8, is a place where information can be temporarily stored. The Clipboard is a feature shared by all Windows applications, which is what makes the transfers possible. You can move or copy text from one application to another, simply by following these steps:

1. Cut or copy selected text from a Windows application. For instance, select text in WordPerfect and choose Edit, Cut. The selected text is placed on the Clipboard.
2. Switch to the other Windows application. One quick method (as previously described in this chapter when discussing how to switch to the Print Manager) is to press (CTRL) + (ESC). A Task List dialog

box appears on screen, with all the open applications listed. Select the application you wish to switch to and choose Switch To.

3. In the other Windows application, position the insertion point where you want to insert the text, and choose Edit, Paste.

Check your Windows manual for details on related issues, such as: how to work with multiple applications; how to use the Clipboard to transfer information between WordPerfect and a non-Windows application; and how to resize and move application windows so that you can display several at one time, which makes the process of cutting and copying even easier. (Chapter 10 also describes how to resize and move the WordPerfect application window.)

You also have the option of creating a link between a WordPerfect document and a *source file*, which is a file created in any other Windows application—whether a text file, spreadsheet file, graphics file, database file, or another type of file. The only stipulation is that the Windows application must support Dynamic Data Exchange (DDE), a medium by which Windows applications transfer information.

The DDE Link feature creates a bond between the source file and the WordPerfect file, so that every time you alter data in the source file, the WordPerfect file can be updated. Before starting the following steps, be sure both the source file and the WordPerfect file are open.

1. Cut or copy selected data from the source file.

2. Switch to WordPerfect and position the insertion point where you want to insert the data.

3. Choose Edit, Link, Paste Link. (If the Paste Link option is dimmed, the source file is not allowing this feature to operate.) A copy of the selected data is placed in the WordPerfect document, and a link is created.

Whenever you change the source file, update the link manually in WordPerfect by choosing Edit, Link, Update and selecting the links you wish to update.

You can also create a DDE link when the source file is not open. With the insertion point in the WordPerfect file where you want to insert the data,

16

choose <u>E</u>dit, <u>L</u>ink, <u>C</u>reate and then indicate the name of the Windows application and the source file that is involved in the link. You will also name the link, and select whether you want the link to update automatically or whether you want to update manually when information changes in the source file.

Spreadsheet Importing and Linking

You may use a spreadsheet application such as Lotus 1-2-3 and its sophisticated mathematical abilities, to calculate numeric information. However, when you're ready to produce a document showing your number-crunching results, these applications don't offer the sophisticated word processing capabilities of WordPerfect. With WordPerfect's Spreadsheet Import and Link features, you can calculate in the Spreadsheet, and then bring the completed results into a final report created in WordPerfect.

Compatible applications for spreadsheet imports and links include: PlanPerfect version 3.0 through 5.1, Lotus 1-2-3 versions 1.0 through 3.1, Excel versions 2.0 through 3.0, Quattro, and Quattro Pro. Thus, this method provides an option for a wider variety of spreadsheet applications than is possible with the DDE Link feature, which was described in the previous section.

There is a difference between importing and linking a spreadsheet. When you *import* the spreadsheet into a WordPerfect document, you are actually retrieving it into the document—either as text (20 columns maximum in a row) or as a table (32 columns maximum). It is a one-time retrieval. Conversely, when you *link* the spreadsheet to a WordPerfect document, you create a bond between those two files; every time you alter the spreadsheet, you can manually or automatically update the data in your WordPerfect document as well.

To import information or create a link, position the insertion point where you want to import the spreadsheet file and choose <u>T</u>ools, Spr<u>e</u>adsheet. Then, choose either <u>I</u>mport or <u>C</u>reate and type the filename of the spreadsheet file into the <u>F</u>ilename text box. (You can also type a range of cells or a range name, when you wish to import only a section of a spreadsheet file.) Finally, select <u>T</u>able or Te<u>x</u>t depending on whether you want to import the spreadsheet file as a table or as text, and choose OK.

If you imported the spreadsheet, it is retrieved into the document, and the process is complete.

If you created a spreadsheet link, [Link] and [Link End] codes are inserted around the imported spreadsheet. Should the contents of the linked spreadsheet file change, you can update the link manually in a WordPerfect document. Choose Tools, Spreadsheet, Update All Links, Yes. Or, you can have the link updated automatically every time you open or retrieve the WordPerfect file containing the link codes, by choosing Tools, Spreadsheet, Link Options and turning on the Update on Retrieve option. At the same time, you can turn on the Show Link Codes option to display beginning and ending link comments for an indication of where a link begins and ends in your document.

Quick Reference

- To preview the layout of a document before printing, choose File, Print Preview. You can view full pages, or zoom in to examine details on a section of page.

- To pause, resume, or cancel a print job after it has been processed by WordPerfect, you must switch to the Print Manager. Press (CTRL) + (ESC), select the Print Manager from the list of open applications that displays, and choose Switch To.

- To select a printer, choose File, Select Printer. You can select a printer that uses either a WordPerfect or Windows printer driver.

- To initialize your printer, downloading soft fonts to your printer's memory, choose File, Print, Initialize Printer. You must initialize your printer when you turn it on if you wish to use any soft fonts that are marked as present when a print job begins.

16

Quick Reference *(continued)*

- To manage files on disk, use features accessed from the Open File dialog box or other dialog boxes where files are listed. You can delete, copy, move, rename, or find a file when you choose Options, and view the contents of a file on disk when you choose View.

- To password-protect a file, choose File, Password. You cannot open or print a file that is locked with a password without knowing the password.

- To create a document summary that contains background information on the contents of a document, choose Layout, Document, Summary.

- To get more direct access to directories you use often, create a Quick List. Turn on the Quick List check box in a dialog box that contains a directory list, such as the Open File dialog box. Choose Edit Quick List if you wish to add, edit, or delete Quick List items.

- To use a document file created by another application in WordPerfect, choose File, Open. The Convert File format dialog box appears so that you can convert the file into WP 5.1 format, the format used in WordPerfect for Windows. You can also paste data created by another application into a WordPerfect document or link data to a WordPerfect document.

17

Tailoring WordPerfect to Your Needs

Chances are that if you dislike how a certain feature or option operates in WordPerfect, you can change it. This chapter describes how to tailor Word-Perfect to your equipment, to your special formatting needs, or to your working habits. For example, you can change the colors displayed so that the screen is as comfortable as possible for your eyes. You can change the initial settings for left/right margins to those that match the margins you use most often. Or, you can change features so that WordPerfect for Windows operates more like WordPerfect 5.1 for DOS does.

You can tailor WordPerfect for Windows in two ways. For procedures that are specific to WordPerfect, you use the Preferences feature. For procedures that affect not only WordPerfect but also other Windows applications, you use the Windows Control Panel. Both are discussed in this chapter.

Working with the Preferences Feature

The designers of WordPerfect made certain assumptions about how the program would operate once installed on your computer. Some of these default or initial settings relate to how a certain WordPerfect feature or option operates—such as how often the Backup feature stores backup copies of documents, or how the ruler works, or whether the scroll bars are displayed. Other initial settings determine a WordPerfect document's layout—such as the initial margin settings, the initial justification settings, or the initial format for the date. A list of WordPerfect's initial settings is displayed in Table 17-1. These represent the settings that WordPerfect Corporation believes most individuals prefer.

Realizing that different individuals have different preferences, however, WordPerfect offers the ability to change any of the initial settings listed in Table 17-1.

You change the settings by choosing File, Preferences and selecting one of the following items from the Preferences cascading menu shown here:

Then you specify the setting you want.

$\overline{\text{CTRL}}$ + $\overline{\text{SHIFT}}$ + $\overline{\text{F1}}$ *is the shortcut for* File, Preferences.

Once you make a change to an initial setting, the change is saved on disk in a file that begins with *wp* and has a *.set* extension, as, for example, *wp{wp}.set*. The file holding your change will be located in the directory where the WordPerfect program is stored, usually *c:\wpwin*.

Sometimes, however, a change is stored in another special file that begins with *wp* and has an *.ini* extension, as, for example, *wpc.ini*. This file will be

Table 17-1. *Initial Settings (As Established by WordPerfect Corporation) that Can Be Altered with Preferences*

Feature	Initial Setting
Auto Code Placement	On
Auto Redisplay in Draft Mode	On
Backup	
Minutes Between Timed Backups	20
Original Document Backup	Off
Times Document Backup	On
Beep	
On Error	Off
On Hyphenation	On
On Search Failure	Off
Columns Side by Side Display	On
Comments Display	On
Confirm on Code Deletion	Off
Date Format	[Month][Day#],[Year ####]
Decimal Alignment Character	. (period)
Document Summary	
Create Summary on Save/Exit	Off
Subject Search Text	RE:
Equations	
Graphical Font Size	Default
Horizontal Alignment	Center
Keyboard	Current WP
Print As Graphics	On
Vertical Alignment	Center
Fast Save	On
Force Odd/Even Current Page	Off

17

Table 17-1.   *Initial Settings (As Established by WordPerfect Corporation) that*
               Can Be Altered with Preferences (continued)

Feature	Initial Setting
Format Retrieved Documents for Default Printer	On
Hard Return Display Character	None
Hyphenation	Off
Hyphenation Dictionary	External
Hyphenation Zone	
Left	10 percent
Right	4 percent
Justification	Left
Kerning	Off
Keyboard Layout	CUA Compatible
Last Open Filenames Display	On
Letter Spacing	WordPerfect Optimal
Line Height	Auto
Line Height Fixed Height	.167 inch
Line Height Adjustment (Leading)	
Between Lines	0 inch
Between Paragraphs	0 inch
Line Numbering	Off
Line Spacing	1
Location of Files	Set during installation
Margins (left/right/top/bottom)	1 inch
Merge Codes Display	On
Merge Field Delimiters	
Begin	None
End	, (comma)
Merge Record Delimiters	
Begin	None

Table 17-1. *Initial Settings (As Established by WordPerfect Corporation) that Can Be Altered with Preferences (continued)*

Feature	Initial Setting
Merge Record Delimiters	
End	[CR]
Page Numbering Position	No Page Numbering
Page Numbering Type	Arabic
Page Size	8.5 x 11 inches (US Version)
Paper Type	Standard
Print Settings	
Binding Offset	0 inch
Fast Graphics Printing	On
Graphics Quality	Medium
Multiple Copies Generated by	WordPerfect
Number of Copies	1
Text Quality	High
Prompt for Hyphenation	When Required
Redline Method	Printer Dependent
Ruler, Automatic Display	Off
Ruler Buttons on Top	Off
Ruler Guides Display	On
Scroll Bar, Vertical Display	On
Scroll Bar, Horizontal Display	Off
Sculptured Dialog Boxes	On
Shortcut Keys Display	On
Size Attribute Ratios (Percent of Normal)	
Fine	60 percent
Small	80 percent
Large	120 percent
Very Large	150 percent

17

Table 17-1.   *Initial Settings (As Established by WordPerfect Corporation) that
                  Can Be Altered with Preferences (continued)*

Feature	Initial Setting
Size Attribute Ratios	
Extra Large	200 percent
Superscript/Subscript	60 percent
Suppress Page Format	Off
Tab Set	0.5-inch intervals
Tab Set Position	Relative to Left Margin
Tabs Snap to Ruler Grid	On
Table of Authorities	
Blank Lines Between Authorities	On
Dot Leaders	On
Underlining Allowed	Off
Undo	On
Units of Measure	
Display and Entry of Numbers	Inches (")
Status Bar Display	Inches (")
Widow/Orphan Protection	Off
Word Spacing	WordPerfect Optimal
Word Spacing Justification Limits	
Compressed to	60 percent
Expanded to	400 percent

found in the *c:\windows* directory. The change goes into effect immediately, and stays in effect until you change the option again.

A description of each item on the Preferences menu is described in the following sections.

Location of Files

Choose File, Preferences, Location of Files to display the dialog box shown in Figure 17-1. This option determines the default directory in effect for certain files—indicating to WordPerfect where files should be stored or looked for—each time you start WordPerfect. (If a location for the files is not specified, WordPerfect assumes that the files are located either in the default directory or in the directory where the main WordPerfect program files are stored, usually *c:\wpwin*.) Each item in Figure 17-1 is explained here.

- *Backup Files* You specify the directory where WordPerfect will store the timed backup files, such as *wp{wp}.bk1*, using the Backup Files text box. (See the "Backup" section following this one for more on the Backup feature.)
- *Documents* You specify the directory where you will store your documents using the Documents text box. The directory you enter

Figure 17-1. *Location of Files dialog box*

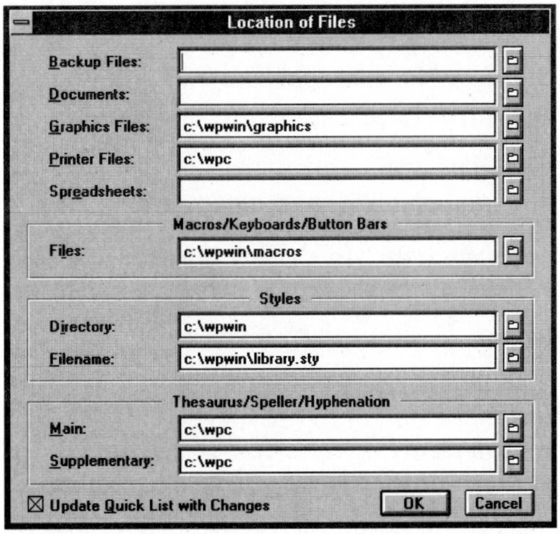

here will become the current (or default) directory in the Open File, Retrieve File, and Save As dialog boxes each time you start Word-Perfect, and will remain the current directory unless you change it for just a single work session (as described in Chapter 16).

- *Graphics Files*   You specify the directory for your graphics files (such as the graphics files ending with the *.wpg* extension that came packaged with WordPerfect) using the Graphics Files text box. The directory you enter will become the default graphics directory each time you start WordPerfect and also the directory where Word-Perfect looks for files when you use the Graphic on Disk option. (See Chapter 12.)

- *Printer Files*   Specify the directory for files with an *.all* or *.prs* extension using the Printer Files text box. The *.all* files are those that contain printer drivers for a variety of printers, (these files are created when you install WordPerfect). The *.prs* files are created by you when you select a specific WordPerfect printer driver.

- *Spreadsheets*   Specify in the Spreadsheets text box the directory that WordPerfect will assume for spreadsheet files when using the Spreadsheet Import or Spreadsheet Link feature.

- *Macros/Keyboards/Button Bars Files*   Specify in the Files text box the directory where WordPerfect will look for macros (files with a *.wcm* extension), keyboards (files with a *.wwk* extension), and button bars (files with a *.wwb* extension).

- *Styles Directory*   Specify in the Directory text box which directory WordPerfect will search for style files.

- *Styles Filename*   In the Filename text box specify the directory and filename for the file that serves as your default style library, that is, your list of styles that is retrieved whenever you display the Styles dialog box for a new document. For instance, if you decide to use the style library that comes packaged with WordPerfect, (assuming that you installed WordPerfect using the basic procedure where it is installed into the directory *c:\wpwin*), the styles filename would be *c:\wpwin\library.sty*. Styles Filename is the only option in the Location of Files dialog box in which you must indicate not only a directory, but also a specific filename.

- *Thesaurus/Speller/Hyphenation <u>M</u>ain*   Specify in the <u>M</u>ain text box which directory WordPerfect will search for the main thesaurus, speller, and hyphenation files.

- *Thesaurus/Speller/Hyphenation <u>S</u>upplementary*   Specify in the Sup-plementary text box which directory WordPerfect will search for the supplementary thesaurus, speller, and hyphenation files.

Choose an option from the Location of Files dialog box, and then type in the directory you desire. You can also choose the file button—the picture of a file folder located just to the right of the option—to search through your hard disk and select a directory.

If you type in a directory name, and that directory does not currently exist on your hard disk, WordPerfect will display a dialog box asking whether you wish to create the directory immediately.

Once you change or add an item in the Location of Files dialog box, be sure that the proper files are located there. For instance, suppose you choose the <u>G</u>raphics Files text box and enter **c:\graphics**. In that case, copy all your graphics files to that new directory.

An Update <u>Q</u>uick List with Changes check box is found at the bottom of the Location of Files dialog box in Figure 17-1. When this option is on (checked), any changes you make in the Location of Files dialog box will cause the Quick List to be updated. For instance, if you choose <u>D</u>ocuments and specify *c:\docs* as the directory, an item named "Documents" is added to the Quick List (or is modified if an item by that name already exists in the Quick List); the Documents item on the Quick List represents the *c:\docs* directory. When the Update <u>Q</u>uick List with Changes check box is off, changes in the Location of Files dialog box will have no effect on the Quick List. (See Chapter 16 for more on the Quick List feature.)

caution   *Many of the directories listed in the Location of Files dialog box are specified automatically by WordPerfect when the program is first installed. Depending on how you installed WordPerfect, there is, however, one important exception—the location for your document files. If the <u>D</u>ocuments text box is blank, WordPerfect assumes your files are opened from and retrieved to the same directory as where the WordPerfect program files are stored (usually c:\wpwin). As discussed in Chapter 4, this is unwise because it creates a poorly organized hard disk and increases the odds that you could inadvertently erase an important program file. Instead, if the <u>D</u>ocuments text box is*

17

blank, be sure to choose Documents and specify the directory that is to be used as the permanent default directory, the directory assumed each time you start WordPerfect. In this book, the permanent default directory suggestion is c:\docs. *You may choose another directory, for instance* c:\files *or* c:\wpwin\docs, *instead. After you specify a new default directory, you may wish to copy some or all of your preexisting document files into it.*

Backup

Choose Eile, Preferences, Backup to display the Backup dialog box shown here:

The Backup dialog box controls two different features that help protect you from the frustration of losing large amounts of work because of a machine or human error.

Timed Document Backup

The Timed Document Backup feature helps protect your work in the event of a machine or power failure. It instructs WordPerfect to save whatever documents you are currently working on into temporary backup files on disk at a specified time interval. For instance, suppose Timed Document Backup is set to save a file every 20 minutes—which is the initial setting. In that case, every 20 minutes, the mouse pointer will momentarily change to an hourglass and you will see the message "Timed Backup" on the status line. (After the first backup, a document is saved again at the time interval specified only if the document has been modified.) Your work is saved on disk. If you experience a power or machine failure, you can open the backup files, thus never losing more than your last 20 minutes of work.

It is advisable to keep the Timed Document Backup feature turned on. You may decide, however, to change the backup time interval. If even losing

20 minutes of work is too much, consider shortening the time interval, perhaps to every 10 minutes. The trade-off for this is that the backup takes a moment of time to store—a bit longer if you're working with a long document—so that a pause every 10 minutes may prove to be too time-consuming.

Backups are stored in files named *wp{wp}.bkn*, where the "n" represents the document window number. For instance, the backup for a document in the Document1 workspace is *wp{wp}.bk1* and in the Document2 workspace is *wp{wp}.bk2*. Backup files are stored in the directory you specify using the Location of Files feature (see the previous section). If no directory is specified, the backup files are stored in the same directory where the WordPerfect program files are stored, usually *c:\wpwin.* (If you're running WordPerfect on a network, the backup filename is *wp{uuu}.bkn,* where the "uuu" represents the user initials you entered when you loaded WordPerfect.)

WordPerfect deletes all these backup files when you exit normally from WordPerfect. However, if you instead experience a power or machine failure, the backup files remain on disk.

When you wish to recover the backup, simply load WordPerfect again. The next time you load (assuming the Timed Document Backup feature is on), a Timed Backup dialog box appears for each document window that was open before the power or machine failure. Here's an example for the Document1 window:

Choose <u>R</u>ename if you want to preserve the backup file but don't wish to examine it immediately. The File Rename dialog box appears so that you can type a new name for the backup file. Later, you can open the document.

Choose <u>O</u>pen if you want to open the backup file immediately and examine its contents. You can then choose to save the file, or to simply close the document without saving it.

Choose <u>D</u>elete if you are sure that you do not need the backup file. For instance, you may have saved the document on screen moments before the power failure. Or, you may have typed just a word or two into a blank document window moments before the power failure. When you choose <u>D</u>elete, the backup file is deleted.

17

Keep in mind that the Timed Document Backup feature is no substitute for saving a document with the Save or Save As feature. Since WordPerfect deletes the temporary files when you exit WordPerfect normally, Timed Backup is only of value in case of a power or machine failure.

Original Document Backup

The Original Document Backup feature helps protect your work if you inadvertently replace a document that you did not intend to replace. When you save a new version of a document on disk, it instructs WordPerfect to save the older (original) file with a *.bk!* extension, rather than delete it, before replacing it with the new version. This feature is turned off as an initial setting.

As an example of how Original Document Backup operates once it is turned on, suppose that you type and save on disk a document named *c:\docs\memo*. Next, you edit the document and save it again with the same filename. The new version is saved as *c:\docs\memo*, and the original version is saved as *c:\docs\memo.bk!*. Both versions are stored in the same directory.

Whenever you wish to recover an original backup file, simply open the file with the *.bk!* extension, and then save it with a name that doesn't have that extension so that you don't accidentally delete it later on when you save it again.

If you elect to turn on the Original Document Backup feature, be aware that files that share the same filename but have different extensions will use the same original backup file. So, for instance, if you have files named *memo.1* and *memo.2*, only one backup file will be created. The file, *memo.bk!* would be the backup for whichever file you last saved. Thus, if you use this feature, consider naming all your documents with a unique name (the eight characters that precede the period in the filename), and don't just give each a unique extension.

Environment

Choose File, Preferences, Environment to display the Environment Settings dialog box shown in Figure 17-2. You can determine how six related groups of features should operate in the WordPerfect environment, as described next.

Figure 17-2. *Environment Settings dialog box*

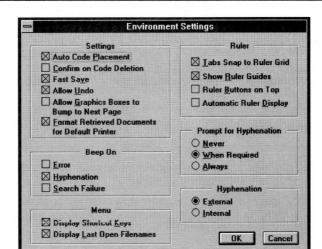

Settings

These items determine basic settings that affect how WordPerfect operates when editing a document and changing its layout.

Auto Code Placement   The default is to have Auto Code Placement turned on, so that certain layout codes are automatically placed in the most appropriate location on the page, depending on whether the format change was designed for insertion at the beginning of the page or the paragraph. If Auto Code Placement is on, two layout codes of the same type will not be duplicated on the same page or in the same paragraph.

The following layout codes are placed at the beginning of the current page, which means the beginning of the page where the insertion point is located when a change is made:

Center Page   Page Numbering
Headers/Footers   Paper Size
Margins—Top/Bottom   Suppress

The following layout codes are placed at the beginning of the current paragraph when a change is made:

Columns	Line Spacing
Hyphenation Zone	Margins—Left/Right
Justification	Outline
Letter Spacing	Tab Set
Line Height	Word Spacing
Line Numbering	Word Spacing Justification Limits

So, for example, if Auto Code Placement is on and you choose Layout, Page, Headers to insert a header, the header code will be inserted at the beginning of the current page. If another header code of the same type already exists on that page, the existing code is deleted when the new code is inserted. As another example, if you choose Layout, Line, Spacing or use the ruler to change line spacing, the line spacing code will be inserted at the beginning of the current paragraph. If another line spacing code already exists at the beginning of that paragraph, the existing code is deleted when the new code is inserted.

On the other hand, when the Auto Code Placement feature is off, all codes are inserted at the insertion point, and each change in the layout of the text will result in a new code. For instance, if you change line spacing twice in the same paragraph, both codes will be inserted. WordPerfect for Windows operates more closely to WordPerfect 5.1 for DOS when this feature is off.

Confirm on Code Deletion   The default is to have Confirm on Code Deletion turned off. As a result, most codes (exceptions include hard returns and Tab codes) cannot be deleted with the (DEL) or (BACKSPACE) key in the document workspace, only if you switch to the reveal codes workspace.

When this item is on, you can delete a code in the document workspace when you press (DEL) or (BACKSPACE). WordPerfect will ask whether you wish to delete the code. WordPerfect for Windows operates more closely to WordPerfect 5.1 for DOS when this feature is on.

Fast Save   The default is to have Fast Save turned on. As a result, WordPerfect saves files without first formatting them, effectively reducing the time it takes to save documents.

When Fast Save is off, saving takes a bit more time. The advantage, however, is that you will print a document from disk faster. If you typically print documents from disk more than from screen, you may wish to turn off this feature.

Allow Undo   The default is to have Allow Undo turned on, so that the Undo feature operates. If this item is turned off, the Undo feature does not operate, which will save you time during procedures involving the Select feature when you wish to work with large sections of text.

Allow Graphics Boxes to Bump to Next Page   The default is to have Allow Graphics Boxes to Bump to Next Page turned off. Thus, when you create a graphics box that is anchored to the page, the graphics box code is placed at the beginning of the current line and the graphics box will remain on the page, even when you type text in front of the code.

   If this item is turned on, the graphics box code is placed at the insertion point when you create a graphics box and WordPerfect moves the graphics box to the next page when you add text before the graphics box. WordPerfect for Windows operates more closely to WordPerfect 5.1 for DOS when this feature is on.

Format Retrieved Documents for Default Printer   The default is to have Format Retrieved Documents for Default Printer turned on. As a result, a document that you open is automatically formatted for the current printer, which may change the appearance of a document you created and saved for a different printer.

   If this item is off, you can work more easily with multiple printers (when you have two or more printers connected to your computer). Whenever you open a document, the printer used when you saved that document is automatically selected for that document. (However, if that printer's *.prs* file is not found, WordPerfect displays a message indicating that the document is not formatted for the current printer, and then formats the document for the current printer.)

Beep On

   These items enable you to determine whether a beep will sound to alert you if: WordPerfect displays an error message; WordPerfect displays a

17

message asking for your assistance in hyphenating a word; or WordPerfect does not find the search text during a Search or Replace operation.

Menu

These items determine how the drop-down menus appear. Display Shortcut Keys specifies whether or not shortcut keys will display beside items on drop-down menus that have them. Display Last Open Filenames will determine whether or not the four most recently opened files will be listed when you select File to display the File menu.

Ruler

These items determine how the ruler operates. Tabs Snap to Ruler Grid determines whether tab and margin markers move (snap) in 1/16th of an inch increments when you drag them, or whether they move without a specific increment setting. (Holding down (SHIFT) while dragging a marker will temporarily reverse this setting.) Show Ruler Guides determines whether or not a vertical guideline appears to help you gauge where a marker aligns on the page while you're dragging it. Ruler Buttons on Top determines whether the row of ruler buttons (including the tab buttons, font button, size button, and so on) appears on the top or the bottom of the ruler. Automatic Ruler Display determines whether or not the ruler is automatically displayed each time you open a document.

Prompt for Hyphenation

These items let you choose whether you wish WordPerfect to: Never prompt you for the location of a hyphen when hyphenating a word; prompt you for the location of a hyphen When Required—or when the word is not found in its hyphenation dictionary or when no hyphenation rule governs the word; Always prompt you for the location of a hyphen—for each and every word it attempts to hyphenate.

Hyphenation

These items allow you to choose whether you wish to use the external or internal method for hyphenating. When you select External, special files outside of the WordPerfect program are used to hyphenate words. These special files, installed when you install WordPerfect (providing that you installed the speller dictionaries), use a dictionary to determine the location of a hyphen when hyphenating a word. When you select Internal, a set of rules is used by WordPerfect to determine the location of a hyphen when hyphenating a word. This second method is less accurate (accurate approximately 70 percent of the time).

Display

Choose File, Preferences, Display to open the Display Settings dialog box shown in Figure 17-3. This dialog box contains six sets of options for specifying how text, graphics, and menus are exhibited on screen as you work in WordPerfect.

Document Window

These items determine the display of text in the document window.

Text in Windows System Colors   If Text in Windows System Colors is turned on, text on screen is displayed according to the color chosen in the Windows Control Panel (described later in this chapter). If this item is turned off, text will display in the color in which it will print (such as in black, or in another color if you selected to print text in another color as described in Chapter 5).

17

Figure 17-3.   *Display Settings dialog box*

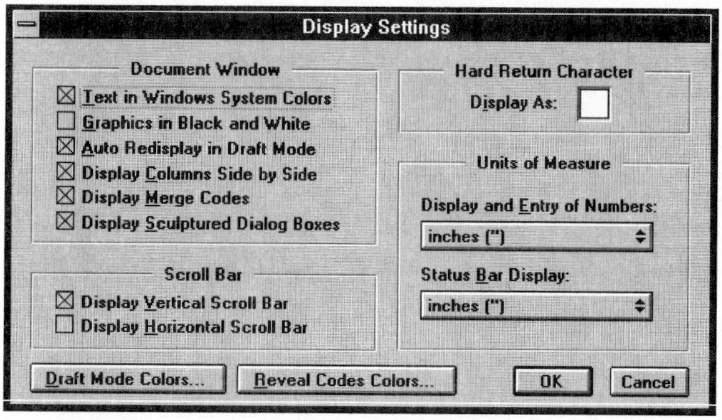

Graphics in Black and White   The default is to have Graphics in Black and White turned off, so that graphics images are shown in color. Turn this feature on to display the graphics in black and white, which is how all but color printers will print them.

Auto Redisplay in Draft Mode   The default is to have Auto Redisplay in Draft Mode turned on, so that when you switch to Draft mode and edit a document, the text is automatically redisplayed. Turn this feature off to redisplay only after you move the insertion point past the editing changes in the document or after you press (CTRL) + (F3).

Display Columns Side by Side   The default is to have Display Columns Side by Side turned on, so that when you turn on the Columns feature, columns of text display side by side just as they appear on the printed page. Turn this feature off if you wish to speed up the reformatting of columns on screen when you make editing changes; the columns will appear on separate pages on screen.

Display Merge Codes   The default is to have Display Merge Codes turned on, so that merge codes are displayed in the document workspace inside curly brackets, such as in {END RECORD}. When this item is turned off, merge codes can be seen only when you switch to the reveal codes workspace.

Display Sculptured Dialog Boxes   The default is to have Display Sculptured Dialog Boxes turned on, so that dialog boxes have a more sculptured, three-dimensional look on certain types of monitors. When this item is turned off, the dialog boxes will appear like those in Windows and other Windows applications. (Sculptured dialog boxes are not available when you are using an EGA and monochrome monitor displays.)

Scroll Bar

By default, only the vertical scroll bar is displayed, although the horizontal scroll bar will display if you turn on the corresponding check box. You can turn on Display Vertical Scroll Bar, Display Horizontal Scroll Bar, turn on both check boxes to display both types of scroll bars, or turn off both so neither scroll bar displays.

Hard Return Character

WordPerfect does not initially show in the document workspace where hard returns are located. (You switch to the reveal codes workspace to find the corresponding [HRt] codes.) You can instead have WordPerfect use a specific character to represent the location of hard returns in the document workspace. Type in a character in the Display As text box. For instance, type the greater than symbol (>), or press (CTRL) + (W) and use the WordPerfect Character dialog box to insert the paragraph symbol (¶) or another special character.

Units of Measure

Numerous features in WordPerfect involve some type of measurement. The default in WordPerfect is to give measurements in inches, with the number followed by an inch mark, as in 1.5" or 6". Because of this initial setting, you can specify a measurement simply by typing in a number, such as **1.5**, which WordPerfect will assume is 1.5 inches. You have other options as well for units of measure.

Option	Explanation	Sample
Inches (")	Default setting	2.5"
Inches (i)	Inches followed by an "i"	2.5i
Centimeters (c)	One centimeter equals .39 inch	6.36c
Points (p)	One point equals 1/72 inch*	180.5p
1200ths inch (w)	1/1200th of an inch	3000w

In publishing, one point equals 1/72.27 inch, a 4 percent difference

By choosing the Display and Entry of Numbers item, you can alter the units of measure for displaying and entering all numbers. For instance, suppose you change the units of measure to centimeters. In that case, if you enter a left margin setting of 6, WordPerfect will assume centimeters rather than inches. In turn, the margin code that is inserted into the text will appear in the new measurement, such as [L/R Mar:6c,6.36c].

17

By choosing the Status <u>B</u>ar Display item, you can alter the units of measure for displaying numbers on the status line and in the ruler bar. For instance, suppose you change the units of measure to 1200ths of an inch. In that case, the status bar will read

```
Doc 1 Pg 1 Ln 1200w Pos 1200w
```

Usually, you will want to make the same selection for both Units of Measure items.

Keep in mind that, regardless of what measurement you select as your default, you can override this setting when entering a particular measurement. Just make sure to enter the measurement followed by the character that indicates the units. WordPerfect will convert to the default units of measure automatically. For instance, suppose you maintain inches as the default setting. When indicating a meaurement, if you type **2.5c**, WordPerfect will convert 2.5 centimeters into .984 inch. Or, type **90p** and WordPerfect will convert 90 points into 1.25 inches.

Draft Mode Colors

This item allows you to select the colors used for the display when you switch to Draft mode. You can choose from predefined display colors, which are useful when you have a laptop with an LCD or plasma display in which the initial settings are difficult to read.

You can also select your own colors. You can choose the item you wish to change (such as Bold to determine the color for bolded text or Underline to select the color for underlined text). You change the color of the characters using the Foreground Palette and the color of the background with the Background Palette. The item changes to reflect the new color choice.

If you choose Reset, WordPerfect will return all the color settings to how they appeared when you first started WordPerfect—which depends on the type of monitor you use.

Reveal Codes Colors

This item, which operates like the <u>D</u>raft Mode Colors option, allows you to select the colors used for the display when you switch to reveal codes. You can select your own colors for text, codes, and for the cursor (the insertion point in the reveal codes workspace).

Print

Choose File, Preferences, Print to display the Print Settings dialog box shown in Figure 17-4. You can change default settings for how WordPerfect prints your documents. These settings are in effect each time you start WordPerfect.

Multiple Copies

These options determine the number of copies and the source for those multiple copies–for each time that you start WordPerfect until you change these options in the Print dialog box prior to printing in a particular work session. Change Number of Copies if you typically need more than one copy for every document you print out. Change Generated By if you want to determine whether WordPerfect or the printer generates the copies. Letting your printer generate copies can be faster (depending on the printer or network), but the document will not be collated because the printer will print multiple copies of page 1, then of page 2, and so on.

Figure 17-4. *Print Settings dialog box*

17

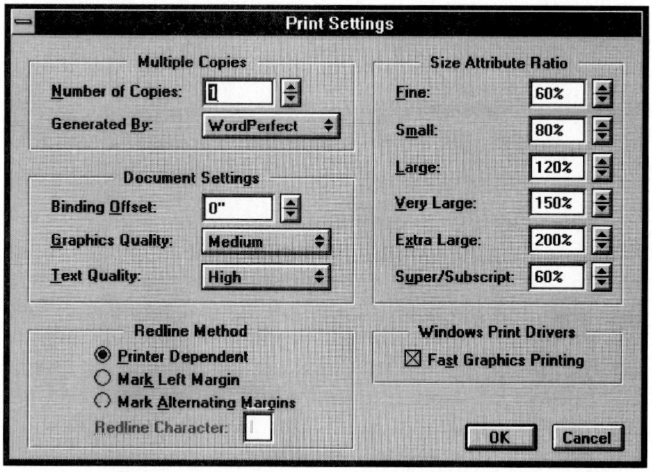

Document Settings

These options determine the binding offset, graphics quality, and text quality for all new documents you create—each time that you start Word-Perfect until you change these options in the Print dialog box. Binding Offset determines the gutter allowance that you'll need when planning to bind your work in book format with two-sided pages. For instance, set a .25-inch offset and WordPerfect will shift the text of even-numbered pages .25 inch to the left and odd-numbered pages .25 inch to the right leaving the right edge of left pages and the left edge of right pages available for binding.

Graphics Quality and Text Quality determine the quality (resolution) with which the graphics and text are printed. The higher the quality, the longer the printing time. (Note that not all printers have different resolution capabilities.)

Redline Method

These options determine the method used to indicate text that is redlined. (See Chapter 5 for more on the Redline feature.) Printer Dependent is the default, which means your printer will either print with red ink, with the background shaded in gray, or, if neither is possible, with a mark in the left margin. You can instead establish an initial setting where redlined text is marked with a character at the left margin or with a character at the left margin on even pages and the right margin on odd pages. The default character is the vertical bar, although this can be changed to any WordPerfect character.

Size Attribute Ratio

These options provide guidelines that will be used when WordPerfect determines the appropriate font to use for the Fine, Small, Large, Very Large, Extra Large, and Super/Subscript attributes. The numbers represent a percentage of the normal font size.

Windows Print Drivers

When the Fast Graphics Printing feature is turned on, graphics will print substantially faster. However, if you are using a Windows printer driver and have problems printing graphics, try turning this feature off.

Keyboard Layout

Choose File, Preferences, Keyboard to display the Keyboard dialog box shown here:

This dialog box enables you to change the setup of the keyboard, customizing it to your needs. You can select from predefined keyboard layouts. For instance, you can change from the Common User Access (CUA) compatible keyboard to the WP 5.1 compatible keyboard, a keyboard layout that mimics many of the keystrokes used in WordPerfect 5.1 for DOS. (You have access to the predefined keyboards if you installed the macros/keyboard/button bar files; if not, see Appendix A.)

You can also create your own keyboard layout, where you assign keys to frequently used features and operations. For instance, you can create one layout tailored for all your legal documents, where you assign special characters like the section sign (§) and paragraph symbol (¶) to individual keystrokes, a macro that defines and generates a table of authorities to another keystroke, and a macro that creates a pleading form to another keystroke.

Choose Select from the Keyboard dialog box to select a different keyboard layout, one that you previously created or that has been predefined by WordPerfect. A list of keyboard filenames is displayed in the Files list box. All the filenames have a *.wwk* extension. For instance, *wpdos51.wwk* is the file where the predefined WP 5.1 compatible keyboard is stored. Or, the file *macros.wwk* stores a predefined keyboard linked to macros that have been shipped with WordPerfect.

To choose a keyboard, type in the filename or select that file from the Files list box, and choose Select. You can also search through the Directories list box if the keyboard files are stored in a different directory. Once you select a new keyboard, choose OK; the Keyboard dialog box clears and you are returned to your document. The selected keyboard stays in effect for the current working session and every time that you load WordPerfect until you select a different layout.

Choose Default (CUA) from the Keyboard dialog box to return to the CUA compatible keyboard if another keyboard had been previously selected. Then choose OK; the Keyboard dialog box clears and you are returned to your document.

Choose Create from the Keyboard dialog box to create a new keyboard layout. You can also select a keyboard (other than the CUA keyboard) and then choose Edit to either examine or edit an existing keyboard. (The CUA keyboard cannot be altered.) Whether you choose to create or edit a keyboard, a Keyboard Editor dialog box appears, as shown in Figure 17-5. If you're creating a new keyboard, the message "Untitled" appears in the upper left corner, next to the heading "Keyboard File". If you're editing an existing keyboard, the name of it appears.

Figure 17-5.   *Keyboard Editor dialog box*

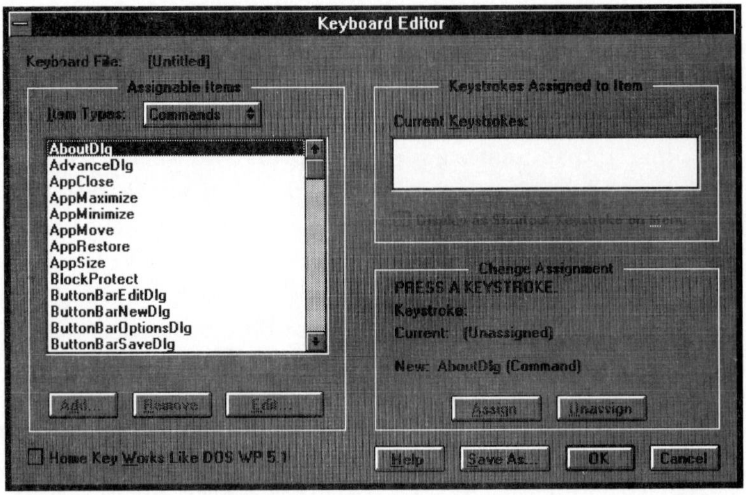

When using the Keyboard Editor to create or edit a keyboard, follow these steps:

1. Choose Item Types, and choose from four different types of items that a key can be assigned to. A list of the corresponding items appears in the Assignable Items list box.

   Commands   Any command that you use, such as turning on underline or retrieving a file can be assigned to a keystroke. The command is abbreviated; for instance, "FileRetrieveDlg" means the File Retrieve Dialog box for retrieving a file.

   Menus   Any menu or submenu in the drop-down menu structure, such as Graphics, Figure, can be assigned to a keystroke. The menu is described in words, such as "Figure Box Menu".

   Text   Any unformatted text, either one character (such as a special character), or a longer string of text (such as your company name or a frequently used paragraph of text) can be assigned to a keystroke.

   Macros   Any macro that you have previously created can be assigned to a keystroke. (When a keystroke is assigned to the macro, the macro is stored with the keyboard. If you later make changes to the macro, you must also edit the keyboard to update this macro.)

2. If you choose Text or Macros from the Item Types pop-up list box, you can choose Add to add text or macros to the list of available items. You can also choose Remove to remove text or macros. (The list of Commands and Menus is predefined by WordPerfect, and items cannot be removed or added from them.)

3. Choose an item from the Assignable Items list box. The item you selected appears in the lower right corner of the Keyboard Editor, next to the heading "New:".

4. Press the keystroke that you want to assign or edit. The *keystroke* can be any key on your keyboard, either alone or in combination with (CTRL), (ALT), (SHIFT), (CTRL) + (SHIFT), or (ALT) + (SHIFT). For instance, a keystroke can be (F6), or (CTRL) + (Y), or (CTRL) + (SHIFT) + (DEL). If the

17

keystroke currently has an assignment, it will be listed in the lower right corner of the Keyboard Editor, next to the heading "Current:". (You can, at this point, choose Unassign to remove the current assignment.)

5. Choose Assign. The keystroke you selected in step 4 will be assigned to the item you selected in step 3.

6. Repeat steps 1 through 5 for each keystroke you wish to assign. You can assign different keystrokes to the same item. (For instance, in the default keyboard, both (SHIFT) + (INS) and (CTRL) + (V) are assigned to the Edit Paste command.)

7. If you're creating a new keyboard, choose Save As and type in a name for the keyboard layout file. WordPerfect automatically adds a *.wwk* extension to the file.

　　If you're editing an existing keyboard, choose OK to save the changes.

When you wish to examine a predefined keyboard to see how it has been set up, you have two approaches in the Keyboard Editor dialog box. To see how a keystroke has been assigned, press the keystroke. The assignment (if the keystroke currently has an assignment) will be listed in the lower right corner of the Keyboard Editor, next to the heading "Current:".

Conversely, to see if an assignable item—such as a command or a menu—has been assigned to a keystroke (that is, to a shortcut key), select the item from the Assignable Items list box. The keystroke (or keystrokes if the item has been assigned more than one) will be listed in the upper right corner of the Keyboard Editor, below the heading "Current Keystrokes:". You can select the keystroke from the Current Keystrokes list box and then turn on or off the Display as Shortcut Keystrokes on Menu check box to determine whether or not the keystroke will appear on the menu structure.

There is one final option that will be of interest to those of you switching from WordPerfect 5.1 for DOS: You can also specify that a keyboard layout makes the (HOME) key work like it does in WordPerfect 5.1 for DOS—where it is used to modify how other keys, such as the arrow keys, operate. To use this option, turn on the Home Key Works Like DOS WP 5.1 check box. (This check box is already turned on for the WP 5.1 compatible keyboard.)

Keep in mind that regardless of the keyboard you select to use in text, you must use the CUA compatible keyboard when you're responding to WordPerfect within dialog boxes. For instance, you may have chosen the WP 5.1 compatible keyboard, where (HOME), (HOME), (→) *moves to the right end of the line. In a dialog box, however, you still must press* (END) *when you wish to move to the end of a line (in a text box, for instance)—because the* (END) *key moves to the end of the line in the CUA compatible keyboard.*

Initial Codes

Choose File, Preferences, Initial Codes to display the Default Initial Codes window shown in Figure 17-6. (As an initial setting, WordPerfect for Windows is set up for left-justified documents; thus a left justification code appears in Figure 17-6.)

In this workspace you can insert additional codes to set a predefined format for all new documents that you create. (This has no effect on existing

Figure 17-6.   *Default Initial Codes window*

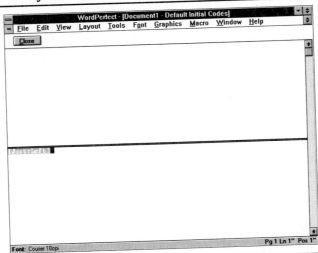

documents.) For instance, WordPerfect is initially set with margins of 1 inch, but you can change this initial setting for all new documents by inserting a margin code that changes left/right margins. Of course, you can change the layout from document to document by inserting formatting codes into the text, as explained in Chapters 6 and 7. But, when you find yourself changing a specific layout setting in the same way for almost every new document, then changing it in the Default Initial Codes workspace will save you time and effort.

You can insert the following codes in the Default Initial Codes workspace:

Column Definition	Letter Spacing
Column On	Line Height
Decimal/Align Character	Line Numbering
Endnote Number	Line Spacing
Endnote Options	Margins
Font	New Page Number
Footnote Number	Page Numbering Style
Footnote Options	Paper Size
Graphics Box Number	Suppress Page Format
Graphics Box Options	Tab Set
Hyphenation On/Off	Text Color
Hyphenation Zone	Underline Spaces and Tabs
Justification	Window/Orphan On/Off
Kerning	Word Spacing
Language	

Other codes or characters you insert into the Default Initial Codes workspace will be deleted when you choose Close to close the workspace.

Document Summary

Choose File, Preferences, Document Summary to display the Document Summary Preferences dialog box shown here:

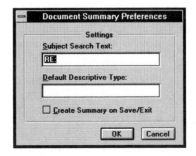

These options affect the Document Summary feature (described in Chapter 16).

Choose Subject Search Text to change the phrase used by WordPerfect to find the subject of a document and to insert that subject as the Subject entry in the document summary. The default is "RE:" because this is a commonly used heading at the top of memos when indicating a memo's subject.

Choose Default Descriptive Type to indicate the text that should automatically be inserted as the Descriptive Type entry in the document summary. For instance, if the majority of your documents are letters, type **letter**. Then, when you create another type of document, you can change the Descriptive Type entry to something else.

Choose Create Summary on Save/Exit if you want WordPerfect to automatically display the Document Summary dialog box when you save a new document and haven't yet created a summary for that document.

Date Format

Choose File, Preferences, Date Format to display the Date/Time Preferences dialog box shown here:

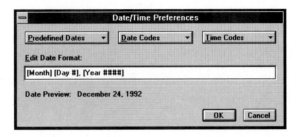

In this dialog box you can change the default date and time format that is used when you choose Tools, Date and insert the date either as text or as a code. The options work the same as in the Document Date/Time Format dialog box, as described in Chapter 8.

Merge

Choose File, Preferences, Merge to display the Merge Preferences dialog box shown here:

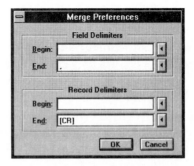

Use this dialog box to let WordPerfect know which characters are used as delimiters to separate each field and each record in a text file (such as a file created in Lotus 1-2-3 or dBASE) that has been converted to an ASCII delimited text (DOS) file. This enables WordPerfect to use the file as a secondary merge file. Some text files have only begin delimiters, while others have end delimiters. You can select from a button with the arrowhead located to the right of each text box when you wish to specify one of four special codes that are used as delimiters—tab, line feed, form feed, and carriage return. (See Chapter 14 for more on the Merge feature.)

Table of Authorities

Choose File, Preferences, Table of Authorities to display the ToA Preferences dialog box shown here:

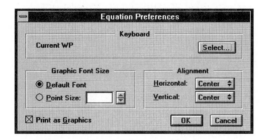

In this dialog box you can change the default settings used when defining a table of authorities. See Chapter 15 for a description of how to create a table of authorities.

Equations

Choose File, Preferences, Equations to display the Equation Preferences dialog box shown here:

You can change the default settings used for working with the Equation Editor, including the font size, the horizontal and vertical position of the equation in the graphics box, and whether the box will print graphically or as text.

In addition, you can select a keyboard layout that will be used automatically whenever you enter the Equation Editor, to help you type special characters and keywords in your equations. When you choose Select, the Keyboard dialog box appears, with the same options as previously described in this chapter (except that in the Equation Editor, the "Default (CUA)" keyboard is instead referred to as the "Current WP" keyboard).

17

Working with the Windows Control Panel

The Windows Control Panel provides a variety of basic settings that affect all applications that run under Windows—including WordPerfect for Windows. Settings include the system colors, the mouse settings, and the date and time that are stored in the computer.

When you wish to customize the basic settings for Windows applications, you must switch out of WordPerfect and into the Windows Control Panel. Follow these steps:

1. Click on the WordPerfect application control-menu box (the box in the upper left corner in the WordPerfect application window) or press (ALT) + (SPACEBAR) to display the control menu.

2. Choose Switch To to display the Task List dialog box.

3. Select (highlight) Program Manager and choose Switch To. This displays the Program Manager.

4. Locate the Main group icon, shown here:

Main

(If the Main group window is already open, skip to step 6.)

5. Double-click the Main group window icon or press (CTRL) + (F6) until the caption of the Main group icon is highlighted and press (ENTER). The Main group window will open.

6. Locate the Control Panel icon, shown here:

Control Panel

7. Double-click the Control Panel icon or use the arrow keys until the caption of the Control Panel icon is highlighted and press (ENTER).

shortcut≡ (CTRL) + (ESC) *is the shortcut for clicking the WordPerfect application control-menu box and choosing Switch To.*

The Control Panel window will open, as shown here:

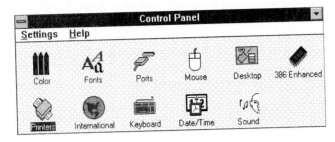

Choose one of the icons in this window, either by double-clicking on the icon, or by using the arrow keys to highlight the caption of the icon you wish to select and then pressing (ENTER). Once you change a setting in the Control Panel, the new setting stays in effect for every working session until you change it again.

The following is a discussion of the options you may wish to change on the Control Panel. For more detail on Control Panel options, be sure to refer to your Windows manual.

Color

Choose the Color icon to display the Color dialog box, which allows you to set the system colors. You can choose from several predefined color schemes or you can create your own color scheme.

To choose a predefined color scheme: click the down arrow located to the right of the Color Schemes list box, or press (ALT) + (↓); select the color scheme that you want, viewing the scheme in the sample window; choose OK.

To create your own color scheme, choose the Color Palette command button, choose a screen element from the Screen Element list box, and the desired color for that element from the Basic Colors palette. Make another selection from the Screen Element list box and Basic Colors palette, viewing the change in the sample window, and repeat for each element you wish to change. Choose OK when you're happy with each.

WordPerfect for Windows will not use the color you selected for window text when displaying text in document windows—unless, within WordPerfect, you choose File, Preferences, Display and turn on the Text in Windows System Colors option, as described previously in this chapter.

17

Mouse

Choose the Mouse icon to display the Mouse dialog box, which lets you change the operations of your mouse. You can choose Mouse Tracking speed and use the associated scroll bar to change the speed at which the mouse pointer travels across the screen. You can also choose Double Click Speed and use the associated scroll bar to change the speed at which Windows registers a double-click. You can then use the TEST box to try out the new double-click setting. Finally, choose Swap Left/Right Buttons to reverse the functions of the left and right buttons; when this box is checked, the effect is immediate (so that if you wish to then choose OK or to choose another option, you must use the right mouse button, instead of the left, to make the selection). Then choose OK.

Keyboard

Choose the Keyboard icon to display the Keyboard dialog box, to adjust the speed with which a key repeats when you hold it down. Choose Key Repeat Speed and use the associated scroll bar to change the repeat speed. You can also test the speed by choosing Test Typematic and holding down any key on the keyboard. Then choose OK.

Printers

Choose the Printers icon to display the Printers dialog box, allowing you to install and configure printers with Windows printer drivers, and also to indicate whether or not you wish to employ the Print Manager. If the Use Print Manager check box is not currently turned on, you may wish to choose Use Print Manager to place an X in the check box. The Print Manager works behind the scenes, enabling you to continue working on a document even while another document is printing.

Date/Time

Choose the Date/Time icon to display the Date & Time dialog box, where you can reset the date and time stored in the computer. Type the correct date into the Date number box or click an arrow in the associated increment box to change the numbers. Type the correct time into the Time number box or click an arrow in the associated increment box to change the numbers. Then choose OK.

Quick Reference

- To change how a certain WordPerfect feature operates or to tailor initial settings for the layout of all new documents, choose File, Preferences to display the Preferences menu. A list of settings that can be changed using the Preferences menu is listed in Table 17-1.

- To set directories that are in effect for different types of files each time you start WordPerfect, choose Location of Files from the Preferences menu.

- To protect against accidentally losing some of your work, choose Backup from the Preferences menu.

- To specify how certain features operate in WordPerfect, choose Environment from the Preferences menu.

- To determine how certain features display in WordPerfect, choose Display from the Preferences menu.

- To establish print settings that are in effect each time you start WordPerfect, choose Print from the Preferences menu.

- To use a predefined keyboard layout or to create a custom keyboard layout where you assign keys to specific features and operations in a customized keyboard layout, choose Keyboard from the Preferences menu.

- To indicate a predefined format for all new documents you create, choose Initial Codes from the Preferences menu.

- To customize the basic system settings for Windows, which in turn affects all programs that run under Windows, such as WordPerfect, use the Windows Control Panel. From WordPerfect's application control menu, choose Switch To, select Program Manager, and choose Switch To. This displays the Program Manager. Then, choose the Main group window icon and finally the Control Panel icon.

17

IV

Reference

A

Installing WordPerfect

You cannot start WordPerfect directly from the master disks that come with the WordPerfect package. The files contained on the master disks are stored in a compressed format, and must be decompressed and copied onto your hard disk before you can use them. Also, certain system files already on your hard disk must be modified. The whole process of preparing WordPerfect to operate on your computer equipment is called *installation*.

One of the master disks contains the Install program, which installs WordPerfect on your computer. You'll learn in this appendix how to use Install.

Before beginning the Install program, make sure that you have the required equipment and software. Your personal computer must have all of these to run WordPerfect:

- An Intel (or compatible) 80286, 80386, or higher processor. For example, these computers can run WordPerfect: IBM AT or another IBM compatible 286 machine, a 386 or 386 SX machine, or a 486 machine.

- A minimum of 2 megabytes of RAM. (Four megabytes is suggested, however, so that WordPerfect doesn't run too slowly.)

- A graphics adapter and monitor supporting EGA, VGA, 8514/A, or a Hercules graphics card.

- A hard disk with a minimum of 6 megabytes of free disk space and a floppy disk drive that accepts either 3.5-inch (1.44M) disks or 5.25-inch (1.2M) disks.

- Windows version 3.0 or higher, already installed on the computer.

In addition, a mouse is recommended because some WordPerfect features are not accessible without one. Both WordPerfect and Windows were designed for use with a mouse.

Using the Install Program

To begin the Install program, start up your computer as you usually do. Then, locate the Install/Program 1 disk, one of the master disks included in the WordPerfect package, and follow these steps:

1. Insert the Install/Program 1 disk into your computer's floppy disk drive.

2. If you are in Windows and viewing the Program Manager, exit to DOS by choosing File, Exit (one way to do so is to press (ALT) + (F) and then press (X)). Then, click OK or press (ENTER) .

3. Once you are viewing a DOS prompt—such as A> or C> or C:\> —type **a:install** and press (ENTER). (Or type **b:install** and press (ENTER) if you inserted the Install/Program 1 disk into drive B.)

4. In moments, a message appears welcoming you to the Install program and asking whether you wish to continue. Type **y**.

The main menu appears for the Install program, listing the menu items shown in Table A-1. You can choose a menu item by either typing the option number, typing the bolded letter in the option's name, or using the arrow keys to move an arrowhead on screen next to the option you wish to select

Table A-1.   *Options on the Install Program's Main Menu*

1 Basic	Install standard files to default locations, such as *c:\wpwin, c:\wpwin\graphics,* and *c:\wpwin\macros.*
2 Custom	Install standard files to locations you specify.
3 Network	Install standard files to a network drive. Only a network supervisor should use this option.
4 Printer	Install additional or updated WordPerfect printer files.
5 Interim	Install Interim Release program files. Use this option only if you are replacing existing WordPerfect for Windows files.
6 Copy	Install every file on a floppy disk to a location you specify (useful for installing all the printer *.all* files).
7 Language	Install additional WordPerfect language modules.
8 README	View WordPerfect for Windows README files.

and pressing (ENTER). You can also press the (F1) key for on-line help, or press (ESC) to exit the Install program.

First-Time Installation

When you are installing WordPerfect for the first time, you will choose one of the first three options shown in Table A-1.

Basic Installation

The first option on Install's main menu, 1 - **Basic**, creates directories on your hard disk and copies files from the WordPerfect master disk to those directories, as follows:

Directory Created	**Files Copied to the Directory**
c:\wpwin	WordPerfect program (*wpwin.exe*) and related files; styles files

A

Directory Created	Files Copied to the Directory
c:\wpwin\graphics	Graphics files (with a *.wpg* extension)
c:\wpc	Printer files (with an *.all* or *.prs* extension); WordPerfect Corporation (WPCORP) shared product files, such as Speller, Thesaurus, and File Manager files; utility files
c:\wpwin\macros	Macros/keyboards/button bars
c:\wpwin\learn	Learning workbook files

The Install program will indicate when you are to insert different master disks so that the appropriate files can be copied, and so the printer(s) that you will use with WordPerfect can also be installed. The Install program will also check to make sure that a specific file on disk, named *autoexec.bat*, is properly set up.

note *After you use the Install program to select a printer (or more than one printer), you may need to change the setup of that printer. For instance, you may need to specify that the printer is hooked into a different port (plug) than WordPerfect assumes. You may need to choose the appropriate sheet feeder. Or, if you purchased additional cartridges or soft fonts for your printer, you will need to select the available fonts. You change the setup after you have started WordPerfect. Chapter 16 describes how to edit the setup for a printer from within WordPerfect.*

Custom Installation

The second option on the Install menu, 2 - **Custom**, is a less automated installation. A new menu appears, that lets you specify where the files will be copied from (that is, where the master disks will be inserted during the installation), as well as where you want the different types of WordPerfect files—the WordPerfect program, graphics, macros/keyboards, styles, learning, WPCORP shared products, and printer files—to be copied to. For instance, if you have previously used WordPerfect 5.1 for DOS, you can use the same printer files in WordPerfect for Windows, and therefore may wish to specify that printer files be copied to the directory where the WordPerfect 5.1 for DOS printer files are already stored (such as *c:\wp51*).

The Custom option also lets you specify a directory where you want your documents to be stored. WordPerfect will create this directory and set up WordPerfect so that your documents will be automatically stored there. For instance, you can specify that all your documents be stored in *c:\docs*. (If you choose the Basic option, rather than the Custom option, you can later specify a location for your document files from within WordPerfect, as discussed in Chapter 4.)

The Custom option is more flexible than the Basic option, allowing you to install only certain files on your hard disk, which is important if space on your hard disk is limited. (Over 9.75 megabytes of free disk space are necessary to install all the WordPerfect files on your hard disk.) Once you choose to perform the custom installation, WordPerfect will pause to explain the functions performed by each group and ask whether you wish to install that group. For reference, a list of the key files in each group is provided in Table A-2. If you have limited disk space, you may decide not to install one or more groups that contain files you will never use. For instance, you may decide not to install the utility, printer program, and learning files.

The Custom option also allows you to decide whether or not you need to check your system's *autoexec.bat* file to make sure the PATH statement in that file is set up correctly for WordPerfect; if you don't allow WordPerfect to check and, if necessary, modify this file, you must do so manually.

Table A-2.   *Program Files Listed in Logical Groupings for Installation*

WordPerfect Program Files
WordPerfect program files are necessary to run WordPerfect for Windows. The key files include:

wpwin.exe	Main program file
wpwpus.dll	Contains help text
wp.qrs	Used with the Equation Editor
standard.prs	Standard printer definition
printer.tst	Printer test file
wp.lrs	Language resource file
wpcprint.drv	Windows printer driver
win2wrs.exe	Used to create Windows printer drivers
install.exe	Install program

A

Table A-2.   *Program Files Listed in Logical Groupings for Installation*
                    (continued)

Shared Product Files

Shared product files are necessary to run all WordPerfect applications that run under Windows, such as WordPerfect, Speller, and Thesaurus. Files include:

wp.drs	Makes it possible to display the Print Preview window and print characters graphically
spwin.exe	Speller
thwin.exe	Thesaurus
wpcdll.exe	Makes it possible to switch between applications

Macro Facility Files

Macro facility files are necessary if you wish to use the Macro feature to record and use macros. Files include:

wfwin.exe	Macro facility program
mcwin.exe	Macro compiler
mxwin.exe	Macro interpreter

File Manager Files

File Manager files are necessary to run the File Manager. Files include:

fmwin.exe	File Manager
wp{fm}.fmb	Default button bar for File Manager

Shared Product Help Files

Shared product help files are necessary to get on-line help with WordPerfect Corporation applications (other than WordPerfect for Windows). Files end with an *.hlp* extension.

Table A-2.   *Program Files Listed in Logical Groupings for Installation (continued)*

Utility Files

Utility files provide utility programs for converting graphics, creating special hyphenation dictionaries for languages that do not use word-based spelling dictionaries, and managing words in the spelling dictionaries. Files include:

graphcnv.exe	Graphics conversion utility
hyphen.exe	Hyphenation utility
spell.exe	Spell utility

Printer Program Files

Printer program files help create or modify files with a *.prs* extension. Files include:

ptr.exe	Printer program
ptr.hlp	Printer program help
charmap.tst	WordPerfect character sets test file
charactr.doc	Lists names of characters in WordPerfect character sets
kern.tst	Kern test file

Button Bar, Keyboard, and Macro Files

Keyboard and macro files provide predefined keyboard layouts, button bars, and macros. Files include:

*.wwk	Keyboard layouts (files with *.wwk* extensions)
wp{wp}.*	Default button bars
*.wwb	Button bars (files with *.wwb* extensions)
*.wcm	Macro files (files with *.wcm* extensions)

A

Table A-2.   *Program Files Listed in Logical Groupings for Installation*
(continued)

Help File

Help files are necessary to get on-line help with WordPerfect for Windows. The main help file is named *wpwp.hlp.*

Style Library File

The style library file provides predefined styles in a file named *library.sty.*

Macro Conversion File

The macro conversion program provides a utility program for converting WordPerfect 5.1 for DOS macros to WordPerfect for Windows.

Button Bar Picture Files

Button bar picture files are necessary if you wish to use the Button Bar feature in WordPerfect. Which you use depends on your monitor:

wpwpega.ddl	Used for EGA monitors with WordPerfect
wpwpherc.ddl	Used for Hercules monitors with WordPerfect
wpwpmvga.ddl	Used for monochrome VGA monitors with WordPerfect
wpwpvga.ddl	Used for color VGA monitors with WordPerfect
wpwp8514.ddl	Used for 8514 monitors with WordPerfect

Learning Workbook Files

Learning files hold the lesson files for going through the WordPerfect workbook. Files include:

*.wkb	Sample documents used with the WordPerfect workbook
*.wpg	Sample graphics images used with the workbook
wplearn.wwb	Button bar for the workbook
wpwork.prs	Printer driver for the workbook

Table A-2. *Program Files Listed in Logical Groupings for Installation (continued)*

Graphics Files

Graphics files provide clip art (different from the clip art provided in WordPerfect 5.1 for DOS) for inserting into graphics boxes in WordPerfect documents. Files have a *.wpg* extension. See Chapter 12 for pictures of the clip art.

Speller/Thesaurus Files

Speller/Thesaurus files are necessary for spell-checking and automatic hyphenation. Files include:

wpcspw.dll	Performs word-based speller functions in English
wpchypus.dll	Hyphenates English words
wp{wp}us.lex	Main work list for the Speller and external dictionary for the Hyphenation feature
wp{wp}us.ths	Contains the word list for the thesaurus

You will also want to install printers during the custom installation, unless you plan to use a printer driver that you have been using in WordPerfect 5.1 for DOS, or unless you will use Windows printer drivers only (*not* recommended).

The final option for a custom installation allows you to view the *readme* files on disk. These files contain information on changes made to your copy of WordPerfect so recently that they are not described in the WordPerfect manual.

Network Installation

The third option on the Install main menu, 3 - Network, installs WordPerfect to a network drive. Only network supervisors should use this option, and they should refer to Appendix M in the WordPerfect manual for more details.

A

Choosing a Keyboard

At the end of the first-time installation process—whether you choose the basic or custom installation—you will be asked to choose a keyboard. You have two keyboards to choose from.

The Common User Access (CUA) compatible keyboard uses keystrokes in accordance with the standards set for all Windows applications. You will want to choose this keyboard if you are unfamiliar with WordPerfect 5.1 for DOS. Or, choose this keyboard if you are familiar with WordPerfect 5.1 for DOS but plan to use other Windows applications besides WordPerfect, in which case learning the CUA keystrokes makes sense.

The WordPerfect (WP) 5.1 for DOS compatible keyboard uses keystrokes that mimic how function keys are used in WordPerfect 5.1 for DOS. If you are a skillfull user of WordPerfect 5.1 for DOS you may wish to switch to the WP 5.1 keyboard—especially if you don't plan on using other Windows applications. (Keep in mind that, if you choose this keyboard, the CUA keystrokes will still apply in dialog boxes. See Appendix D for more information.)

You can always change your mind later and switch to another keyboard. From within WordPerfect, you would use the File, Preferences, Keyboard command; see Chapter 17 for details.

Repeat Installation

There may be cases after installing WordPerfect in which you need to run the Install program again. For example, you might need to run it to install certain files that you didn't install originally, or to install additional printer files. Various options on the Install main menu are used to modify the WordPerfect installation.

The 2 - Custom option can be used if you wish to install certain groups of files that you did not install during the first-time installation procedures.

The 4 - Printer option enables you to install additional or updated WordPerfect printer files. For instance, if you purchase a new printer for your computer, you may need to use this option to install a file with an *.all* extension that contains the printer driver that instructs WordPerfect how to work with your printer.

The 5 - Interim option allows you to update the WordPerfect files on your hard disk. This is necessary if you receive new master disks that update the WordPerfect program.

The 6 - Copy option is useful if you have plenty of room on your hard disk and wish to install all the printer files with an *.all* extension. This way you don't have to return to the Install program each time you need to create a printer driver for a new printer that you wish to use with WordPerfect.

The 7 - Language option enables you to install WordPerfect language modules, which you can purchase and use with the Speller, Thesaurus, and other features. (See Chapter 9 for more information.)

The 8 - **README** option displays the contents of files named *readme*, which are stored on the different master disks. You can read about last-minute changes to the WordPerfect program, in files stored either on the original master disks that came packaged with WordPerfect or on new master disks that you receive later. These changes are so recent that they are not described in the WordPerfect manual.

Starting WordPerfect and Startup Options

After you have performed the installation of WordPerfect, you are ready to turn to Chapter 1 to learn how to start and use WordPerfect on your computer.

However, depending on your equipment and needs, you may be better off loading WordPerfect in a slightly different way than is described in Chapter 1. Chapter 1 describes how you can start WordPerfect using the WordPerfect group icon and the WordPerfect program item icon. If one of these icons is not displayed after you have started Windows and you are viewing the Program Manager, load WordPerfect using these steps:

1. From the Program Manager, choose File, Run. (One way to do so is to press (ALT) + (F) and then press (R).)

2. In the Run dialog box that appears, type as a command the path where the main WordPerfect program is stored. For instance, if you performed a basic installation, then the main WordPerfect program

A

file, named *wpwin.exe*, is stored in the directory *c:\wpwin*. In that case, type **c:\wpwin\wpwin.exe**. You can abbreviate this by simply typing **c:\wpwin\wpwin**.

3. Choose OK or press (ENTER). WordPerfect will begin to load.

You can run startup options when you load WordPerfect. Some of these startup options may be necessary to run WordPerfect on your equipment; others are more for your convenience. Startup options usually consist of a slash (/) followed by one or more letters. They can be entered when you use the Program Manager to start WordPerfect. Type them as part of the command that you type in step 2 of the preceding instructions. These startup options take effect until you exit WordPerfect.

- */d-drive\directory* Redirect the location of temporary files that WordPerfect creates while it is running by typing **/d-** and your drive and directory. For instance, type **c:\wpwin\wpwin/d-d:** in step 2 of the instructions if you have established a RAM disk as drive D and wish to redirect temporary files to the RAM disk.

- *filename* Open the specified file. For instance, type **c:\wpwin\ wpwin first** in step 2 to open the file named *first* from the current directory after WordPerfect is loaded.

- */m-macroname* Start the specified macro by typing **/m-** and the macro name. For instance, type **c:\wpwin\wpwin/m-rr** to start the macro named "rr" from the current directory after WordPerfect is loaded.

- */nb* Overwrite the original document when you save and replace a file, without creating a backup. This is useful if you have insufficient disk space to hold two copies of your files. (Note: This can be risky; if a power failure occurs while you are saving a file, you could lose the document.) Type **c:\wpwin\wpwin\nb** in step 2 in the instructions.

- */nt-network* # Indicate which network software you are using, where each supported network has a number or letter as follows: Novell Netware—1; Banyan VINES—2; TOPS Network—3; IBM LAN Network—4; Nokia PC-Net—5; 3COM 3+—6; 10NET—7; LANtastic—8; AT&T StarGROUP—9; DEC PCSA—A; 3COM 3+ OPEN—B;

StreetTalk—C. For instance, type **c:\wpwin\wpwin/nt=network 1** in step 2 to indicate a Novell Netware network.

- */ps-directory path*   Instruct WordPerfect to use a certain directory for the location where individual personal setup files (with a *.set* extension) will be located.

- */sa*   Instruct WordPerfect to load in stand-alone mode. This lets you operate as if not on the network even if a network environment exists.

- */u-username*   Indicate to WordPerfect that multiple users can run WordPerfect on a network. For instance, type **c:\wpwin\wpwin /u-mrm** in step 2 to indicate you are starting WordPerfect with the user initials "mrm".

- */x*   Instruct WordPerfect to restore all the default settings that you may have changed using the Preferences feature (see Chapter 17) to the original default settings as established by WordPerfect Corporation.

A

B

WordPerfect Commands and Codes

This appendix contains quick reference information for WordPerfect's commands and codes. The first section provides a summary of WordPerfect's commands. The second section lists the WordPerfect codes that you will encounter when you open the reveal codes workspace to edit your WordPerfect documents.

Command Summary

In the following summary, commands are listed according to the drop-down menu on which they can be found.

File Menu

Command	Purpose
New	Opens a new document window
Open	Recalls an existing file into a new document window

627

Retrieve	Recalls an existing file into the active document window at the insertion point location
Close	Closes the active document window
Save	Saves a document
Save As	Saves a document with a different name or file format
Password	Sets or removes password protection for the current document
File Manager	Activates WordPerfect's File Manager
Preferences	Changes initial WordPerfect and document settings
Print	Prints a document
Print Preview	Views a formatted document before printing
Select Printer	Selects a printer and changes printer options
Exit	Quits WordPerfect

Edit Menu

Command	**Purpose**
Undo	Reverses the last change to the text
Undelete	Restores a recent deletion
Cut	Moves selected text to the Clipboard
Copy	Copies selected text to the Clipboard
Paste	Places a copy of the contents of the Clipboard at the insertion point location
Append	Adds a copy of selected text to the Clipboard
Link	Establishes, edits, or updates DDE links in a document
Select	Selects (highlights) a block of text
Convert Case	Switches selected text to uppercase (if text is lowercase) or lowercase (if text is uppercase)
Search	Looks for text or codes
Search Next	Looks for the next occurrence of the search string

Search Previous	Looks for the previous occurrence of the search string
Replace	Replaces existing text or codes with other text or codes
Go To	Relocates the insertion point on the current page or another page

View Menu

Command	Purpose
Ruler	Shows/Hides the ruler
Reveal Codes	Shows/Hides the reveal codes workspace
Draft Mode	Shows/Hides Draft mode
Graphics	Shows/Hides graphics in documents
Comments	Shows/Hides comments in documents
Button Bar	Shows/Hides the current button bar
Button Bar Setup	Creates, edits, selects, changes display options for a button bar
Short Menus	Shows/Hides short menus

Layout Menu

Command	Purpose
Line	Changes the format of lines, including tab settings, line spacing, line height, and hyphenation
Paragraph	Changes the format of paragraphs including indent, double indent, hanging indent, and margin release
Page	Changes the format of pages, including paper size, headers, footers, and page numbering
Columns	Defines, creates, and edits text columns
Tables	Defines and creates tables
Document	Changes the document format, including document summary, initial font, and initial codes
Footnote	Creates, edits, and formats footnotes

B

Endnote	Creates, edits, and formats endnotes
Advance	Positions text horizontally or vertically
Typesetting	Adjusts typesetting features such as kerning, word spacing, and letter spacing
Justification	Aligns text
Margins	Changes left/right/top/bottom margins
Styles	Establishes and applies styles that format text

Tools Menu

Command	**Purpose**
Speller	Checks for misspellings, double words, or irregular capitalization
Thesaurus	Lists synonyms and antonyms for words
Word Count	Tallies the number of words in the current document
Language	Specifies the language of the text
Date	Defines and inserts the date and/or time
Outline	Creates and edits outlines
Sort	Rearranges text alphabetically or numerically
Merge	Creates merge documents and performs merges
Mark Text	Marks text for a list, index, table of contents, table of authorities, or cross-reference
Define	Defines the location and numbering style for a list, index, table of contents, or table of authorities
Generate	Creates/updates defined lists, indexes, tables of contents, tables of authorities, cross-references, or endnote placement codes
Document Compare	Compares two versions of a document
Master Document	Creates, condenses, or expands a master document
Spreadsheet	Extracts information from a spreadsheet into a WordPerfect document

| Comment | Creates or edits a nonprinting comment in a document |
| Line Draw | Draws lines with text and special characters |

Font Menu

Command	**Purpose**
Font	Changes the font or font attribute
Color	Changes the text color on the printed page
Normal	Removes all font attributes
Bold	Turns On/Off bold attribute
Italic	Turns On/Off italics attribute
Underline	Turns On/Off underline attribute
Double Underline	Turns On/Off double underline attribute
Redline	Turns On/Off redline attribute
Strikeout	Turns On/Off strikeout attribute
Subscript	Turns On/Off subscript attribute
Superscript	Turns On/Off superscript attribute
Size	Changes the size attribute
Overstrike	Creates new characters by combining keyboard characters
WP Characters	Inserts special characters from the WordPerfect character sets

Graphics Menu

Command	**Purpose**
Figure	Creates and edits figure boxes
Text Box	Creates and edits text boxes
Equation	Creates and edits equations
Table Box	Creates and edits table boxes
User Box	Creates and edits user boxes
Line	Creates and edits vertical and horizontal lines

B

Macro Menu

Command	Purpose
Play	Plays back a recorded series of commands (a macro)
Record	Records a macro
Stop	Quits the recording of a macro
Pause	Pauses during the recording or playback of a macro
Assign to Menu	Adds an existing macro to the Macro menu

Window Menu

Command	Purpose
Cascade	Arranges document windows in a stack with the title bars showing
Tile	Arranges document windows so that the contents of all of them are displayed

Help Menu

Command	Purpose
Index	Lists help topics alphabetically
Keyboard	Displays templates and keystroke information
How Do I	Tells how to perform common tasks
Glossary	Lists alphabetically definitions for important terms
Using Help	Explains how to use the Help feature
What Is	Lets you use the keyboard and mouse to select items on which you want help
About WordPerfect	Displays version and license information

WordPerfect Codes

In the following list, codes are listed alphabetically. Use this list of codes to discover which feature is being activated or deactivated by a certain code found in your document. Remember that in order to show codes, you must open the reveal codes workspace by choosing <u>V</u>iew, Reveal <u>C</u>odes or pressing (ALT) + (F3).

This list is also useful when you are working with the Search and the Replace features (described in Chapter 8) and wish to look for or swap codes in your document.

Keep in mind that there are two types of codes. Open codes are single codes that activate a feature starting from the insertion point and continuing to the end of the document, unless another code of the same type is found farther forward in the document. For instance, an [L/R Mar:2",2"] code establishes left and right margins of 2 inches to the end of the document or up to the location of another [L/R Mar:] code with different margin settings. As another example, a [W/O On] code turns on the Widow/Orphan feature to the end of the document or up to the location of a [W/O Off] code.

Paired codes *always* come in sets of two. With paired codes, the On code marks the location where the feature begins, and the Off code marks the location where the feature ends. Paired codes—which cannot have an On code without an accompanying Off code—are listed on the same line in the first column of the following list.

Code	Name of Code
-	Soft Hyphen
[-]	Hyphen Character

A

Code	Name of Code
[AdvDn:]	Advance Down
[AdvLft:]	Advance Left
[AdvRgt:]	Advance Right
[AdvToLn:]	Advance To Line
[AdvToPos:]	Advance To Position
[AdvUp:]	Advance Up

B

B

[Bline:Off]	Baseline Placement Off
[Bline:On]	Baseline Placement On
[Block Pro:On][Block Pro:Off]	Block Protection (begin and end)
[Bold On][Bold Off]	Bold (begin and end)
[Box Num]	Box Number for a Graphics Box Caption

C

[Cell]	Cell in a Table
[Center]	Center
[Center Pg]	Center Page Top to Bottom
[Cndl EOP:]	Conditional End of Page
[Cntr Tab]	Centered Tab
[Col Def:]	Text Columns Definition
[Col Off]	Text Columns Off
[Col On]	Text Columns On
[Color:]	Text Color
[Comment]	Document Comment

D

[Date:]	Date/Time Format
[Dbl Indent]	Double Indent
[Dbl Und On][Dbl Und Off]	Double Underline (begin and end)
[DDE Link Begin]	DDE Link Begin
[DDE Link End]	DDE Link End
[Dec Tab]	Decimal Tab Align
[Decml/Algn Char:]	Decimal Align and Thousands Separator Characters
[Def Mark:Index]	Index Definition
[Def Mark:List,*n*]	List Definition (*n* = list number)

[Def Mark:ToA,*n*]	Table of Authorities Definition (*n* = section number)
[Def Mark:ToC,*n*]	Table of Contents Definition (*n* = ToC level)
[Dorm HRt]	Dormant Hard Return
[DSRt]	Deletable Soft Return

E

[Embedded]	Embedded Code for Macro
[End C/A]	End of Centering/Alignment
[End Def]	End of Index, List, or Table (after generation)
[End Mark:List,*n*]	End Marked Text for List (*n* = list number)
[End Mark:ToC,*n*]	End Marked Text for Table of Contents (*n* = ToC level)
[End Opt]	Endnote Options
[Endnote:*n*;[Note Num]*text*]	Endnote (*n* = note number)
[Endnote Placement]	Endnote Placement
[Equ Box:*n*;]	Equation Box (*n* = box number)
[Equ Opt]	Equation Box Options
[Ext Large On][Ext Large Off]	Extra Large Print (begin and end)

F

[Fig Box:*n*;]	Figure Box (*n* = box number)
[Fig Opt]	Figure Box Options
[Fine On][Fine Off]	Fine Print (begin and end)
[Flsh Rgt]	Flush Right
[Font:]	Base Font
[Footer *N*:*n*;*text*]	Footer (*N* = type, A or B) (*n* = frequency)
[Footnote:*n*;[Note Num]*text*]	Footnote (*n* = note number)

B

| [Force:] | Force Odd or Force Even |
| [Ftn Opt] | Footnote Options |

H

[HdCntrTab]	Hard Centered Tab
[HdDecTab]	Hard Decimal Aligned Tab
[HdRgtTab]	Hard Right Aligned Tab
[HdSpc]	Hard Space
[HdTab]	Hard Left Aligned Tab
[Header *N:n;text*]	Header (N = type, A or B) (n = frequency)
[HLine:]	Horizontal Line
[HPg]	Hard Page
[Hrd Row]	Hard Row in a Table
[HRt]	Hard Return
[HRt-SPg]	Hard Return—Soft Page
[Hyph Ign Wrd]	Hyphenation Ignore Word
[Hyph Off]	Hyphenation Off
[Hyph On]	Hyphenation On
[HyphSRt]	Hyphenation Soft Return
[HZone:*n,n*]	Hyphenation Zone (n = left, right)

I

[Indent]	Indent
[Index:*heading;subheading*]	Index Entry
[Insert Pg Num]	Insert Page Number
[Italc On][Italc Off]	Italics Print (begin and end)

J

| [Just:] | Justification |
| [Just Lim:] | Justification Limits for Word/Letter Spacing |

K

[Kern:Off]	Kerning Off
[Kern:On]	Kerning On

L

[L/R Mar:]	Left and Right Margins
[Lang:]	Language (for Speller, Thesaurus, and Hyphenation Module)
[Large On][Large Off]	Large Print (begin and end)
[Line Height Adj]	Line Height (leading) Adjustment
[Link]	Spreadsheet Link
[Link End]	Spreadsheet Link End
[Ln Height:]	Line Height
[Ln Num:Off]	Line Numbering Off
[Ln Num:On]	Line Numbering On
[Ln Spacing:]	Line Spacing

M

[Mar Rel]	Left Margin Release
[Mark:List,*n*] [End Mark:List,*n*]	List Entry Mark (*n* = list number) (begin and end)
[Mark:ToC,*n*] [End Mark:ToC,*n*]	Table of Contents Entry Mark (*n* = ToC level) (begin and end)

N

[New End Num:]	New Endnote Number
[New Equ Num:]	New Equation Number
[New Fig Num:]	New Figure Box Number
[New Ftn Num:]	New Footnote Number
[New Tbl Num:]	New Table Number
[New Txt Num:]	New Text Box Number

B

[New Usr Num:]   New User-Defined Box Number

[Note Num]   Footnote/Endnote Reference
                                        Number

O

[Open Style:*name*]   Open Style (*name* = style name)

[Outline Lvl Open Style]   Outline Open Style

[Outline Lvl Style On]   Paired Outline Style (begin and
   [Outline Lvl Style Off]   end)

[Outline Off]   Outline Feature Off

[Outline On]   Outline Feature On

[Outln On][Outln Off]   Outline Attribute (begin and end)

[Ovrstk:]   Overstrike

P

[Paper Sz/Typ:*s,t*]   Paper Size and Type (*s* = size,
                                        t = type)

[Par Num:Auto]   Paragraph Number, Automatic

[Par Num:*n*]   Paragraph Number (*n* = paragraph
                                        level)

[Par Num Def:]   Paragraph Number Definition

[Pg Num:]   New Page Number

[Pg Num Style:]   Page Number Style

[Pg Numbering:]   Page Numbering Position

[Ptr Cmnd:]   Printer Command

R

[Redln On][Redln Off]   Redline (begin and end)

[Ref(*name*) *t*]   Cross Reference (*name* = target
                                        name) (*t* = what reference is tied to)

[Rgt Tab]   Right Tab Align

[Row]   Row in a Table

S

[Select]	Beginning of Selection
[Shadw On][Shadw Off]	Shadow (begin and end)
[Sm Cap On][Sm Cap Off]	Small Caps (begin and end)
[Small On][Small Off]	Small Print (begin and end)
[SPg]	Soft Page
[SRt]	Soft Return
[Stkout On][Stkout Off]	Strikeout (begin and end)
[Style On:*name*] [Style Off:*name*]	Paired Style (begin and end) (*name* = style name)
[Subdoc:]	Subdocument in a Master Document
[Subdoc Start:][Subdoc End:]	Subdocument after being generated (begin and end)
[Subscpt On][Subscpt Off]	Subscript (begin and end)
[Suppress:]	Suppress Page Format Options
[Suprscpt On][Suprscpt Off]	Superscript (begin and end)

T

[T/B Mar:]	Top and Bottom Margins
[Tab]	Left Align Tab
[Tab Set:]	Tab Set
[Target(*name*)]	Target in Cross Reference (*name* = target name)
[Tbl Box:*n*;]	Table Box (*n* = box number)
[Tbl Def:*n*;]	Table Definition (*n* = table number)
[Tbl Off]	Table Off
[Tbl Opt]	Table Box Options
[Text Box:*n*;]	Text Box (*n* = box number)
[ToA:;*text*]	Table of Authorities Short Form (*text* = text of Short Form)

B

[ToA:*n*;*text*;Full Form]	Table of Authorities Full Form (*n* = section number) (*text* = text of Short Form)
[Txt Opt]	Text Box Options

U

[Und On][Und Off]	Underlining (begin and end)
[Undrln:]	Underline Spaces and/or Tabs
[Unknown]	Non-WP 5.1 code
[Usr Box:*n*;]	User-Defined Box (*n* = box number)
[Usr Opt]	User-Defined Box Options

V

[VLine:]	Vertical Line
[Vry Large On][Vry Large Off]	Very Large Print (begin and end)

W

[Wrd/Ltr Spacing:]	Word and Letter Spacing
[W/O Off]	Widow/Orphan Off
[W/O On]	Widow/Orphan On

C

Getting Help

This appendix lists several resources available when you need additional help using WordPerfect for Windows. You'll first learn how to use the Help feature, so you can learn how to answer many of your own questions. You'll also learn how to get a knowledgeable voice at the other end of your telephone if you have a question or problem that you can't solve on your own.

Using the Help Feature

By displaying the Help application window, you can discover which features are available to you, how specific features work, and how to access them. It's like having an abbreviated version of the WordPerfect manual on screen.

The Help feature is driven by Windows, which means you can get both Windows Help and WordPerfect Help. If you did not install the Help files when you installed WordPerfect, the Help feature is unavailable until you run the Install program again (as described in Appendix A) and install those files.

The Basic Procedure

The basic steps of using Help are as follows:

1. Choose Help. A menu appears, as shown here:

2. Choose a menu item. A Help application window appears so that
   you can look through a list for the topic you wish to learn about.

   An example of the Help window is shown in Figure C-1. This
   window contains a control-menu box, resizing buttons, a menu bar,
   a scroll bar, and buttons on a button bar.

3. Choose a topic—any of the underlined or green-colored items. Your
   mouse pointer changes to a hand when pointing to a topic; click the
   topic to choose it. With your keyboard, press (TAB) or (SHIFT) + (TAB)
   to move forward and backward between topics. When the topic you
   wish to choose is highlighted, press (ENTER).

4. Read the information provided on the topic you chose.

5. Choose another topic or choose from the Help menu bar or Help
   buttons.

6. When you're finished using help, close the Help window the same
   way that you exit the WordPerfect window: either choose File, Exit;
   double-click the Help Control-menu box; or press (ALT) + (F4). The
   Help window will close.

These steps will vary slightly, depending on the Help menu item you
choose. Each item represents a different approach to getting the help you
need. The seven menu items on the Help menu, covered in the following
sections, are Index, Keyboard, How Do I, Glossary, Using Help, What Is, and
About WordPerfect.

Figure C-1. *Help application window*

Index

Choose <u>H</u>elp, <u>I</u>ndex to access the main WordPerfect Help Index, where you can look up a specific topic alphabetically. Choose the letter with which your topic begins, and then from all the topics with that first letter choose your topic.

shortcut (F1) *is the shortcut for <u>H</u>elp, <u>I</u>ndex as long as the document window is the only active feature. ((F1) is used in other shortcuts as well, as described later in this chapter.)*

Keyboard

Choose <u>H</u>elp, <u>K</u>eyboard to view the templates and information on the shortcut keys of the CUA compatible keyboard and the WP 5.1 keyboard.

How Do I

Choose <u>H</u>elp, <u>H</u>ow Do I to look up information about how to perform a common task. For instance, you may wonder, "How do I print a document?", or "How do I save a document?". Topics are organized into the following categories: Basics; Changing Defaults; Edit; Format; Graphics; Menu Bar; Printing; Special Features; Tables; and Utilities.

C

Glossary

Choose Help, Glossary to look up definitions for the terminology used in WordPerfect and Windows, such as "application window" or "macro". Once you select a topic in the glossary, you must click and hold on the mouse, or hold down the (ENTER) key, to read the definition.

Using Help

Choose Help, Using Help to learn how to use the Help system.

What Is

Choose Help, What Is to get context-sensitive help, which means you can access Help for something on your screen without having to search through an index, list, or glossary. The mouse pointer changes to an image of an arrow/question mark. You can now press a key (such as (PGDN) or (F2)) to display the Help window with information on the function of that key. Or, you can click any element on screen (such as a menu name or dialog box or button) to display the Help window with information on that element. You must have a mouse to access context-sensitive help.

shortcut (SHIFT) + (F1) *is the shortcut for* Help, What Is.

Whenever you want context-sensitive help on a dialog box, drop-down menus, and certain special windows displayed in the document window, you cannot press Help, What Is because the dialog box, drop-down menu, or special window will close. Instead, you have two alternatives. First, press (F1) to get general information on the box, menu, or window. For instance, with the Open File dialog box displayed, press (F1) to get help on this dialog box.

Second, you can press (SHIFT) + (F1) and click an item or element to get specific information on that item or element. For instance, with the Open File dialog box displayed, press (SHIFT) + (F1) and click the View command button to get information on the View feature.

About WordPerfect

Choose Help, About WordPerfect to display your license number (provided that you entered your license number the first time you loaded WordPerfect after installation) and other information about your version of WordPerfect, such as the date of release. You'll need these and other important facts provided by About WordPerfect when you call WordPerfect Corporation's customer support to discuss a problem or ask a question (as described later in this appendix).

Buttons in the Help Window

As shown in Figure C-1, there are five buttons in the Help window. These buttons provide other ways to access topics.

- *Index*   Choose Index to display the main WordPerfect Help Index from anywhere within the Help window. (This option is equivalent to exiting the Help window, and then choosing Help, Index.)

- *Back*   Choose Back to move back one topic at a time through as many as 40 topics that you previously viewed in the current Help session. If you have yet to look up a topic, this button is dimmed.

- *Browse* << and *Browse* >>   Choose Browse << to move back through a sequence of related topics. Choose Browse >> to move forward to the next topic in a sequence. When you reach the first or last topic of the sequence, the corresponding button becomes dimmed.

- *Search*   Choose Search to open a dialog box that lists key words and phrases. Double-click the word/phrase or select the word/phrase and press (ENTER) to get a list of associated topics. Then, select a topic and choose Go To to get help on that topic.

Menus in the Help Window

As shown in Figure C-1, there are four menu names listed on the Help window's menu bar.

- *File*   Choose File and then choose from three menu items. Open recalls another Help file. Print Topic prints the topic currently displayed in the Help window. Printer Setup selects the appropriate printer (which uses a Windows printer driver).

C

- *Edit*   Choose Edit and then choose from two menu items. Copy places a copy of the topic currently displayed in the Help window into the Clipboard (after which you can paste the Clipboard contents into a document). Annotate adds a comment to the topic currently displayed in the Help window. A paper clip symbol is inserted beside the topic title; choose the paper clip any time you wish to redisplay the comment.

- *Bookmark*   Choose Bookmark and then choose Define to mark a topic that you know you'll want to return to later. You can type a new name for the topic or accept the current name. The name is added to the Bookmark menu. To return to a topic that has been marked, choose Bookmark and then choose the corresponding topic name.

- *Help*   Choose Help and then choose from two menu items. Help displays information on how to use Windows Help topics. About displays information about your version of Windows Help.

shortcut   (F1) *is the shortcut for Help, Help once you are viewing the Help window.*

You can maximize the Help window to make it easier to read the information displayed. You maximize the Help window just as you would the WordPerfect window. Double-click the maximize button in the upper right corner of the Help window, or press (ALT) + (SPACEBAR) to display the Help control menu, and choose Maximize. To restore the Help window to a medium-sized window, double-click the Restore button in the upper right corner or press (ALT) + (SPACEBAR), Restore. (You can also minimize the Help window so that subsequent references to Help can be executed faster. See Chapter 10 for more on resizing the WordPerfect application windows—the Help window is resized in the same way.)

Talking to a WordPerfect Expert

If you wish to talk to a WordPerfect expert, you could contact your computer dealer, a users group devoted to your brand of computer, or a users group devoted to WordPerfect for Windows. The names and addresses of users groups are listed in regional and national computer magazines.

To report software problems or to get answers to specific questions on WordPerfect, contact WordPerfect Corporation. Their telephone support service is frequently hailed as the best in the business. Their customer support center has hundreds of people on staff, ready to answer your questions about installation, printers, or general items on all WordPerfect Corporation products. Staff members are extremely responsive once you get through to them, but you may be placed on hold during peak hours (11:00 a.m. to 3:00 p.m. mountain standard time). Customer support is available from 7:00 a.m. to 6:00 p.m. mountain standard time, Monday through Friday. Which phone number you dial depends on your needs. All of these telephone numbers are toll-free:

Installation	(800) 228-6076
Features	(800) 228-1029
Graphics/Tables/Equations	(800) 228-6013
Macro/Merge/Labels	(800) 228-1032
Laser/PostScript Printers	(800) 228-1023
Dot-Matrix/All Other Printers	(800) 228-1017
Networks	(800) 228-6066

If you are in an area where toll-free numbers are not supported, call (801) 228-9907. WordPerfect Corporation also offers after-hours customer support, from 6:00 p.m. to 7:00 a.m. mountain standard time, Monday morning through Friday evening: (801) 228-9908. Note that the after-hours support number is *not* toll-free.

When you call, make sure that you're at your computer, with WordPerfect loaded. That way, you can duplicate the problem you're encountering keystroke by keystroke for the customer support representative.

C

D

WordPerfect 5.1: Switching from DOS to Windows

This appendix is written specifically for the knowledgeable WordPerfect user—those of you who have for months or years used WordPerfect in the DOS environment. When you switch to the Windows environment, you'll initially lose the comfort of knowing exactly how to do everyday word processing tasks. You'll undoubtedly want to make the adjustment to Word-Perfect for Windows as quick and effortless as possible. Your questions may be these: What are the advantages and disadvantages of making the switch? Do I have to use a mouse? Do the function keys work the same way? How will I do the tasks in Windows that I've been doing all along under DOS? What things does WordPerfect for Windows do that WordPerfect for DOS doesn't? What things won't it do? What do I have to do with my documents to use them in WordPerfect for Windows?

Answers to such questions are provided in this appendix. The discussion is general and includes many references to the chapters where each topic is covered more fully. You'll want to turn to chapters 1 and 2 after reading this appendix if you're a Windows novice; learning the fundamentals of the

Windows environment first will enable you to more quickly feel comfortable with WordPerfect for Windows.

note   *The abbreviation used in this appendix for WordPerfect 5.1 for Windows is WPWIN, and the abbreviation used for WordPerfect 5.1 for DOS is WPDOS.*

The Advantages and Disadvantages of Switching from DOS

Windows is a graphics environment, which gives you many advantages. One is that complex formatting and font control becomes much easier. Unlike WPDOS, which is a character-based environment, in WPWIN you can view font sizes and attributes (such as italic and bold) on screen just as they will appear in your printed document. You can also view graphics boxes and graphics lines on screen as you work, without going into a Preview mode, which makes desktop publishing applications quicker and easier. The result is a much more accurate image of the printed page.

The Windows environment also allows for multitasking. What that means is that you can run more than one application at a time, and transfer information between applications. For instance, you can load WordPerfect, switch back to Windows' Program Manager, and load another application, such as Lotus 1-2-3 for Windows. Then, you can switch back and forth between WordPerfect and Lotus 1-2-3, and swap data between the two by cutting and pasting information.

With few exceptions, all the features in WPDOS are found in WPWIN. Some have been enhanced, so they are easier to use. New features have been added, some of which are spectacular; these are described later in this appendix.

A disadvantage of making the switch to WPWIN is that you may need to upgrade your computer equipment. Minimum requirements are a 286 machine with at least 2MB of memory. However, to get the most out of WPWIN, you will want to have at least a 386 machine with 4MB of memory. You will need at least 8MB of free space on your hard disk. And, you won't be able to take advantage of some new features if you don't have a mouse.

Even if you upgrade to a faster computer, when you switch to WPWIN you will probably sacrifice some speed. How much speed depends on your computer equipment. Certain features, such as Search, Replace, the Speller, and even scrolling through your document, will take longer. At first, the sluggishness may prove frustrating. However, if you stick with WPWIN, you may determine that slower computing is a small price to pay for working on a graphically oriented, easier-to-use system that offers some exciting new features.

Interacting with WordPerfect for Windows

How you interact with WordPerfect has changed quite a bit—from how to use the mouse, to how you issue commands, to how you respond to WordPerfect's questions. The following sections will help you acclimate to the changes.

The Mouse

In WPDOS, you may or may not have used a mouse. If you used a mouse, it was for only a limited number of tasks, such as blocking text or scrolling through a document, and there was no clear advantage to using the mouse over the keyboard.

In WPWIN, a mouse can perform all the tasks that you can do with the keyboard except for typing text. In fact, there are certain tasks that are much easier to perform with a mouse. For example, with a mouse you can move a graphics box on screen to exactly where you want it.

Some features in WPWIN cannot be used unless you have a mouse. For instance, you cannot use the Button Bar feature, a shortcut for issuing commands, without one.

Chapters 1 and 2 start you on your way to using a mouse, by giving you some practice with it. Allow yourself some time and practice to become comfortable using the mouse. You'll probably find that it makes your work easier in the long run. If you never become comfortable with the mouse, you may rely on the keyboard for the majority of tasks, and use the mouse only for tasks that can't be done otherwise. The choice is up to you.

The Screen

Once you load WPWIN (as described in Chapter 1), you may feel that the screen is a bit more cluttered than in WPDOS; fortunately, the clutter is confined to the edges of the window. Chapter 1 explains all the elements you will see on the screen.

You'll also note that the cursor in WPWIN is different from the WPDOS cursor. In WPWIN, it is called the *insertion point*. It is a vertical (rather than horizontal) bar that moves between characters (rather than below characters). The insertion point moves inside the *document workspace*, which is simply the space where the text of your document appears.

As you begin to type, you'll see that the text on screen is black against a white background—just the reverse of the screen in WPDOS. The characters in WPWIN display just as they will appear when printed—with features such as proportional spacing, italics, different font sizes, and so on.

You can change the text color and background color on screen. For instance, you can change to a black background with white letters to replicate the colors in WPDOS. This way, you can still see font changes and graphics on screen, but opt for a color choice that you are more accustomed to and that you may find easier on your eyes. You use the Windows Control Panel to change the background and text colors. The Windows Control Panel affects not only WordPerfect applications, but other Windows applications as well. See Chapter 17 for more on the Windows Control Panel.

If you want to make the document on screen more closely resemble a document in WPDOS, you can switch to Draft mode. In Draft mode, text is monospaced, font sizes and attributes are shown with a different color rather than a different typeface or type size, and graphics images and lines are hidden. To switch to Draft mode, choose View, Draft Mode. Chapter 5 describes the Draft Mode feature. You can even change the colors used for the text and the background in Draft mode. You choose File, Preferences, Display and then select the Draft Mode Colors option to choose the colors you want for the text and the background. See Chapter 17 for more on this procedure.

The Menu Bar

Another basic change in how you interact with WordPerfect is the menu bar, the horizontal bar containing the names of menus. In WPWIN, the menu bar remains on screen at all times (whereas in WPDOS it displayed only when you requested to view it).

The menu bar in WPWIN features more prominently than it did in WPDOS. You are more reliant on it because certain features and commands can *only* be accessed from the menu bar. (In WPDOS, on the other hand, every command accessed on the menu bar could also be accessed via function keys. As a result, you may have been unaware that WPDOS even had a menu bar.)

You'll want to become familiar with how the menu bar is organized and how it works. By being oriented to the menu bar, you may find that certain features and commands are much more accessible to you than in WPDOS. For instance, if you don't know where to find a command, you can search through the menu items until you find it.

The menu bar in WPWIN is organized into ten menus, listed here:

Menu	**Action**
File	Open and save documents
Edit	Change a document
View	Change what you see in the WordPerfect window
Layout	Change the text format in a document
Tools	Use tools to assist in creating and editing a document
Font	Change the appearance of printed text
Graphics	Add graphics lines, graphics boxes, and equations to your document
Macro	Record or play back a series of commands
Window	Change the document window display
Help	Get onscreen help

You can issue commands from the menu bar with your mouse by clicking a menu name and then a menu item. You can also use your keyboard by pressing (ALT) + the mnemonic of the menu name (or the letter underlined on screen), and then pressing the mnemonic of the menu item. For instance, to choose File, Save—which means selecting the Save menu item from the File

menu—you can click F̲ile and then click S̲ave. You can also press (ALT) + (F)
and then (S). See Chapter 2 for details.

The Function Keys

Because the menu bar has such prominence in WPWIN, the function keys
are viewed as shortcut keys; they are shortcuts to accessing commands because
you bypass the menu bar entirely. For instance, rather than reveal codes by
choosing V̲iew, Reveal C̲odes from the menu bar, you can press (ALT) +
(F3)—which is the same keystroke as in WPDOS. It is a good idea to become
familiar with the shortcut keys for those features you use regularly.

You can choose from two different sets of shortcut keys:

- The WP 5.1 compatible keyboard has shortcut keys designed to
  mimic how function keys are used in WPDOS. About 85 percent of
  the WPDOS function keys are the same or similar, so you can still
  press (SHIFT) + (F7) to print a document, or (F8) to underline text, or
  (ALT) + (F1) to access the Thesaurus, for example.

- The Common User Access (CUA) compatible keyboard has only a
  few function keys that work the same way in WPDOS. The rest of
  the function keys have been reassigned so that the shortcuts are
  consistent with CUA guidelines—meaning the same shortcuts apply
  in other applications. For instance, (ALT) + (F4) always exits the
  application—whether you press (ALT) + (F4) in WordPerfect or press
  it in some other Windows application.

A plastic template packaged with WordPerfect lists the shortcut keys for
the WP 5.1 keyboard on one side and the CUA keyboard on the other.

If you don't plan to use a Windows application other than WPWIN, you
may wish to use the WP 5.1 compatible keyboard. Turn the plastic template
to the side that reads "WP 5.1 Compatible". Refer to Table D-1, which lists
commands alphabetically in the left column, and provides the corresponding
shortcut keys in the right column. Many shortcut keys are the same; some are
new. You'll also notice that WPWIN uses more key combinations than
WPDOS. In addition to those that combine a modifier key ((SHIFT) or (ALT) or
(CTRL)) and a function key, some shortcut keys combine two modifiers and a

Table D-1. *Shortcut Keys for Issuing Commands (WP 5.1 Keyboard)*

Command	Key Combination
Bold	`F6` (or `CTRL` + `B`)
Cancel	`ESC`
Center	`SHIFT` + `F6`
Center Justify	`CTRL` + `J`
Clear	`CTRL` + `SHIFT` + `F7`
Close	`F7`
Copy	`CTRL` + `C` (or `CTRL` + `INS`)
Cut	`CTRL` + `X` (or `SHIFT` + `DEL`)
Date/Outline	`SHIFT` + `F5`
Decimal Tab	`CTRL` + `F6`
Double Indent	`SHIFT` + `F4`
Draft Mode	`CTRL` + `SHIFT` + `F3` (or `ALT` + `F11`)
End Field	`F9` (or `ALT` + `ENTER`)
End Record	`ALT` + `SHIFT` + `ENTER`
File Manager	`F5`
Flush Right	`ALT` + `F6`
Font	`CTRL` + `F8`
Footnote	`CTRL` + `F7`
Full Justify	`CTRL` + `F`
Generate	`ALT` + `SHIFT` + `F5`
Goto	`CTRL` + `G` (or `CTRL` + `HOME`)
Graphics	`ALT` + `F9`
Hard Hyphen	`HOME`, `-`
Hard Page	`CTRL` + `ENTER`
Hard Space	`HOME`, `SPACEBAR` (or `CTRL` + `SPACEBAR`)
Help	`F1`
Indent	`F4`
Italics	`CTRL` + `I`

Table D-1.   *Shortcut Keys for Issuing Commands (WP 5.1 Keyboard)*
(continued)

Command	Key Combination
Layout	(SHIFT) + (F9)
Left Justify	(CTRL) + (L)
Line Draw	(CTRL) + (D)
Macro Play	(ALT) + (F10)
Macro Record	(CTRL) + (F10)
Macro Stop	(CTRL) + (SHIFT) + (F10)
Mark Text	(ALT) + (F5)
Menu Bar	(ALT)
Merge	(SHIFT) + (F9)
Merge/Sort	(CTRL) + (F9)
Next Document	(SHIFT) + (F3)
Next Pane	(CTRL) + (F1)
Next Window	(ALT) + (SHIFT) + (F6)
Normal	(CTRL) + (N)
Open	(SHIFT) + (F10)
Paste	(CTRL) + (V) (or (SHIFT) + (INS))
Preferences	(SHIFT) + (F1)
Previous Document	(ALT) + (SHIFT) + (F3)
Previous Pane	(CTRL) + (SHIFT) + (F1)
Print	(SHIFT) + (F7)
Print Full Document	(CTRL) + (P)
Print Preview	(ALT) + (SHIFT) + (F7)
Redisplay	(CTRL) + (F3)
Replace	(ALT) + (F2)
Reveal Codes	(ALT) + (F3) (or (F11))
Right Justify	(CTRL) + (R)
Ruler	(SHIFT) + (F11)

D

Table D-1. *Shortcut Keys for Issuing Commands (WP 5.1 Keyboard)*
(continued)

Command	Key Combination
Save As	(F10)
Search	(F2)
Search Next	(SHIFT) + (F2)
Search Previous	(ALT) + (SHIFT) + (F2)
Select	(ALT) + (F4) (or (F12))
Select Cell	(ALT) + (SHIFT) + (F4) (or (SHIFT) + (F12))
Select Paragraph	(CTRL) + (SHIFT) + (F4)
Select Sentence	(CTRL) + (F4)
Size	(CTRL) + (S)
Special Codes	(ALT) + (SHIFT) + (F8)
Speller	(CTRL) + (F2)
Styles	(ALT) + (F8)
Tables/Columns	(ALT) + (F7)
Thesaurus	(ALT) + (F1)
Undelete	(F3) (or (ALT) + (SHIFT) + (BACKSPACE))
Underline	(F8) (or (CTRL) + (U))
Undo	(CTRL) + (Z) (or (ALT) + (BACKSPACE))
WP Characters	(CTRL) + (W)

function key, such as (ALT) + (SHIFT) + (F2) or (CTRL) + (SHIFT) + (F4). Others use a combination of (CTRL) and a letter, such as (CTRL) + (S).

On the other hand, if you plan to use other Windows applications in addition to WordPerfect, you may want to use the CUA compatible keyboard. Turn the plastic template to the side that reads "CUA Compatible" and refer to Table 2-1 in Chapter 2. You'll have to endure the process of learning a whole new set of keystrokes. Once you learn those keystrokes, however, you'll find that many will apply in other Windows applications as well. Knowing those keystrokes will make learning new Windows applications much easier.

≡note≡ Wherever shortcuts are provided in this book, the keystrokes will refer to the CUA compatible keyboard. If you want to know the corresponding WP 5.1 keyboard shortcut key, refer to Table D-1.

The CUA keyboard is the default, but you may have switched to the WP 5.1 keyboard during installation (provided that you elected to install the Macro/Keyboard Button Bar files during the installation). Even after installation, you can change your mind at any time, and switch to the other keyboard. A command on the Preferences menu (which is called the Setup menu in WPDOS) is used to switch to another keyboard. The entire procedure is described in Chapter 17.

The following steps give you the procedure to switch to the CUA keyboard in brief:

1. Choose File, Preferences, Keyboard. (One method to do this is to press (ALT) + (F), then press (E), then press (K).)

2. Choose Default (CUA) and then choose OK. (One method to do this is to press (ALT) + (D), then press (ENTER).)

Here's the procedure in brief to switch to the WP 5.1 keyboard:

1. Choose File, Preferences, Keyboard. (One method to do this is to press (ALT) + (F), then press (E), then press (K).)

2. Choose Select. (One method to do this is to press (ALT) + (S).)

3. Select *wpdos51.wwk* and then choose OK. (One method to do this is to type **wpdos51.wwk**, and press (ENTER) twice.)

Whichever keyboard you select remains in effect for the current working session and all future working sessions—until you select a different keyboard.

The Insertion Point

In WPWIN, there are also shortcut keys for moving the insertion point, depending on the keyboard you selected. If you're using the WP 5.1 keyboard, the shortcuts are almost all the same as in WPDOS, (a list of them is provided in Table D-2). Also, (CTRL) + (END) still deletes text from the insertion point to

Table D-2. *Shortcut Keys for Moving the Insertion Point (WP 5.1 Keyboard)*

Movement	Key Combination
Word Left	(CTRL) + (←)
Word Right	(CTRL) + (→)
Paragraph Up	(CTRL) + (↑)
Paragraph Down	(CTRL) + (↓)
Screen Left	(HOME), (←)
Screen Right	(HOME), (→)
Screen Up	(HOME), (↑) or (-)
Screen Down	(HOME), (↓) or (•)
Top of Page	(CTRL) + (HOME), Position, Top of current page
Bottom of Page	(CTRL) + (HOME), Position, Bottom of current page
Previous Page	(PGUP)
Next Page	(PGDN)
Beginning of Line	(HOME), (HOME), (←)
End of Line	(HOME), (HOME), (→) (or (END))
Beginning of Document	(HOME), (HOME), (↑)
End of Document	(HOME), (HOME), (↓)

the end of the line, and (CTRL) + (PGDN) still deletes text from the insertion point to the end of the page.

If you're using the CUA keyboard, most of the shortcuts are new; a list of the shortcuts for moving the insertion point is provided in Table 3-1, in Chapter 3.

You should also know that you can now scroll through your document with the mouse. You can point the mouse pointer and click; the insertion point moves to that location. You can also use a vertical or horizontal scroll bar, as described in Chapter 3. The important thing to remember when using the scroll bar is that as you move through the document with the scroll bar, the display moves but the insertion point stays fixed. The insertion point can thus disappear off screen. Once you've scrolled to a new section of your document, remember to point and click the mouse or press an arrow key to relocate the insertion point onto the screen.

You'll notice as you move the insertion point in WPWIN that hidden codes are skipped over. For instance, suppose the insertion point is just past a hidden code. When you press ⊖, the insertion point will skip the code and move to the left of the next character. This is different from WPDOS, where when you press ⊖, the insertion point will seem not to move, when in actuality it has moved to the left of the code—something that is apparent only when you reveal codes.

The Prompts and Menus

In WPDOS, certain commands bring up either a full screen menu, a line menu, or a prompt such as "Save document? Y̲es (No)". In WPWIN, all prompts have been standardized. Whenever it is necessary for you to communicate with WordPerfect, a dialog box appears on screen. A dialog box is like a menu surrounded by a rectangular border, and contains a menu, a prompt, or some other message.

Dialog boxes allow you to choose from several or many options as a way of responding to WordPerfect. It is essential to understand the elements in dialog boxes. Be sure to review Chapter 2, where they are explained fully. Also, note that in dialog boxes, only the CUA keyboard applies. So, even if you're using the WP 5.1 keyboard, you will want to become familiar with a small set of CUA keyboard shortcut keys, as listed in Table D-3. The shortcut keys in Table D-3 always operate in dialog boxes—regardless of the keyboard that you have selected to use on your computer.

Table D-3.   *Shortcut Keys in Dialog Boxes*

Command	Key Combination
Execute the preselected command button	`ENTER`
Cancel the dialog box	`ESC`
Exit the dialog box	`ALT` + `F4`
Move to the next element in the dialog box	`TAB`
Move to the previous element in the dialog box	`SHIFT` + `TAB`
Move to the beginning of the line in a text box element	`HOME`
Move to the end of the line in a text box element	`END`
Open the dialog box's Control menu	`ALT` + `SPACEBAR`

Blocking Text

The all-important ability to block text has changed also. The terminology has changed from "block" to "select". You'll find that selecting text is now easier than ever before. There are two basic methods. First, you can use the Select mode, which is like the Block mode in WPDOS: press `F8` (CUA keyboard) or `ALT` + `F4` (WP 5.1 keyboard) and move the insertion point to select the text or type a character to extend the selection up to the next occurrence of that character.

Second, you can select text without turning on Select mode. With the mouse, click and drag the insertion point to highlight text. With the keyboard, press `SHIFT` and, while holding `SHIFT` down, use the arrow keys to highlight text. Chapter 3 describes the procedure in more detail and lists some shortcuts as well. (Keep in mind that if you use this second method to select text, you cannot type a character to extend the selection up to the next occurrence of that character. Instead, what happens is that the selected text is deleted, and the character you type is inserted in its place.)

Text remains highlighted even after you perform a task on the text (except when you cut or delete the text). This provides you the opportunity to make multiple changes without having to reselect the text. For instance, you can select text, underline it, and then boldface it. To turn off the selection if you turned on Select mode, press (F8) (CUA keyboard) or (ALT) + (F4) (WP 5.1 keyboard) again. To turn off the selection when you used the second method, click the mouse or press an arrow key.

Getting Help

The Help facility in WPWIN is comprehensive, and can answer your specific questions fast. You can use Help to learn how to perform common tasks and to display templates and keystrokes of the CUA keyboard or the WP 5.1 keyboard. See Appendix C for detailed information on using Help.

Changes in the Features

Some features are brand-new; others have been enhanced. A few have been eliminated—for the most part made obsolete because of the new or enhanced features.

New Features

Here are the most significant of the new features in WPWIN:

- You can now work with up to nine documents at one time (depending on the amount of RAM in your computer). Each document is placed in a separate document window. You can switch back and forth between documents, or display all of them on screen at the same time. (See Chapter 10.) As previously mentioned, you can also multitask, running WordPerfect and other applications at the same time.

- The ruler simplifies the task of adjusting margins, tab settings, justification, and line spacing. (See Chapter 6.) It also makes it easy to create or modify columns and tables (Chapter 11), change fonts (Chapter 5), and use styles (Chapter 15).

- The Button Bar feature lets you display menu items and macros as icons (pictures with captions) on screen. You can create your own button bar or use one that is already defined. Your access to commands becomes as fast and easy as a click of a mouse on the button bar. You must have a mouse to use the Button Bar feature. (See Chapter 10.)

- The Quick List feature lets you assign descriptive names to directories. For instance, you can assign the name "Reports" to the directory *c:\wpwin\business\reports*. You can thus avoid the hassle of maneuvering through directories or typing long, cumbersome path names. (See Chapter 16.)

- The Undo feature reverses the last change you made to your text. So, for instance, suppose you rearrange a paragraph and decide you preferred the paragraph in its original layout. You can undo the rearranging. Or, suppose you set new margins for your document and then decide you prefer the margins with their original settings. You can undo the margin change. (See Chapter 3.)

- The Auto Code Placement feature means that WordPerfect automatically places layout codes at the top of the paragraph or page, even if the insertion point is in the middle of the paragraph or page when you make the change. This allows you to make formatting changes without precisely placing the insertion point. For instance, to change margin settings beginning at a specific paragraph, you can position the insertion point anywhere in the paragraph before initiating the margin change.

  Auto Code Placement also eliminates the need for deleting extra codes. For instance, if you change margins once and then change them again in the same paragraph, the first margin code is deleted, and the second margin code is inserted in its place at the beginning of the paragraph.

  You can turn off this feature if you want WPWIN to operate more like WPDOS. (See Chapter 17.)

Enhanced Features

Here is a list of some of the major enhancements you'll find in WPWIN:

- You can now confine a formatting or font change to a section of text in one operation. For instance, to change from single- to double-spacing in the third paragraph only, select the paragraph and then specify double-spacing. A double-spacing code is placed at the beginning of the selected paragraph, and a single-spacing code is placed at the end of the selected paragraph. In WPDOS, you had to change the line spacing twice, once before the paragraph and once afterward.

- With the Confirm on Code Deletion feature, you no longer delete certain formatting codes without revealing codes first. In WPDOS, when you were deleting with (BACKSPACE) or (DEL) and bumped up against a code, a prompt such as "Delete [L/R Mar:1.5",1"]? No (Yes)" would appear. In WPWIN, except for a few codes (such as indent and footnote), no such prompt appears; the code is skipped over, and you must reveal codes to delete it. (Because of the Auto Code Placement feature, you will probably find you seldom need to delete formatting codes anyway.) You can turn off this feature if you want WPWIN to operate more like WPDOS. (See Chapter 17.)

- The procedure to move and copy text has been modified. You either "cut" text (whereby you remove the text from its original spot and place it in temporary storage), or you "copy" text (whereby you place a copy in temporary storage). The temporary storage place is called the Clipboard, which is provided by Windows. When you're ready to relocate the text stored in the Clipboard into the document, you "paste" the text. In this way, you can move or copy within a document, or between documents.

  Also, the procedure is much simpler because of new shortcut keys. For instance, cut text by selecting the text and pressing (CTRL) + (X). Then paste the text into a new location by repositioning the insertion point and pressing (CTRL) + (V). (See Chapter 8.)

- Graphics boxes and lines are easier to place, move, and resize. You can do so directly in your documents with a mouse; click on the box or line, and then drag to change its position or size. (See Chapter 12.)

- When you preview how your document will appear when printed, you can zoom in for a closer look at a specific section of the page. (See Chapter 16.)

- You can change the size of the area in which you want to reveal codes. Using a mouse, you can have half of your screen show the text with codes revealed, which is like WPDOS. Or, you can have just one line, two lines, or almost all of the screen show the text with codes revealed. (See Chapter 3.)

- To print your documents, you have the option of using either a WordPerfect printer driver (to select from over 900 printers) or a Windows printer driver. (See Chapter 16.)

- What was called the Setup menu in WPDOS is referred to as the Preferences menu in WPWIN. This menu offers you most of the options you are accustomed to, and some new ones, including options that let you make WPWIN operate more like WPDOS. (See Chapter 17.)

Excluded Features

A few features have been eliminated in WPWIN, including these:

- You can no longer display numbers and the status line in 4.2 units. You can choose inches, centimeters, points, or 1200ths of an inch.

- The (ESC) key no longer repeats any character that you type a specified number of times. The (ESC) key is used to cancel a menu item or command (which is a task performed by (F1) in WPDOS).

- There is no longer a Math feature. Instead, you create your columns and rows of numbers using the Tables feature, and then use the

Formula and Calculate commands to have WPWIN figure out the totals for you. (See Chapter 11.)

- There are no settings within WordPerfect for controlling the mouse, speed of the insertion point, or screen colors; you must use the Windows Control Panel instead. (See Chapter 17.)

- You can continue to work in a document on screen while a print job is printing, but WordPerfect no longer controls the behind-the-scenes printing. Once a print job is processed by WordPerfect, it is sent to Windows' Print Manager. You must then switch to the Print Manager if you wish to cancel, pause, or resume the print job. (See Chapter 16.)

Changes in How Files Are Retrieved and Saved

The procedures for working with document files has changed in WPWIN. There are two methods for retrieving files, and four methods for saving them. The terminology has changed, too, so that WPWIN remains consistent with other Windows applications. (See Chapter 4 for more information on what is described next.)

Methods for Retrieving Files

There are two ways to recall a document from disk onto the screen. You can "open" a document, which means you recall the contents of a file into a clear document workspace. Using the Open feature is comparable in WPDOS to clearing the workspace (either by exiting a document so that the Document1 workspace is clear or by switching to the Document2 workspace), and then retrieving a file.

The second method is to "retrieve" a document, which means you insert the contents of a file into the current document workspace wherever the insertion point is positioned, whether the workspace is clear or not. Using the Retrieve feature in WPWIN is the same as using the Retrieve feature in WPDOS. But, in Windows applications, the Open feature is used more often;

D

it is more common to recall a file into a clear document workspace, and this is ensured when you use Open.

You can also open a clear document workspace without recalling a document into that workspace. You do so with the New feature. (See Chapter 10.)

Methods for Saving Files

In WPWIN, there are four basic methods to save a document. The Save As feature saves a document on disk, prompting you for the document's filename and also asking you to confirm the replacement if a file by that name already exists. The Save As feature is comparable to pressing F10 in WPDOS.

The Save feature is new, and is convenient when you wish to save your document at regular intervals to safeguard against losing it to a power or machine failure. After the first time you save your text, choose the Save feature if you wish to resave the text using the same filename and without being prompted to confirm the replacement. Keep in mind that the Save feature replaces an existing file *without any warning message.*

The Close feature closes a document as well as the window where it was located. If the document has been modified since it was last saved on disk, WordPerfect will ask whether you wish to save the changes. The Close feature is comparable to pressing "F7, Yes or No, No" in WPDOS.

The Exit feature closes all document windows and exits you from Word-Perfect. If any of the documents have been modified since they were last saved on disk, WordPerfect will ask whether you wish to save the changes. This feature is comparable to pressing "F7, Yes or No, Yes" in WPDOS.

Working with WPDOS Files and Files in Other Formats

The document files you created in WPDOS are completely compatible with WPWIN. Both products use the same format, which is called "Word-Perfect 5.1" format. No special conversion is required—just recall the file with the Open or Retrieve feature. In fact, the compatibility is so good that you may decide to use WPDOS to type the raw text of a document (especially for long documents and when WPDOS is much speedier on your computer than WPWIN), and switch to WPWIN when you want to edit and format it, especially when you want to change fonts, insert graphics lines and boxes, produce newsletters, design letterheads, and do other types of desktop publishing.

To recall document files from a different format (including WordPerfect 5.0, WordPerfect 4.2, and other word processing applications), you can also use the Open or Retrieve feature. WPWIN indicates the file's current format, and then converts the file to WordPerfect 5.1 format "on the fly".

To save document files into a different format, use the Save As feature. The Save As dialog box that displays once you activate Save As lets you select from a variety of formats. (See Chapter 16.)

The macros you created in WPDOS are *not* compatible with WPWIN because of the graphical environment. They are very different. In WPWIN, macros are based on the task performed, rather than on the keystroke involved. For instance, a macro to turn on bold in WPWIN includes the result of turning on italics with this macro command: FontItalic (State:On!). In WPDOS, the same macro includes three keystrokes to turn on italics: {Font}ai. (Every task in WPWIN has an associated macro command, which is documented in the WordPerfect macros manual. You can order the manual by calling WordPerfect at 800-321-4566.)

A macro conversion utility comes with WPWIN to aid in the conversion of some WPDOS macros. The utility is stored in a file named *mfwin.exe*, which is usually installed in the directory *c:\wpc*. You can load this file from WordPerfect by choosing File, File Manager to load WordPerfect's File Manager. Then, choose File, Run, type **c:\wpc\mfwin.exe**, and press (ENTER) to load the macro utility. Next, press Macro, Convert and the name of the file you wish to convert. After the conversion, one way to return to WordPerfect is to press (ALT) + (F4) to exit the macro utility and (ALT) + (F4) again to exit the File Manager.

Even after you convert a macro, you will probably need to make some (or many) changes manually. A WPWIN macro is an ordinary document file, which can be edited by recalling it to the screen.

The printer drivers you created in WPDOS—which are files with a *.prs* extension—are compatible with WPWIN. You can copy the printer drivers from WPDOS into the directory where the printer drivers for WPWIN have been installed, which is typically *c:\wpc*. (However, if you use a LaserMaster or fax-card driver, you must install a new printer driver–a Windows printer driver.)

WPDOS dictionaries can be used with the WPWIN Speller.

A Few Warnings

As a last bit of information, once you switch to WPWIN be cautious about pressing these keys:

- Don't cancel or undelete text by pressing (F1). Instead, press (ALT) or (ESC) to cancel a command on the menu bar. Press (ALT) + (F4) to close a dialog box (sometimes (ESC) will work as well). Press (ALT) + (SHIFT) + (BACKSPACE) or choose Edit, Undelete to undelete text. (Or press (F3) if you're using the WP 5.1 keyboard).

  The (F1) key is now a shortcut to getting onscreen help, whether you use the CUA or WP 5.1 keyboard. If you accidentally press (F1), it will take a few moments for the Help window to appear. Then, quickly clear this dialog box; one option is to press (ALT) + (F4). (If you can't seem to get out of the habit of pressing (F1) and you're using the WP 5.1 keyboard, you can reassign the (F1) key; see Chapter 17 for more on the Keyboard Layout feature.)

- Don't automatically press (ENTER) after making a selection from a dialog box. In WPDOS, you pressed (ENTER) after making each change on a menu, such as after typing new margin measurements. In WPWIN, pressing (ENTER) may execute a command prematurely, before you have made all the selections you wish to make. Press (ENTER) only after you make all the selections you desire in a dialog box.

- Don't press (ALT) + (F4) to block text or press (CTRL) + (F4) to move text if you're using the CUA keyboard. Pressing (ALT) + (F4) on the CUA keyboard will exit you from WordPerfect. Pressing (CTRL) + (F4) will close the current document. So be careful to get out of the habit of pressing these key combinations when editing text.

- Don't press (CTRL) + (END) to erase a line of text if you're using the CUA keyboard. Press (CTRL) + (DEL) instead. Pressing (CTRL) + (END) on the CUA keyboard will position the insertion point at the bottom of the document. If you press (CTRL) + (END) by mistake, press (CTRL) + (G), (ALT) + (L), which displays the Go To dialog box and moves the insertion point back to its last position.

- Don't press (F5) if you simply want to recall a file to the screen. Use the <u>F</u>ile, <u>O</u>pen command instead, whose shortcut is (F4) in the CUA keyboard and (SHIFT) + (F10) in the WP 5.1 keyboard. (Pressing (F5) in the WP 5.1 keyboard will enable you to open a file, but via the File Manager, which involves a lengthier process.)

Index

M